ROOFED TOWERS

The image of the ivory tower symbolizes higher education and academia in the Western context, evoking a flavour of transcendence. The curved roof is a well-known feature of the low structures which house traditional Chinese academies and ceremonial buildings. The roof carries the eye from heaven to earth, giving a sense of immanence. When these roofs are perched on Western-style highrises on modern Chinese campuses, the aesthetic incongruence is striking. The photograph here, from a campus in the Northeastern city of Changchun, is typical of a large number of university buildings erected under Soviet influence during the 1950s.

Interestingly, the Chinese characters for university, in the modern context, also constitute the title of the first of *The Four Books and Five Classics: The Great Learning*.

I am indebted to my niece, Jane Francisco, founding editor of Venue Magazine in Toronto, for the design of this frontispiece. The many hours of our fruitful discussion resulted in the concept of "Roofed Towers" as a way of imaging the cultural conflict at the heart of the modern Chinese university. — RH

CHINA'S UNIVERSITIES 1895 - 1995:

A Century of Cultural Conflict

by RUTH HAYHOE

GARLAND STUDIES IN HIGHER EDUCATION
VOLUME 4
GARLAND REFERENCE LIBRARY OF SOCIAL SCIENCE
VOLUME 997

GARLAND STUDIES IN HIGHER EDUCATION

This series is published in cooperation with the Program in Higher Education, School of Education, Boston College, Chestnut Hill, Massachusetts.

PHILIP G. ALTBACH, *Series Editor*

THE FUNDING OF
HIGHER EDUCATION
International Perspectives
edited by Philip G. Altbach and
D. Bruce Johnstone

REFORM AND CHANGE
IN HIGHER EDUCATION
International Perspectives
edited by James E. Mauch and
Paula L.W. Sabloff

THE LIBERAL ARTS COLLEGE
ADAPTING TO CHANGE
The Survival of Small Schools
by Gary Bonvillian
and Robert Murphy

SCIENCE AND TECHNOLOGY IN
CENTRAL AND EASTERN EUROPE
*The Reform of Higher
Education*
edited by A.D. Tillett
and Barry Lesser

THE SOCIAL ROLE OF HIGHER
EDUCATION
Comparative Perspectives
edited by Ken Kempner
and William Tierney

HIGHER EDUCATION IN CRISIS
*New York in National
Perspective*
edited by William C. Barba

JESUIT EDUCATION AND SOCIAL
CHANGE IN EL SALVADOR
by Charles J. Beirne

CHINA'S UNIVERSITIES,
1895–1995
A Century of Cultural Conflict
by Ruth Hayhoe

DIMENSIONS OF THE COMMUNITY
COLLEGE
*International, Intercultural, and
Multicultural Perspectives*
edited by Rosalind Latiner Raby and
Norma Tarrow

CHINA'S UNIVERSITIES 1895–1995
A CENTURY OF CULTURAL CONFLICT

RUTH HAYHOE

GARLAND PUBLISHING, INC.
NEW YORK AND LONDON
1996

Copyright © 1996 by Ruth Hayhoe

Library of Congress Cataloging-in-Publication Data

Hayhoe, Ruth.
    China's universities, 1895–1995 : a century of cultural conflict / Ruth
Hayhoe.
        p.   cm. — (Garland reference library of social science ; vol. 997.
Garland studies in higher education ; v. 4)
    Includes bibliographical references and index.
    ISBN 0-8153-1859-6 (alk. paper)
    1. Universities and colleges—China—History—20th century.   2. Univer-
sities and colleges—China—Sociological aspects.   3. China—History—20th
century.   4. China—Politics and government—20th century.   I. Title.
II. Series: Garland reference library of social science ; v. 997.   III. Series:
Garland reference library of social science. Garland studies in higher
education ; vol. 4.
LA1133.H388   1996
378.51'09'04—dc20   95-44021
                                                                              CIP

Printed on acid-free, 250-year-life paper
Manufactured in the United States of America

Contents

Abbreviations

AID	Agency for International Development (U.S.)
CAS	Chinese Academy of Sciences
CASS	Chinese Academy of Social Sciences
CIDA	Canadian International Development Agency
FBIS	Foreign Broadcast Information Service (U.S.)
IDRC	International Development Research Center (Canada)
JICA	Japan International Cooperation Agency
NPC	National People's Congress (China)
NNSF	National Natural Sciences Foundation (China)
NSSF	National Social Sciences Foundation (China)
OECD	Organization for Economic Cooperation and Development
UNDP	United Nations Development Program
UNESCO	United Nations Educational, Scientific, and Cultural Organization
UNFPA	United Nations Fund for Population Activity
UNICEF	United Nations International Children's Emergency Fund

SERIES EDITOR'S PREFACE

Higher education is a multifaceted phenomenon in modern society, combining a variety of institutions and an increasing diversity of students, a range of purposes and functions, and different orientations. The series combines research-based monographs, analyses, and discussions of broader issues and reference books related to all aspects of higher education. It is concerned with policy as well as practice from a global perspective. The series is dedicated to illuminating the reality of higher and postsecondary education in contemporary society.

Philip G. Altbach
Boston College

INTRODUCTION: A STORY, NOT
A HISTORY

Although there are many informative books about the differing dimensions of Chinese higher education over the twentieth century, there is no general account of the development of the Chinese university during this period of momentous social, economic, cultural, and political change. Such is the situation as far as the English language is concerned, at least. Accordingly, there exists a need for a volume that can bring together reflections on the Chinese university and its role in the two great experiments of modern China: Nationalist efforts to create a modern state under the broad rubric of capitalist modernization, and the Communist project of socialist construction under Soviet tutelage.

In addition to these two general frames of discourse, other models and patterns also cry out for attention. For example, there are patterns in the culture that continued to shape conceptions of knowledge in the university long after traditional institutions had disappeared, and there are dimensions of Maoist revolutionary thought that called into question the very existence of universities in a society such as China. There is also a variety of external influences that have come from distinctive civilizational contexts in different periods. The challenge is to weave together these different threads in such a way as to be able to reflect on the resources China's universities may draw upon for the tasks that face them in the coming century. How might they integrate the experiences gained under the programmatic influences of these two external narratives in shaping a future that cannot be predicted on the basis of either?

Though a history of modern Chinese higher education is clearly needed, I hesitate in face of such an undertaking. My own intellectual training has been in the area of comparative education, and the character of my research on Chinese higher education over the past decade makes me more at ease with the notion of a story than a history. A historical work would call for painstaking archival research and the extensive use of both primary and secondary sources, while the telling of a story may focus on broad themes and concepts. I see it as a search for interpretative understanding that probes the unique while connecting it to one or several global narratives by the very terms in which it is phrased. Comparative education provides the tools for doing this in a somewhat different way than would the historian.

The methodology of comparative education has been characterized over many years by a dichotomy between tendencies to seek universally valid explanations of educational-societal connections on the one hand, and to identify and understand the particular in educational, cultural, and societal patterns on the other. Thus the researcher takes up concepts such as university, college, and academy with a critical awareness that their very use may hide the cultural features of greatest interest in a particular context. To give up universality and attempts at the definition of common terms could result in a relativism that admits of no dialogue. However, by using these terms tentatively and critically, in ways that open up insight into the culturally particular, we may be able to identify alternatives to the dominating narratives that have tended to shape our perceptions and our vocabulary.[1]

A second dichotomy runs through the literature of comparative education. On the one hand are methodologies that call for strict adherence to the objectivity associated with inductive method in the natural sciences, or to the critical dualism between factual knowledge and moral imperative that Karl Popper and others have seen as fundamental to the open society of Western liberalism.[2] These have been mainly associated with the narrative of modernization, and with evolutionary or structural functionalist views of social change. On the other hand are methodologies that are characterized by a holism or monism in their epistemological basis and regard scientific understanding as going beyond factual knowledge to moral prescription and political direction. These are linked to the Marxist or socialist narrative and the various versions of it that entered the Western scholarly discourse in the postwar period of decolonization and nation-building: dependency theory, world systems theory, world order modeling, etc.[3]

Much of the research on China in the West falls within the modernization discourse, with a scrupulous adherence to objectivity and little or no comment made on preferred directions for China's future. Research within China, by contrast, has been largely phrased within a classical Marxist framework, though the use of Marxist terminology is often perfunctory, even ceremonial. Soviet sinology of the 1950s might be the best example of research that operated within a clear framework of traditional Marxist thought, with

a prescriptive grasp of future directions for the building of Chinese socialism. China's failure to adhere to these directions in the Great Leap Forward
and Cultural Revolution periods seemed to have been the cause for considerable puzzlement on the Soviet side.[4]

In telling the story of China's universities, it is my intention to find a
way somewhere between these two discourses. I have been greatly influenced
by the work of Juergen Habermas, in seeking what he calls a "redemption"
of Western modernity through an expanded understanding of rationality that
reconnects the moral, affective, and cognitive domains.[5] I have also found
in Johann Galtung's "structural theory of imperialism" a helpful approach
to understanding patterns of domination and subjugation in the international
milieu. Rather than assuming the primacy of economic dynamics in the global capitalist system, Galtung identifies structural patterns that might be
modified through interventions in the domains of culture and communications, as well as through political or economic means.[6]

Thus my intention is to go beyond the kinds of explanation associated with the modernization narrative, which traditionally tried to discover
contextual "causes" of particular phenomena or make predictions on the
basis of deductive theory and then test them in a carefully defined context.[7]
It is not, however, to offer a prescription for the next stage, derived from
the socialist narrative. Rather, I hope to tell the story in such a way that there
is an integral link between understanding what is, or what has been, and
reaching forward toward what should be, or what might be, the case in the
future. There should be room for openness, and a sense of possibility, a recognition that moral direction can be derived from a logical working out of
a preferred future within the university community. University scholars are
not merely in a position to provide the technical expertise needed by the
Chinese leadership in its ambitious drive for economic and social development, as critical dualism would suggest. They are also capable of defining a
preferred future for Chinese society, and working out, with logic and com-
passion, the kinds of intervention that could contribute to the realization of
that future.[8]

It is with this kind of vision in mind that I hope to tell the story of
China's universities. The emphasis will be both on understanding what are
the unique characteristics of these institutions in the context of Chinese culture and Chinese historical experience, and on anticipating what might be
the kinds of contribution they might make to the shaping of Chinese society in the twenty-first century. Much research on Chinese education has been
done by political scientists, whose explanations of educational policy and
practice tend to link them very closely to the major struggles over social, po-

litical, and economic policy of factions within the Communist party. Without doubt, this kind of explanation is of primary importance and validity for China. However, it has long been my sense that, beyond the political, there are patterns in the culture and epistemology that may give another layer of explanation to the great educational crises that have convulsed China at various times over the century, seemingly with increasing intensity, if the Cultural Revolution is taken as a kind of apogee of cultural conflict. The uncovering of this layer will be a major objective of the storytelling process.

A DISTILLATION FROM PERSONAL EXPERIENCE

A story may not call for the rigorous data collection required by history, yet sources it must have. In coming to this point, something needs to be said about the storyteller, as the collection of information used for this book has a logic that has emerged from her personal story. That story began with an eleven-year stint teaching secondary school in Hong Kong, over a period that coincided almost exactly with China's Cultural Revolution decade—1967 to 1978. Thus initial insights into Chinese schooling came from a setting where British colonialism had provided conditions for a remarkably dynamic southern Chinese society.

Subsequently, a master's program in comparative education at the University of London, 1978–1979, was followed by two years of teaching in Shanghai. There was a tremendous sense of elation over the first freedoms of China's open-door policy at that time, and Fudan University provided a setting for stimulating encounters with six different classes from the 1977–1978 cohorts, the first two groups of university students recruited nationwide in competitive examinations after the Cultural Revolution. The Shanghai experience was followed by doctoral work at the University of London, culminating in a dissertation that attempted to examine the impact of German, French, American, and Soviet models of the university on Chinese higher education policy from 1911 to the early 1980s.[9]

This dissertation, prepared under the direction of Professor Brian Holmes, was my first attempt to tell the story of China's universities. While many of the insights gained in this work have informed my later research and publications, the dissertation itself was never published. With the exception of *China's Universities and the Open Door*, a study in Chinese higher education in the 1980s, most of my work has been of a cooperative and collaborative nature.[10] Somehow, the task of preparing a book on Chinese education always seemed to require the involvement of numerous scholars who could provide a multifaceted account. The challenge to attempt this monograph was put to me at my last meeting with Brian Holmes in Tokyo, January 1993, six months before his untimely death in July of that year. The writing process is therefore offered as a tribute to Brian Holmes, whose richly elaborated approach to method and stimulating criticism have left a lasting imprint on my work, even though I have come to disagree with him on some fundamental points.

Since completing the dissertation and returning to Canada in 1984, I have been privileged to make numerous research visits to China, which have allowed me to spend time at more than 100 universities in all of the six major regions of the country. The first two visits in 1985 and 1987 were funded through an exchange program between the Social Sciences and Humanities Research Council of Canada (SSHRCC), and the Chinese Academy of Social Sciences (CASS), and allowed me to visit the Northeast and East China, respectively. A subsequent three visits were funded by the Canadian International Development Agency (CIDA), and enabled me to focus my research on North China in 1989, the Central South in 1992, and the Northwest in 1993. Each visit lasted approximately four to six weeks, and detailed interviews were held with provincial higher education authorities, university leaders in areas such as curriculum, research, international activity, finance, and student affairs.[11] Also, a total of about 200 scholars who had returned from abroad in many different institutions were individually interviewed.[12] In 1994 I visited universities in Sichuan Province under the auspices of a World Bank mission, and so got a sense of reforms in the Southwest.

One of the remarkable characteristics of Chinese universities is the degree to which they are highly stable communities. Many middle-aged and younger faculty have spent their whole adult lives in one institution, due to a practice in place since the 1950s whereby universities mainly appoint their own graduates to faculty positions. Some are the children of faculty or staff, and so have been born and lived out their whole lives on one campus! Older faculty whose careers stretch back before 1949 can recall the revolutionary period and the conditions under which a whole new higher education system was designed in the early 1950s, while middle-aged faculty have vivid memories of the way in which the Cultural Revolution affected their campuses.

This makes an ideal setting for storytelling, as each faculty member and administrator is able to give a detailed account of his or her section, department, or field, in some cases back to its earliest days. The interview notes collected on these extensive visits thus reflect a kind of oral history, carrying with them a flavor of the retrospective emotions of persons experiencing an immense sense of relief at the greater freedom of the 1980s. These emotions, of course, shaped the way in which they interpreted the eventful years of their own institution's history. Institutions too have a kind of personality of their own, a group identity formed by a faculty who have been together for a long period of time, and weathered periods of upheaval and intense suffering.

In addition to these oral accounts, I have been able to collect a considerable number of university histories over this period. The writing of these histories has been part of a process of reconstructing the particular identities of each institution. The massive reorganization of 1952, instituted under the guidance of Soviet experts, tore apart whole institutions and reconstituted academic departments in an entirely new constellation, with the result that universities lost many of their links to the prerevolutionary period. The subsequent maelstrom of the Cultural Revolution made it positively dangerous to look back with nostalgia on any but the revolutionary colleges of Yan'an and other border regions. One of the great new freedoms of the 1980s was the freedom for universities to reflect on their own identities and focus on the particular strengths they could separately bring to China's development tasks. In some cases this may have related to their experience during the Nationalist period with a specific Western country— Germany, France, Britain, the United States—where many of their older scholars had been educated, in other cases to aspects of regional history over that period.[13]

Thus research and writing for these institutional histories was more than an academic exercise; it was part and parcel of the construction of a new or renewed identity. Universities were no longer seen as simply cogs in a large machine, training specialists according to plan for each sector of the country, but could rediscover themselves as communities of scholars with a distinct identity. Great pride was taken, in some cases, in restoring the name that had been used in the pre-Liberation period.[14] In other cases, universities that had been founded in the 1950s sought to trace their lineage back to distinguished Nationalist institutions from which specific departments had been separated out in the reorganization of 1952, and which created the basis for their establishment. At first, most histories ended in 1949, it being too painful to recount what had been lost in the reorganization of 1952,[15] and, in many cases, too politically sensitive to describe what had happened in the Cultural Revolution decade. However, by the late 1980s, many of the histories have carried the story right through to the contemporary period. As I have traveled around visiting universities and listening to their accounts of both the past and present, these institutional histories have greatly helped to put things in perspective.

The main sources for this volume are thus stories that have already been constructed, both orally and in the form of institutional histories. There should be a certain inner logic and authenticity coming from these many narratives. Yet there is also a need to test and refine these stories from within against the scholarly literature developed through a rigorous sinological tradition.

THE SINOLOGICAL LITERATURE

I must acknowledge a great debt over the years to the research of others in three particular areas. First, there are writings in Chinese classical history that have focused on schools and scholarly institutions at different periods: the work of W. Theodore de Bary, John Chaffee, and Thomas Lee on the Song dynasty,[16] John Meskill on the Ming,[17] Benjamin Elman and Alexander Woodside on the Qing,[18] Marianne Bastid on the late Qing,[19] He Bingdi on the ladder of success in traditional China,[20] Zhang Zongli on the Chinese gentry[21]—the list could go on and on. Let me just say at this point how grateful I am for the clarity of this highly erudite scholarship and its accessibility to someone like myself, who is seeking to make use of its insights to explore the cultural and epistemological dynamics that underlay contemporary Chinese educational development. This literature makes it possible to identify and highlight core values and patterns of education and scholarship within the world of classical Chinese culture and thought.

The second literature is that of the Republican period, from 1911 to 1949. Here again are numerous excellent studies on different dimensions of higher education: John Israel on student movements in the 1930s,[22] Jessie Lutz on the Christian colleges,[23] Ming Chan and Arif Dirlik on the Labor University,[24] Peter Seybolt on Yan'an higher education,[25] Barry Keenan on Deweyan influences on Chinese education,[26] and Yeh Wen-hsin's beautifully crafted interpretive history of universities in the Republican era that exemplify evolving patterns for higher education.[27] This literature is fundamental for understanding the models and patterns that had come to be associated with the term "university" in modern China, and which were important, though often misused, resources in the building of a socialist higher education system in the early 1950s. Several of these models have been a source of great pride, and some have come to constitute the image of a preferred future as well as of a respected past in the greater freedom of the 1980s. As a pragmatic leadership has moved toward forms of pluralism in the economy and society that have some parallels with the Nationalist period, an understanding of the Republican experience in higher education has become important once again for interpreting changes in higher education in the 1980s and 1990s.

Finally, there is the well-developed sinological literature on the post-Liberation period, which has had many interesting works devoted to particular periods and aspects of education—Irving Epstein, John Hawkins, Juergen Henze, Julia Kwong, Karen Minden, Leo A. Orleans, Lynn Paine, Suzanne Pepper, Gerard Postiglione, Ronald Price, Stanley Rosen, Heidi Ross—the list could go on and on. These scholars have constituted a community for me, a community in which the constant stimulus of critical discussion over research findings and their interpretation has been complemented by friendship, and, I believe, a shared hope and vision for positive change in China.

INTIMATIONS FROM PRACTICE

At this point I should note that my understanding has also been integrally linked with opportunities for action, as well as for teaching and reflection, in a decade or more of life within the university community. The most striking such opportunity came early in 1989, when I agreed to accept a secondment to External Affairs and International Trade Canada, and to a position that involved coordinating the cultural, educational, and academic relations between Canada and China from the Canadian embassy in Beijing. When I accepted the appointment, I had no idea of the conditions under which it would be taken up—in the somber summer that followed the Tiananmen events in Beijing.

While in this position I was able to visit a large number of university campuses over a two-year period, and to see them in a mood very different from the optimism of the early to mid-1980s, or the iconoclasm of the heady months that led up to the June events. The fact that I had spent one month living on the campus of People's University and doing a study of the North China region in May of the same year gave me a vivid sense of these contrasts. The two years from the summer of 1989 to that of 1991 saw the continuation of practical programs of academic and educational interchange at the people-to-people level that flourished even under conditions of severe strain in bilateral political and economic relations. It was a delicate line to draw between supporting universities that had been the victims of governmental violence on the one hand, and withholding support from political authorities in their efforts to dismiss these events and restore international respectability.[28]

After the two years of academic diplomacy in Beijing, a strong practical streak remained a part of my academic work at the Ontario Institute for Studies in Education (OISE), due to the fact that I had initiated and continued to be responsible for a joint program in doctoral training and course development with seven Chinese normal universities, with support from CIDA. The task of facilitating a large group of doctoral students and young faculty during periods of six months to a year in Canada, and after their return to China, as well as enabling Canadian doctoral students and faculty to learn from their Chinese counterparts through visits and research in China, was an exacting one. There have been many pitfalls and some failed promises on both sides, but it seems likely that at the end of six years there will be a strong set of relationships between scholars on both sides, capable of sustaining the next phase of cooperation, in which the focus will be on joint research.

The writing of this book has thus been constantly interlinked with practice in ways that might be seen as a kind of test of its validity. Also, a growth process has taken place, with new concerns coming to the fore over time. For example, in the doctoral dissertation, little attention was given to women and their role in the story of China's universities. As women faculty and students began to experience certain adverse affects in the new freedoms of the 1980s, I realized their story needed some special attention, and so oriented the last regional study in the Northwest particularly to women's issues. On the practical level, the same concern came to the fore with our joint doctoral program. Only after we insisted on a fair participation of young women faculty and doctoral students were we able to get a substantial number of women applicants for consideration. Apparently they were there, but their names simply did not come up when decisions were made about who might qualify for study and research abroad until affirmative action was adopted. The subsequent selection of nine Chinese women for the project has enhanced this interest in understanding women's perspectives on Chinese higher education.

It remains now to say something about who I think you, the readers of this volume, might be. My intention has been to craft a story that will be illuminating to scholars, policymakers, and academic administrators in areas other than sinology, who may be involved in the increasingly wide network of China's international academic relations. Naturally, I would welcome also sinologists and comparative educationists who may wish to call into question some of my interpretations and findings. My purpose is both to contribute to the cumulative literature aimed at understanding Chinese education in a national and international milieu, and to provide suggestive insights into how particular interventions, whether individual, institutional, or national in scope, might have a positive impact on China's future society.

There is thus an explicit normative purpose, in addition to the explanatory intent. I hope to tell the story in such a way that readers will be able to understand it in terms of the discourses of modernization and socialist construction that we know, but will also be able to see around the edges of these narratives and be enriched by idiographic elements in the Chinese context that may open up unique possibilities for its future development.

OUTLINE OF CONTENTS

Chapter 1 of the volume deals critically with the main concepts that will be used in telling the story of China's universities, and the substantive content implied by each. It then puts China's modern story in the broader context of global modernization and the way in which various versions of the European university found their way to all parts of the world. It identifies some of the particularities of China's response, with highly developed traditional knowledge patterns shaping the modern institutions that emerged under the influences of Western capitalism in the first instance, then of Western socialism. The counter model to these Western influences posed by the Yan'an experience is also looked at. Chapter 1 provides the definitional context for the story.

Chapter 2 tells the story of the Republican period. It begins with a discussion of evolving policy and legislation under successive Republican governments that tried, with increasing sophistication, to weave together into one system the various institutions for higher learning that had come into being during a long transition out of empire. Of key interest are the contradictions around efforts to integrate the values of autonomy and academic freedom, introduced along with Western models, into Chinese concepts of the relation between higher learning and the state. The various channels whereby foreign influences continued to affect Chinese universities, keeping this tension alive, are also discussed.

Three main themes are developed in chapter 2 and used throughout the volume thereafter. The gender map is explored in terms of some reflections on the nature of Chinese women's struggle in the modern era, and a discussion of available information on women's experience in universities of the Nationalist period. Curricular development, or the knowledge map of Nationalist universities, was an area of considerable experimentation and contestation over the whole Nationalist period. The geographical distribution of higher education was a third main issue of concern, with various schemes of geographical rationalization failing in the face of institutional autonomy up until the dramatic events of the Sino-Japanese War. These resulted in a great migration from coastal areas to the hinterland.

Chapter 3 tells the story of Chinese higher education under socialism. It deals first with the massive reorganization of the system in 1952 under Soviet tutelage, and the implications of this for knowledge patterns, geographical rationalization, and the participation of women. The new constellation of higher institutions that took shape had many parallels with late Qing patterns, I argue, since there were cultural dynamics at work that linked elements of the Soviet academic tradition with persisting patterns from the Confucian past.

With the leading role given by the Communist party to People's University, and the establishment of an all-embracing national network of intellectual institutions, a new Hanlin Academy came into being. Autonomy and academic freedom were subsumed under a new intellectual authority and scholarly monopoly of the socialist bureaucracy. The Great Leap Forward and the Cultural Revolution are seen as response from below, the first relatively moderate and leading to the establishment of provincial level institutions, curricular diversification, and the integration of research into the university; the second a much more radical explosion resulting in the abolition of all formal institutions of higher learning. Chapter 3 attempts to reflect on these movements from a cultural perspective, probing beyond the explanations provided by analyses of factional politics.

Chapter 4 tells the story of the reform decade from 1978 to 1990. The main trends of curricular reform are seen in relation to the creation of new and more diverse identities for China's universities. Issues of geographical distribution and women's participation under the new conditions of "market socialism" are discussed. In addition, the various channels of external influence are identified and outlined, and some attempt is made to assess their contribution. Chapter 4 shows a new synthesis emerging as the two poles of China's own traditions come into balanced tension once again, and diverse external influences are introduced and absorbed.

Chapters 5 and 6 move down to the regional level, and give a detailed account of how different types of universities in two contrasting regions have fared in the reform decade. The Central South region is in the forefront of economic reform, and this is reflected in the situation facing universities of different types and levels. The Northwest region is experiencing slower economic growth, and a severe internal brain drain. The issues of curricular change, geographic distribution, and female participation in these two regions are considered in detail and linked both to historical and contemporary dimensions of the broader picture. These two chapters also include the stories of particular institutions, and perspectives from scholars who have returned from abroad.

Finally, chapter 7 considers the situation of Chinese universities in the

1990s, as they stand on the brink of a transition to mass higher education, and as they face the rapid and sweeping social change process brought about under the market reforms. Both historical and comparative analysis indicate that there are real choices to be made on the cultural level at this momentous time. In this chapter, I attempt to sketch out a preferred future for China's universities, and for Chinese society, a future characterized by authenticity in terms of the cultural context, and justice in terms of preserving and building on the achievements of both modern experiments, the socialist and the Nationalist.

ACKNOWLEDGMENTS

I owe a heavy debt of gratitude to my institute, OISE, for providing me with a stimulating and supportive teaching and research environment over nearly a decade. The unfailing patience, appreciation, and understanding shown by students, colleagues, and administrative superiors in face of my frequent absences in China, and my obsessive absorption with Chinese affairs, has made it possible for me to write this book. In addition, I must express special thanks to SSHRCC and CIDA for providing funds for the research visits to China.

I would also like to acknowledge the important contribution made to the book by colleagues and friends who read and commented on parts or the whole of the manuscript. Dr. J.H. Higginson of Canterbury, a long-time friend and mentor of my doctoral studies, made detailed comments on this introductory section. Professor Edward Shils made extremely valuable and incisive editorial suggestions for an earlier version of chapter 1, which appeared in *Minerva* in December 1994 under the title, "Ideas of Higher Learning East and West." Dr. Ding Gang of East China Normal University in Shanghai gave helpful suggestions for the historical analysis in chapters 1 and 2. Dr. Ronald Price took time to read the complete manuscript, sent to him in Australia through the Internet, and gave me a detailed written response, which challenged me to think through many points more deeply. Dr. Irving Epstein made a similar contribution, suggesting areas of reading I had overlooked, stimulating me to greater clarity of expression on some issues, and giving me enormous encouragement along the way. Dr. Nina Borevskaya, a China specialist from the Institute for East Asian Studies of the Russian Academy of Sciences, gave me some significant feedback on my interpretation of Soviet-Chinese relations in education. Dr. Heidi Ross commented on the first three chapters, giving some especially helpful ideas on gender issues in Chinese education. My doctoral student, Lu Yongling, gave the whole manuscript a critical reading, and made some suggestions based on her background in Chinese classical history and education. I also received consistent support from Professor Philip Altbach, general editor of the series, who invited me to undertake the project.

NOTES

   1. The journal *Alternatives*, which is edited by Ashis Nandy at the Center for the Study of Developing Societies in Delhi, India, and affiliated with the World Order Models Project (WOMP), plays a leading role in this kind of effort.

   2. Karl Popper, *The Open Society and Its Enemies* (London: Routledge and Kegan Paul, 1970) and F.A. Hayek, *The Counter Revolution of Science* (Indianapolis, Indiana: Liberty Press, 1979).

   3. Martin Carnoy's *Education and Cultural Imperialism* (London: Mackay, 1974) provides what still stands as a useful outline of these theories. See also Kelly and Altbach, *Education and the Colonial Experience* (London: Transaction Books, 1984); Martin McLean, "Educational Dependency" in *Compare* 13:1, 1983, pp. 25–42; and R. Hayhoe, "China, Comparative Education, and World Order Models Theory," in *Compare*, 16:1, 1986, pp. 65–80.

   4. O.B. Borisov and B.T. Koloskov, *Soviet-Chinese Relations 1945–1970* (Bloomington and London: Indiana University Press, 1975).

   5. Juergen Habermas, *The Theory of Communicative Action*, (Boston: Beacon Press, 1984, 1987) Vols. 1 and 2.

   6. J. Galtung, "A Structural Theory of Imperialism," *Journal of Peace Research*, Vol. 8, 1972, pp. 81–117.

   7. Brian Holmes, "The Positivist Debate in Comparative Education," in B. Holmes, *Comparative Education: Some Considerations of Method* (London: George Allen and Unwin, 1981). This chapter gives a refutation of inductive scientific method as applied to comparative education, and suggests in its place hypothetico-deductive method as a means whereby comparative education methodology can continue to model itself on scientific research in the post-Einsteinian paradigm of science.

   8. The contrast here is between Holmes's idea of comparative education as a kind of "social technology" within a broader notion of "piecemeal social engineering" as against the more broadly inclusive rationality of scholars in the World Order Models Project (WOMP), seeking to establish models of a preferred future through rational dialogue, a task Holmes and Popper would place outside the realm of scientific rationality. Examples include J. Galtung, *The True Worlds* (New York: Free Press, 1980); Ali Mazrui, *A World Federation of Cultures* (New York: Free Press, 1976); and Rajni Kothari, *Footsteps into the Future* (New York: Free Press, 1974). Just as there have been few attempts to work out the implications of Holmes's methodology in comparative research, beyond the work of his doctoral students, the development of comparative education research within a WOMP framework has been very limited. This approach is usually subsumed under various Marxist or neo-Marxist methodologies, which are somewhat more tied to economic determinacy, I would argue.

   9. R. Hayhoe, "German, French, Soviet, and American University Models and the Evaluation of Chinese Higher Education Policy since 1911," thesis submitted in fulfilment of the requirements of the doctor of philosophy degree, University of London, April 1984.

   10. R. Hayhoe, *Contemporary Chinese Education* (London: Croom Helm, 1984); R. Hayhoe and M. Bastid, *China's Education and the Industrialized World: Studies in Cultural Transfer* (New York: M.E. Sharpe, and Toronto: OISE Press, 1987); R. Hayhoe, *Education and Modernization: The Chinese Experience* (Oxford: Pergamon, and Toronto: OISE Press, 1992).

   11. Detailed reports were submitted to CIDA after these research missions, but the results have never been published elsewhere.

12. For an analysis of some of this interview data, see R. Hayhoe, "China's Scholars Returned from Abroad: A View From Shanghai," parts 1 and 2, in *China Exchange News*, 17:3, 1989, pp. 3–8, 17:4, 1989, pp. 2–9. See also R. Hayhoe, "China's Returned Scholars and the Democracy Movement," in *China Quarterly*, 122, June 1990, pp. 293–302.

13. See Liu Haifeng, "Zhongguo gaodeng xuexiao de xiaoshi zhuisu wenti," [The Problem of Founding Dates in the Institutional Histories of Chinese Higher Education] in *Jiaoyu yanjiu* [Educational Research], no. 5, 1994, pp. 63–75, for a sensitive discussion of these institutional histories. Liu identifies six periods in which modern higher education went through great changes, making it difficult, in many cases, to trace the history of a particular institution accurately: 1902–1904, 1912–1913, 1937–1940, 1949–1953, 1958–1960, 1966–1970. Each of these were periods of political upheaval and change, which led to the reshaping of institutional identities.

14. Examples of this include the Sichuan Medical College, derived from the pre-Liberation North American Missionary University, West China Union University, and renamed West China University of Medical Sciences in 1985. Another interesting example is that of Beijing University, which has recently proudly restored its English name from the 1920s—Peking University. A third example is that of Nanjing Institute of Technology, which has adopted the name of an illustrious university of the 1920s—Southeast University (Dongnan University), that had later become National Central University under the Nationalists. Many other examples of such name changes could be cited, and they create a considerable problem in Western graduate registries trying to check the academic background of Chinese applicants.

15. The case of Qinghua University is interesting in this regard. Its institutional history up to 1949 was one of the earliest to be published, in 1982, but so far it has not been followed up with a history of the post-Liberation period. While Qinghua had been distinguished for its scholarship in areas like classical Chinese history and philosophy, also literature and the social sciences before Liberation, these departments were all removed, along with its basic science departments, to re-create it as a polytechnical university in 1952. Efforts since the mid-1980s to restore some of its arts and social science programs have left the community with a sense of how much was lost in 1952, and a reluctance to tell the story of that period.

16. W. Theodore de Bary and John Chaffee (eds.), *Neo-Confucian Education: The Formative Stage* (Berkeley: University of California Press, 1989); John Chaffee, *The Thorny Gates of Learning in Sung China* (Cambridge: Cambridge University Press, 1985); Thomas H.C. Lee, *Government Education and Examinations in Sung China* (Hong Kong: Chinese University Press, 1985).

17. John Meskill, *Academies in the Ming Dynasty* (Tucson: University of Arizona Press, 1982).

18. Benjamin Elman and Alexander Woodside (eds.), *Education and Society in Late Imperial China, 1600–1900* (Berkeley: University of California Press, 1994).

19. Marianne Bastid, *Educational Reform in Early Twentieth-Century China*, translated by Paul Bailey (Ann Arbor: Center for Chinese Studies, University of Michigan, 1988).

20. Ho Ping-ti, *The Ladder of Success in Imperial China: Aspects of Social Mobility, 1368–1911* (New York and London: Columbia University Press, 1962).

21. Chang Chung-li, *The Chinese Gentry* (Seattle: University of Washington Press, 1955).

22. John Israel, *Student Nationalism in China 1927–1937* (Stanford, Calif.: Stanford University Press, 1966).

23. Jessie Lutz, *China and the Christian Colleges* (Ithaca, N.Y. and London: Cornell University Press, 1971).

24. Ming K. Chan and Arif Dirlik, *Schools into Fields and Factories: Anarchists, The Guomindang, and the National Labor University in Shanghai, 1927–1937* (Durham, N.C., and London: Duke University Press, 1991).

25. Peter Seybolt, "Yenan Education and the Chinese Revolution," unpublished Ph.D. thesis, Harvard University, 1969.

26. Barry Keenan, *The Dewey Experiment in China* (Cambridge, Mass.: Harvard University Press, 1977).

27. Yeh Wen–hsin, *The Alienated Academy: Culture and Politics in Republican China, 1919–1937* (Cambridge, Mass.: Council on East Asian Studies, Harvard University, 1990).

28. R. Hayhoe, "Canada–China Cultural Relations: Some Reflections on Practice," *Higher Education Group Annual*, 1991, pp. 139–154.

CHINA'S UNIVERSITIES
1895–1995

I Concepts and Frameworks for Telling the Story

A story cannot be told without words, and yet words carry with them assumptions and connotations that may hide as much as they reveal. Thus the term "university" has a rich legacy of history in the European and North American context, yet is sometimes used to denote an entirely different constellation of scholarly institutions in China and other Eastern civilizations. A historically accurate use of the term in China would have to limit itself to the period since the late nineteenth century, when modern higher institutions were established on a new basis, as traditional ones gradually disintegrated. In fact, the widely accepted date for the founding of the first modern university in most Chinese research on higher education history is 1895, when *Beiyang gongxue*, the forerunner of Tianjin University was founded, followed by *Nanyang gongxue* (later Jiaotong University) in 1896, and the Imperial University (Peking University) in 1898. Traditional institutions had more or less disappeared by the time of the 1911 revolution, yet the values associated with them persisted and have informed struggles and conflicts in the development of higher education right up to the present time.

The main purpose of this opening chapter is to clarify the terms that will be used in telling the story of China's universities, and to draw attention to the underlying patterns of persisting cultural values in Chinese higher education, which may be helpful for interpreting some dimensions of the story. The literature on classical Chinese institutions of education and scholarship is so extensive and rich, and covers such a lengthy period of time, that it is extremely difficult, if not impossible, to summarize it. However, one way to approach it is through the comparative method, by identifying the characteristic values and structures of the medieval university of Europe, and then asking what the corresponding values and structures in the Chinese tradition of scholarship were. Such a task obviously involves a high degree of conceptual synthesis, and Max Weber's invention and use of ideal types provides some inspiration for it.[1] The values and patterns of another civilization can ultimately be seen only through the screen of one's own, so that bias is unavoidable in this exercise. However, it is a bias that is explicit and open to critical discussion.

In this chapter, I will, therefore, first sketch out the main connotations associated with the term university in the European historical experience, and then develop a contrasting picture of traditional Chinese higher education, its characteristic values and patterns, and its commonalities with other Eastern civilizations. The story of how the European university became a kind of universal institution, an essential accoutrement of every modernizing society, is integrally linked to the story of imperialism and the expansion of European civilization. The development of China's modern universities is part of this pattern.

Nevertheless, certain dimensions mark out China's experience as distinct from that of other Asian societies: it was never extensively colonized by European powers, in the way that India, Malaysia, and Vietnam were, nor did Japan ever have the same degree of colonial power as it exercised in Korea and Taiwan. Therefore, China's experience in establishing universities differed somewhat from that of other Asian nations.

This chapter ends with the consideration of a kind of higher institution unique to China. The Yan'an model might be seen as a kind of counterformation to set against all of the experiments with Western university models from the late nineteenth century up to the 1950s. Its patterns and values can best be understood in relation to China's own scholarly traditions, as both their antithesis and their reincarnation.

THE MEDIEVAL UNIVERSITIES OF EUROPE

The fundamental scholarly values of the European university might be summed up in the twin concepts of autonomy and academic freedom. In his great history, Rashdall notes how the university found its place as studium between sacerdotium and imperium, a kind of intermediate force in the structure of power of medieval society.[2] The emergence of cities and guilds of merchants[3] had provided the context for guilds of scholars to form and subsequently to gain recognition separately through papal charters, and collectively through the *ius ubique docendi*, which gave masters the right teach in any university throughout Europe.[4] The guild of scholars was known as the *universitas* and it provided the basis for intellectual and scholarly autonomy in relation to local state and church jurisdictions. Rashdall provides a fascinating discussion of the two mechanisms that could be used by medieval scholars to protect the autonomy of their guild: *migratio* or the right to move to another city in the case of the students; and *cessatio* or the withdrawal of labor by all graduates of the university working within church or state.[5]

The autonomy of the medieval universities was always relative, of course, but it was expressed in control over what should be taught in the university, the selection of students, their admission into the responsibilities and privileges of masters, and most aspects of internal structure and organization. They were communities of scholars who set their own standards of knowledge, much in the way craftspersons set their standards within guilds, and who gradually gained an important influence in medieval society as their degrees became recognized as qualifications for appointments to positions in both the church and civil states.[6] At no time, however, were universities exclusively the arm of either state or church for the purpose of training and recruitment into leadership positions. There was always a degree of autonomy around the institutionalization of the professions of law, medicine, and theology.

Academic freedom, the other great value of the medieval university, could be interpreted as the essential precondition for individual scholars within the community to search out and advance knowledge in their particular fields, in accordance with the traditions and rules they regarded as valid. It was associated to some degree with the early divisions of the curriculum into the faculties of arts, medicine, law, and theology, with theology as the overarching or integrative discipline.[7] Unlike the situation in the church, where theology defined and laid out truths that were to be unquestioningly accepted, theology within the university community provided an arena for debate and discussion over the truths being discovered in various specialist fields, and their integration into a broader web of understanding. There were clearly limits on academic freedom that came from the dominance of theology, and these were only dealt with effectively in the distinction made between scientific and moral truth in Kantian philosophy. Nevertheless, there is much evidence of a creative tension between specialist and general truth, and debates that were remarkably free in comparison to the absolutism of religious and political authority in the wider society. Rashdall comments on this in the following way: "In that age a theological dictatorship of some kind was inevitable. It was something that such a dictatorship should be vested in a large and popularly constituted body of secular theologians, eminently amenable to the influences of public opinion and always favorable within certain limits to free discussion and theological ingenuity, and without motive for unnecessary or malignant persecution."[8]

A second significant aspect of academic freedom was its link to an epistemology that emphasized the growth of knowledge through logical disputation[9] or theoretical debate rather than through application to practice in the natural or social worlds. Experimental science came only with the scientific revolution of the seventeenth and eighteenth centuries, and the notion of knowledge being advanced through experimentation or social practice even later. Thus it was a pure, theoretical or speculative knowledge that was advanced by the academic freedom of scholars within the university. The freedom to raise any question or dispute any received opinion was premised on the assumption that their pursuit of truth would not lead to any direct intervention into the affairs of state or church. In a sense, this was part of the legacy of the monasteries, whose preservation of books and whose communities of scholars through the Dark Ages had bequeathed institutional patterns almost as important as those of the guild.

These two values of autonomy and academic freedom were preserved and transformed in the changes that took place with the emergence of nation-states in Europe of the eighteenth and nineteenth centuries. They were accentuated differently in the different national experiences of such colonial powers as France, Germany, and Britain, also in what might be termed the neocolonial powers of the United States and the Soviet Union, the two superpowers that were to dominate much of the twentieth century. A comparison of the academic patterns of these five countries should provide grounds for some interesting reflection on Chinese universities as they developed from the late nineteenth to the mid-twentieth centuries.

France was perhaps the first modern nation, and the French Revolution swept away the last remnants of traditional universities in favor of new style *grandes écoles* that were to provide the personnel needed by the modern state at a high level.[10] When Napoleon reestablished the university in 1810, it was as a national system of academic and professional faculties, rationally distributed across the country according to academic districts, and headed by a *grand maître* and council in Paris directly responsible to the emperor.[11] It has been characterized as *l'Etat enseignant* in its dominant position over the entire national education system.[12] However, as academic members of the university struggled for control of the council, they gained a kind of autonomy that was seen as the right to regulate all aspects of education, not in subservience to successive governments, but in loyalty to the higher moral and intellectual interests of the state.[13] Academic freedom was closely linked by these proponents of the Napoleonic ideal to the concept of the scholar-specialist, and the freedom necessary for the unhindered growth of specialist knowledge in various fields through rational inquiry.[14] Academic freedom in France may also be seen in the context of the ascendancy of bourgeois values, which marked the French intellectual establishment more thoroughly than the German, as Fritz Ringer has shown.[15]

The German state came into being as a unified entity much later than the French, and its universities evolved gradually into their modern form. If the Napoleonic university set the pattern for France, probably the University of Berlin, founded by Humboldt in 1810, is the best prototype for the German university.[16] While its professorate was an integrated part of the civil service, as in France, it enjoyed greater autonomy in its relation to the state. This autonomy was predicated on Hegelian notions of the state, and the way its higher interests would be served by allowing the free pursuit of idealist knowledge in the university.[17] Academic freedom in Germany was linked to the Kantian distinction between factual and moral knowledge, which had given free rein to scientific investigation, and a new role for philosophy as the arbiter and synthesist of all other fields of knowledge.[18] Theory was emphasized over practice.[19] In fact, practical studies in areas such as engineering and administration were relegated to *Technische Hochschulen*, which were clearly of lower status than universities and enjoyed less autonomy and academic freedom in their early period of development.[20]

The modern British university differed from that of France or Germany in that the members of its teaching faculty never became a part of the civil service, and thus its autonomy from the state had a stronger tradition. On the other hand, the influence of the church over matters such as the curriculum, the appointment of faculty, and the recruitment of students, remained strong, especially in the ancient universities such as Oxford and Cambridge.[21] Once the grip of the church was relaxed in the course of the nineteenth century, academic freedom gradually increased. There was no theory of academic freedom, as in Germany, nor was there any agitation for it, as in France under the Second Empire. It was regarded as right and proper, to be practiced, not talked about. A tendency toward empiricism in philosophy marks out British intellectual life from the rationalism of France and the idealism of Germany.

The persistence of the college within the university in England also gave a special mark to British higher education. As a community retaining similarities to early monastic communities, the college fostered close personal relations between students and their tutors, and retained a sense of practical and religious integration that distinguished its ethos from the more impersonal and theoretical views of knowledge characteristic of universities on the Continent.[22] It was the collegiate model that was first transferred to North America, both in the English-speaking colonial colleges and, somewhat differently, in the Jesuit classical colleges established in Quebec.[23] Only in the nineteenth century did the more diverse patterns of the European university find their way to the New World.

In the American college of the seventeenth to nineteenth centuries, neither the values of autonomy nor of academic freedom were consciously cultivated. The colleges were mainly local institutions, dominated by churchmen, whose governmental style they reflected and whose members dominated their boards. With pragmatism as the main epistemological orientation, there was little place for the kind of academic freedom associated with idealist philosophy in the German case and with rationalism and specialization in the French case. Only with the development of the graduate school and the increased influence of German universities in the nineteenth century did major universities emerge. They faced a struggle for academic freedom that was surprisingly difficult, in spite of the degree of civil liberty and democracy present in the political context.[24] The integration of practical and theoretical knowledge and professional and academic knowledge, has been a characteristic feature of the American model, in contrast to the greater dualism between these areas in the European context.[25]

If the American university traces its roots to the English tradition of the college, the Soviet university has a considerable debt to both the German and French models, each of which had a significant impact in prerevolutionary Russia.[26] Although Marxist epistemology is characterized by a dialectical holism that should support a broad intellectual freedom, Leninist views of the state resulted in a limited academic freedom and a circumscribed autonomy for the university. This seemed to be a compromise that encouraged high standards of scholarship while causing minimal threat to political order. It is thus interesting to note how these values persisted, especially in the institutions that were called "comprehensive universities," which were characterized by a purity of knowledge far stricter than Humboldt's German model.[27] Professors were appointed by the state and formed an integral part of its personnel, as in the German and French cases. They managed to exercise a considerable degree of control over the curriculum, the selection of students, and many aspects of educational policy.[28] The academic freedom they enjoyed was firmly rooted in the European tradition, probably more that of France than of Germany. It was their command of specialist knowledge, and their ability to advance this knowledge in the basic and applied sciences, that made them most valuable to the regime.

Andrei Sakharov made the following fascinating comment on the tendency to standardization and authoritarianism in the Soviet Union: "A system of education under government control, separation of school and church, universal free education—all these are great achievements of social progress.

But everything has a reverse side. In this case it is the excessive standardization, extending to the teaching process itself, to the curriculum, especially in literature, history . . . geography, and to the system of examinations. One cannot but see a danger in excessive reference to authority and in the limitation of discussion and intellectual boldness at an age when personal convictions are beginning to be formed. In the old China, the systems of examinations for official positions led to mental stagnation and to the canonizing of the reactionary aspects of Confucianism. It is highly undesirable to have anything like that in a modern society."[29]

In the Soviet Union, another institution central to European scholarship found its fullest development—the academy. After its adoption by Plato and Aristotle, the term connoted a kind of informal society for learning and teaching. This was true right up to the seventeenth and eighteenth centuries. (It has thus been a fairly appropriate translation for the Chinese term *shuyuan* or the Arabic *madrasseh*.) However, when a group of French scholars who met regularly to discuss the maintenance of scholarly and linguistic standards were persuaded by the French king to form a national body, the *Académie française*, the term took on an entirely new connotation.[30] In various other European societies it became associated also with scientific enterprises originating outside of the university and gaining national recognition and prestige. Even in this new meaning, the term academy in most of Western Europe denoted an elite association of scholars, who had a nationally recognized intellectual authority, yet retained an institutional basis for their scholarly activities in universities or other types of institutions for research and higher learning.

Only in the Soviet Union and the Communist states within its orbit did the academy become a powerful research institution in its own right, which provided a setting for the careers of scholars occupied with major state research projects and a counterbalance to the university's focus on teaching.[31] The clear separation of research and teaching, which was antithetical to the values of the German model, resulted in the derogation of the universities, as the faculties had been derogated by the Napoleonic system in France in the preceding century. The canons of knowledge to be taught were not necessarily subjected to challenges arising from new research findings. Rather, university and academy stood side by side as primary intellectual forces, enjoying a measure of autonomy and academic freedom, yet separated by function and institutional framework.

We can see the resilience of the fundamental values of autonomy and academic freedom, in spite of somewhat different emphases and connotations, in each of the national cases outlined above. It is interesting to note their persistence within the socialist as well as the capitalist narrative. In many ways the cultural and epistemological bases of American society made them as difficult to achieve and maintain, as did the political and ideological constraints of the Soviet context. In spite of these constraints, however, they persisted as an integral part of the historical legacy of each nation.

CHINESE SCHOLARLY INSTITUTIONS AND VALUES

In China, a very different set of scholarly values arose over a long historical process. Given China's cultural and linguistic domination of East Asia, an understanding of some of the main values of the Chinese scholarly tradition is helpful also for interpreting the experience of other East Asian societies.

It is difficult to characterize several thousand years of Chinese scholarly institutions by reference to two or three core values. We can say with some certainty, however, that they were neither autonomy nor academic freedom, and that there was no institution in Chinese tradition that could accurately be called a university. Many years of reflection and reading have led me to believe that parallels to these European values and patterns have to be sought at two opposite poles of the Chinese experience. On the one hand there was the civil service examination system and its cognate institutions—the Hanlin Academy,[32] the college for the sons of the emperor (*guozijian*), the institution of supreme learning (*taixue*), and the whole system of institutions at provincial, prefectural, and county levels that made possible a "ladder of success" through a series of examinations, culminating in the palace examination in the presence of the emperor himself.[33] On the other hand, there were the *shuyuan*, scholarly societies or academies, that were often financially independent through bequests of land, and usually headed by one great scholar, who attracted disciples and colleagues through the virtuosity of his scholarship.[34]

The imperial examination system began to take form around 400 C.E. and reached its full institutional development in the Tang dynasty (618–907 C.E.). During the Song (960–1279 C.E.), it crystallized into patterns that were to last right up to 1911. While the medieval university of Europe had faculties of medicine, law, and arts, the imperial examination system of the Song, which developed at around the same time, standardized for examination purposes an integrated canon of classical texts, the Four Books and Five Classics, as arranged and annotated by the great neo-Confucian scholar Zhu Xi.[35] The specialized examinations in medicine and law that had been developed alongside those in more general classical knowledge in the Tang were discontinued. Zhu Xi himself was somewhat of an iconoclast, yet the canon he and his disciples formed was to become one of the most long-lasting and resilient codes of curricular knowledge in human history. It was only in the late nineteenth century that it was challenged by additional examinations introduced in areas such as mathematics and foreign languages, and finally abolished in favor of a modern curriculum in 1905.[36]

The academies or *shuyuan* also took their definitive form in the Song dynasty, as what had been originally libraries or centers for scholarly discussion developed into academies that provided a structured learning environment separate from, yet interacting with, state institutions associated with the civil service examination system. In a certain sense, the academies were oppositional to state power, drawing on texts and ideas that criticized and revised successive versions of classical orthodoxy. However, in another sense, they were essential to the maintenance of the imperial system, providing for a revitalization of the classical texts that served imperial power. There is a particular irony in the case of Zhu Xi's scholarship. While it was closely associated with the establishment of independent academies, and constituted a critique of governmental abuses of the time, it was to provide a foundation for the orthodox classical doctrine that dominated the imperial examinations of most succeeding dynasties.[37]

Ding Gang and Liu Qi give the following assessment of the role of the *shuyuan*: "From the process of development of traditional education Confucian culture was always the main current. Due to certain factors of the times, its ability to revitalize itself enabled it, in the process of its struggles and contentions with Buddhist, Daoist, and other educational traditions, to absorb valuable experience from them and renew itself. Thus it always succeeded in meeting the challenges and attacks from Buddhism and Daoism on its supremacy as the orthodox tradition. The academies were the product of this process of struggle between Confucian education, and Buddhist, and Daoist education."[38]

Neither the *shuyuan* nor the institutions for the imperial examination system were characterized by the kind of autonomy enjoyed by the European university. The latter were clearly an arm of the state for the recruitment and training of civil officials.[39] The content of the examinations, and therefore of such teaching as was done, was based on classical texts, and regulated through the Hanlin Academy, which held a dominant role in the Ming and Qing dynasties, with all those aspiring to highest office seeking appointment there. The "college for the sons of the empire" (*guozijian*), which can be traced back to 278 B.C., was both a kind of administrative office for educational and examination processes throughout the empire, and a college for sons of the aristocracy and high officials. The institute of supreme learning (*taixue*) provided a location at the center of empire where youth of other social strata could prepare for the examinations. More than autonomy, the community of scholar-officials could be said to hold a scholarly monopoly over the imperial bureaucracy, a monopoly that was predicated on their loyalty to the emperor and the classical texts. One English admirer of the early nineteenth century commented on the system in this way: "The whole of China may be said to resemble one vast university, which is governed by the scholars who have been educated within its walls."[40]

In striking contrast to this scholarly monopoly was the position of the *shuyuan*, which were characterized by an autonomy both fragile and fragmented. Having nothing equivalent to the papal charters to protect their institutional development, their rise and decline often reflected the fate of particular scholars and the groups of disciples around them.[41] At no time was there an officially established group of *shuyuan*, with collective rights for its members such as the *ius ubique docendi* of the medieval universities of Europe. The fragile autonomy they managed de facto to secure in certain periods enabled them to introduce heterodox texts from varying sources and encourage lively and iconoclastic teaching and learning methods, which often challenged imperial intellectual authority. As a result, in some periods, they were ruthlessly suppressed on the grounds that they were subversive to imperial authority.[42] In other periods they were successfully coopted into the service of the imperial examination system, and given funds to ensure that they played a subservient and supportive role in the system.[43] In contrast to the broadly based autonomy of the European university, we detect patterns of a scholarly monopoly of empire at one pole of Chinese scholarship, and a fragile and fragmented autonomy at the other pole.[44]

What about academic freedom? Can we find any value in the Chinese tradition that might be seen as its equivalent? We have already noted in the European context the association of academic freedom with increasing specialization of knowledge, and also with an epistemology that leaned toward the growth of knowledge through theoretical disputation and logical or empirical testing, rather than through application to practice. However, the Chinese tradition remained resistant to specialization up to the nineteenth century, in consequence of the breadth of content of the classical texts.[45] It was also more oriented toward practice than theory, in the sense that the highest knowledge could only be tested by scholar-officials through its use in the practice of government. Scholars who did not succeed in becoming officials and dedicated themselves rather to teaching or specialist research were always in a secondary and subordinate position.

There was thus no real parallel in the Chinese tradition to the notion of academic freedom that emerged in Europe. At one pole was the absolute intellectual authority of the inner circle of scholar-officials, who set the examinations and controlled canonical knowledge within the Hanlin Academy. This authority permitted them to censure the emperor himself, if his practice of government strayed from the principles enshrined in the classical texts.[46] It did not, however, allow them to participate in critical questioning or debates about the validity of these principles.[47] At the other pole was the broad intellectual freedom exercised at certain periods by scholars within the *shuyuan*, who seldom restricted themselves to a specialist field of knowledge, nor to merely theoretical dimensions of understanding. They too dealt with issues around the definition and interpretation of the classical texts and their application to affairs of government.[48] In contrast with the academic freedom of Western universities was an intellectual authority that extended over the whole imperial system at one pole, and at the other an intermittent intellectual freedom that at times offered a direct challenge to imperial authority through criticisms of and interventions into the practice of government.

With the identification of these two opposing sets of scholarly values, we can get the sense of a cultural dialectic, an ongoing tension that could not easily be synthesized into the kind of compromise with governmental and ecclesiastical authority achieved in the autonomy and academic freedom of the European university. It is also possible to make interesting comparisons with various threads of the European experience. In terms of a practice-based epistemology and a resistance to specialization, certain shared sensitivities with Anglo-American scholarly traditions might be discerned, and thus problems with academic freedom in the experience of those traditions might have some resonance with China's modern experience. In its hierarchy and the bureaucratization of higher institutions, with one clear central intellectual authority dominating the scene, there are parallels between China's patterns, on the one side, and the ethos of the Napoleonic university in France and the Soviet university and academy under Lenin and Stalin, on the other.

EASTERN TRADITIONS AND PATTERNS

Among other Asian societies, Japan, Korea, and Vietnam owe the most to Chinese scholarly traditions. In the Japanese case, the classical texts held an equally important position, but neither an elaborate system of civil service examinations, nor their antithesis in independent academies developed, possibly because of the more important role played by the military class in feudal government.[49] Perhaps that is why the adoption of French and German patterns for the modern Japanese university seems to have been a smoother and less troubled process than for China. In the Korean case, there were much stronger parallels, with both a civil service examination system, and institutions called *sowon* that were similar to the Chinese *shuyuan*.[50] Korea's modern universities developed under the shadow of Japanese imperialism, and it is not surprising that it was the American model, supported by the legacy of *sowon* values, which was to facilitate effective cultural resistance to Japanese domination.[51] In the case of Vietnam, a civil service examination system was closely related to Chinese patterns, but there were no equivalent institutions to the *shuyuan*.[52]

Beyond these obvious links among countries that shared a Confucian heritage, it might be interesting to ask how far the Chinese tradition could be regarded as an "Eastern tradition" having some characteristics in common with institutions of Arabic philosophy, for example. In his exhaustive study of the rise of Islamic colleges, George Makdisi makes interesting comparisons between the college and the university, and notes how the university was unique to Europe, and never took form in the Arabic world, in spite of the profound influences of Arabic scholarship on the European university. The colleges or *madrassehs* of the Arabic world were based on charitable trusts or *waqf*, which never became incorporated. The license to teach was essentially granted by individuals, who held it by right of their scholarly competence in the laws. "There being no church in Islam, no ecclesiastical hierarchy, no university, that is to say no guild of masters, no one but the individual master-jurisconsult granted the license. The line of religious authority rested, not with sovereign power but rather with the religious scholars, the *ulama*. Moreover, the institutions in which the *ulama* taught were creations completely independent of the sovereign as such, and in no need of his sanction to come into existence . . . Islamic education, like Islamic law, is basically individualist, personalist."[53]

Makdisi goes on to suggest that it was the incorporation of the colleges in Europe, and their integration within the university as the guild of scholars, having a separate and collective institutional identity recognized by church and feudal and city states, that made possible the dynamism of the European scholarly community and its movement to carry forward all it had gained from the Arabic world in terms of scholarly texts and methods of disputation. In contrast, the colleges of Islam, always private and never incorporated, remained static and gradually fell under the total control of the governing power of the caliphs. The rationalism and breadth of scholarship of the eleventh and twelfth centuries, with the freedom for disputation and rational debate that had sustained it, were to be snuffed out.[54]

There seem to be one main point of similarity here with China. This was the identity of scholarly or religious authority ultimately with a person, the interpreter of the text, as against the texts themselves or a group who might collectively interpret them within the protections afforded by an incorporated institution. As in the case of Islam, the Chinese had no institutions of independent academic or religious authority. Rather, they had the tension between the authority of individual scholars of great virtuosity, who often founded or revived *shuyuan* as a basis for the dissemination of new teachings, and the imperial learning institutions, presided over by the emperor as Son of Heaven, and gaining their legitimacy ultimately from the imperial throne, if not from the emperor himself. This sense of knowledge being authorized by the person, whether the emperor or a scholar recognized as having received the mantle of truth, seems to be a persisting element of Eastern scholarly orientation. It stands in fundamental contrast with the ethos of the university as a corporation or guild whose scholars consensually establish abstract criteria of truth and substantive propositions.

THE TRIUMPH OF THE EUROPEAN UNIVERSITY

The nineteenth century saw the diffusion of the European model of the university throughout much of the world, under conditions of imperialism and colonialism, which might be understood as an integral part of the history of capitalism,[55] or might be seen in terms of broader and more comprehensive structures of imperialism.[56] If the guild, the corporation, and the mercantile city are seen as foundations of capitalist development, then the university was closely linked to this history from its earliest days.

However, the Soviet Union also bears reflection from the perspective of views of imperialism and colonialism. There, values of the European university tradition managed to persist after the October revolution, and informed a socialist higher education system, which took upon itself responsibility for academic leadership in most of the countries that found themselves within the Soviet orbit, including Eastern Europe, North Korea, China, and Vietnam. These relations came to be viewed as imperialistic, by China at least, and perhaps can be best understood in terms of a structural theory of imperialism.[57] Soviet socialism was, after all, also a product of the rationalism and idealism of nineteenth-century French and German thought. It is notable how the university has been integral to both the capitalist and the socialist versions of the Western narrative of development.

Eric Ashby gives a splendid conspectus on the process whereby the British university, specifically the University of London, which operated more as an examining body than a teaching institution, was transferred to India in the nineteenth century. He suggests that values of autonomy and academic freedom, never as clearly articulated in Britain as in France and Germany, were limited in the course of the transfer, partly with the intention of ensuring the university's subordination to British colonial interests.[58] In the African context, where this process took place much later, Ashby suggests that British colonial authorities had learned from some of the lessons of the Indian experience, and gave a little more leeway for new African institutions to reflect their own cultural traditions.[59] However, English was the main language of instruction, and the curricular content was highly Eurocentric (in the early period, at least). The development of French universities in the African context provides an even more compelling example of the propensity of the European institution to extend the domain of the metropole.[60]

What was the particular character of the Asian experience? First, we must take into account the role of scholarship in the empire of classical China, which had bequeathed institutional patterns, authoritative texts, and even the linguistic forms expressing them, to Japan, Korea, and Vietnam. In Japan's historical experience as a colonial power, exercising control over Korea and Taiwan for a moderately long period, the overt pattern of the university was Western, a combination of influences from several European countries, with French and German patterns predominant.[61] Underlying this, however, lay a Confucianist conception of the state and its intellectual prerogatives that had shaped Asian thought for more than a millennium.[62] It could be argued that this combination of Confucian intellectual authority and French patterns of centralized academic administration made for a more repressive and exclusivist university in Korea and Taiwan than had been the case for most universities established in Western colonies. This seems to have been particularly the case in Korea,[63] less so in Taiwan.[64]

The other point of note in the Asian experience of university development is that of the diversity of Western colonial powers and their respective influences—Britain in India, Malaysia, Hong Kong and Singapore, France in Vietnam, Holland in Indonesia, the United States in the Philippines, and subsequently as a kind of quasi-colonial power in Japan, Korea, and Taiwan after World War II. China and Thailand stand out in this picture as countries that never fell under the complete domination of any one foreign power. China, however, experienced inroads and periods of domination from most of the Western powers, as well as Japan, at different periods of its history. The nearest China came to being fully colonized by any one power, with the possible exception of Japan, was when it came under the influence of the Soviet Union in the period from 1949 to 1957, an experience that came to be seen by the Chinese as "social imperialism."[65] That may account for the intensity of the backlash against external domination, and the deep psychosis about external aggression and deculturation that characterized the Great Leap Forward period and the Cultural Revolution.

In spite of the Leninist adage that imperialism is the highest stage of capitalism, the Chinese were to experience imperialism in its most bruising form at the hands of its socialist big brother, the Soviet Union, and it was felt more in the arenas of politics and culture than economy. While clear patterns of economic domination can be detected in the relations between China and the Soviet Union, there is also strong evidence of tremendous economic benefits accruing to China, especially in the development of heavy industry, under Soviet tutelage.[66] Probably cultural and political imperialism were more responsible for China's explosive counterreaction than perceptions of economic exploitation. China's universities were to be integrally caught up in the interface between political and cultural domination, as centers for the propagation of a socialist orthodoxy that was clearly Western in its roots and that provided the main legitimation for the new regime.

It may be worthwhile at this point to reflect on the question of whether or not imperialism needs a broader definition than that common to the Marxist corpus and Lenin's characterization of the phenomenon. In contrast to the view that it is fundamentally rooted in the economic patterns of domination associated with capitalism, Johann Galtung has identified and characterized structures of domination that can be found congruently in cultural, political, economic, communications, and military spheres in his "structural theory of imperialism."[67] He calls upon researchers to explore in particular historical contexts the interconnections among these spheres. This way of posing the problem of imperialism carries within it suggestions for reducing degrees of domination through structural changes toward what he terms "horizontalization" and "de-feudalization."

Values of equity, autonomy, solidarity, and participation can be explicitly drawn upon in constructing versions of a preferred future, and interventions can be identified in the cultural, political, or economic arenas that would reduce patterns of domination.[68] Many of the efforts of developing nations in U.N. organizations since the late 1960s, such as the New International Economic Order and the New World Information Order, have exemplified this approach,[69] as has a considerable amount of research in comparative education.[70]

A second methodological point that merits discussion at this point relates to the issue of scientific method. Some of the work on imperialism and educational or cultural influences operates within an implicit positivism of method. Attempts are made to "prove" the coherence between economic patterns of exploitation and cultural or educational patterns that reinforce that exploitation, and make it appear normal.[71] Less attention is given to situations where educational and cultural influences can be seen to diverge from economic or political patterns of domination. Yet surely it is these cases that are of the greatest interest, if our intention is to understand the complexity of patterns of domination and their interrelations in all spheres, not only the economic. Thus I would suggest that a sense of the confluence of economic, political, and cultural imperialism in specific geographic and historic time contexts makes for excellent hypothesis generation. However, the most interesting and scientifically sound research efforts around these hypotheses would be those that attempt to falsify them, rather than those that amass extensive data to prove them. Popper's views on critical method and fallibilism in scientific research might well be relevant to this kind of research agenda.[72]

The story of how universities developed in China provides an ideal testing ground for a critical exploration of the links between cultural institution-building and a whole range of different forms of imperialism, each having a somewhat different combination of emphasis on the economic, the political, the cultural, and the military dimension of the relationship. It was my privilege in the mid-1980s to work with the French sinologist, Marianne Bastid, on a volume in which we tried to separate these threads as we considered the creation of modern Chinese institutions of education.[73] The volume was only partially successful, as not every contributor was interested in the linkages we were trying to probe. Nevertheless, it attempted a differentiated picture of China's experience of imperialism and the building of modern educational institutions. I will attempt at this point to summarize some of its main findings as part of my efforts to set the context for the story of China's universities in the period after 1911.

The British were by far the most important colonial power in terms of economic involvement in Chinese development, from the time of the Opium Wars. Yet it is striking how limited was British influence on Chinese education, especially at the tertiary level. This can be explained fairly simply in terms of the character of British missionary endeavor in China. Few British missionaries were themselves university educated, in contrast to their American fellows, and the evangelical wing, intent on grass-roots evangelization, tended to dominate. The most interesting English figure in terms of higher education was the Baptist missionary, Timothy Richards, whose involvement with Chinese intellectual circles in the late nineteenth and early twentieth centuries resulted in the founding of Shanxi University in 1901. It used British Boxer indemnity funds and had a definite British imprint. What is fascinating about this institution is the smooth way in which it became sinicized, with most traces of British influence disappearing by the 1920s. The question of how far the first statutes for modern higher education, issued by imperial edicts of 1902 and 1903, were influenced by this model remains one yet to be researched. Apart from this, the only university in China that could be linked to British colonialism was the University of Hong Kong, and its influence in mainland China was to be minimal.[74]

Probably the second most important imperial power, in terms of economic and military involvement in China, was Japan. It is interesting to note that Japanese educational influences predated its most extensive economic and military incursions. In effect, the whole modern Chinese education system was designed by imperial officials who admired, perhaps grudgingly, Japan's success with modernization, and who were proud of its military victory over Russia in 1904–1905.[75] While designing institutions intended to introduce modern techniques yet preserve the essence of Confucian loyalty and social harmony, these same officials provided for large numbers of Chinese youth to study in Japan. Contrary to their expectations and plans, many were exposed to radical and critical currents of thought in Japan, and some became revolutionary activists.[76]

The Imperial University, founded in 1898, was almost the only institution introduced under the influence of progressive intellectuals involved in the brief Hundred-Day Reform Movement of 1898 to survive the conservative backlash to this movement. It was patterned after the University of Tokyo, which in turn had been influenced by both French and German academic patterns. Conservative political leaders in China were apparently attracted to the ways in which Japan had introduced Western institutions and techniques while maintaining imperial authority and Confucian cultural supremacy, as is fairly clear in the legislation for a modern educational system patterned after Japan that was passed in 1902 and 1903.[77] This legislation gave the Imperial University a leading position over the entire education system.

With the revolution of 1911, this explicit commitment to Confucian ideology became more and more contested, and by the time Japan's imperialist ambitions became obvious in the 21 Demands of 1915, China had already begun to turn from Japanese educational patterns toward the more emancipatory patterns of America and Europe. It is thus difficult to prove a strong connection between Japan's educational influences on China and Japanese imperialist ambitions.

The rest of the story of China's experience with foreign models of higher education really lies within chapter 2 of this volume, which will treat the period from 1911 to 1949. Still, a few comments may be useful at this point to highlight aspects of the Chinese experience with foreign models of education in the period up to the 1950s, and contrasts with the period of Soviet influence from 1949 to 1960. A wide range of models or types of higher institution were introduced, some through initiatives taken by foreign missionaries or governments, others through efforts undertaken by individual Chinese scholars and successive Chinese regimes. The diversity of influence and variety of experimentation over this period makes for a striking contrast with the period of Soviet influence after 1949, when there was a uniformity in the patterns introduced and a congruence among cultural, political, and economic interactions that had not been experienced in China before or since.

From the American side, both the model of the college and that of the university had considerable impact. In the early period, most American missionaries sought to establish colleges modeled after their own educational experiences in American colleges. Only gradually did these institutions develop into universities in China, and then the direct and unified authority exercised over them by the Western Christian establishment cast them into a different form from universities in the United States at the same period.[78] The American university model was pioneered by Qinghua University, originally a language school set up with American Boxer indemnity funds, but by the late 1920s one of China's premier national universities, under the leadership of some outstanding American-returned Chinese scholars. Thus, while missionaries had introduced the college model, Chinese scholarly circles had chosen to emulate the American university model.

The French case is equally interesting. On the one hand, Jesuit missionaries established a "French Catholic university in China" with support and recognition from the French government, which, in spite of its secularism, had not hesitated to maintain a high profile in China through the French Protectorate.[79] In the absence of extensive economic interests, opportunities for cultural presence seem to have been highly valued. However, when it came to the support of a secular, socialist-oriented university, the Université Franco-Chinoise, established in the 1920s by such distinguished Chinese scholars as Cai Yuanpei, Wu Zhihui, and Li Shizeng, French government support was more tentative. This institution never got the kind of support from French Boxer indemnity funds that did so much to make Qinghua University excel.[80]

The German case has an interesting twist of its own. German authorities seemed to be particularly interested in potential linkages between higher education and their economic interests in China. Thus the model they wished to introduce was that of the *Technische Hochschule*, with its focus on higher engineering education and its absence of a tradition of autonomy or academic freedom. This area, together with medical education, thus became the main emphasis of institutions supported by the German government in China.[81] It was left to Cai Yuanpei to introduce the Humboldtian university model to China when he was appointed president of Peking University in 1917.[82] The patterns of autonomy and academic freedom instituted at that time led to contradictions in the Chinese context that have reverberated through Chinese history from the May 4th Movement of 1919 up to the Tiananmen events of 1989, with Peking University constantly finding itself at the center of these movements. As for the technical education introduced with German government help, the fact of Germany's defeat in World War I made it particularly easy for Chinese scholarly and governmental circles to embrace this part of the German heritage.

These brief sketches of Chinese-Western interaction over the period up to 1949 are intended simply to illustrate the complexity of the interconnections among diverse cultural and educational patterns, and the economic and political interests of the various colonial powers on the one side, and the Chinese ideas of their own practical needs, their pride in their own culture, and their distrustful respect for Western intellectual traditions on the other. Just as there were diverse influences coming through channels that were more or less linked to overt governmental concerns on the Western side, within China there were diverse interlocutors, from individual scholars who exercised enormous influence over the development of one or several institutions at times, to various educational interest groups, to governmental representatives initiating policy and legislation at the national level.

What makes the experience of Soviet influence in the 1950s so strikingly different is the uniformity of initiative and response on each side. On the Soviet side were strong and centralized governmental interests, with the scholarly community involved only to the degree that it exercised intellectual authority on behalf of the government. On the Chinese side there was a corresponding uniformity. Not only were all private higher institutions dissolved in the early 1950s, very few local or provincial level institutions were allowed to survive, with the exception of a few teacher training colleges. The focus of the early 1950s was on establishing a highly centralized national system of higher educational institutions, which would directly serve the task of "socialist construction" along lines that imitated the experience of the Soviet Union as closely as possible.[83] Scholars were able to be involved in this process only to the degree that they identified closely with both the patterns and the ideology imported from the Soviet Union.

The central intellectual institution, People's University, held a position that enabled it to dominate and regulate all teaching and research in the social sciences, to educate or reeducate all leading cadres in the crucial areas of national planning, finance, trade, and related areas, and finally to train an army of political instructors whose task was to ensure absolute intellectual orthodoxy throughout the university community and in the wider professional milieu.[84] The Soviet Union achieved a degree of congruence among patterns of educational, cultural, economic, and political domination that had never been achieved by any other colonial power that had been active in China.

I am aware of the complexities of the points of conflict that emerged between China and the Soviet Union in the 1950s, and do not intend to convey an over-simplified view of the reasons for these conflicts. Yet the degree to which Chinese educational policy in the Great Leap Forward and the Cultural Revolution may have been a reaction to this last and most penetrating experience of educational imperialism has perhaps been underestimated in what has been written about these two periods. Valuable as Soviet expertise was in many important areas, especially those of industrial and technological development, it seems to have led to a reaction on the Chinese side of explosive proportions.

The model that the Chinese returned to, after their experience with "Soviet social imperialism" was the one that had been developed in Yan'an during a period of self-reliance and minimal influence from any external source. The institutions of the border region during the revolutionary struggle were, of course, developed under circumstances of limited resources and considerable difficulty. They were really colleges for training cadres to work in military and party organizations, and in the fledgling bureaucratic institutions of the border region governments. One of the most famous institutions, the Anti-Japanese Military College (*Kangda*), was directly administered by the army, and had training programs in military and political strategy that lasted for about six months. Yan'an University was directly under Communist party administration, and had somewhat greater academic pretensions, with colleges of arts, sciences, public administration, and medicine. Its programs lasted for two to three years, depending on the field. Most of the faculty in both of these institutions held dual positions as lecturers and as cadres within government, party, or military administration, and there was certainly neither autonomy nor academic freedom.[85]

There was, however, an informality in the teaching and learning process, a concern with social practice, and a tendency toward multidisciplinarity that reflected aspects of the *shuyuan* tradition. In writing for the inauguration of the Hunan Self-Study University in the 1920s, Mao had made the following comments on this tradition: "In looking back at the *shuyuan*, although there were faults in their form of organization, there were not the faults of schools listed above (a mechanistic style of teaching that does injury to human personality, too many hours of class and too complex a curriculum so that students can't use their own ideas to initiate research). First, affectionate bonds between students and teachers were sincere. Second, there was no 'academic government by professors' (the Chinese term for university autonomy) but a free spirit and free research. Thirdly, the curriculum was simple and discussion ranged broadly, it was possible to work in a leisurely and carefree way and to play a little."[86] In the early years of the Yan'an institutions there was a similar intellectual spirit, as this group of revolutionary intellectuals planned the remaking of China. Marxist thought and theory were explored in an experimental way, and applied to the particularities of the Chinese context.

As Mao's star rose, however, this intellectual freedom was transmuted into a new authority, a new orthodoxy. From being a scholar able to prove the virtuosity of his knowledge in the practice of government, Mao gradually adopted the position of an emperor figure, able to impose his own words and thoughts as a new intellectual orthodoxy. The beginnings of this can be seen in the rectification movements of the early 1940s, and the culmination in the reverence given to Mao's thoughts and words during the Cultural Revolution decade.

Can there be such an institution as the university in a context characterized by these cultural dynamics? This is the main question that will be explored throughout this volume. If not, what sort of hybrid institution has emerged at the interface of these value complexes? What is its potential and likely trajectory of development? Does it have any lessons worth pondering in relation to the future of university and society in a global context?

NOTES

1. Max Weber, *The Methodology of the Social Sciences* [translated and edited by Edward Shils and Henry Find] (New York: Free Press, 1949), pp. 93ff. Weber's discussion of the creation and use of ideal types in this passage is particularly incisive.

2. Hastings Rashdall, *The Universities of Europe in the Middle Ages*, (Oxford: Clarendon Press, 1895), Vol. I, chapter 1.

3. A graphic discussion of the significance of the emergence of early medieval towns is found in Karl Marx's *German Ideology* (Moscow: Progress Publishers, 1976), pp. 71–80.

4. Rashdall, *The Universities of Europe*, Vol. I, p. 16.

5. Rashdall, *The Universities of Europe*, Vol. I, pp. 189, 401, 421; see also Gabriel Compayré, *Abelard and the Origin and Early History of Universities* (New York: Ams Press, 1969), pp. 87–90.

6. John Baldwin, "The Penetration of University Personnel into French and

English Administration at the Turn of the Twelfth and Thirteenth Centuries," in *Revue des Etudes Islamiques*, XLIV, Special issue on "Medieval Education in Islam and the West," 1976, pp. 199–211.

7. Ibid., Vol. I, 527–529; Vol. II, pp. 692ff.

8. See Charles Thurot, *De l'organisation de l'enseignement dans l'Université de Paris au Moyen age* (Paris, 1850), quoted in George Makdisi, *The Rise of Colleges* (Edinburgh: Edinburgh University Press, 1981) for a discussion of the remarkable authority exercised by members of the faculty of theology of the University of Paris in matters of theological dogma. Rashdall, *The Universities of Europe*, Vol. I, pp. 548–549.

9. Compayré, *Abelard and the Origin and Early History of Universities*, pp. 185 ff. gives a detailed depiction of the method of disputation for advancing knowledge.

10. H.C. Barnard, *Education and the French Revolution* (Cambridge: Cambridge University Press, 1969). See also Frederick Artz, *The Development of Technical Education in France, 1500–1850* (Cambridge, Mass., and London: Society for the History of Technology and M.I.T. Press, 1966), and Emile Durkheim, *The Evolution of Educational Thought* (London: Routledge and Kegan Paul, 1977).

11. Antoine Prost, *L'Enseignement en France, 1800–1967* (Paris: Armand Colin, 1968); Joseph Moody, *French Education Since Napoleon* (New York: Syracuse University Press, 1978).

12. Pascale Gruson, *L'Etat Enseignant* (Paris: Mouton, 1978).

13. Ibid., p. 150.

14. Ibid., p.91; Prost, *L'Enseignement*, p. 300.

15. Fritz Ringer, *Education and Society in Modern Europe* (Bloomington and London: Indiana University Press, 1979); Fritz Ringer, *Fields of Knowledge: French Academic Culture in Comparative Perspective, 1890–1920* (Cambridge: Cambridge University Press, 1992).

16. Wilhelm von Humboldt, "On the Spirit and the Organizational Framework of Intellectual Institutions," in *Minerva*, Vol. 8, April 1970, pp. 242–250.

17. Charles McLelland, *State, Society and University in Germany, 1700–1914* (Cambridge: Cambridge University Press, 1980); Fritz Ringer, *The Decline of the German Mandarins* (Cambridge, Mass.: Harvard University Press, 1969).

18. Frederic Lilge, *The Abuse of Learning: The Failure of the German University* (New York: Macmillan, 1948), p. 48ff discusses Fichte's interpretation of this role. For a critical discussion of the effects of the rule of philosophy on the natural and social sciences, see Ralf Dahrendorf, *Society and Democracy in Germany* (London: Wiedenfield and Nicolson, 1965), p. 156ff.

19. The connotations of academic freedom in the German context can also be understood in relation to the social background of the intellectual class. Fritz Ringer has shown how the educated middle classes in Germany continued to be infused by aristocratic values and developed rather separately from the industrial or economically defined middle class.

20. Isolde Guenther, "A Study of the Evolution of the German Technische Hochschule," unpublished Ph.D. dissertation, University of London Institute of Education, 1972.

21. Eric Ashby, *Universities: British, Indian, African* (London: Weidenfield and Nicolson, 1966) provides an incisive summary of the nineteenth-century British university in chapter 1, pp. 19–29.

22. Sheldon Rothblatt, *The Revolution of the Dons: Cambridge and Society in Victorian England* (London: Faber and Faber, 1968), especially chapter 7, "The Idea of a College," pp. 209–247.

23. Robin Harris, *A History of Higher Education in Canada* (Toronto: University of Toronto Press, 1978), pp. 14–26.

24. Richard Hofstadter and Walter Metzger, *The Development of Academic Freedom in the United States* (New York and London: Columbia University Press, 1955) provides an illuminating historical exploration of this contradiction. See also

Richard Hofstadter and Wilson Smith, *American Higher Education Documentary History*, 2 vols. (Chicago and London: University of Chicago Press, 1961).

25. Joseph Ben-David, *American Higher Education: Directions Old and New* (New York: McGraw-Hill, 1972).

26. William Johnson, *Russia's Educational Heritage* (Pittsburgh, Pa.: Carnegie Press, 1950), chapter 3.

27. Nicholas DeWitt, *Soviet Professional Manpower* (Washington, D.C.: National Science Foundation, 1955), provides a useful historical overview of the development of universities within the higher education system after the 1917 Revolution.

28. L.G. Churchward, *The Soviet Intelligentsia* (London: Routledge and Kegan Paul, 1973).

29. Andrei Sakharov, "The Threat to Intellectual Freedom," in J.L. Nogee, *Man, State, and Society in the Soviet Union* (London: Pall Mall Press, 1972). p. 494–5.

30. Frances Yates, *The French Academy of the Sixteenth Century* (The Warburg Institute, University of London, 1947); D. MacLaren Robertson, *A History of the French Academy, 1635–1910* (New York: G.W. Dillingham, 1910).

31. Alexander Korol, *Soviet Education for Science and Technology* (New York: John Wiley and Sons, and Technology Press of M.I.T., 1957), p. 297ff provides a discussion of the distinctions and interconnections between research institutes of the academy of sciences and higher education institutions.

32. Adam Yuen-chung Lui, *The Hanlin Academy: Training Ground for the Ambitious, 1644–1850* (Hamden, Conn.: Archon Books, 1981), gives a thorough discussion of the character and role of this institution in the last imperial dynasty—the Qing, ending his study just sixty-one years before the collapse of the Qing empire in 1911.

33. Ho Ping-ti, *The Ladder of Success in Imperial China: Aspects of Social Mobility, 1368 to 1911* (New York and London: Columbia University Press, 1962); Ichisada Miyazaki, *China's Examination Hell: The Civil Service Examinations of Imperial China* (New York and Tokyo: Weatherhill, 1977). These two volumes give a succinct overall picture over a long time period. For a detailed study of the examinations in one important period, the Song, see John Chaffee, *The Thorny Gates of Learning in Sung China* (Cambridge: Cambridge University Press, 1985).

34. For a good study of these institutions during the Ming dynasty, see John Meskill, *Academies in Ming China*, (Tucson: University of Arizona Press, 1982). For several excellent essays on their early development and role in the Song period, see Theodore de Bary and John Chaffee (eds.), *Neo-Confucian Education: The Formative Stage* (Berkeley: University of California Press, 1989). For their role in the late Qing dynasty, see Barry Keenan, "Lung-men Academy in Shanghai and the Expansion of Kiangsu's Educated Elite, 1865–1911," in Benjamin A. Elman and Alexander Woodside (eds.), *Education and Society in Late Imperial China, 1600–1900* (Berkeley: University of California Press, 1994), pp. 493–524.

35. Chan Wing-tsit, *Chu Hsi: Life and Thought* (Hong Kong: Chinese University Press, 1984).

36. Wolfgang Franke, *The Reform and Abolition of the Traditional Chinese Examination System* (Cambridge, Mass.: Harvard University Press, 1960).

37. Zhu Weizheng, "Confucius and Traditional Chinese Education: An Assessment," in R. Hayhoe (ed.), *Education and Modernization: The Chinese Experience* (Oxford: Pergamon, Toronto: OISE Press, 1992), pp. 15–17.

38. Ding Gang and Liu Qi, *Shuyuan yu Zhongguo wenhua* [Academies and Chinese Culture] (Shanghai: Shanghai jiaoyu chubanshe, 1992) p. 19.

39. Thomas Lee, *Government Education and Examinations in Song China* (Hong Kong: Chinese University of Hong Kong Press, 1985); Joanna Menzel, *The Chinese Civil Service: Career Open to Talent* (Boston: D.C. Heath, 1963).

40. Teng Ssu-yu, "Chinese Influence on the Western Examination System," in *Harvard Journal of Asiatic Studies*, Vol. 7, no. 4, 1942, p. 290. Teng quotes this statement from an English writer, C.T. Downey, in a book published in 1838.

41. Liu Boji, *Guangdong shuyuan zhidu* (Taiwan: Taiwan Shudian, 1958). Li Caidong (ed.), *Bailudong shuyuan shilue* [The Evolution of the White Deer Academy] (Beijing: Jiaoyu kexue chubanshe, 1989), especially chapter 1.

42. One of the most famous cases of a *shuyuan* becoming a center for political dissidence is the Donglin Academy. See Charles Hucker, "The Tong-lin Movement of the Late Ming Period," in John Fairbank (ed.), *Chinese Thought and Institutions* (Chicago: University of Chicago Press, 1957), pp. 132–162.

43. Chen Dongyuan, *Zhongguo jiaoyu shi* [A History of Chinese Education] (Shanghai: Commercial Press, 1936) describes the Qing government legislation designed to bring the *shuyuan* into conformity with state needs. Benjamin Elman, *From Philosophy to Philology: Intellectual and Social Aspects of Change in Late Imperial China* (Cambridge, Mass.: Harvard East Asian Monographs, 1984), pp. 120–127, has a thoughtful and informed discussion of the tensions between cooptation to government service and the maintenance of space for free intellectual debate.

44. There is a wealth of literature in Chinese on the *shuyuan*. Three volumes that I have found particularly helpful are Liu Boji, *Guangdong shuyuan zhidu* [The Guangdong Shuyuan System] (Taiwan: Taiwan shudian, 1958; Sheng Langxi, *Zhongguo shuyuan zhidu* [The Chinese Shuyuan System] (Shanghai: Zhonghua shuju, 1934); Zhang Liuquan, *Zhongguo shuyuan shihua* [The Evolution of Chinese Shuyuan] (Beijing: Jiaoyu kexue chubanshe, 1981).

45. See Joseph Levenson, *Confucian China and Its Modern Fate* (London: Routledge and Kegan Paul, 1958), Vol. I, chapter 2, "The Amateur Ideal in Ming and Ch'ing Society," and John Dardess, *Confucianism and Autocracy: Professional Elites in the Founding of the Ming Dynasty* (Berkeley: University of California Press, 1983) for a response. See also Chang Chung-li, *The Chinese Gentry: Studies in Their Role in the Nineteenth Century* (Seattle: University of Washington Press, 1962).

46. The American Presbyterian missionary, W.A.P. Martin, in *Hanlin Papers* (London: Trubner and Co., 1880), p. 114, provides the following description of where this took place: "In an adjacent block or square (to the Confucian temple and the College of the Sons of the Emperor) stands a pavilion known as the 'Imperial Lecture Room,' because it is incumbent on each occupant of the dragon throne to go there at least once in his lifetime, to hear a discourse on the nature and responsibilities of his office—thus confirming to the Chowle, which makes it the duty of the officers of the university to administer reproofs and exhortation to their sovereign, and doing homage to the university, by going in person to receive its instructions."

47. R. Kent Guy, *The Emperor's Four Treasuries: Scholars and the State in the Late Ch'ien-Lung Era* (Cambridge, Mass.: Harvard University Press, 1987), provides an illuminating study of the great book collection put together by scholar officials during the Qianlong reign of the Qing dynasty, and the subsequent literary inquisition. He describes the compilation itself as a process whereby "intellectuals and rulers together defined the nature of imperial authority and explored its limits" (p. 2).

48. See Charles Hucker, "The Tong-lin Movement," p. 161.

49. Ronald Dore, *Education in Tokagawa Japan* (London: Athlone, 1984).

50. William Theodore de Bary and JaJyun Kim Haboush (eds.), *The Rise of Neo-Confucianism in Korea* (New York: Columbia University Press, 1985). See especially Yi Songmu, "The Influence of Neo-Confucianism on Education and the Civil Service Examination System in Fourteenth- and Fifteenth-Century Korea," pp. 125–160.

51. Songho Lee, "The Emergence of the Modern University in Korea," in Philip Altbach and Viswanathan Selvaratnam, *From Dependence to Autonomy: The Development of Asian Universities* (Amsterdam: Kluwer Academic Publishers, 1989, pp. 227–256. Uchang Kim, "The Autonomous Development of the University in Korea," in *The University and the Future World* (Seoul: Yonsei University Press, 1985), pp. 151–153 discusses the Korean tradition of the *sowon* and the important heritage of values it left to modern institutions in their struggle for independence.

52. Alexander Woodside, *Vietnam and the Chinese Model: A Comparative*

Study of Vietnamese and Chinese Government in the First Half of the Nineteenth Century (Cambridge, Mass.: Council on East Asian Studies, Harvard University, 1988). See especially chapter 4, "Education and Examinations in Nguyen Vietnam."

53. George Makdisi, *The Rise of Colleges: Institutions of Learning in Islam and the West* (Edinburgh: Edinburgh University Press, 1981), p. 271.

54. For somewhat different perspectives on the Madrasseh, see A.L. Tibawi, "Origin and Character of Al-Madrasah," in A.L. Tibawi, *Arabic and Islamic Themes* (London: Luzac and Company, 1974; R.W. Bulliet, *The Patricians of Nishapur: A Study in Medieval Islamic Social History* (Cambridge, Mass.: Harvard University Press, 1972), especially chapter 4 (pp. 47–60) and Appendix I, "The Madrasa," pp. 249–255; Dominique Sourdel, "Reflexions sur la Diffusion de la Madrasa en Orient du XIe au XIIIe siecle," in *Revue des Etudes Islamiques*, XLIV, 1976, pp. 165–184.

55. V. Lenin, *Imperialism, the Highest Stage of Capitalism* (New York: International Publishers, 1939) is, of course, the classic text on this subject. Martin Carnoy's *Education as Cultural Imperialism* (New York: MacKay, 1974) was one of the early texts suggesting this perspective as a framework for comparative educational research.

56. Johann Galtung, "A Structural Theory of Imperialism," *Journal of Peace Research*, Vol. 8, 1972, pp. 81–117.

57. Johann Galtung, "Conflict on a Global Scale: Social Imperialism and Sub-Imperialism—Continuities in the Structural Theory of Imperialism," *World Development*, Vol. 4, no. 3, March 1976, pp. 153–165.

58. E. Ashby, *Universities*, pp. 47–54.

59. Ibid., pp. 142–143.

60. Ibid., pp. 364–375. See also Ali Mazrui, "The African University as a Multi-National Corporation," in A. Mazrui, *Political Values and the Educated Class in Africa* (London: Heinneman, 1978).

61. Shigeru Nakayama, "Independence and Choice: Western Impacts on Japanese Higher Education," in P. Altbach and V. Selvaratnam, *From Independence to Autonomy*, pp. 97–104.

62. Teruhisa Horio, *Educational Thought and Ideology in Modern Japan* (Tokyo: University of Tokyo Press, 1988). See especially Horio's analysis of how "the practicality of Western science" was fused with "the virtues of Confucian moralism" (p. 47) in "The Meiji Enlightenment" (pp. 24–64) and "Education and Human Cultivation in the Emperor State," pp. 65–104.

63. Sungho Lee, "The Emergence of the Modern Korean University," pp. 234–237.

64. E. Patricia Tsurumi, *Japanese Colonial Education in Taiwan, 1895–1945* (Cambridge, Mass.: Harvard University Press, 1977), provides an excellent analysis of the Taiwan experience of Japanese colonialism. See especially chapters 8 and 9. See also Douglas Smith, "Foundations of Modern Chinese Education and the Taiwan Experience," in D. Smith (ed.), *The Confucian Continuum: Educational Modernization in Taiwan* (New York: Praeger, 1991), pp. 39–43.

65. See Galtung, "Conflict on a Global Scale: Social Imperialism and Sub-Imperialism." There is also an interesting historical reassessment underway of the relationship between the Soviet and Chinese Communist parties, going back to the 1920s. See Bruce A. Elleman, "The Soviet Union's Secret Diplomacy Concerning the Chinese Eastern Railway, 1924–1925," *Journal of Asian Studies,* Vol. 53, no. 2 (May 1994): 459–486.

66. *Ten Great Years* (Beijing: Foreign Language Press, 1960) gives a Chinese summary of economic achievements. For a Russian view, see Borisov and Koloskov, *Soviet-Chinese Relations, 1945–1970*, especially chapter 5.

67. J. Galtung, "A Structural Theory of Imperialism," *Journal of Peace Studies*, Vol. 8, 1972, pp. 81–117.

68. J. Galtung, *The True Worlds: A Transnational Perspective* (New York: Free Press, 1980). In his structural theory of imperialism, Galtung breaks down patterns of domination into four categories: exploitation, penetration, marginalization, and fragmentation.

69. Samuel Kim, *The Quest for a Just World Order* (Boulder, Colo.: Westview Press, 1984).

70. I would see much of the work of Philip Altbach in this light. His analyses of the inequalities of the international knowledge system, and international publishing are almost always accompanied by recommendations on how to strengthen peripheral countries in these areas. See, for example, *The Knowledge Context* (Albany, N.Y.: SUNY Press, 1986).

71. Robert Arnove, "World Systems Theory and Comparative Education," in *Comparative Education Review*, Vol. 24, no. 2, February, 1980, pp. 48–62. Arnove writes approvingly of "the empirical verification of linkages between the flow of ideas and the movement of goods, the connection between cultural capital and economic capital," on p. 56.

72. Karl Popper, *The Logic of Scientific Discovery* (London: Hutchinson, 1959), and *Conjectures and Refutations* (London: Routledge and Kegan Paul, 1963).

73. R. Hayhoe and M. Bastid, *China's Education and the Industrialized World: Studies in Cultural Transfer* (New York: M.E. Sharpe, and Toronto: OISE Press, 1987).

74. Delia Davin, "Imperialism and the Diffusion of Liberal Thought: British Influences on Chinese Education," in Ibid., pp. 33–56.

75. For an excellent recent study of the Japanese influence at this time, which distinguishes it from later imperialist ambitions, see Douglas J. Reynolds, *China 1898–1912: The Xinzheng Revolution and Japan* (Cambridge, Mass.: Council on East Asian Studies, Harvard University, 1993).

76. See Paula Harrell, *Sowing the Seeds of Change: Chinese Students, Japanese Teachers, 1895–1905* (Stanford, Calif.: Stanford University Press, 1992).

77. Hiroshi Abe, "Borrowing from Japan: China's First Modern Education System," in R. Hayhoe and M. Bastid, *China's Education and the Industrialized World*, pp. 57–80.

78. Jessie Lutz, *China and the Christian Colleges* (Ithaca, N.Y., and London: Cornell University Press, 1971).

79. Under the French Protectorate, France was responsible for all Catholic missionaries on Chinese soil, not only those from France. See J.B. Piolet, *La France en dehors: les missions catholiques françaises au XIXe siècle*, Tome III (Paris: Librairie Armand Colin, c. 1900); Paul Cohen, *China and Christianity: The Missionary Movement and the Growth of Chinese Anti-Foreignism, 1860–1870* (Cambridge, Mass.: Harvard University Press, 1963).

80. Ruth Hayhoe, "Catholics and Socialists: The Paradox of French Educational Interaction with China," in R. Hayhoe and M. Bastid, *China's Education and the Industrialized World*, pp. 97–119.

81. Francoise Kreissler, "Technical Education as a Key to Cultural Cooperation: The Sino-German Case," in Ibid., pp. 81–96.

82. William Duiker, *Ts'ai Yuan-p'ei: Educator of Modern China* (University Park and London: Pennsylvania State University Press, 1977).

83. Chung Shih, *Higher Education in China* (Hong Kong: Union Research Institute, 1953).

84. C.T. Hu, "Chinese People's University: Bastion of Marxism-Leninism," in R.F. Butts and W.B. Niblett (eds.), *The World Yearbook of Education: Universities Facing the Future* (London: Evans Bros., 1972), pp. 63–74.

85. Michael Lindsay, *Notes on Educational Problems in Communist China, 1941–1947* (New York: Institute of Pacific Relations, 1950); Peter Seybolt, "Yenan Education and the Chinese Revolution, 1937–1945," unpublished Ph.D. dissertation, Harvard University, 1969; Wang Hsueh-wen, *Chinese Communist Education: The Yenan Period* (Taiwan: Institute of International Relations, 1975).

86. Mao Zedong "The Hunan Self-Study University Inauguration Manifesto," in Zhang Liuquan, *Zhongguo shuyuan shihua*, p. 135.

2 THE NATIONALIST STORY, 1911–1949

Chapter 1 considered how the ideals of the European university and the structures of knowledge associated with them were transferred to the Chinese context, and what sort of ground they had to take root in. It also noted a dualism in epistemology that allowed the university to champion academic freedom on the theoretical level, while abstaining from direct political participation. The highly academic forms of theoretical and professional knowledge fostered in universities culminated in the emergence of modern science and its universalization through the capitalist world system. Set against that were patterns of knowledge in traditional Chinese society that reflected an integration of theory and practice, focusing on central issues of good governance, and a resistance to specialization beyond the broad categories of classics, philosophy, history, and literature.[1] During the whole twentieth century, it is possible to see a struggle going on in China to achieve the economic and social benefits of Western science and technology, while asserting its own patterns of culture and knowledge in ways that would maintain Chinese identity.

At the same time, the Western academic and scientific tradition has itself been subjected to critical reexamination in recent years, with the gender implications of its knowledge patterns being one interesting dimension of this critique. Research has shown striking parallels in the ways in which women in the West have been marginalized in the development of the university within the capitalist system,[2] and the kinds of exploitation experienced by other peoples and cultures in the movements of imperialism and colonialism that dominated the eighteenth and nineteenth centuries.[3] Chinese women have thus faced a dual challenge in their struggle for participation in modern higher education, internally that of Confucian patriarchy, and externally that of the structures of the Western-style university.

On the one hand, it could be argued that the holism and monism of traditional Chinese epistemology silenced women even more effectively than the dualistic and mechanistic knowledge patterns of Western science.[4] At least, that is the stereotype most common in the West.[5] On the other hand, in dimensions of the Buddhist and Daoist legacy, Chinese women have had a space in the scheme of things that made for a different quality and kind of resistance to male domination than was possible for Western women.[6] There are certain parallels, it seems, in the interaction between female and male, yin and yang, in Chinese society with the character of the polar dichotomy between academy and civil service examination system sketched out in chapter 1. There was a clear recognition that both poles were essential, and their holding in balanced tension constituted health.[7] The supremacy of Zhu Xi's canons of Neo-Confucianism from the Song to the Qing dynasties solidified an emphasis on male supremacy and Confucian patriarchy at about the same time as the exclusion of women from the mainstream of scholarly and religious life took place in Europe.[8] However, Daoist and Buddhist challenges to Confucian views remained a strong undercurrent of intellectual and cultural life in China right up to the Qing dynasty.[9] Furthermore, Song Neo-Confucianism never developed the mechanistic approach to modern science that so effectively suppressed women's holistic and interactive views of nature in the West. In a certain sense, Chinese women have never lost their roots in the grounded and integrative approaches to knowledge that Western feminists have struggled to re-create in recent decades.[10]

Chapter 2 of this book might thus be seen as the struggle for China's "modernization" along lines that constituted a kind of four-way interaction, among patterns of the capitalist and socialist West, as they were adopted for specific nationalist purposes, and patterns of polar tension and integration in Chinese culture, which undergirded the ways in which these Western patterns were seen and adapted. Subthemes that call for exploration are the cultural differences among the various Western patterns emulated, and the range of different emphases in the threads of Chinese traditional epistemology. Women's story, a kind of gender mapping of the period, is an integral part of these tensions.

The knowledge map constitutes a second theme, with an exploration of the way a "modern" curriculum was negotiated through the introduction of models from Japan and the West and their adaptation on the basis of persisting, initially visible, later often hidden, dimensions of the Chinese knowledge tradition. The difficulty of external patterns becoming fully rooted became evident in the Cultural Revolution, when the disciplines were unceremoniously tossed out, in spite of nearly a century of development in the Chinese context, and a new holism of knowledge and society, in rhetoric at least, replaced the fragmented patterns of specialization that characterized the Soviet model.[11] The struggle to define a modern curriculum had begun in the late nineteenth century, and continued through to the early Nationalist period, when fairly clear patterns were set down in legislation of the late 1920s and early 1930s. These were adjusted to fit Soviet-defined categories in the 1950s, and reemerged after the Cultural Revolution decade in 1978.

Thirdly, we will consider the geographical map of modern higher education. The struggle to ensure that all regions of China participated in the change process, not merely a few advanced coastal cities, forms an important part of the story. This concern recurred in reform schemes of the early Republican period, and in attempts at rationalization by the Nationalist government, but took concrete form only during the Sino-Japanese War, when many coastal institutions moved to the hinterland under wartime conditions.

How are we to view the Western influences? What relative weight should be given to differences in cultural pattern, as against the broadly common influences of capitalist economic and political systems? This period was marked by a diversity of types of influence and interaction, a diversity based on real cultural and historical differences on both sides. This marks it out from the subsequent experiment with Soviet socialist patterns, which had a much higher degree of unity and coherence, and thus culminated in a much more extreme reaction or antithesis from the Chinese side.

Some sort of periodization is needed in laying out a story of this complexity, yet I hope it will be possible to connect the threads from one period to the next, in terms of the themes of gender, knowledge, and geography, and the interaction between various foreign influences and persisting aspects of the polar tensions within China's own cultural patterns. The first section deals with the period roughly between the 1860s and 1911, the gradual fading out of traditional institutions, and the development of "modern" universities and colleges, also of legislation that was designed to integrate attractive external patterns within an explicit and persisting set of Chinese definitions.

The second section deals with the period from 1911 to 1927, a time of revolution followed by near anarchy, which gave considerable space for experimentation at the levels of policy, legislation, and practice in higher education. In many ways the May 4th Movement of 1919, the center-point of this period, was more important for the establishment of "modern" universities in China than any other single event.

The third section deals with the story of universities under the Nationalist government, the first unified modern political context for their development. As in the nineteenth century in the West, universities were seen as essential accoutrements of state building, and it is interesting to consider the policy and legislation adopted by the Nationalist government for its universities and the ways in which values of autonomy and academic freedom were shaped to Nationalist ends. The period of the Sino-Japanese War, 1937–1945, was perhaps the greatest test China's modern universities had to undergo, and in many ways it laid both the geographical and the cultural foundation for a more authentically Chinese university system.

Finally, the fourth section of this chapter deals with the alternate higher institutions that developed in the border regions under Communist control, and which were to set a model both modern and purely Chinese in form. It ensured an ongoing tension with the patterns to be introduced from the former Soviet Union, a tension that will be the main subject of chapter 3.

In each of the three periods under discussion, there was a diversity of foreign influences to be drawn upon,[12] but one or two tended to dominate. Thus in the period before 1911, Japan was the most important model, both for imperial bureaucrats and for large numbers of young teachers, writers, artists, and revolutionaries who went to study in Japan. In the period between 1911 and 1927, one can see first an attempt at conscious emulation of European models, particularly those of Germany and France, then considerable interest in the American model, culminating in the establishment of Qinghua University as a national institution in 1926. After the Nationalist government came to power in 1927, there was an intentional reorientation toward European models, and national policy for higher education was strongly influenced by the advice of a delegation of high-level European intellectuals who came under the auspices of the League of Nations to study the education system and make recommendations for reform.

In spite of the domination of specific national influences in particular periods, a large number of private and missionary institutions, which exemplified a range of models, were active throughout the whole period from the late nineteenth century to 1949. Only after the Communist government took power were all institutions forced to conform to a single centrally prescribed pattern.

THE TRANSITION: HIGHER EDUCATION FROM 1860 TO 1911

This was a period dominated by warfare, from the Opium Wars (1839–1842), to the Taiping Rebellion (1850–1864), war with France (1884–1885), with Japan (1895), the Boxer Rebellion (1900) and finally the Japanese defeat of Russia (1904–1905).[13] Qing dynasty officials launched a self-strengthening movement, which was to introduce Western technology for the purpose of national salvation, while keeping intact the basic character of the Chinese empire. In the brief Hundred Day Reform of 1898, it looked as if some fundamental changes might take place, making possible political reform toward a constitutional monarchy. However, the dowager empress took it upon herself to arrest the reformist young emperor and stem the tide of reform. Only after the Boxer Rebellion of 1900 was she forced to start a reform process that came too late to prevent the collapse of the dynasty in 1911.

Traditional institutions of higher learning—both those responsible for the civil service examinations and the academies (*shuyuan*)—continued in place, yet gradually lost their legitimacy and viability.[14] In the 1860s, efforts were made to reform the examination system by removing corrupt practices and making sure that the classical content be applied to real problems of government. In the 1870s, there was a plan to broaden the examination content on two fronts—adding knowledge in mathematics, and a new category defined as "foreign subjects" (*yangwu*). However, neither of these initiatives was successful. Only in 1887 did mathematics get included, and then candidates who passed in this field had to fulfill all of the classics requirements as well.[15]

In the 1890s, Kang Youwei proposed a complete revision of the examination system, which would allow for numerous categories of specialist and professional knowledge to be recognized, somewhat in the pattern of the Tang dynasty system. Alongside of this he proposed an examination in Confucianism as a religion, and the development of a Chinese clergy. However, this notion of separating secular and spiritual authority was not acceptable. Various other schemes were suggested that would preserve the unity of the examination content, while linking the examination system to a system of schools that would teach some of the practical and professional subjects needed for self-strengthening.[16]

In the late Qing period, the *shuyuan* had become more and more integrated with the examination system in efforts to revitalize Confucian learning,[17] and so it was not surprising that there were repeated suggestions for *shuyuan* to be converted into modern schools in various specialist areas, that would still continue to prepare the best students for the imperial examinations. In the various proposals made for this, a hierarchy of institutions was suggested, based on level of administration and geographical location. Each province was to have one university (*daxue*), presumably converted from a *shuyuan* in the provincial capital, while *shuyuan* in prefectural seats, the next lower level of government, were to become middle schools (*zhongxue*), and those at lower levels were to become primary schools (*xiaoxue*).[18] The hierarchy was, of course, drawn from long-lasting patterns of the examination system, which had operated mainly at prefectural, provincial, and imperial levels. It has persisted to this day, with basically the same hierarchy of administrative level in contemporary Chinese higher education, and differential prestige and influence according to the level at which an institution is administered: national, provincial, or local.

Women were entirely excluded from the examination system. There are stories of aspiring women scholars who disguised themselves as men in order to take the examinations, but the notion of a woman becoming a scholar-official was simply unthinkable within the Confucian order. Song neo-Confucianism, which dominated the examination system up to the Qing, specified a wholly subservient role for women.[19] It was supported by a canon of women's literature that provided detailed historical examples to illustrate the ideal female role.[20]

Women were also excluded from formal participation in the *shuyuan*, though at periods marked by an openness to local society, they may well have attended lectures and participated in scholarly discussion. During the Tang dynasty, Buddhist convents had been established where women scholars studied and taught both Buddhist and Confucian texts,[21] and Buddhist communities of both monks and nuns continued to be active in subsequent dynasties. It seems there was always some space for women within Buddhist education and scholarship. Buddhist patterns of thought and organization in turn influenced the *shuyuan*, and it has been argued that they were particularly important as an indigenous reference point in the nineteenth-century period of opening to the West.[22]

The leaders of the Taiping Rebellion in the mid-nineteenth century made a point of allowing girls to be educated alongside boys in their early initiatives.[23] This may have made the idea particularly subversive and threatening to officials of the late Qing in their desperate efforts to save the dynasty. Not surprisingly, it was only through the various alternatives to governmental education that sprung up—missionary schools and schools established by revolutionary intellectuals—that women found a way into higher education during this period.

The new curricular patterns established were conceived entirely in relation to the male population, with the expectation that women would continue to be educated within the family being explicitly stated in legislation of 1902–1903, and appropriate textbooks recommended. Only with regulations passed in 1907 was direction given for the establishment of primary schools for girls and normal schools for female teachers.[24] These were intended to be separate from the education ladder that was to harmonize new Western subjects and persisting Confucian patterns.

Although it was never realized in practice, it is interesting to see the conception that underlay the creation of the first modern system of education in legislation passed in 1902 and 1903, with the Japanese model as the main point of reference. At the pinnacle of the system was to be a Confucian academy for high-level research. Presumably, it was also to maintain a role similar to that of the Hanlin Academy in terms of regulating all scholarship at lower levels. Under it were to be eight kinds of university (*daxue*) in the following order of precedence: classics universities (*jingxueke daxue*), with specializations in the Four Books and Five Classics; political science universities (*zhengzhike daxue*), with specializations in politics and law; arts universities (*wenke daxue*), with specializations in languages, literatures, geography, and history; medical universities (*yike daxue*), with specializations in medicine and pharmacy; natural science universities (*gezhike daxue*), with specializations in mathematics, astronomy, physics, chemistry, biology, and geology; agricultural universities (*nongke daxue*), with specializations in agriculture, agro-chemistry, forestry, and animal husbandry; engineering universities (*gongke daxue*), with specializations in a range of engineering areas, and commerce universities (*shangke daxue*), with specializations in banking and insurance, trade, and transportation, and customs.[25]

I have provided a complete outline of this "modern" system from the 1903 legislation, not because it represents the reality of what was happening in higher education at the time, but as a kind of vision of how new practical subjects, including many areas introduced from the West, could be adopted under the guidance of a Confucian academy and a university of the classics. It is fascinating to reflect on the fact that a set of patterns close to these was to be realized the 1950s, when the Soviet model of higher education was adopted.

The terminology used in this legislation shows traditional and modern terms in relation. The Confucian academy and the classics university were an explicit expression of the determination to maintain a framework for the specialist fields of modern knowledge in classical culture and Confucian ideology. Notably, natural science universities were conceived in Confucian terms, with the classical term *gezhi*, taken from the Great Learning, used for science, rather than the modern term borrowed from Japan, *like* or *kexue*. This reflected an interesting debate around language at the time—how far should classical Chinese terms, such as *zhizhi* for philosophy, and *licai* for economics, be used, as against newfangled terms introduced from Japan, *zhexue* for philosophy, and *jingji* for economics.

Scholars such as Yan Fu and Ma Xiangbo, through their writings and translations, prepared texts in which Western content was expressed in classical language connected to Chinese traditional learning. However, the new terminology seemed to offer a quick route to Western learning through a large body of material that had already been translated into Japanese. In this situation Confucian ideology could hardly avoid becoming ossified, as it was limited to the role of an instrument for maintaining orthodoxy. The Marxist canon of orthodox texts, adopted officially in 1949 and formulated as Marxism-Leninism-Mao Zedong thought, met a similar fate, I would argue, within Chinese socialist education. Neither version of Chinese ideology, the Confucian or the Marxist, has been well able to integrate the findings of the disparate disciplines and professional areas of knowledge in a mutually transformative process. It might be argued that theology in the Western context was more successful at certain periods.

A second point of interest in this legislation, compared to later such documents, is the lack of any special concern or provision for a geographical balance in the modern schooling and higher education system. This seems to reflect an ingenuous confidence in persisting traditional patterns, which had been fairly equitably spread throughout the empire through means of a quota system for examination candidates, established as early as the Song dynasty.[26] A concern over emerging geographical imbalances in educational participation was to come mainly in the years after the 1911 revolution, when the proliferation of new institutions in coastal areas and the lack of a parallel development in the hinterland became more and more evident.

As stated earlier, legislation and policy were something entirely separate from what was really happening in higher education over the period. They expressed, perhaps, an attempt to make sense of a process of change that was many dimensional. The actual building of modern higher institutions was carried out by diverse individuals: high-level bureaucrats, scholar-gentry, revolutionary intellectuals, missionaries, and in many cases a combination of these.

The earliest modern government schools were created to provide education in specific areas needed to deal with the Western incursion. The *Tongwenguan*, established in 1860, focused first on foreign languages, and gradually introduced departments of mathematics and astronomy, and later social sciences and medicine. The fact that it could be headed for a long period by the American Presbyterian missionary, W.A.P. Martin, showed a remarkable degree of cooperation between official circles and progressive missionaries. It also reflected the fact that the *Tongwenguan* was always seen by Chinese officials as a subsidiary form of higher education to that of the examination system. A parallel institution in Shanghai was linked to the

Kiangnan Arsenal, where engineering and technical subjects were taught in addition to languages, and considerable work in the translation of Western texts of science and technology was undertaken. American missionary Young J. Allen was involved in this school. A third official institution in the south, the Fuzhou Navy Yard School, focused on naval technology, and had both English and French divisions. Students were sent to France and England for further training.[27]

In terms of our story of China's universities, it is important to remember that these imperial institutions for self-strengthening were simply high-level training institutes; there was at no time any thought of them as universities in the Western sense. They were consciously created by official decree to provide the kinds of practical knowledge that would enable China to resist incursions from the West and maintain the integrity of its own culture and polity. They were never integrated into the civil service examination system, in spite of many recommendations that they should be, in order to attract superior students.

Parallel to these imperial institutions were many other modern schools, set up by provincial gentry and scholar-officials in specific regions or locations as their contribution to self-strengthening. Some of the best and most famous of these became the basis for modern universities, such as *Beiyang gongxue*, set up in Tianjin in 1895, and *Nanyang gongxue*, established in Shanghai in 1896 with the support of industrialist Sheng Xuanhuai.[28]

One of the most active of those scholar-bureaucrats in the area of modern school building was Zhang Zhidong, who established a total of eight modern schools in Guangdong and Hubei between 1886 and 1899, most having an orientation toward the military.[29] Zhang subsequently played an important role in drafting the legislation for a modern higher education system outlined earlier, and he is well known for the slogan "Chinese learning as the essence, Western learning for its usefulness," which guided the overall thinking behind this legislation.[30] The idea seems to have been that Western knowledge specializing in particular areas should be mastered and applied to specific purposes, while a Chinese essence should remain at the core, directing the choice and orientation of those purposes. The antithesis of this conservatism was a revolutionary opposition that called for the complete overthrow of Chinese learning in favor of all-out Westernization. It came to a head in the May 4th Movement.[31]

In between these opposite positions, however, there were some interesting efforts at mediating the different world views. A Shanghai historian, Li Tiangang, has argued convincingly that the Anglo-Chinese College (*Zhongxi shuyuan*)[32] established cooperatively between Sheng Yugui and

American missionary Young J. Allen in Shanghai in 1881, represented an effort to create a kind of higher institution that would integrate Chinese and Western learning in ways that would lead to the transformation of both. Equal importance was given to Chinese classical studies and Western religious study, as well as new disciplines and techniques introduced from the West. Students were encouraged to take the civil service examinations, and quite a few were successful, enhancing the prestige of the school.

Li has argued that the origin of Zhang Zhidong's slogan—"Chinese learning as the essence, Western learning for its usefulness"—was the thinking around the curriculum in this institution. The original intention was that Chinese knowledge and culture should be mastered as the means through which Western learning could be fully understood and integrated into Chinese scholarship. This can be contrasted with the instrumentalist view of Western learning put forward by Zhang Zhidong, and persisting in official perspectives on Chinese higher education right up to the 1980s.[33]

The program of the College St. Ignace (*Xuhui gongxue*), a Jesuit institution in Shanghai, was similar to that of the Anglo-Chinese College. While Ma Xiangbo was principal in the early 1870s, he insisted that all students first develop a solid grounding in Chinese classical study, and many were able to try for the civil service examinations. This knowledge of the Chinese classics was seen as the essential basis for an introduction to Western learning that drew upon the Jesuit curriculum, and embraced philosophy, mathematics, and theology, as well as more practical subjects.

Ma was frustrated by Jesuit suspicions of his emphasis on Chinese studies and finally left the order. However, when he established *l'Université l'Aurore* in 1903, using his family inheritance as a kind of endowment, he invited members of the Jesuit order to participate, feeling that their approach to education introduced Western learning in a coherent and holistic way, not simply as a set of techniques that could be manipulated to Chinese ends. His efforts in writing textbooks, such as the first Western-style grammatical analysis of the Chinese language, which was entitled *The Ma Brothers Grammar (Mashi wentong)*,[34] and a philosophy text that introduced Aristotle, scholasticism, and the history of Western philosophy in classical Chinese terminology, entitled *A Simple Introduction to Philosophy (Zhizhi qianshuo)*,[35] were an expression of his vision for a process of mutual transformation between Chinese and Western scholarship.[36]

A third very important group of higher institutions over this period were the missionary colleges, most founded by American missionaries, and only a small number reaching a college level in their programs before 1911. These institutions were modeled after American denominational colleges, and their curricular patterns reflected this.[37] In the earliest period, efforts were made to do most of the teaching in Chinese, but gradually English was adopted as the main language of instruction, especially for Western subjects. The main purposes of the colleges were to convert students to Christianity, and to provide them with knowledge and skills that would enable them to contribute to China's development from a Christian perspective.[38] The attitude toward the Chinese language, and Chinese subjects was utilitarian in the sense that these were to enable students to bring about the Christianization of China through their continuing connectedness to Chinese culture. Their intention to use Chinese learning for Western ends provides a fascinating antithesis to the utilitarianism of government schools, which proposed to use Western learning for purely Chinese purposes.

Finally there were the revolutionary schools, set up by Chinese intellectuals who found themselves fundamentally at odds with official efforts to preserve the essence of Chinese identity, and who wished to see the imperial dynasty overthrown in favor of a republic. These institutions were mainly short-lived, often a front for revolutionary activities, and their curricula stressed practical and military studies that would contribute to the revolutionary struggle. Mary Rankin gives the following depiction of one of the best known of them: "As much a society as a school, it offered unusual freedom and ample time for philosophical discussion and political demonstration. Modern subjects dominated the curriculum. Military drill and P.E. were to foster the skills and attitudes needed by a militant citizenry. The aim of developing an independent, pioneering spirit overshadowed considerations of academic excellence. Of course, as a practical matter the educational input of the school was negligible, but its political contribution was considerable. The radicalizing influence of its environment on both students and teachers was almost immediate."[39]

The only institutions among the four types outlined above where women found a place were the missionary schools and the revolutionary schools—in other words, those that were farthest removed from Chinese tradition—a telling comment on how completely women had been excluded from that tradition in its late nineteenth-century form. Missionary schools for girls at the primary and secondary level were established from early in the nineteenth century, and a few began to operate at the tertiary level in the decade that preceded the revolution of 1911. The Bridgman Academy became part of the North China Union College for Women in 1904 and the Huanan College for Women was established in 1908 on the basis of earlier girls' schools. Jinling College in Nanjing was opened in 1913, after five or six years of planning for a girls' college on the part of several missions. Parallel to these Protestant girls colleges was *l'Etoile de Matin*, a Catholic girls' college in Shanghai that was linked to *Aurore*, and gradually developed tertiary level programs.[40] Apart from these colleges specifically for women, other missionary colleges did not begin to enroll women until after 1911.[41]

A number of China's best known intellectuals of the late Qing spoke out strongly in support of women's education, including Liang Qichao, Kang Youwei, and others. However, it was another matter to establish tertiary-level schools for girls. The one that has drawn most attention was the Patriotic Girls School established by Cai Yuanpei in 1903, after he left *Nanyang gongxue* in protest.[42] This school only continued for a few years, as was the situation with many of the revolutionary schools, and its most obvious purpose was one of revolutionary activism.[43] In this same period, one of China's most famous woman activists, Qiu Jin, returned from study in Japan and went to take up the directorship of a new school for girls in Shaoxing. She was involved in organizing an uprising and was assassinated by Qing loyalists in 1907, only shortly after assuming her duties at the school.[44] This event did much to stir women to action in the period.

Diverse foreign influences were felt over this period, and it may be helpful to consider the channels by which they entered. We have already noted the increasing numbers of missionaries, both Protestant and Catholic, who saw education as an important means of spreading their message. In addition, a growing number of young Chinese were being sent abroad over this period, beginning with the first group of 120 young boys sent to the United States between 1872 and 1875, continuing with small numbers being sent to European countries after graduation from institutions such as the Fuzhou Navy Yard School, and culminating in what was almost a mass movement of study in Japan between 1900 and 1911. In the period between 1890 and 1910, a total of 492 students went to the United States; of these, thirty were women. In the period between 1906 and 1910, several thousand students and intellectuals went to Japan. Exact figures are tenuous, but the high point seemed to be in 1906, when 7,283 were there, forty-five of them women.[45] The number declined to 3,180 in 1910, 118 being women.[46] One of the interesting anomalies of the period lay in the fact that women were allowed to participate in programs for study abroad from the beginning, in spite of the fact that government higher institutions within China did not open their doors to women until 1919.[47]

Those who returned from study abroad were an important channel of influence, especially the large number of returnees from Japan who taught in Chinese schools over the period from 1902 to 1911,[48] and there were many teachers from Japan working in China.[49] Other forms of influence included translations, reports, and texts written by the numerous delegations who were sent to study various foreign systems of education, and the proliferating journals and newspapers of the period, which contained many articles about foreign matters.[50]

Japanese achievements and models had a dominant influence over practical educational thinking, also over specific technical and institutional changes needed in areas such as agriculture and engineering, and in the patterns for a modern school system in this period.[51] However, European and American ideas were also widely discussed in intellectual circles, with a whole range of philosophical and ideological perspectives being introduced. Some of the missionaries who contributed to this dialogue were Young J. Allen, Timothy Richards, and W.A.P. Martin. On the Chinese side, perhaps the most famous contributor was Yan Fu, who was sent to England to study naval engineering after graduating from the Fuzhou Navy Yard School, but who instead developed an interest in philosophy and the social sciences, and translated the works of Huxley, Spencer, Mill, Montesquieu, Smith, and others into elegant classical Chinese.[52]

Nevertheless, I would argue that the spirit of the European university was neither well understood, nor seriously emulated during this period. The system of higher education, as all other levels, was clearly modeled on that of Japan in the legislation of 1902 and 1903. The Imperial University, founded in 1898 as a part of the Hundred Day Reform Movement, was closely linked to the Ministry of Education, and was supposed to have a kind of supervisory role over all levels of the education system.[53] It was thus more an arm of bureaucratic power, as had been the Hanlin Academy and the College for the Sons of the Emperor (*guozijian*), than an autonomous institution, having any aspirations toward academic freedom. To some extent it had been patterned after the University of Tokyo, which in turn had been influenced by both French and German models. In conception, it may thus have been close to the Napoleonic university of nineteenth-century France. However, the ideas of university autonomy and academic freedom were only taken up seriously in Chinese intellectual circles a decade or more later, as we will see in the next section of this chapter.

The last few years before the collapse of the Qing dynasty saw a rapid proliferation of modern schools, mostly either private or gentry-run schools, rather than government schools, and reflecting in their geographic distribution the rapid industrialization going on in coastal areas. Marianne Bastid has noted the emergence of a kind of oppositional mentality in the gentry of this period, who were hoping to see evolutionary change rather than the stability espoused by conservative officials, and who were more concerned with national studies (*guoxue*) than the preservation of classical studies (*jingxue*).[54] Their vigorous activity in educational development is reflected in the huge number of educational societies that were organized at the local level. In 1908, there were 506 such societies with 37,118 members, and this had grown to 723 in 1909, with 48,432 members.[55] The impetus for mass education began to take off at around this time, and might be seen as an important, even essential, concomitant force to that of modern higher education.[56]

By 1909, there were three universities (*daxue*), with 749 students, twenty-four provincial higher institutions with 4,203 students, and 101 specialist colleges with 6,431 students.[57] The geographical focus of these new institutions was biased toward the east coast, yet the only province that had no institution was Heilongjiang. Xinjiang, Guizhou, and Guangxi each had only one small college of law and politics, whereas provinces such as Jiangsu, Anhui, Fujian, Hunan, and Guangdong had six to eight institutions, and more than 1,000 students each. Zhili (including Beijing) had eighteen institutions and 4,028 students, 37 percent of the national total. Unfortunately, we do not have details on curricular emphasis in the universities and provincial higher institutions, but it is likely they reflected the emphasis evident in the specialist colleges, where 50 percent of students were in law and politics, 35 percent in humanities, 7 percent in fine arts, 5 percent in medicine and 3 percent in science and engineering.[58] All of these students were male.

The growth in schools for women at lower levels, however, was dramatic, indicating the degree to which the first regulations for girls' primary schools and normal colleges promulgated in 1907 had lagged behind the actual social impetus for women's education. In 1907, the year in which the regulations were made, there were already estimated to be 428 schools for girls throughout the country, with 15,496 students enrolled. The geographical distribution of these schools showed drastic imbalances, with 121 schools in Zhili, seventy-two in Jiangsu, seventy in Sichuan, thirty-two in Zhejiang, and numbers between ten and zero in most other provinces.[59] Importantly, however, a foundation had been laid in secondary and normal education for young women in some regions that provided conditions for them to press for entry to higher education.

UNIVERSITY, COLLEGE, AND ACADEMY IN THE TRANSITION TO A MODERN REPUBLIC, 1911–1927

The period from 1911 to 1927 was an important one for education, since the lack of a strong central government meant that there was the possibility of vigorous experimentation at all levels. The fledgling republic established by Sun Yat Sen in Nanjing in 1911 quickly gave way to a takeover from the north, with Yuan Shikai moving the new government to Beijing in 1913, then working to reinstate a monarchy and restore an emphasis on classical knowledge in education. After Yuan's death in 1917, the country was essentially ruled by warlords, with their local and regional armies, until southern forces reorganized themselves and initiated the Northern Expedition of 1927, culminating in the establishment of the Nationalist government.[60]

This period, I would argue, saw the first real effort to establish a "university," in the sense of the defining values of autonomy and academic freedom. The most important figure in this effort, Cai Yuanpei, had spent the years from 1906 to 1910 in Germany and France, and subsequently returned to Europe in 1912 for another five-year period[61] after his brief tenure as minister of education in 1912. In this role, he had been responsible for educational legislation that set forth five goals for Republican education, in place of the Confucian values that had informed earlier legislation. Three were intended to offer a direct service to political development—military education, education for citizenship, and practical education in technical fields. The other two goals, education for a world view and aesthetic education, were to foster new social values that stood above politics.[62] Cai had a particular commitment to aesthetic education, which he felt could take the place of religion in modern Chinese society.

The new legislation for higher education, passed in 1912, made a clear distinction between specialist higher schools, which would focus on practical areas of knowledge, and universities, which were to have a curriculum including both arts and sciences; other combinations permitted for the university were arts along with law and commerce, or sciences along with engineering, agriculture, and medicine. There was to be a commitment to advancing theoretical knowledge, as well as teaching, and universities were to have graduate schools for high-level research.

Explicit indications were given in the legislation concerning the internal government of universities, through a senate (*pingyi hui*) consisting of the deans of each subject area, and representatives elected from all full professors, who would decide on curriculum, teaching, internal regulations, and issues of student graduation and faculty promotion.[63] Although the terms academic freedom and university autonomy do not appear in this document, it laid down conditions to protect them along the lines of the German model, which made them the prerogative of universities, not of specialist higher schools.[64]

The idea of university autonomy, however, was not to be worked out in a practical way within government institutions until Cai returned from Germany in 1917 to take up the chancellorship of Peking University. In the meantime, his one-time teacher and mentor, Ma Xiangbo, was taking up the struggle for the autonomy of scholarship and academic freedom in another context. Ma had been deeply influenced by French thought, through his long-time association with the Jesuits, and was a great admirer of the Académie Française. As a high-level advisor to Yuan Shikai's government in Beijing in 1913, he attempted to persuade the government to provide support for a Chinese national academy that would be modeled after the French academy. Ma was familiar with the Royal Society and its branch in China, the North China Branch of the Royal Asia Society also with other European academies, but he felt the French model was most suited to China's needs, possibly due to its particular attention to issues of the development of the national language.

Ma used the term *Hanxia kaowenyuan* for the academy he wished to establish, *Hanxia* being a classical term for China, and *kaowenyuan* suggesting an institution for critical literary studies. The purpose of the academy was to set the highest standards of scholarship in all important fields of endeavor, and to take responsibility for raising the level of Chinese civilization more broadly through encouraging, recognizing, and rewarding the best fruits of scholarship, wherever they were found. While initial financial support from the government, in terms of some endowments of land, was essential, the academy was to stand independent of government as an arbiter of knowledge and culture.

We have noted earlier Ma's concern with the development of the Chinese language, and his efforts to ensure continuity between new terms being developed and the classical language, in face of an influx of neologisms that had been coined in Japan. This concern was shared with Zhang Taiyan, Yan Fu, and others, and was seen as essential to a critical and holistic absorption of knowledge from the West, as against either the conservative focus on techniques that could be shaped by Confucian ideology, or various radical moves to "all-out Westernization."

Ma persuaded Zhang Taiyuan, Yan Fu, and Liang Qichao to join him in designing an institution that was to have forty members, and would set standards for scholarship in the following areas: law, rhetoric, philosophy, classics, history, mathematics, aesthetics, music, and Buddhism. They selected fifteen scholars as the founding group, among whom noted proponents of Confucianism as a religion, such as Kang Youwei, were conspicuously absent. Elaborate plans were laid whereby the remaining twenty-five members would be gradually selected, and the academy would gain both property and various kinds of financial support.

The project, however, was never to be realized. It would be easy to assume the main reason for this failure lay with Yuan Shikai, who was working toward the restoration of a Confucian-style monarchy at this period. However, there were many other problems and obstacles. Chinese intellectual circles were still far from the kind of development of scientific knowledge that had been the main force in the emergence of academies in Europe. Among the fifteen scholars named in the academy plans, the only scientist Ma felt to have adequate standing was Hua Hengfang, an engineer from the Jiangnan Manufacturing Bureau in Shanghai, who had been trained in the West.[65]

Only after Cai Yuanpei returned from his second stay in Europe in 1917 did the ideals of autonomy and academic freedom find institutional form, first in Peking University, later in the Academica Sinica. Cai had been deeply influenced by his early studies of Latin and European philosophy under Ma, and by his two lengthy periods of study in Germany and France. In his vision of a modern Chinese university, the internal dimensions were shaped by a German-inspired view of autonomy and academic freedom. The idea of "professorial rule" (*jiaoshou zhixiao*) that he adopted, had already been envisioned in provisions of the 1912 legislation that he drafted, as noted earlier. He was now to take vigorous action to reorganize Peking University in such a way that it could be realized in practice. As for academic freedom, Cai felt it was essential that the university provide an atmosphere where any viewpoint, provided it was based on scholarship, could be aired, debated, and discussed.[66]

While Cai's vision for the internal constitution of the university came largely from the German model, his ideas for the university in its relation to the rest of the education system and to society more generally were influenced by the French model. His intense involvement in the work-study movement in France, and subsequently the setting up of the *Université Franco-chinoise*, had brought him into contact with French anarchists and socialists during a period of French history sometimes dubbed the "republic of professors," due to the broad influence of the *École Normale*.[67] Thus the institution of autonomy and academic freedom within the university was expected to contribute indirectly to broader social transformation.

The fact that the May 4th Movement broke out at Peking University (*Beida*) only two years after Cai took over its leadership is noteworthy. Vera Schwarcz has shown how it was largely Beida faculty who were writers for the *New Youth*, and it was Beida students who were responsible for *New Tides*, the two most influential journals of the movement. She argues that this group of intellectuals continued throughout their lives to seek for the fulfilment of an enlightenment process that was repeatedly broken off due to pressures for rapid political change.[68] The fact that such a group had come to find themselves at one university at such a crucial time must be linked to Cai's determination to institute academic freedom, to his concerted efforts to attract and protect the best scholars across the spectrum from radical to conservative, and to his commitment to providing conditions for free and unrestrained academic debate.

In terms of curriculum, it is also possible to see a clear German influence in Cai's views. He saw arts and sciences as being at the heart of the university's mission, and he set patterns at Beida as early as 1919 whereby all students had to take courses in the core areas of philosophy, psychology, and education, in addition to specialist courses in the sciences or arts.[69] Cai arranged for programs in engineering to be moved to Beiyang University in Tianjin,[70] since he felt that applied and professional studies were best pursued in institutions such as the *Technische Hochschule*. He also tried unsuccessfully to move Beida's law program out to form an independent specialist higher school. This was an expression of his efforts to change the ethos of Peking University in a fundamental way, separating it from the role it had had since 1898 as a school dominated by programs in law and politics for young people aspiring to bureaucratic careers.[71]

We have noted Cai's institution of aesthetics and education for a world view as areas of education that should rise above politics in the legislation of 1912. The university, with its focus on theoretical discourse in a broad yet interconnected range of knowledge areas, was vital to the development of these areas, in Cai's view. As an anarchist in his own political orientation, he hoped to see a thriving university community that would relate indirectly, through critical debates, rather than directly, through political activism, to the wider society.

Cai was therefore ambivalent over the direct political involvement of Beida's students and teachers in the May 4th Movement. He felt this contravened principles of political detachment for the university that were essential to a realization of academic freedom. Shortly after his resignation on May 7, in an open letter to all university students of the time, Cai appealed to them to refrain from participation in politics and concentrate rather on "pure scientific research," so as to be prepared for the longer-term task of laying "the foundation for a new national culture for China."[72] Cai came back to Beida soon after, but in subsequent higher education developments, it was American-returned Chinese who had the greater influence, and a rather different idea of the university became evident.

In legislation passed in 1922 and 1924, which was largely the work of these reform-minded intellectuals, a strong American influence can be seen. The legislation stated that no firm aims for education could be laid down in a changing environment, but that the following standards should guide educational development: "adapt to the evolution of society, give full play to the spirit of education for the common person, seek the development of individuality, take into consideration the strength of the national economy, pay attention to education for life, universalize education, and be flexible in giving space for local initiative."[73]

The provisions this legislation made for higher education suggested the influence of an American ethos in several ways. First, the definition of university was broadened to include any higher institution, including specialist higher schools. Cai's distinction between a university focusing on theoretical disciplines, and an institution for professional or applied studies disappeared. The second change was a move away from Cai's emphasis on autonomy, in terms of the rule of professors within the university, to a concern for social responsibility in terms of an American-style board of managers for each university. It was to be responsible for finance, planning, and major policy decisions.[74] Thirdly, a credit system was initiated, leading to innovative and largely unregulated approaches to the university curriculum.

Intellectually, this period was dominated by debates between Hu Shi, whose pragmatist philosophical tendencies differed considerably from Cai's European essentialism, and Marxist scholars such as Chen Duxiu, over the relative merits of "piecemeal problem solving" as against "isms" such as socialism and communism, which offered a holistic analysis of China's dilemma.[75] Marxists saw little value in either university autonomy or academic freedom, except for an appreciation of the fact that Cai's espousal of these values had given them a foothold in the university world of the time. Pragmatists such as Hu Shi favored an approach to knowledge through problem solving that stressed more the university's social responsibility than its autonomy and academic freedom.[76]

As a result of the legislation of 1922 and 1924, the number of higher institutions that called themselves universities burgeoned, and most of these included instruction in basic disciplines and various applied fields of study. In 1917, there had been eight universities, but by 1923 there were reported to be thirty-five. Meanwhile, other forms of specialized higher education in law, medicine, agriculture, and engineering grew in number from eighty-two to ninety-eight, with law schools predominating. Total enrollments grew from 23,334 in 1917 to 34,880 in 1923, with university enrollments growing from 3,511 to 13,098.[77] It was a broader and less elitist definition of a university, closer to the American model than the European.

This period was of the greatest importance for women's participation in higher education. In 1912, a group of women suffragettes had marched into the new parliament and demanded representation, but they had been ignored.[78] However, their increasing participation in formal education meant they were soon to become a force that could no longer be ignored. In legislation of 1907, they had gained the right to primary education and normal education, and legislation of 1917 mandated both general secondary schools and vocational schools for girls.[79] However, women did not gain entrance to government universities until 1919.

This was the year in which the Beijing Girls Normal School, which had been founded in 1908, was raised to tertiary level, and became a leading institution for women's higher education. It was also a center for women's social and political activism, in terms of well-articulated demands for political participation and effective protests against government corruption.[80] In addition, most government universities opened their doors to women over the period between 1920 and 1927. Thus by 1922, there were reported to be 665 women in thirty-one universities, 236 of them in the Beijing Women's Normal College.[81] This does not include those in missionary colleges and universities at the time. In total, women made up about 2.5 percent of all students in higher education, while at the secondary level they made up 17.5 percent in normal schools, 3.1 percent in general academic schools, and 7.9 percent in vocational schools.[82]

In terms of the geographical map, this was a period of minimal central guidance for the development of higher institutions, due to prevailing conditions of political chaos and warlordism. The development of higher education was haphazard and very much reflected economic resources, as well as degrees of interest and initiative in various localities. The skewing of emphasis toward coastal areas, which had already begun in the period before and after 1911, now became more pronounced, with a particularly large concentration of new institutions in Beijing and Shanghai. Concern over this tendency by successive officials can be clearly seen in efforts to organize a university district scheme along the French model, which would ensure a fair geographic distribution throughout the country. Thus Yuan Shikai suggested four major districts in 1914, Tang Hualong mapped out six in 1917, and Fan Yuanlian, who was minister of education three times between 1912 and 1921, identified seven in 1918.[83] In spite of this high level of concern, the fragmented state of political authority, and a lack of funds, made it impossible to rectify these increasing imbalances in regional access to higher education. This was to be of primary concern to the new government in 1927.

Overall, this period saw a tremendous range of new higher institutions develop and flourish, in spite of extremely difficult economic conditions. The diversity probably reflected the ways in which different strands of China's own evolving traditions linked up with various foreign influences. Study abroad continued during this period, with America becoming an increasingly favored destination. From a total of ninety reported to be in the U.S. in 1910, numbers rose to a peak of 426 in 1924, with at least thirty-two of those being women. Meanwhile, numbers in Japan declined from 3,328 in 1911 to 2,116 in 1921, the last year for which there is a record.[84] There were considerable numbers also in France, Germany, Britain, and other European countries.[85] Chinese scholars who returned from all of these countries played a key role in the vigorous development of higher education, many of them being university presidents and deans at a young age. This was in striking contrast to the lot of scholars such as Yan Fu at an earlier period, who were given only marginal roles by traditional bureaucrats.

The role of missionaries went through a different kind of reversal. Earlier figures such as Timothy Richards, Young J. Allen, and W.A.P. Martin had been able to gain the confidence of high-level bureaucrats and work with them. In this period, however, Chinese intellectual and political leaders largely ignored the missionaries and their institutions, until a rising tide of nationalism in the mid-1920s resulted in demands that all missionary colleges and universities be brought under Chinese control.[86] More broadly influential than the missionary presence in the story of this period were the visits of distinguished intellectuals from abroad—Bertrand Russell from England, John Dewey[87] and Paul Monroe[88] from the USA, Rabinath Tagore from India,[89] and many others. In the ferment of change that characterized the period, the lectures and writings of these visitors gained wide attention.

It is difficult in a few strokes of the pen to do justice to the variety of new institutions that sprung up, and the different roles that they played. There can be little doubt that Beida under Cai Yuanpei was the first real university, but before long it was to be challenged by Qinghua, which became a national university in 1926, having developed from a language school for preparing young Chinese to study in America established with Boxer indemnity funds in 1908. It had the luxury of a substantial income and a degree of independence coming from its American connection. On this basis it developed into a highly visible comprehensive university, with programs in the basic arts and sciences, as well as professional areas such as law and engineering. One of its areas of focus in research was the critical reordering of Chinese classical studies, and for this it attracted some of China's best-known historians and literary figures.[90] Other government institutions that achieved some prominence over this period include Zhejiang University, Wuhan University, and Jiaotong University.

Private institutions flourished, and a few of them began to establish formidable reputations in the latter part of the period. Nankai University, with its focus on economics and applied arts and sciences, was among the most distinguished.[91] Missionary institutions continued largely in the mode of the college, yet some developed into universities of some academic standing, including Yanjing in Beijing,[92] Jinling in Nanjing, Dongwu in Suzhou, and St. Johns in Shanghai.[93] There were also European models such as *Aurore*, a French Catholic university under Jesuit control,[94] and Tongji University, which kept its links with the German government and German industrialists even after becoming a national university in the late 1920s.[95]

For the sciences, the challenge of the period was a very basic one—how to develop research and teaching in scientific disciplines to a standard that made it possible to contribute to fields that had been given a definite modern form in the West much earlier: physics, chemistry, geology, biology, and mathematics.[96] For the humanities, it was a matter of seeking a balance between a critical rethinking of China's vast heritage of classical thought on the one hand, and attention to new works of literature, history, and philosophy, as well an influx of academic literature from the West. Perhaps the task facing the social sciences was the most difficult—how to develop fields such as sociology, anthropology, political science, law, and economics—disciplines that had emerged in the context of nineteenth-century capitalist development,[97] in ways that had some authenticity in the Chinese context.

I have argued elsewhere that the social sciences in China have been fragmented throughout the modern period, due to the different emphases in the universities where they took shape. This can be seen already in the 1920s, with Nankai and Yanjing adopting quantitative survey methods for community-oriented social research, Qinghua and Beida focusing on critical theoretical study linked to a rethinking of the Chinese classical heritage,[98] and Shanghai University introducing Marxist approaches.[99] Unfortunately, the approach developed by Nationalist leaders in the institutions under their direct control in the 1930s tended to predominate. This was a thoroughly utilitarian insistence that all social knowledge be shaped to the task of legitimating the regime and offering practical support for its policies.[100] Communist leaders were to adopt a very similar approach, once they came to power, and they have been able to enforce it with even greater rigor.

UNIVERSITY, COLLEGE, AND ACADEMY UNDER THE NATIONALIST GOVERNMENT, 1927–1949

In wake of the Northern Expedition of joint Guomindang and Communist forces in 1927, a new Nationalist government established itself in Nanjing in 1927, and one of its first acts was to purge Communist supporters in 1928. This led in turn to the Communist Long March to central and western border regions in 1934, while the Nationalists worked to develop a one-party state under conditions of economic difficulty and a growing threat from Japan. Japanese incursions into Manchuria in the early 1930s finally culminated in a full-scale invasion in 1937 and a war that lasted until Japan's defeat in 1945. Over this period, the Nationalist regime received considerable support from the Americans, especially in the anti-Japanese struggle, but also continued to be influenced by European models in some areas, including education. This was the first relatively strong national government China had had since the collapse of the Qing dynasty in 1911. Although the extent of its jurisdiction was limited, moderate intellectuals in the university community held great hopes for the transformative potential of education in the early part of this period.

Cai Yuanpei exemplifies these hopes, and it is with him that we once again take up the story of the university. Intellectually an anarchist, he was nevertheless a supporter of the Guomindang party, and found himself in a position to take the initiative in creating an integrated set of national institutions to protect education from direct political interference. Cai persuaded the new political authorities to allow the establishment of a university council (*daxue yuan*) in July of 1927, which was to manage all of the scholarly and educational work of the nation, and was to stand independent of the national government. Under the university council would be such national cultural institutions as universities, libraries, and museums, and a bureau of educational administration that would operate essentially as a Ministry of Education and be responsible for school education at all levels, social education, and educational legislation.

It was a remarkably bold concept, in which Cai attempted to apply the autonomy and academic freedom he had introduced to Beida in 1917 to the whole educational and cultural life of the nation. One part of the vision was to establish a national academy, which should be responsible for setting and maintaining the highest levels of scholarship in all fields, and another was to address the issue of geographical imbalance in higher education, which had become more and more acute. Cai's plan for a university district scheme, whereby China would be divided into regions and each region assured of reasonable higher education provision, may have been what led to the downfall of the whole plan. Universities had gained considerable real autonomy in the previous period, and were unwilling to be subjected to a rationalization that could destroy their identities, while educators at lower levels were also suspicious of structures that would subject them to supervision by the university. [101]

By 1928, the plan had clearly failed to find acceptance, and a Ministry of Education was formed as an integral part of the new government. From this time forward, Cai focused his energies on building up the Academica Sinica, where a senate was established with the membership of China's most distinguished scholars across the sciences, humanities, and social sciences.[102] The large wave of returned scholars in all of these fields meant that the areas of physics, chemistry, biology, geology, and meteorology were represented by excellent scholars, as was the case also for the humanities and social sciences.[103] This situation makes an interesting contrast with Ma Xiangbo's efforts to recruit scholars for his academy a decade earlier.

The new Ministry of Education proceeded to develop policies and legislation for education that put a strong emphasis on practical knowledge and skills, as well as setting in place patterns that would ensure strong central control and ideological conformity to Sun Yat Sen's "Three Principles of the People," a kind of nationalist credo. In legislation passed in April of 1928, the aims of higher education were expressed as follows: "Universities and professional schools must emphasize the applied sciences, enrich the scientific content of their courses, nurture people with specialized knowledge and skills, and mould healthy character for the service of nation and society."[104] In spite of this practical emphasis, some remnant of Cai's concern for the integration of the disciplines can be seen in the requirement that a university have at least three colleges out of a possible eight (arts, sciences, engineering, commerce, medicine, agriculture, law, education). One of these was to be in the basic or applied sciences. All other institutions specializing in one or two areas were to be known as colleges.[105]

In 1930, China had thirty-nine universities, seventeen colleges, and twenty-three professional schools. Of the universities and colleges, fifteen were national-level institutions, eighteen were provincial level, and twenty-three were private.[106] An important consideration in these regulations was the registration and control of private institutions, to ensure they served Nationalist ends. The total student enrollment at university and college level was 28,677, and 36.6 percent of all students were studying law and politics, 22.5 percent liberal arts, followed by engineering (11.5 percent), sciences (9.7 percent), commerce (6.2 percent), education (6.1 percent), medicine (3.7 percent), and agriculture (3.1 percent).[107] There were another 8,889 in professional schools.

Geographical distribution was extremely unbalanced, with twenty-two institutions in Shanghai, fifteen in Beijing, eight each in Guangdong and Hebei; six each in Hubei and Shandong; five in Jiangsu; four each in Zhejiang, Jiangxi, and Fujian; two each in Hunan, Guangxi, Yunnan, Henan, Shandong, and Liaoning; one each in Anhui, Sichuan, Xinjiang, Gansu, Jilin, and Chahar; none in Shaanxi, Suiyuan, Guizhou, Qinghai, Ningxia, Xikang,

Xizang, Heilongjiang, and Mongolia.[108] Of the total student body, 60 percent were studying in either Beijing or Shanghai.

Two main concerns of the new regime were how to shape curricular emphasis and content toward practical tasks of nation-building, and how to bring about greater equity of access from a geographical perspective. They were also deeply worried about how to deal with student activism, which now threatened the government, though it had contributed to the success of the Northern Expedition. Although defeated over the university council scheme, for his part, Cai continued to struggle for greater autonomy of education, especially in the matter of blocking the establishment of a national student organization directly under the Guomindang party, for the purpose of channelling the energies of university students to political ends.[109]

Generally, this was a period characterized by considerable maturity and independence of educational thought, with eclectic foreign influences being introduced by Chinese scholars who had returned from abroad and at a young age held positions of considerable power.[110] In the educational legislation it is possible to see both American and European influences integrated within patterns that were to serve Nationalist goals. There was a sense, however, that the American-inspired patterns of the 1920s, with their emphasis on decentralization and democracy at the local level, had resulted in an over-activist student population and the constant disruption of schooling for political involvement. There was also concern about academic standards and the lack of clear curricular requirements in most fields. Therefore, European patterns of greater centralization and standardization appealed to Nationalist leaders, and they turned to Europe for assistance.

> At the May 1931 session of the Council of the League of Nations, the Chinese government asked the technical organization of the League to collaborate in the creation and execution of a scheme of reform.[111]

These are the opening lines of the document that was to bring a direct European influence to bear on Chinese higher education policy in the 1930s. The European intellectuals who came to China in 1932 under a League of Nations project to study the education system included C.H. Becker of Germany, P. Langevin of France, M. Falski of Poland, and R.H. Tawney of England. Although they tended to the left politically, a clear European perspective can be seen in their assumptions about the university. The aims of the university they assumed to be the "advancement of knowledge," and "the formation of leadership in the world of science and public affairs," also "the maintenance of the cultural standards of the nation."[112] They were disturbed by American influences on the higher curriculum, which they thought was being fragmented by the use of the credit system and lacked a sense of the cumulative development of knowledge within the disciplines.[113] Thus they recommended the regulation of entry to the university through nationwide entrance examinations in the basic disciplines, the establishment of chairs for each discipline, and final examinations for graduating students. Concerned about the lack of adequate numbers studying basic and applied sciences, and the geographical imbalance of higher education provision, they suggested vigorous action by the government to rationalize these areas. Finally, they recommended a central advisory council for universities, to ensure high academic standards in the appointment of professors, and strict academic criteria for faculty at all levels, combined with a tenure system, which would make for better teaching quality.

The Nationalist government did not follow all of these recommendations. For example, a chair system was not adopted, nor was a university council set up. However, city and provincial-level entrance examinations were initiated, as well as examinations for graduation. Also, legislation was passed establishing national criteria for the appointment of faculty. These measures at the central level made it possible to exercise tighter political control on Chinese campuses under the guise of protecting academic standards, an outcome that was far from the intention of the European advisors.

While there was still little success with geographical rationalization, the Nationalist government did succeed in enrolling larger numbers of students in fields of science and engineering during the 1930s. By 1937, of a total of 31,188 students enrolled in universities and colleges, 18 percent were in engineering, 14 percent in basic sciences, 11 percent in medicine, 6 percent in agriculture, 8 percent in education, 13 percent in humanities, 23 percent in law, and 6 percent in commerce.[114] There were another 3,262 in professional higher schools.

There is a dearth of information about the situation of women students and faculty over this period. We do know that only 10 percent of all university students in 1931 were women, as this was reported in the League study.[115] Yet gender imbalance was not a matter of interest to the four European intellectuals who expressed so much concern about geographical and curricular imbalances in their report. The question of women's participation is never raised in this study, and probably was never asked. University students are referred to as "young men" on several occasions in the document.

In 1931, Beijing Woman's Normal College, which had been so active in promoting the cause of women, was quietly merged with Beiping Normal College to become National Beiping Normal University. This seems to have come about in the aftermath of the university district experiment, which had been fiercely opposed by almost all higher institutions in Beijing.[116] It seems also to have been symptomatic of a move away from women's activism in Nationalist circles. Even though there were Nationalist women's organizations throughout the 1930s and 1940s, and they had some success in new legislation protecting women and in the organization of resistance against Japan, the revival of Confucian values in the New Life Movement of 1934 seems to have brought some restraint to the women's movement.[117]

There is little reference to women in the research literature on Nationalist universities, yet statistics of the period indicate that their participation rate in higher education rose to 15 percent in 1935, 18 percent in 1940, and 19 percent in 1945. Reflecting Nationalist efforts to increase enrollments in applied sciences, 35 percent of them were enrolled in engineering, science, medicine, or business in 1935, and this rose to 43 percent in 1940, then fell back to 41 percent in 1945.[118]

Even in research done outside of China on Nationalist higher education, little attention has been paid to women. In her richly evocative depiction of university life over the period up to 1937, Yeh Wen-hsin limits herself to a single brief and incorrect comment on women—that they gained entrance to the major universities only in 1929.[119] This may reflect a general lack of interest in and information on women's issues over this period. Even in the chapter where the mood on Chinese campuses is depicted through a sensitive summary of important literature of the period, no writings by women are included.[120] Similarly Chan and Dirlik give no attention to women in their important study of the National Labor University, which constituted an interesting attempt to build an intellectual institution around the anarchist ideas of a leading group within the Nationalist party. Statistics in the appendices indicate there were eleven women in a student body of 138 in 1931, and twenty-eight in a student body of 408 a year earlier.[121] The main women's agenda seems to have passed to the Communist party at this time, and the role of women in higher education in the liberated areas will be considered in the next section.

We turn now to issues of the geographical map and the knowledge map, which were of great concern in Nationalist higher education. A Taiwan doctoral dissertation on higher education during the Anti-Japanese War period gives thorough and painstaking detail on both of these issues, using a large number of original source materials.[122] Zhuang Hunming shows that the period between the League of Nations report and the outbreak of war in 1937 saw no real progress in geographical rationalization, in spite of various initiatives on the part of central administration.[123] The actual autonomy of universities was such that attempts to merge or move them were futile. The main change was that the Shanghai and Jiangsu area, with the national capital now in Nanjing, outpaced the number of institutions in the Beijing area.[124] With the Japanese takeover of Manchuria in 1931, Dongbei University refused to cooperate with Japanese authorities and moved to the Beijing area. Its experience was a kind of model for the large exodus that was to take place after the Japanese invasion reached Beijing in 1937 and then the whole southeastern region.[125]

While a certain number of private and missionary institutions retreated to the foreign concessions, or stayed on under Japanese occupation after 1937, and a few southern institutions took refuge in Hong Kong, the majority of institutions, including all government institutions, moved either to rural areas within their province, or westward to areas the Japanese had not occupied. Some moved once, others three or four times, as wartime conditions required. The story is a heroic one, with much of the travel being done under very difficult circumstances due to poor transportation, and to the fact that books and instruments were carried along in many cases.[126]

The Nationalist government endorsed a policy of supporting the universities in their academic work during the war, and it is quite remarkable to see the growth in enrollments and in the number of institutions over the wartime period, from eighty-five universities, colleges, and professional schools with 37,566 students in 1930, to 141 higher institutions with 83,498 students in 1945, 19 percent of them being women.[127] By 1947, there were a total of 207 higher institutions and 154,612 students enrolled. Of these, 27,600, or 17.9 percent, were women.[128]

A radical change in the geographical map took place with the moves to the hinterland, and the provinces that had the most striking benefits were Sichuan, Shaanxi, Gansu, and Yunnan. However, Zhuang points out that even under wartime conditions there continued to be geographical discrepancies. Efforts made by Minister of Education Zhu Jiahua to use the wartime situation as a means of achieving the rationalization that had long been talked about were not very successful. With Chongqing as the new national capital, a very large number of institutions clustered there, even though constant bombing put them in considerable peril. Meanwhile, genuinely remote border regions such as Qinghai, Western Mongolia, Xinjiang, and Ningxia still had no higher education.[129] When the war ended in 1945, the central government had little control over the movement of institutions back to their original locations, although a substantial result of the wartime circumstances was the growth of higher education in central and hinterland regions, in many cases on foundations left by institutions that returned to the coastal regions.

It is quite striking to see the tenacity with which institutions were able to maintain and build distinctive identities over this period, probably a tribute to Cai's early emphasis on autonomy and academic freedom. Two of the most famous institutions that emerged in the process of this westward trek were the Southwest Associated University, and the Northwest Associated University. The former is well known. A combination of Qinghua University, Peking University, and Nankai University, it was located in Kunming through the war years, and produced a remarkable quality of scholarship across the disciplines. It also educated a generation that was to take on important intellectual leadership. Its geographical location in the province of Yunnan under a warlord government and far from interference by Chongqing authorities enabled it to operate with considerable academic freedom and autonomy.[130]

The story of the three universities that moved to the Northwest is less well known and somewhat different. Beiping University, Beijing Normal University, and Beiyang Engineering University first located in Xi'an, forming the Northwest Associated University. However, due to concerns on the part of the Nationalist authorities about its proximity to Yan'an in the North, it was soon disbanded, and separate colleges of agriculture and engineering were relocated to southern Shaanxi province. The part of the institution made up by Beijing Normal University moved to Lanzhou in 1939, and formed the basis for Northwest Normal University. Much closer both to the civil war and the Anti-Japanese War, these institutions were not able to develop with the same cohesion and academic brilliance as Southwest Associated. Nevertheless, an intellectual foundation was laid in the Northwest over the period that was very important for the subsequent development of the region.[131]

We have noted already the concern about curriculum in the early 1930s, and the recommendations for stricter and more unified standards given by the League of Nations delegation. These were taken very seriously by the Nationalist government, yet by 1935, the only field in which clear standards for each course content had been established was medicine.[132] In 1937, the Nationalist government published a report on curricular patterns and textbooks used across the disciplines in major universities, with a critical comparative analysis that pointed to a whole series of weaknesses: lack of uniformity in the definition of programs and courses, inadequate attention to basic content as against specialist areas of interest, lack of good teaching material, and an over-dependence on Western texts whose content had little relevance to China.[133] After Chen Lifu took over as minister of education in 1938, in his visits to universities to assist in plans for the westward migration, he commented that he felt as if he were entering foreign territory culturally, due to the preponderance of foreign material and models in the teaching content.[134]

Over the following two years, the Ministry of Education organized committees in all of the major fields of knowledge, and published standards for required courses, which were to be the same across all institutions, as well as guidelines for elective courses. New textbooks were prepared, and there was a considerable effort made to give greater emphasis to Chinese history, and to Chinese content in areas such as economics, sociology, and political science. Standards were also established for teaching faculty, as had been recommended by the League, and an elaborate process of faculty evaluation was initiated. This was a convenient instrument whereby Nationalist authorities could exert pressure on leftist and Communist faculty within their institutions.[135] Political orthodoxy was also a consideration in the new teaching material. Still, it would be a mistake to dismiss all of the work done toward improving academic standards and indigenizing teaching content as simply a matter of ideological struggle, as is often done in Communist accounts of the period.[136]

In fact, the whole wartime period was a kind of baptism by fire for Chinese intellectuals, many of whom had gained the basic tools of their disciplines in study abroad, and then had worked in universities in major coastal cities where there was little challenge to these ideas and theories, until the war drove them to the hinterland. Here they did important anthropological and sociological research, which was locally based, as well as continuing historical and literary studies. In scientific fields also, there was a new interest in researching practical topics related to agricultural and industrial development in the hinterland, as well as areas urgently needed for the military struggle, such as aeronautics and various kinds of military engineering.[137] Zhuang gives interesting details on an intense debate that went on in political and intellectual circles over how far higher education should be reorganized into a series of research institutes focused directly on wartime needs, as against being allowed to maintain greater autonomy and academic direction over teaching and research topics.[138] The actual outcome of this debate was decided partly by distance, with those institutions in regions more remote from Chongqing able to retain greater control over their academic work.

In her study of the civil war in China, Suzanne Pepper devotes a chapter to universities and their students in the Nationalist areas. She shows how determined they were in their opposition to the civil war, and their wish to support a coalition government, including both the Communist and Nationalist parties. While Communist historians were later to give credit to the Chinese Communist party for much of the patriotic activism that marked this period, in fact it seems most of it was a genuine expression of intellectual freedom and social responsibility. Faculty and students were determined not to offer blind support to an increasingly repressive and corrupt regime, yet most were moderate in their political views, and hopeful of political pluralism as a context in which they could contribute their knowledge and skills to nation-building.[139]

In many ways the whole Republican era was one in that the university had gone through a process of adaptation and indigenization that might be compared to the development of American universities in the nineteenth century, under the joint influences of German scholarship and the emergence of modern scientific studies.[140] In China, university autonomy and academic freedom on European lines were neither easily acceptable in terms of their epistemological connotations, nor practically possible, given the series of political and economic crises the nation was passing through. However, one can see new intellectual institutions evolving over this period that combined elements of China's academy tradition of scholarship, with its ethos of intellectual freedom and social responsibility, and dimensions of both the American and European patterns that had been introduced.

Rapid curricular change involved the development of natural sciences, social sciences, and humanities in new ways, and new interrelationships. Modern universities were varied in form, but achieved a degree of autonomy and intellectual freedom that enabled them to be an effective independent force in the wartime struggle, contributing in positive ways to national development, yet resisting negative aspects of Nationalist regimentation. Also in this period, modern higher education finally reached most parts of the country, thereby becoming both more accessible and more connected to its indigenous roots.

Unfortunately, few of the lessons learned from the integration of Chinese and Western patterns that took place in this period were to be appreciated and drawn upon in the subsequent period. This could be blamed on the global context of imperialism, and the way in which China became pitted against the United States in the Korean War. Yet it was also due to mistakes and excesses in the policy of the Communist party after it came to power in 1949.

In the 1950s, a new set of tensions and oppositions between Chinese and Western patterns of higher education emerged, with the institutions of the border regions, which represented a pure Chinese Communist model, being set against a highly sophisticated set of patterns introduced from the

Soviet Union, which for China was the "other West." The tension between these two poles was to prove highly explosive in the Cultural Revolution decade, I will argue, because there were not the shades of experimentation and diversity at this time that had characterized Chinese-Western interaction in the Republican period. Chapter 2 concludes with a few comments on this new model of higher education that grew up in the liberated areas under the Chinese Communist party.

THE EVOLUTION OF COMMUNIST HIGHER EDUCATION

The first Communist institution of higher education, Shanghai University, was founded in the same year in which the Communist party was formed, 1921, and had explicit links to the party. The aims of the university were to "nurture talented people for national construction and to promote cultural work." Due to very limited resources, the curriculum focused first on literature and fine arts, then social sciences, with a sociology department established in 1923. In explicit reaction to the ways in which social sciences in other Shanghai universities of the time tended to ape foreign theories and contexts, the intention was to develop a Chinese sociology that was rooted in active theoretical and practical involvement in China's revolutionary transformation. The well-known theorist, Qu Qiubai, was one of several Communist intellectuals involved in this institution.[141] In 1928, it was closed down by Nationalist authorities, and the National Labor University was established on its campus. It attempted to develop an anarchist approach to social theory, in contrast to the Marxist one of Shanghai University.

During the period of the Jiangxi Soviet, from around 1929 to 1933, it is difficult to speak of any real higher education under the difficult situation of increasing military pressure from the Guomindang, but there was certainly an active program for short-term cadre training, which probably laid the basis for later educational patterns in Yan'an. Educational content was almost entirely political and military, with study periods being rather brief. A significant feature of this period was the passing of the first Communist legislation to guarantee equal rights to women, and the relatively high representation of women in various political councils and other representative organizations.[142]

About fifty Chinese women were reported to have participated in the Long March of 1934, among them such legendary figures as Kang Keqing, Ding Ling, and Deng Yingchao.[143] Over the period when Yan'an was the center of the revolutionary regime, large numbers of young intellectuals joined the movement there. In the period between May and August of 1938, a total of 2,288 arrived, 30 percent of these being young women.[144]

A range of diverse higher institutions developed in Yan'an and other border regions. The Anti-Japanese Resistance University (Kangda) provided short-term courses of around six months to young people in military and strategic affairs, and it had branches spread throughout the border regions. The Shaanbei Public Institute (*Shaanbei gongxue*) focused on the training of political cadres, in a program complementary to that of Kangda. In 1939, it moved to the Pu Cha Yi military base, and thereafter moved several times, ending up as the North China United University in Shi Jia Zhuang. Both of these institutions focused on very specific training ends, yet also provided courses in broader social science and literary areas.

In 1939, the China Women's University was established in Yan'an as an institution somewhat similar to Kangda and the Shaanbei gongxue, with a focus on training women cadres for political and military work. It was also to foster women activists who would carry forward the women's movement. Its student numbers are variously reported as between 400 and 1,000.[145]

Meanwhile, more specialized institutions with a longer-term academic orientation gradually came into being, including the Yan'an College of Natural Sciences (1939), the Lu Xun Academy of the Arts (1938), and the China Medical University (1940). In 1941, Yan'an University was established on the basis of the Shaanbei Public Institute, the China Women's University, and a cadre school, and in 1943, the Yan'an College of Natural Sciences and the Lu Xun Academy of Arts were combined with it to form a comprehensive university. By 1944, it had an enrollment of 1,302 students, but only seventy-four were women.[146]

Programs were to last three or four years, with a broad range of academic subjects organized within four colleges, and subordinate departments. Considerable debate went on over how far the university should uphold academic goals, as against focusing on very specific training for immediate wartime needs. Inevitably, it was the latter emphasis that dominated, but the very fact of an attempt to create a "regular" higher institution under these circumstances was remarkable. The curriculum was organized both around the disciplines and practical applications. Teaching quality was generally high on both counts, given the presence of some distinguished intellectuals on the faculty, including a few returnees from Europe, and the fact that many of the revolutionary leaders came often to lecture on issues of policy and strategy. Some of Mao's well-known speeches of the time were delivered as lectures to the university community.

In the first years of higher education at Yan'an, there is much to suggest an informal atmosphere in which the approach to study characteristic of the *shuyuan* was common. Class and lecture time was flexible, and students were expected to do a great deal of reading and self-study, as well as to be involved in practical tasks. Students wrote reports on their own study, and participated actively in debates and discussions over both theoretical and practical issues.[147] There was considerable intellectual freedom in a situation where knowledge was thought to be advanced through revolutionary practice. However, this should be distinguished from the associations of academic freedom in the Western sense.

As for autonomy, this was neither an aspiration nor a possibility under circumstances of the time. The university was very much an arm of the border-region government for the training of its cadres. Yan'an University was administered by the party, Kangda by the army, and the majority of university administrators and faculty were concurrently responsible members of the border-region bureaucracy. In this sense, Yan'an institutions represented a kind of continuity with classical Chinese bureaucratic patterns of higher education as preparation for public office.[148]

The Rectification Campaign of 1942–1944 laid down conditions for the suppression of the intellectual freedom that characterized an earlier period, and the consolidation of an approach to higher education that made Mao's adaptation of Marxism and Leninism to Chinese conditions a new epistemological orthodoxy. In several important speeches related to the movement, Mao outlined ideas that set out the main lines of this epistemology. In "Reform Our Study," he called for the integrated study of Chinese history, current conditions, and ways in which Marxism-Leninism could be applied to the Chinese situation and so become a new concrete Chinese system of thought. Set against this was a "subjectivism" that Mao associated with a purely theoretical understanding of Marxism-Leninism. In "Oppose Stereotyped Party Writing," Mao attacked what he regarded as modern versions of the traditional "eight-legged essay," which adopt a highly theoretical and pretentious approach to introducing Marxism-Leninism as a tool for control and manipulation of the people, rather than a flexible scholarship in the language of the people, which would make sense of their experience and conditions. In the "Yan'an Forum on Art and Literature," Mao called for the direct subordination of all literary writing to the political struggle, identifying literature that was critical of revolutionary efforts as bourgeois, and showing the need for its creators to join the party ideologically as well as organizationally.[149]

While there was much good sense in the criticisms of tendencies to theoretical dogmatism and academicism in these essays, Mao's epistemological formula, from practice to perception to conceptual understanding, had serious and long-term implications for intellectual life. It suggested that differences of view could not be worked out through argument, debate, and theoretical discussion, but only through practice-based social and political struggle. Added to this was Mao's growing prestige as a revolutionary intellectual who was literally able to remold China by the application of his views to revolutionary practice, and who was therefore becoming a new emperor figure, a transformation well under way even before 1949. Mao's immense personal prestige put a kind of personal authority at the core of Maoist epistemology, which was to be pitted against the European rationalist and specialist approach to knowledge in the Soviet model.

Thus Yan'an University and Kangda, after they had been purified in the Rectification Campaign of 1942–1944, were to be the models for the Cultural Revolution decade, when the Soviet model came under intense attack, as an instrument of social imperialism.

CONCLUSION

This chapter has given a brief overview of a century during which modern higher institutions evolved in China. The Western idea of the university was introduced about halfway through the period, and through a series of interactions and adaptations, ideals of academic freedom and autonomy were transformed into forms of intellectual freedom and social responsibility suited to the Chinese context. The Chinese university of the Republican era gradually developed into a mature institution, which achieved a balance between its Chinese identity and its ability to link up to a world community of universities.

Meanwhile, in the harsher and more extreme conditions of the Communist guerilla struggle, another set of higher institutions emerged that were untouched by Western values of the university and remained close to certain elements of Chinese epistemological and revolutionary tradition. With the success of the Communist revolution, these patterns were to form the antithesis to a new attempt at Westernization, this time in its socialist form, with the adoption of the Soviet model of higher education in 1952. All that had been learned in the Nationalist period was shelved at this time, to make way for the new agenda of socialist nation-building. It was only to become relevant again in the 1980s, after the powerful opposing tensions of the Soviet way and the Yan'an way had worked themselves out in the violence of the Cultural Revolution.

NOTES

1. Benjamin Elman, *From Philosophy to Philology: Intellectual Aspects of Social Change in Late Imperial China* (Cambridge, Mass.: Council on East Asian Stud-

ies, Harvard University, 1984), esp. pp. 163–169.

2. David Noble, *A World without Women: The Christian Clerical Culture of Western Science* (New York: Alfred Knopf, 1992); Carolyn Merchant, *The Death of Nature: Women, Ecology, and the Scientific Revolution* (San Francisco: Harper and Row, 1980).

3. In an article written for *Xin Qingnian* (New Youth) in 1916, Chen Duxiu made this point, and called for a rectification of the shameful way women had been treated in Chinese society as part of the movement to oppose foreign domination. See Chen Dongyuan, *Zhongguo funu shenghuo shi* [A History of the Life of Chinese Women] (Shanghai: Shangwu chubanshe, 1937), pp. 366–368. See also Bobby Siu, *Women of China: Imperialism and Women's Resistance, 1900–1949* (London: Zed Press, 1982).

4. Catherine Jami, "Learning Mathematical Sciences during the Early and Mid-Ch'ing," in B. Elman and A. Woodside, *Education and Society in Late Imperial China*, pp. 223–256, looks at the role of science in the intellectual life of late imperial China, rather than focusing on the question of why "modern science" did not develop, suggesting that the latter was itself a cultural artifact.

5. Richard Guisso and Stanley Johannesen (eds.), *Women in China: Current Directions in Historical Scholarship* (Lewiston, N.Y.: Edwin Mellen Press, 1981), Introduction, pp. vii–x.

6. Kathryn A. Tsai, "The Chinese Buddhist Monastic Order for Women: The First Two Centuries," in Ibid., pp. 1–20. Roger T. Ames, "Taoism and the Androgynous Ideal," in Ibid., pp. 21–46.

7. Julia Kristeva, *About Chinese Women* (London: Marion Boyars, 1974), explores this dynamic in the situation of Chinese women.

8. D. Noble, *A World without Women*. It is fascinating to reflect on the parallels between the activity of women in Buddhist circles during the Tang, and that of European women, such as the abbesses of the Ely Cathedral, with whom Noble begins his account. It was from the Song dynasty, and specifically the ideas of Zhu Xi, that the notion of a lack of talent being women's greatest virtue (*funu wucai ji shi de*) began in China. See Esther Lee Yao, *Chinese Women Past and Present* (Mesquite, Tex.: Ide House, 1983), pp. 75–82.

9. Ding Gang, *Zhongguo fojiao jiaoyu: Ru fo dao jiaoyu bijiao yanjiu* [Chinese Buddhist Education: Comparative Research on Confucian, Buddhist, and Daoist Education] (Chengdu: Sichuan jiaoyu chubanshe, 1988). Charlotte Furth, "Rethinking Van Gulik: Sexuality and Reproduction in Traditional Chinese Medicine," in C. Gilmartin, G. Hershatter, L. Rofel, and T. White (eds.), *Engendering China* (Cambridge, Mass.: Harvard University Press, 1994), suggests that Daoism may not have been as supportive to women's interests as has been thought.

10. M. Belenky et al., *Women's Ways of Knowing: The Development of Self, Voice, and Mind* (New York: Basic Books, 1986).

11. Chan Hoiman, "Modernity and Revolution in Chinese Education: Towards an Analytical Agenda of the Great Leap Forward and the Cultural Revolution," in R. Hayhoe (ed.), *Education and Modernization: The Chinese Experience* (Oxford: Pergamon, Toronto: OISE Press, 1992), pp. 73–102. Here Chan gives a sensitive depiction of the attempt to create a totalistic integration of education and society in ways that made the disciplines of knowledge irrelevant in the Cultural Revolution decade.

12. Paul Bailey, *Reform the People: Changing Attitudes towards Popular Education in Early Twentieth Century China* (Edinburgh: Edinburgh University Press, 1990). In the last chapter of this excellent monograph, which covers the period from 1900 to 1920, Bailey emphasizes the diversity of foreign influences, and the ambiguities in the way Chinese thinkers drew eclectically upon various dimensions of Japanese, European, and American patterns.

13. Jonathan Spence, *The Search for Modern China* (New York: W.W. Norton, 1990), pp. 137–268, provides a wonderfully reflective panorama of the period.

14. We are indebted to recent Chinese educational scholarship for a wealth of documentary material on this period that has been collected in several major series: *Zhongguo jindai xuezhi shiliao* [Historical Materials on the Educational System in Recent Chinese History], edited by Zhu Youxian and published by Huadong Shida chubanshe, Shanghai in six volumes between 1983 and 1991, and *Zhongguo jindai jiaoyushi ziliao huibian* [A Collection of Material on Recent Chinese Educational History], edited by Chen Yuanhui, and published by Shanghai jiaoyu chubanshe in three volumes in 1990 and 1991. In Vol. 1, part 2 of Zhu Youxian's series, there is a great deal of documentary information on traditional and new *shuyuan* in the late Qing period.

15. Wolfgang Franke, *The Reform and Abolition of the Traditional Examination System* (Cambridge, Mass.: East Asian Research Center, Harvard University, 1963), pp. 28–32.

16. Ibid., pp. 32–43.

17. Barry Keenan, *Academy Revival and the Management of China's Education in the Lower Yangtze Region, 1865–1911* (Berkeley: Institute of East Asian Studies, University of California, 1994).

18. Ibid., p. 54.

19. Lin Yu-t'ang, "Feminist Thought in Ancient China," in Li Yu-ning (ed.), *Chinese Women through Chinese Eyes* (New York: M.E. Sharpe, 1992), pp. 34–58. Lin blames Buddhist influences for the treatment of women, a rather different view than that of Ding Gang, who felt Buddhist institutions were generally more open to women.

20. Marina H. Sung, "The Chinese Lie-nu Tradition," in Guisso and Johannesen, *Women in China*, pp. 63–74. See note 5 above.

21. Kathryn A. Tsai, "The Chinese Buddhist Monastic Order for Women: The First Two Centuries," in Guisso and Johannesen, *Women in China*, pp. 1–20.

22. Ding Gang, *Zhongguo fojiao jiaoyu*, especially chapters 5 and 6.

23. As the Taipings gained greater power, women were gradually pushed back into more traditional roles. Ju Jin (ed.) *Yapian zhanzheng shiqi jiaoyu* [Education in the Period of the Opium Wars], part of the series *Zhongguo jindai jiaoyushi ziliao huibian* [A Collection of Materials on Recent Chinese Educational History] (Shanghai: Shanghai jiaoyu chubanshe, 1990), pp. 507–508. See also Mao Lirui, Shen Guanqun (eds.) *Zhongguo jiaoyu tongshi* [A Comprehensive History of Chinese Education] (Jinan: Shandong jiaoyu chubanshe, 1988), Vol. 4, p. 63, and Elizabeth Croll, *Feminism and Socialism in China* (London: Routledge and Kegan Paul, 1978), pp. 38–41.

24. Shu Xincheng, *Zhongguo jindai jiaoyushi ziliao* [Materials on Recent Chinese Educational History], Vol. 3 (Beijing: Renmin jiaoyu chubanshe, 1979), pp. 800–818. See Esther Lee Yao, *Chinese Women Past and Present*, pp. 116–120, for an interesting comparison of courses for girls in government normal schools and missionary colleges.

25. Shu Xincheng, *Zhongguo jindai jiaoyushi ziliao*, Vol. 2, pp. 578–624.

26. John Chaffee, *The Thorny Gates of Learning in Sung China* (Cambridge: Cambridge University Press, 1985), Chapter 6, "The Geography of Success," pp. 119–142.

27. Knight Biggerstaff, *The Earliest Modern Government Schools in China* (Port Washington, New York: Kennikat Press, 1972).

28. Yeh Wen-hsin, *The Alienated Academy: Culture and Politics in Republican China, 1919–1937* (Cambridge, Mass.: Harvard University Press, 1990), pp. 93–102. Chinese histories of higher education normally take 1895 as the date for the first modern university, which makes 1995 their centenary date.

29. William Ayers, *Chang Chih-tung and Educational Reform in China* (Cambridge, Mass.: Harvard University Press, 1971), pp. 104–133.

30. Ibid., pp. 159–160, 253–254.

31. Mary B. Rankin, *Early Chinese Revolutionaries: Radical Intellectuals in Shanghai and Chekiang, 1902–1911* (Cambridge, Mass.: Harvard University Press, 1971). This volume provides an interesting discussion of the revolutionary alternatives to Qing government schooling.

32. Ding Gang and Liu Qi, *Shuyuan yu Zhongguo wenhua* [Academics and Chinese Culture], (Shanghai: Shanghai jiaoyu chubanshe, 1992) has a whole section on missionary educators and *shuyuan*, pp. 131–147. While many missionary institutions used this term as a translation for college, only a few were inspired by the ethos of the classical *shuyuan*, and this seems to have been one of them.

33. Li Tiangang, "The Anglo-Chinese College and East-West Cultural Understanding," paper presented at the conference, "Knowledge Across Cultures: Universities East and West," OISE, Toronto, Canada, October 11–14, 1992.

34. This has recently been republished in China: Lu Shuxiang and Wang Haifen (eds.) *Mashi wentong duben* [A Reader on the Ma Brothers' Grammar] (Shanghai: Shanghai jiaoyu chubanshe, 1986).

35. This was published by the Commercial Press, Shanghai, in 1926.

36. Lu Yongling, "Standing Between Two Worlds: Ma Xiangbo's Educational Thought and Practice," in R. Hayhoe and Lu Yongling, *Ma Xiangbo and the Mind of Modern China* (New York: M.E. Sharpe, forthcoming).

37. Jessie Lutz, *China and the Christian Colleges, 1850–1950* (Ithaca, N.Y., and London: Cornell University Press, 1971), pp. 59–73, 187–190.

38. Karen Minden, *Bamboo Stone: The Evolution of a Chinese Medical Elite* (Toronto: University of Toronto Press, 1994) gives an illuminating picture of how this was done by Canadian missionaries in the context of a medical school.

39. Rankin, *Early Chinese Revolutionaries*, p. 69.

40. "Un Oeuvre de Haut Enseignement pour les Jeunes Païennes: L'Etoile de Matin de Zi-ka-Wei," in *Relations de Chine*, Mai-Août, 1923 to Janvier, 1924. See also Martine Raibaud, "L'enseignement catholique en Chine sous la Republique de 1912 a 1949," thèse de doctorat, Université de Paris VII, 1991, pp. 101–112, and Charles Meyer, *Histoire de la Femme Chinoise* (Paris: J. Clattes, 1986), p. 154.

41. J. Lutz, *China and the Christian Colleges*, pp. 132–138.

42. For original documents on this school, see *Zhongguo jindai xuezhi shiliao* [Historical Materials on the Educational System in Recent Chinese History] (Shanghai Huadong shida chubanshi, Vol. 2, part 2, 1989, pp. 609–631.

43. Croll, *Feminism and Socialism in China*, pp. 45–79, gives a good overview of women's revolutionary activity in this early period.

44. Mary Bacchus Rankin, "The Emergence of Women at the End of the Ch'ing: The Case of Ch'iu Chin," in Marjorie Wolfe and Roxane Witke (eds.), *Women in Chinese Society* (Stanford, Calif.: Stanford University Press, 1975), gives an excellent overview of her life and achievements in the context of the general situation of women in the late Qing period.

45. Ono Kozuko, *Chinese Women in a Century of Revolution, 1850–1950* (Stanford, Calif.: Stanford University Press, 1989), pp. 54–70, gives a vivid depiction of the experience of these women, facing both conservative forces and revolutionary ideas.

46. Hiroshi Abe, "Borrowing from Japan: China's First Modern Education System," in R. Hayhoe and M. Bastid (eds.), *China's Education and the Industrialized World: Studies in Cultural Transfer*, pp. 73–79; Chen Xuexun and Tian Zhengping (eds.), *Liuxue jiaoyu* [The Education of Students Abroad], in the series Chen Yuanhui (ed.), *Zhongguo jindai jiaoyushi ziliao huibian* (see note 14 above) (Shanghai: Shanghai jiaoyu chubanshe, 1991), pp. 686–689. This book gives valuable details on the whole study abroad movement through the many original documents collected in it.

47. Y.C. Wang, *Chinese Intellectuals and the West* (Chapel Hill: University of North Carolina Press, 1966), pp. 72–3; Chen Dongyuan, *Zhongguo funu shenghuo shi* (see note 3 above), p. 350.

48. Douglas Reynolds, *China 1898–1912: The Xinzheng Revolution and Japan* (Cambridge, Mass.: Council on East Asian Studies, Harvard University, 1993).

49. Wang Xiangrong, *Riben jiaoxi* [Japanese Teachers] (Beijing: Sanlian, 1987).

50. Paul Bailey, *Reform the People*, especially chapter 2.

51. Marianne Bastid, *Educational Reform in Early Twentieth-Century China*, translated by Paul Bailey, (Ann Arbor: Center for Chinese Studies, University of Michigan, 1988), pp. 44–50.

52. Benjamin Schwartz, *In Search of Wealth and Power: Yen Fu and the West* (Cambridge, Mass.: Harvard University Press, 1964).

53. Paul Bailey, *Reform the People*, pp. 29–30.

54. Marianne Bastid, *Educational Reform in Early Twentieth-Century China*, chapter 3, pp. 59–88.

55. Ibid., p. 63.

56. See, for example, Paul Bailey, *Reform the People*, and Charles Hayford, *To the People: James Yen and Village China* (New York: Columbia University Press, 1990).

57. Zhou Yutong, *Zhongguo xiandai jiaoyushi* [A History of Contemporary Chinese Education] (Shanghai: Liangyou tushu gongsi, 1934), pp. 223–4.

58. Ibid.

59. *Zhongguo jindai xuezhi shiliao* (see note 14 above), Vol. 2, part 2, 1989, pp. 649–650.

60. Spence, *The Search for Modern China*, pp. 275–360.

61. William Duiker, *Ts'ai Yuan-p'ei: Educator of Modern China* (University Park and London: Pennsylvania State University Press, 1977); Eugene Lubot, "Ts'ai Yuan-p'ei: From Confucian Scholar to Chancellor of Peking University," unpublished Ph.D. dissertation, Ohio State University, 1970.

62. For an interesting discussion of these ideas see Zhou Yutong, *Zhongguo xiandai jiaoyushi* (see note 57 above), pp. 28–29, p. 206ff. Zhou felt that Cai's ideas about aesthetic education and education for a world view were not widely understood. For a retrospective view from the 1980s, see Mao Lirui and Shen Guanqun, *Zhongguo jiaoyu tongshi* (see note 23 above), Vol. 4, pp. 379–407

63. One commonly used term in Chinese for university autonomy is *jiaoshou zhixiao* [professors rule the school], which reflects these provisions. We have already noted Mao Zedong's contempt for this notion in the Inauguration Manifesto he wrote for the Hunan Self-Study University, which is quoted in chapter 1.

64. Shu Xincheng, *Zhongguo jindai jiaoyushi ziliao* (see note 24 above), Vol. 2, pp. 646–7.

65. Most of these details concerning the academy project come from Li Tiangang, "The Chinese Academy of Literary Standards and Ma Xiangbo's Educational Thought," paper delivered at the Conference on the History of Chinese Missionary Universities, Nanjing Normal University, June 1991. See also Lu Yongling, "Standing Between Two Worlds."

66. Lubot, "Ts'ai Yuan-p'ei," pp. 64–75.

67. Robert Smith, *The École Normale Supérieure and the Third Republic* (Albany, N.Y.: SUNY Press, 1982). R. Hayhoe, "Catholics and Socialists: The Paradox of French Educational Interaction with China," in R. Hayhoe and M. Bastid (eds.), *China's Education and the Industrialized World*, pp. 97–119.

68. Vera Schwarcz, *The Chinese Enlightenment: Intellectuals and the Legacy of the May 4th Movement of 1919* (Berkeley: University of California Press, 1986).

69. Xiao Chaoren et al., *Beijing daxue xiaoshi* [A History of Beijing University] (Shanghai: Shanghai jiaoyu chubanshe, 1981), pp. 43–4, 136ff.

70. Ibid, p. 32.

71. Lubot, E. "Ts'ai Yuan-p'ei," p. 64, noted that there were 532 students in law at Beida in 1918, 341 in arts, and 134 in sciences.

72. Cai Yuanpei, *Cai Yuanpei xuanji* [Selected Writings of Cai Yuanpei] (Beijing: Zhongguo shuju, 1959), p. 98.

73. Zhou Yutong, *Zhongguo xiandai jiaoyushi* (see note 57 above), pp. 30–33.

74. Ibid., p. 201–202. See also Yin Chiling, *Reconstruction of Modern Educational Organizations in China* (Shanghai: Commercial Press, 1924), and Djung, Ludzai, *A History of Democratic Education in Modern China* (Shanghai: Commercial Press, 1934), for a sense of the spirit of the period.

75. Y.C. Wang, *Chinese Intellectuals and the West*, chapter 12, pp. 378–421; Jerome Grieder, *Hu Shi and the Chinese Renaissance: Liberalism in the Chinese Revolution, 1917–1937* (Cambridge, Mass.: Harvard University Press, 1970).

76. Lin Yusheng, *The Crisis of Chinese Consciousness: Radical Antitraditionalism in the May Fourth Era* (Madison: University of Wisconsin Press, 1979) provides a sensitive exploration of the intellectual struggle of younger Chinese scholars during this period, with particular attention given to Chen Duxiu, Hu shi and Xiand.

77. Zhou Yutong, *Zhongguo xiandai jiaoyushi*, pp. 223–225.

78. Chen Dongyuan, *Zhongguo funu shenghuo shi*, pp. 359–60.

79. Chen Qingzhi, *Zhongguo jiaoyushi*, (Shanghai: Commercial Press, 1936), pp. 686–687.

80. Chen Dongyuan, *Zhongguo funu shenghuo shi*, pp. 416–417. See also Roxane Witke, "Woman as Politician in China of the 1920s," in Marilyn Young, *Women in China: Studies in Social Change and Feminism* (Ann Arbor: Center for Chinese Studies, University of Michigan, 1973), pp. 33–46, and Croll, *Feminism and Socialism in China*, pp. 80–116.

81. Ibid., pp. 389–392.

82. Zhongguo jiaoyu gaijin hui [China Educational Progress Society] (ed.), *Zhongguo jiaoyu tongji gailan* [A Survey of Chinese Educational Statistics] (Shanghai: Commercial Press, 1923). This book was put together by progressive educators, and reflects the concern about women's participation that was strong at the time.

83. Chen, *Zhongguo jiaoyushi*, p. 631.

84. Chen Xuexun, Tan Zhengping, *Liuxue jiaoyu*, pp. 687, 689. (Part of the series edited by Chen Yuanhui, *Zhongguo jindai jiaoyushi ziliao huibian*).

85. Y.C. Wang, *Chinese Intellectuals and the West*, chapter 5, pp. 99–120.

86. Jessie Lutz, *China and the Christian Colleges*, chapter 7.

87. Barry Keenan, *The Dewey Experiment in China* (Cambridge, Mass.: Harvard University Press, 1977).

88. Paul Monroe, *China: A Nation in Evolution* (New York: Macmillan, 1928). Monroe was very well known in educational theory and comparative education at the time, so his comments on Chinese schools of the period are most interesting.

89. Stephen Hay, *Asian Ideas of East and West: Tagore and His Critics in Japan, China, and India* (Cambridge, Mass.: Harvard University Press, 1970).

90. *Qinghua daxue xiaoshi gao* [Draft History of Qinghua University] (Beijing: Zhonghua shuju, 1981). John Israel, "The Idea of Liberal Education in China" in Ronald A. Morse (ed.) *The Limits of Reform in China* (Boulder, Colo.: Westview Press, 1983), pp. 87–118. This article by Israel gives a fascinating reflection on the liberal university ethos developed at Qinghua, Beida, and Nankai, both separately and later jointly in the Sino-Japanese War period, then applies this to a considerations of university reform in China in the 1980s. In his comments on the official Qinghua University history, Israel notes the lack of appreciation of this liberal tradition.

91. Chiang Yung-chen, "Social Engineering and the Social Sciences in China, 1898–1949," unpublished Ph.D. dissertation, Harvard University, 1986, chapters 4 and 5, pp. 133–229.

92. Philip West, *Yenching University and Sino-Western Relations, 1916–1952* (Cambridge, Mass.: Harvard University Press, 1976).

93. Yeh Wen-hsin, *The Alienated Academy: Culture and Politics in Republican China, 1919–1937* (Cambridge, Mass.: Harvard University Press, 1990), pp. 59–88.

94. R. Hayhoe, "Catholics and Socialists," pp. 105–107.

95. Françoise Kreissler, "Technical Education as a Key to Cultural Cooperation: The Sino-German Experience," in R. Hayhoe and M. Bastid, *China's Education and the Industrialized World*, pp. 91–96.

96. Y.C. Wang, *Chinese Intellectuals and the West*, pp. 377–393, gives a good assessment of achievements in the sciences.

97. Immanuel Wallerstein, *The Politics of the World Economy: The States, the Movements, and the Civilizations* (Cambridge: Cambridge University Press, 1984), chapter 17, "The Development of the Concept of Development," pp. 173–185.

98. Yeh Wen-hsin, *The Alienated Academy*, pp. 37–48, gives a wonderfully insightful account of these efforts.

99. Ruth Hayhoe, "Chinese Universities and the Social Sciences," *Minerva*, Vol. XXXI, no. 4, 1993, pp. 478–503.

100. Yeh Wen-hsin, *The Alienated Academy*, pp. 172–182, gives an excellent analysis of the process of "partification" at Zhongshan University in Guangzhou, National Zhejiang University in Hangzhou, and National Central University in Nanjing.

101. Cai's plan was patterned after the French model, and had been introduced in an article he published in *New Education* [Xin jiaoyu] in 1922, at a time of great concern over the protection of individual freedom. It had originally left much of the initiative in the hands of university district councils, who were to elect members to the national council. See Allen B. Linden, "Politics and Education in Nationalist China: The Case of the University Council, 1927–1928," in *Journal of Asian Studies*, Vol. XXVIII, no. 4, August 1968, pp. 763–776. See also R. Hayhoe, "Catholics and Socialists."

102. Tao Yinghui, "Cai Yuanpei yu zhongyang yanjiuyuan" [Cai Yuanpei and the Academica Sinica], in Zhongyang yanjiuyuan, *Jindaishi yanjiusuo jikan*, Vol. 7, June 1978, pp. 1–51.

103. E-Tu Zen Sun, "The Growth of the Academic Community, 1912–1949," in John Fairbank and Albert Feuerwerker (eds.), *The Cambridge History of China*, Vol. XIII, part 2 (Cambridge: Cambridge University Press, 1986), pp. 396–412, gives a good overview of scientific developments in the period.

104. *Zhongguo jiaoyu nianjian* [China Education Yearbook] (Shanghai: Kaiming shudian, 1934), part A, p. 16.

105. This was stated in Articles 1 and 2 of the "Daxue zuzhi fa" [Regulations on University Organization]. See *Jiaoyu faling* [Educational Laws and Regulations] (Shanghai: Zhonghua shuju, 1947), p. 141.

106. Zhou Yutong, *Zhongguo xiandai jiaoyushi*, pp. 229–234, gives a full listing of all institutions by category.

107. C.H. Becker, M. Falski, P. Langevin, and R.H. Tawney, *The Reorganization of Education in China* (Paris: League of Nations Institute of Intellectual Cooperation, 1932), p. 151.

108. Mao Lirui and Shen Guanqun, *Zhongguo jiaoyu tongshi* (see note 23 above), Vol. 5, p. 294.

109. John Israel, *Student Nationalism in China, 1927–1937* (Stanford, Calif.: Stanford University Press, 1966), pp. 22–25; A. Linden, "Politics and Education in Nationalist China," pp. 770–775.

110. Marianne Bastid, "Servitude or Liberation? The Introduction of Foreign Educational Practices and Systems to China from 1840 to the Present," in R. Hayhoe and M. Bastid (eds.), *China's Education and the Industrialized World*, pp. 14–17.

111. C.H. Becker et al., *The Reorganization of Education in China*, p. 11; for a detailed historical analysis of the background and documents related to this mission, see Ernst Neugebauer, *Anfange pädagogischer Entwicklungshilfe unter dem Völkerbund in China 1931 bis 1935* (Hamburg: Mitteilungen des Instituts für Asienkunde, 1971).

112. Becker et al., *The Reorganization of Education in China*, p. 139.

113. For the American response to this criticism, see Stephen Duggan, *A Critique of the Report of the League of Nations Mission of Educational Experts to China* (New York: Institute of International Education, January 1933).

114. Xiong Mingan, *Zhongguo gaodeng jiaoyushi* [A History of Chinese Higher Education] (Chongqing: Chongqing chubanshe, 1983), p. 385.

115. Becker et al., *The Reorganization of Education in China*, p. 141.

116. *Beijing shifan daxue xiaoshi 1902–1982* [A History of Beijing Normal University] (Beijing: Beijing shifan daxue chubanshe, 1982, pp. 84–85. A list of accomplished women scholars, writers, and activists who were educated at the women's normal college during the 1920s is given here.

117. Croll, *Feminism and Socialist in China*, "The Feminine Mystique: Guomindang China," pp. 153–184; Esther Lee Yao, *Chinese Women Past and Present*, pp. 136–142. For some vivid autobiographical accounts of women's lives during the period, see Li Yu-ming (ed.) *Chinese Women Through Chinese Eyes* (New York: M.E. Sharpe, 1992).

118. Akigoro Taga, *Kin-dai Chu-goku kyo-iku-shi shiryo* [Historical Materials on Recent Chinese Educational History] (Tokyo: Nihon Gakujutsu Shinkokai, 1973–1975), Table 18-2. See also Wen-Lang Li, "Changing Status of Women in the PRC," in Shao-chuan Leng (ed.), *Changes in China: Party, State, and Society* (New York: University Press of America, 1989), pp. 216–218.

119. Yeh, *The Alienated Academy*, p. 225. As noted earlier, Chen Dongyuan, *Zhongguo funu shenghuo shi*, pp. 390–393, provides details on the numbers in each of thirty universities in 1922.

120. Yeh, *The Alienated Academy*, pp. 229–247.

121. Ming K. Chan and Arif Dirlik, *Schools into Fields and Factories: Anarchists, the Guomindang and the National Labor University 1927–1932* (Durham, N.C., and London: Duke University Press, 1991).

122. Zhuang Hunming, *Kangri shiqi Zhongguo gaodeng jiaoyu zhi yanjiu* [Research on Chinese Higher Education in the Period of the Anti-Japanese War] (unpublished Ph.D dissertation, Sili Zhongguo wenhua xueyuan, lishixue yanjiusuo, Taipei, 1979).

123. Ibid., p. 145ff.

124. Ibid., p. 152. There were 35 higher institutions in Jiangsu, including Shanghai in 1937, and 26 in Hebei, including Beijing.

125. Ibid., pp. 163–164.

126. Ibid., pp. 162–178 for details. See also the vivid contemporary account by Hubert Freyn, *Chinese Education in the War* (Shanghai: Kelly and Walsh, 1940).

127. Zhuang, *Kangzhan shiqi Zhongguo gaodeng jiaoyu*, p. 394.

128. *Achievement of Education in China: Statistics, 1949–1983* (Beijing: People's Education Press, 1984), p. 40.

129. Zhuang, *Kangri shiqi Zhongguo gaodeng jiaoyu*, pp. 169–178.

130. John Israel, "Southwest Associated University: Preservation as an Ultimate Value," in Paul K.T. Sih (ed.), *Nationalist China during the Sino-Japanese War, 1937–1945* (Hicksville, N.Y.: Exposition Press, 1977), pp. 131–154. John Israel, "The Idea of Liberal Education in China," in Ronald A. Morse (ed.), *The Limits of Reform in China* (Boulder, Colo.: Westview Press, 1983). Memorial statements from many graduates now in influential positions are found in *Xinan lianda ji Yunnan shida jianxiao wushi zhounian jinian ji* [A Memorial Collection of the Fiftieth Anniversary of the Establishment of Southwest Associated University and Yunnan Normal University] (Kunming: special issue of Yunnan shida xuebao, 1988).

131. For the Nationalist side of the story, see Zhuang, *Kangzhan shiqi Zhongguo gaodeng jiaoyu*, pp. 199–201. For a retrospective from the Communist side, see the histories of several of the key institutions that have been recently published: *Xibei daxue xiaoshi gao* [A Draft History of Northwest University] (Xi'an: Xibei daxue

chubanshe, 1987); *Xibei nongye daxue xiaoshi* [An Institutional History of North-west Agricultural University] (Xi'an: Shaanxi renmin chubanshe, 1986); *Xibei shifan daxue xiaoshi* [An Institutional History of Northwest Normal University] (Xining: Qinghai renmin chubanshe, 1989).

132. Zhuang, p. 300.

133. Ibid., pp. 301–304.

134. Ibid., p. 311. Chen Lifu, *Zhanshi jiaoyu xingzheng huiyi* [Recollections of Educational Administration During the War] (Taiwan: Commercial Press, 1973), p. 20.

135. Ibid., pp. 317–325.

136. Mao Lirui, Shen Guanqun, *Zhongguo jiaoyu tongshi*, Vol. 5, pp. 296–301.

137. Freyn, *Chinese Education in the War*, pp. 94–102, gives details on some of the research and teaching going on.

138. Zhuang, *Kangzhan shiqi Zhongguo gaodeng jiaoyu*, pp. 307–311.

139. Suzanne Pepper, *Civil War in China: The Political Struggle, 1945–1949* (Berkeley: University of California Press, 1980), part I, chapter 3 "The Student Anti-war Movement," pp. 42–94.

140. R. Hofstadter and W. Metzger, *The Development of Academic Freedom in the United States* (New York and London: Columbia University Press, 1955).

141. Huang Meizhen, Shi Yanhua, and Zhang Yun (eds.) *Shanghai daxue shiliao* [Historical Materials on Shanghai University] (Shanghai: Fudan daxue chubanshe, 1984); Yeh, *The Alienated Academy*, pp. 129–164.

142. Croll, *Feminism and Socialism in China*, chapter 7; Judith Stacey, *Patriarchy and Socialist Revolution in China* (Berkeley: University of California Press, 1983). Delia Davin, "Women in the Liberated Areas," in Marilyn Young, *Women in China*, pp. 73–87.

143. Several scholars have noted the fact that there have been no autobiographical accounts by women describing their experiences on the Long March.

144. Qu Shipei, *Kangri zhanzheng shiqi jiefang qu gaodeng jiaoyu* [Higher Education in Liberated Areas during the Anti-Japanese War Period] (Beijing: Beijing daxue chubanshe, 1985), p. 18.

145. Ibid., pp. 146–148.

146. Patricia Stranahan, *Yan'an Women and the Communist Party* (Berkeley: Center for Chinese Studies, Institute of East Asian Studies, 1983), pp. 98–101.

147. Wu Wei and Li Zhengxin, "Mao Zedong yu Zhongguo chuantong jiaoyu," [Mao Zedong and Chinese Traditional Education], in *Jiaoyu yanjiu* [Educational Research], no. 4, 1994, p. 11. This article contains a thoughtful discussion of Mao's assessment of the *shuyuan* tradition, and some comments on the ways it influenced the approach to learning in early Communist schools.

148. Much material is available on Yan'an education. In English, excellent sources include Peter Seybolt, "Yenan Education and the Chinese Revolution," unpublished Ph.D. dissertation, Harvard University, 1969; Wang Hsueh-wen, *Chinese Communist Education: The Yenan Period* (Taiwan: Institute of International Relations, 1975); Mark Selden, *The Yenan Way in Revolutionary China* (Cambridge, Mass.: Harvard University Press, 1971). In Chinese, numerous recent sources include a three-volume history: Dong Chuncai (ed.), *Zhongguo geming gendi jiaoyu shi* [A History of Education in the Chinese Revolutionary Base Areas] (Beijing: Jiaoyu kexue chubanshe, Vol. 1, 1991, Vol. 2, 1991, Vol. 3, 1993). For a fascinating set of documents on the Yan'an College of Natural Sciences, see *Yan'an ziran kexueyuan shiliao* [Historical Materials on the Yan'an Natural Sciences College] (Beijing: Zhonggong dangshi ziliao chubanshe, 1986).

149. For English versions of these essays, see *Selected Works of Mao Tse-tung*, Vol. III (Peking: Foreign Languages Press, 1967).

3 THE SOCIALIST STORY, 1949–1978

Few modern governments have experienced the degree of euphoria and wide popular support that surrounded the new Communist administration in the first year or two after it took power in China. After a century of military incursions, culminating in the devastation of the Sino-Japanese War, World War II, and the civil war that followed, it seemed the nation was finally to have a chance to build itself according to a self-chosen socialist vision. The elements to be selectively integrated into this vision from international experience might have been more diverse and eclectic if the external climate of the Cold War, and the Korean War, had not pressed the new Communist leadership into a close relationship with the Soviet Union.[1] There seemed to be little concern in the early years of cooperation about the possibility that this alternative Western narrative of modernization might prove as imperialistic and prone to cultural conflict as had the earlier capitalist narrative. There was, rather, a sense of urgency to catch up on the years lost to war and build a strong economy and polity as rapidly as possible. Naturally, higher education and scientific research were to be important dimensions of this process of socialist construction.

In this chapter, we will consider the next phase of the story of China's modern universities, with a focus on uncovering the ongoing cultural dynamic that underlay the framework of political change. Three main periods will be discussed: the early period of socialist construction from 1949 to 1957, the efforts to radicalize and sinify the socialist vision from 1958 to 1965, and finally, the Cultural Revolution decade from 1966 to 1976. Much has been written on all of these periods, with a focus on the struggle among factions within the Communist party with different visions of Chinese socialism. The burden of this chapter will be entirely with developments in higher education, and I will seek to connect them to deeper-level patterns of cultural conflict between ideas and values of higher learning in China and the West. It is important to remember that while the Soviet Union has always been thought of as the East, in terms of the Cold War and East-West political conflict, for China it represented the West, at least culturally, if not politically. Its patterns of higher education were strongly rooted in the European tradition, perhaps most notably that of France. The Soviet vision of socialist construction, as a kind of gigantic machine whose separate and highly specialist parts were coordinated through a centralized planning process, was also intellectually and culturally close to nineteenth-century French rationalism.

Thus the stage was set for a new phase of cultural conflict between Chinese and Western patterns of higher learning, which had once again become highly polarized due to historical conditions, and the silencing of the institutions and voices that had done so much to mediate and integrate the two sides in the 1930s and 1940s. On the one hand stood the university, an institution carrying values of autonomy and academic freedom at its core in the Western tradition and continuing these values under authoritarian conditions in the Soviet Union. Set against this on the Chinese side was a tradition of intellectual authority and a scholarly monopoly of bureaucratic power at one pole, balanced by the fragile autonomy and intellectual freedom associated with the *shuyuan* and other nonformal institutions. This chapter will attempt to trace the cultural conflicts around these value orientations in the development of higher education over the period.

Continuing sub-themes to the story are the knowledge map, the geographical map, and the gender map. There were striking achievements in the redesign of the geographical map and the knowledge map in the early 1950s. Few governments have ever had the degree of cooperation that was required to implement a total restructuring of the curricular patterns and identities of a whole higher education system, and their reordering according to a geographic plan. The rationalist dream of macro-planning was carried out with an exquisite thoroughness, and hopes were high that it would contribute to building a peaceful, strong, and self-confident socialist nation. Instead, however, it aroused deep-seated resistance on both the cultural and political fronts. This was expressed first in new initiatives before and during the Great Leap Forward, and later in the violent conflicts of the Cultural Revolution.

As for the gender map, much was achieved in terms of enhanced female participation in higher education, at both the student and faculty levels, in the context of new legal protections for women, yet women themselves had only limited opportunity to shape the struggle. It is also remarkably difficult to find detailed information on women's contribution to the new higher education, beyond some basic statistics relating to participation.

The first nationwide education conference of the new regime was held in December 1949, with the main normative directions for education being defined within the Common Program of the Chinese People's Consultative Conference, which had been passed in September of that year. Chapter 5 of this program dealt with cultural and educational policy, and set as goals of the new education system the task of raising the cultural level of the people and training personnel for national construction work. Core values laid down were patriotism, love of labor, and love of science. There was a commitment to the development of the natural sciences in the service of industry, agriculture, and national defense, and the application of a scientific and historical viewpoint to the study and interpretation of history, economics, politics, culture, and international affairs. Literature and art were to be promoted to serve the people and heighten their political consciousness and labor enthusiasm.[2]

The first higher education conference was held in June 1950, presided over by Ma Xulun, for many years a professor of philosophy at Beijing University and a highly respected non-party intellectual.[3] He summed up the situation in terms of the 227 higher institutions that were the legacy of the Nationalist government, and the "people's universities" that had been set up as short-term cadre training institutions following the model of Yan'an University and Kangda, as the Red Army moved into the different regions of the country. The most serious problems were seen as geographical imbalance, with the majority of institutions being on the east coast, and the fact that few worker and peasant students had had access to formal higher education. The formal system was called upon to undergo curricular and administrative reforms that would ensure that it adapted to the new circumstances. The revolutionary institutions were also to adapt to the new situation, with People's University chosen as the center and prototype of a new kind of higher education, designed to serve the socialist polity in a special way.

The main task for future higher education development set forth at the conference was to "serve the economic construction, which is the foundation for all the other construction" (i.e., politics, culture, and national defense).[4] There was a call for careful curricular development to this end, which would ensure both a strong theoretical basis and the application of the curriculum to national needs. Special provision was to be made through affiliated rapid secondary schools to open up higher institutions to workers and peasants. There was also a call for much greater integration and uniformity among all institutions in the system, with the central Ministry of

Education exercising overall central leadership, and other ministries taking control over institutions in their particular areas.

Neither autonomy nor academic freedom were at issue in these deliberations, with the overriding emphasis being on how higher education could be shaped to serve the new socialist economy and polity. However, there was a healthy respect for the achievements of a system that had enjoyed a considerable measure of both under the Nationalists. As a part of their ethos of social responsibility, these institutions had done much to support the Liberation struggle and welcome the new regime. Thus, leading professors were entrusted with the important task of undertaking a total revision of the curriculum, with four committees set up at the June conference to cover the areas of humanities, law, science, and engineering. The humanities committee had subcommittees for Chinese, foreign languages, philosophy, history, and education, the law committee for politics, economics, law, and sociology. In the sciences and engineering, there were parallel subcommittees for the various fields.[5]

The plan was to keep in place the credit system and allow for some diversity of program, but lay down clear guidelines and teaching material that would gradually shape the different fields toward the new goals and conditions of the socialist state.[6] Even the field of sociology, which was later to be summarily abolished, continued in place for a brief period. Private institutions and missionary institutions maintained their identities and received some state support over the first two to three years of the new regime, with the expectation that they would gradually adapt themselves to the new guidelines. The only fairly radical area of curricular change was the abolition of the political education practices of the Nationalist government and their replacement by new programs based on Marxist-Leninist texts.

The leading figures in the curricular reform process were sympathetically inclined to the task of integrating the new Marxist teachings into the curriculum in an appropriate way. This can be clearly seen in statements of persons such as Ma Xulun, minister of education from 1950 to 1953, then of higher education from 1953 to 1956, Ma Yinchu, president of Beida, and Qian Duansheng, a highly respected political scientist and historian of Nationalist politics who became president of the Beijing College of Political Science and Law in 1952.[7] Unfortunately, however, this cautious approach, which encouraged gradual change and adaptation in higher education reform, was to be short-lived.

The international political climate, particularly the intensification of the Cold War, and China's participation in the Korean War from October 1950 to 1953, was leading Chinese leaders to closer and closer identification with the Soviet Union at this time. In education, this was manifested in a movement away from self-reliance and gradual reform toward an all-out emulation of Soviet patterns and practices, with the assistance of a large number of Soviet experts as advisors to the various ministries, and as teachers and researchers within specific institutions. As a result, higher education increasingly took on patterns of intellectual authority and a kind of identification with the bureaucracy that resonated with state Confucian patterns at one extreme, and stimulated a strong reaction from the other pole of Chinese tradition—that of the nonformal, fragmented yet dynamic tendencies represented by institutions oriented toward populism and social criticism. The tension between these two poles was to rock the whole system over the three decades under consideration, I will argue, reaching a high point of intensity in Cultural Revolution attempts to completely eliminate universities as such.

The reforms carried out under Soviet guidance as a part of the efforts associated with the First Five-year Plan (1953–1957) have been summarized under the term "the reordering of colleges and departments" (*yuanxi tiaozheng*). These reforms involved both a geographical rationalization of higher education provision and a complete rethinking of curricular patterns and institutional identities. Universities that had grown up over decades with fairly comprehensive programs including humanities, basic sciences, engineering, education, agriculture, and medicine were now dismembered, with their various departments required to amalgamate into an entirely new constellation of institutions. For some private and missionary colleges, the consolidation and redeployment of areas of strength was perhaps inevitable, since there was not much possibility of their continued survival and healthy development under the new socialist state. For national universities, however, the loss of an ethos expressed in curricular patterns unique to each institution's history was felt right up to the 1980s, when many tried to restore programs that had been lopped off in 1952.[8]

The new knowledge map was remarkably similar to that envisaged by late Qing reformers in 1902. Instead of classics universities, at the head of the system was a new revolutionary university—People's University— which had the task of developing an authoritative Marxist-Leninist-Maoist canon for the social sciences. Next to these in prestige were new polytechnic universities whose broad programs in applied sciences were to train engineers for the socialist machine.[9] Whereas the late Qing plan had envisaged separate institutions for arts and sciences, the new Soviet-inspired map allowed for "comprehensive universities" that were, in fact, limited to the classic disciplines of the European tradition, embodying the German ethos, which

Cai Yuanpei had tried to introduce to Beijing University in 1917. Normal universities were to have a similar set of departments, with the addition of education, fine arts, and music. All other institutions were highly specialized and identified closely with particular governmental sectors or product areas: agriculture, health, finance, justice, metallurgy, mechanical engineering, textiles, etc.

The fundamental principle that was supposed to underlie this knowledge map was the unity of theory and practice, yet, in fact, theoretical and practical subjects were separated by firm institutional barriers. Biology and physics were found in comprehensive universities that had no link to separate institutions for agriculture, medicine, and engineering, law in political science institutions that had no connection to philosophy departments. All major scientific research was organized within institutes of the Chinese Academy of Sciences, quite separate from the higher education system. This meant there was minimal support for research carried on within universities, and a canonical approach to knowledge and teaching as the transmission of authoritative and unchanging texts became common.[10]

The primary concern was to restructure the whole higher education system in ways that would ensure its direct service to the economic and social goals of the First Five-Year Plan. Thus, the main consideration in the patterns of knowledge was a functional one in terms of personnel training. It led to an eclectic set of institutional types, each with its own distinctive curricular rationale. People's University, and the institutes of political science and law, finance and economics under its guidance, provided the ideological core of the system, responsible for training socialist planners and teachers of political theory for the whole system. The new polytechnical universities emphasized breadth of technological and theoretical knowledge as both a scientifically sound and ideologically progressive kind of education. The comprehensive universities, and to a lesser degree the normal universities, maintained the old European ethos associated with the basic theoretical disciplines of knowledge and their interconnection. Finally, the large number of specialist institutions had knowledge patterns that were conceived in relation to product or sector.

In this kind of a situation, the unity of theory and practice could find expression only in an emphasis on linking the practical training outcome needed in each field to the particular area of scientific theory to which it related. Thus, in the planning of the program for each narrowly defined specialization, there was a carefully constructed combination of common courses (politics, foreign languages, physical education), basic theory courses, specialist theory courses, and specialist courses. By 1953, 249 distinct specializations had been identified, a number that was to grow to 627 by 1962, and ultimately to a high point of more than 1,000 in the 1980s.[11] Whereas the main organizing structure of knowledge in the Nationalist universities had been at the level of the college, with related departments coordinated within colleges, the specialization at the sub-department level now became the main organizing unit, and each was assigned a specific quota of students annually by the state. The program for each specialization was operated in a self-sufficient way, with little regard even for other specializations within the same department. The credit system, which had allowed for common courses across the university, college, and department in the old system, was terminated in favor of uniform curricular requirements for each student that were arranged in entirety within one specialization.

This reordering of knowledge from above, and its close link to industrial development plans and student enrollment planning, left little scope for the work of the curriculum reform committees that had been set up in 1950 under distinguished professors in broadly defined fields of knowledge.[12] The quickest and most efficient way of developing courses for each specialization seemed to be to translate teaching outlines and textbooks from the Soviet Union. This was done in a top-down manner, with three or four leading institutions being selected as centers. Thus, sixty-seven Soviet experts were invited to Harbin Polytechnical University, the designated leader of polytechnical education; ninety-eight were located at People's University for the task of rewriting social science textbooks; and a further critical mass were located at Beijing Normal University to lead the way in reconstituting programs for the education of teachers.[13]

Once the new knowledge map had been established, it remained to redraw the geographical map in ways that ensured a rational geographic distribution of each functional type of higher institution across the country. In 1950, six major regions became the basic units for political-administrative planning. The Northwest, the Southwest, the Central South, and East China remained under military supervision, while North China and the Northeast led the way in developing civilian government.[14] Each region had an administrative center—Shanghai for East China, Shenyang for the Northeast, Wuhan for the Central South, Chongqing for the Southwest, and Xi'an for the Northwest, with an educational bureau responsible for regional planning and the coordination of all levels of education. In a sense, it was finally possible to fulfill the rationalist dream of a university district system of the early part of the century, combining a knowledge map adjusted to macroplanning for rapid industrialization, and a geographic map that included the center and hinterland parts of the country more fully than ever before.

Beginning in 1951 with North China, East China, and the Central South, all institutions were put under scrutiny, and reorganized by department and specialization according to a plan that allowed for one or two comprehensive universities, one or two polytechnical universities, one major normal university, one to three agricultural universities, and other specialist institutions in each region. Thus Qinghua University and Zhejiang University were designated as the leading polytechnical institutions for North China and East China, respectively, and had their main programs in the arts, basic sciences, and professions moved to comprehensive or specialized institutions. Beijing University and Fudan University lost all of their applied and most of their professional programs, and were limited to teaching the basic arts and sciences as the leading comprehensive universities for North China and East China, respectively. Many other comprehensive universities followed the same pattern, Wuhan and Zhongshan in the Central South, Sichuan in the Southwest, Lanzhou in the Northwest, and Jilin in the Northeast. North China had Nankai University in addition to Beijing University, and East China had Nanjing and Shandong Universities, in addition to Fudan.

Beijing Normal University set the tone for the new normal universities in each region, which were established on the basis of interesting amalgamations. East China Normal University, for example, was founded in Shanghai in 1951 on the basis of two private universities, Daxia and Guanghua, with departments of education from Fudan and St. Johns University combined into it. Zhonghua University in Wuhan, a former missionary institution, and another private university, Huazhong, became the basis for the Huazhong Normal University, which was the leading institution for the Central South.[15] Parallel institutions were Southwest Normal in Beipei, near Chongqing, Northeast Normal in Changchun and Northwest Normal in Lanzhou.

In the process of adjustment, particular emphasis was placed on the development of new engineering universities, both polytechnical and specialized. Thus the Huazhong University of Science and Technology, set up to be the leading polytechnical institution for the Central South in Wuhan in 1952, was built upon engineering departments moved there from Wuhan University, Hunan University, Nanchang University, and Guangxi University. What had been excellent institutions in different parts of the region were required to dedicate engineering programs they had built up as part of local comprehensive universities during the Nationalist period to the support of this new central institution located in Wuhan.[16] This illustrates a main principle of the reform, which was to ensure a concentration of the best resources in certain key centers; these were then to be responsible for high-level training for the whole region.

By the end of this period of readjustment, the total number of institutions had been reduced from 227 to 181, with most institutions now being specialized in function, and administered by the national ministry appropriate to their knowledge area. Only comprehensive, polytechnical, and normal universities were directly administered by the Ministry of Higher Education. The only institutions administered at the provincial level were local teachers colleges.

While this restructuring process had done much to improve the geographical spread, the hinterland still remained disadvantaged. With the intensification of the Cold War, and perceived threats due to the American naval presence in the Taiwan Strait, a renewed effort to industrialize and strengthen the hinterland began in the mid-1950s, and its ripples were felt in higher education planning. A new process of restructuring was initiated in 1955, intended to right continuing imbalances with ninety-seven institutions—51 percent of the total, and 61 percent of students and faculty—still in coastal cities. Between 1955 and 1957, there was a plan to move five major coastal universities to central and hinterland locations, while also building twelve new institutions in the hinterland.

The most celebrated case of moving a whole institution was that of Shanghai Jiaotong University, which was moved to Xi'an in 1955.[17] Shandong University, then located in the coastal city of Qingdao, was to be moved to Zhengzhou in Henan province, but in the end it was moved instead to Jinan, the capital city of Shandong province. The East China Aeronautic University in Nanjing was moved to Xi'an and combined with a local engineering institution to form the basis for the Northwest Engineering University under the Ministry of Aeronautical Industry. Other new and reorganized institutions in this period included the Xi'an Institute of Construction for the Metallurgical Industry that was formed from the departments of several institutions moved there from Shenyang and Qingdao, and the Chengdu Institute of Telecommunications Engineering, administered by the Ministry of Machine Building and built on departments of electronics from Shanghai Jiaotong University, the Nanjing Institute of Technology, and the South China Institute of Technology.[18]

By 1955, a tightly structured national system of higher education had emerged. People's University, which was administered jointly by the Ministry of Higher Education and the Central Committee of the Communist party was at its head. Next in prestige were the polytechnical and comprehensive universities directly controlled by the Ministry of Higher Education, then the highly specialized sectoral institutions controlled by other national ministries and commissions. The system operated almost entirely at the national level, and every effort had been made to ensure the appropriate geographical distribution of each type of institution and to establish uniformity of standards and content within each narrowly defined specialization, which was designed to serve specific development goals. Although the principle of the unity of theory and practice was touted, theory was actually tightly controlled from above, with little possibility of local practice, either social or productive, having an impact upon it. For each area of knowledge there was one center that laid down orthodoxy from above, and the teaching of Marxist-Leninist theory exemplifies this best.

People's University, a descendant of one of the most important of the revolutionary institutions, the Shaanbei Public Institute, had been opened with much fanfare in 1950. It was designated as an institution devoted to training cadres for the new socialist state and carrying forward the traditions of the revolutionary universities that had emerged in the Liberation struggle. In a speech at its inauguration, Liu Shaoqi made clear its mission as an institution responsible for creating a whole new pattern for the social sciences, based on the advanced experience of the Soviet Union, which was to replace the capitalist social sciences of an earlier era. There was little sense here of the new social sciences evolving in a Chinese context, in interaction with the natural sciences and other fields. Rather, Liu made the point that People's University would not compete for students with the other universities having programs in the sciences, but would be exclusively a center for the new social sciences.[19] Liu went on to link the authority of this new area of knowledge in the socialist state to that of the Confucian canon in traditional China, mentioning in his speech how Confucius had not tolerated other schools. The new orthodoxy, emanating from People's University, was to be the foundation of party and state ideology.

People's University led a massive program for the translation of Soviet texts in the social sciences, and their dissemination to all levels within the system. Because the Soviet Union had little tolerance of sociology at the time, it was abolished, while anthropology was moved to specialized institutions for national minorities. The new social sciences consisted of Marxist economics, finance, trade, law, politics, and various kinds of planning. As well as preparing specialized texts, teaching plans, and course outlines for each of these areas, professors at People's University developed new textbooks and course outlines for political education, which were to be used in all higher institutions throughout the country. A large number of Soviet experts acted as advisors in this process.

At the regional level, specialized institutes of finance and economics, political science and law were set up, which operated under the intellectual leadership of People's University, while being administered by national ministries of justice and finance and the People's Bank.[20] Meanwhile, only a few comprehensive universities were allowed to retain departments of philosophy, law, and economics, in spite of their highly developed traditions in the social sciences. The role of these departments was to be a theoretical rather than a professional one, and their faculty were all expected to be retrained at People's University. One of the excuses used for this drastic limiting of the social sciences was the job assignment plan, and the perception that only a limited number of specialists in these areas were needed in the new cadre system.

Just as the Confucian classics had been preserved as a unique category of knowledge, responsible for ordering an array of narrowly defined specialist knowledge areas toward state defined ends in the late Qing patterns, the new state orthodoxy, Marxism-Leninism-Mao Zedong thought, was given a guiding role in the new system. The very structure of the system ensured that there would be little possibility of its integration and mutual transformation in relation to other knowledge areas.

The field of education is a case in point. Education departments had been integrated within faculties of arts and social sciences in comprehensive universities during the Nationalist period, but they were now separated out in a network of newly established normal universities and colleges. One major normal university took leadership in each of the six major regions. Teachers were an extremely important group for the new regime, and the intention was that all should be brought to accept party orthodoxy as quickly as possible, so that they could bring up a new generation of youth.

The old education departments were roundly criticized as being out of touch with reality in China, and dominated by a bourgeois mentality. The closure of these departments in favor of a totally separate system of higher normal institutions was regarded as an important advance. Educational theory was borrowed from the Soviet Union, and the president of the Soviet Academy of Educational Sciences, I.A. Kairov, was taken as the new authority. A textbook he had written, entitled *Pedagogy*, was translated into Chinese in several editions, and adopted as the main text of educational theory for the training of teachers. Only four academic departments of education were allowed to survive, due to the fact that subject area teachers were in much greater demand for employment than specialists in education, per se. Thus the education department at Beijing Normal University, and those at East China Normal in Shanghai, Northeast Normal in Changchun, and

Central China Normal in Wuhan, held the monopoly over the definition of the field. Actually, Beijing Normal was the leading department, and the large number of Soviet experts located there exercised a significant influence on the whole system through specially organized short-term courses and conferences for faculty from normal universities and colleges throughout the country.[21]

In February 1955, the vice-minister of education, Liao Di, did an inspection tour of four normal universities—Nanjing Normal, East China Normal, Zhejiang Normal, and Huazhong Normal in Wuhan. He noted the energy with which the Soviet model had been followed, and the total transformation that had taken place in teaching content. Thus at Zhejiang Normal, of the 153 courses being taught, forty-one were based on texts directly translated from the Soviet Union, and another seventy-nine had been newly developed on the basis of Soviet models. His main criticisms were that there was a tendency to dogmatism in teaching, and that educational research was not closely enough connected to the actual problems of secondary schools. In a sense, this reflected the overall problem of this elaborately structured system—the fact that its connection to China's own cultural context was so tenuous.[22]

Between 1950 and 1954, students were selected and enrolled by examination at the level of the six major regions, but in 1955, a national unified examination system was put in place to ensure a fair distribution of candidates to the different institutions according to their academic standing.[23] This was also the year in which a nationwide system for assigning graduates to jobs was set in place. While considerable effort had been made to expand primary education provision over this period, with a rise in enrollments from 24 million in 1949 to 64 million in 1955, secondary education had remained very selective, with total enrollments in the general stream rising from around 1 million in 1949 to 3.9 million in 1955, and only 15 percent of these being at the upper secondary level.[24] Thus the number of entrants to higher education in some years exceeded graduates from the regular secondary system.[25] Provision had been made for accelerated secondary study opportunities that were to help working class and peasant youth enter higher education, and the estimated percentage of students of worker-peasant origin in higher education rose from 20.5 in 1953 to 36.4 in 1957.[26] This was a substantial change, yet the children of cadres and intellectuals still dominated higher education enrollments, and the impulse to press for higher working-class participation had begun to fade by 1955.[27]

The emphasis in higher education under Soviet influence was very much on the formation of a highly disciplined elite corps of specialists in all of the areas needed by the new socialist state. On the political level, this fitted with the ideas of what has often been defined as the moderate or pragmatist faction within the Chinese Communist party. It went against the grain, however, for Mao Zedong and others within the party who were seeking a more radical revolutionary transformation of society. The roots of Mao's more populist vision actually go back to concerns expressed by educators of various political persuasions in the Republican period for a kind of educational change more deeply rooted in Chinese soil.

In discussing the Hunan Self-Study University in the 1920s, Mao had talked about the value of the *shuyuan* as institutions closely linked to local concerns and open to the people. As informal institutions, they had allowed for the lively discussion of a broad range of knowledge areas and non-authoritarian relations between students and teachers.[28] Other scholars and educators who had emphasized this aspect of Chinese tradition included Liang Shuming, Tao Xingzhi, Xu Chongqing, Huang Yanpei, Yan Yangchu, and Chen Qingzhi.[29] The struggle that was to unfold thus had an important cultural dimension, in addition to the way it reflected the differing political views of radicals and pragmatists within the party.

The patterns of the Soviet system also had an interesting ancestry. In his history of *Education and the French Revolution*, British comparativist H.C. Barnard describes the educational outcomes of the revolution in a way that shows how far cultural patterns persisted through political change, reconstituting themselves for a new version of autocracy under Napoleon. In his view, "the centralized absolutism of the *ancien régime* was reproduced and even emphasized, and in its rather different way the rule of Napoleon was as complete and autocratic as that of Louis XIV, as well as being administratively more efficient."[30] He goes on to describe how the Imperial University, as a teaching corporation holding a monopoly over national education, made it possible for a thoroughgoing regimentation of popular thought at all levels, and the use of religious teaching as a means of strengthening the political regime. "The educational system was organized to subserve the state and to be an agent of propaganda for the government."[31]

The direct influence of French higher education in prerevolutionary Russian historical experience is well known,[32] while broader aspects of nineteenth-century French social thought were one thread in the socialist ideology that became state orthodoxy after the revolution. The higher education system that emerged in the Soviet Union in the 1930s, after the failure of various experiments with progressivism in the 1920s, was very close in spirit to nineteenth-century French patterns, I would argue, taking the principle of specialization beyond the traditional disciplines to new fields of knowledge defined by function and product. These were closely linked to the personnel needs of successive five-year plans.[33]

Basil Bernstein's framework for analyzing curricular change identifies the integrated code at one extreme and the collection code at the other. He uses the term "classification" to define the strength of boundary maintenance between different specialist subjects or fields of knowledge in the curriculum, and between curricular knowledge and ordinary life knowledge. The term framing defines the pedagogical style of the teacher and the nature of relations between teacher and student.[34] Strong classification and strong framing, which characterize the collection code, are a significant feature of French educational patterns, in contrast to the strong classification but weak framing of the English system, and the weak classification and framing of the American system, in Bernstein's view. From this perspective, Soviet patterns at the higher level could be described as exhibiting extremely strong classification and framing. Hierarchical authority patterns within higher education reinforced and were strengthened by such patterns more generally in the planned socialist society.

These patterns were introduced into the Chinese context under the conditions described above, with narrow knowledge areas rigidly defined by specialization and largely isolated in institutions defined with a specialist identity. On the economic level, there was an intense concern with rapid economic growth, particularly in heavy industry, and this was achieved under the First Five-year Plan, especially in terms of industrial growth.[35] However, it may be worth reflecting on how the political and ideological dimensions of these patterns penetrated right down to the daily life of intellectuals.

To understand this, we need to look at the actual campus environment and consider how the lives of students and teachers were affected by this Soviet-derived system. The core unit within each university was no longer the college or department, but the specialization, as this was the unit that was assigned a quota of students within the state plan each year. Each student's total program was carried out entirely within the auspices of one specialization. While faculty belonged to departments (the level of colleges within a university had been abolished), their work and lives were now organized within teaching and research groups, newly established on a Soviet model in the early 1950s. Each group consisted of from five to twenty faculty, and several groups were responsible for different parts of the teaching done in a particular specialization. For example, one group might be responsible for the specialist courses, another for the basic theory courses, and a third for the specialist theory courses. Specialist courses tended to have highest prestige, as these were offered mainly in the upper years, and had the highest level of academic content.

Students belonging to a particular class within one specialization lived in the same dormitory on campus, and were in one another's company for nearly twenty-four hours of the day. Faculty belonging to the same teaching and research group often lived in the same campus housing unit, and also spent much of their time in one another's company.[36] The lowest unit of the Communist party and the Communist Youth League were organized at the level of the specialization and the teaching and research group, with political advisors assigned to offer guidance to each member of faculty and each student. Students were expected to write a review of their ideological progress every term, and this document was read and commented on by the political advisors, and even by the department party secretary in some cases, then kept on the individual's file. Such vitally important decisions for students as their job assignments on graduation were decided by political authorities at the department level. Faculty promotions or transfers were also affected in important ways by the content of these files, which were accessible only to party authorities, not to the individual in question or to the university's academic leadership.

Under these circumstances the higher curriculum operated as a kind of framework for every aspect of the lives of students and faculty. The classification and framing that Bernstein identified in the context of European schools penetrated to the very core of daily life in this Chinese context. Perhaps only an understanding of how deep that penetration was can explain the bitter energy with which the system was criticized, first in the Great Leap Forward, later in the Cultural Revolution.

There was an almost mechanical efficiency in the ways in which higher professional training was adjusted to the precise needs of industrialization and socialist nation-building. The percentage of students enrolled in engineering rose from 26 percent in 1949 to 37 percent in 1957, teacher training from 10.3 to 26 percent, basic sciences from 6.0 to 6.5 percent, with a concomitant decline in social science and humanities and their reshaping to new needs. A centrally controlled job assignment system, buttressed by forms of political study and social organization throughout university life, made it possible to match graduates in a mechanistic way to positions in state enterprises and government ministries where most were assigned over these years.

Perhaps the image that best captures the cultural patterns of this period is that of the massive new central administration building erected on most university campuses opposite to the main gate, usually a six- to eight-story building, sometimes higher, whose stark lines proclaimed tremendous confidence in the new age of industrialization and technology. In some cases, Chinese style roofs were added to these buildings to give a touch of local authenticity, and the aesthetic incongruence of this combination gave visual expression to the cultural conflicts between mechanistic, specialist, and functional views of knowledge, coming from Western influence, and the holistic, integrative, and organic views of knowledge that had emphasized social practice and had been resistant to specialization in Chinese tradition. In a certain sense, all of the efforts of the First Five-year Plan, so successful in terms of industrialization and economic growth, were standing on highly volatile cultural soil.[37]

The success of geographical rationalization may have had a close correspondence with long-term concerns about the unbalanced distribution of higher education throughout the country, but here too there was an artificial and mechanistic character to the way in which the redistribution had been achieved. From the perspective of the six broad regions, there was no doubt that redistribution had been effected, and, in fact, right up to the 1980s, hinterland regions have been able to maintain fairly high proportions of enrollment relative to their population density. However, within each region, the principle of specialization and a concentration of resources in one or two main centers prevailed.

If we take the case of the Northwest, the massive geographical reordering of resources had focused on Xi'an, as a main center for the region, with Lanzhou as the secondary center, while far-flung parts of the region such as Xinjiang, Qinghai, and Ningxia had little or no higher education development over this period. In the case of the Central South region, from Henan down to Guangdong province, the decision to make Wuhan the center of the region led to a massive transfer of resources in areas like engineering and technology education from the provinces of Henan, Hunan, and Guangxi, to Wuhan. This has left these provinces disadvantaged right up to the 1980s. We noted in chapter 2 how the exigencies of the Sino-Japanese War failed to bring about the degree of geographical redistribution of higher education that had been hoped for. In a certain sense the same could be said of the radical efforts at geographical rationalization in the 1950s.

What about the gender map and the participation of women in higher education over this period? The Common Program of 1949 had stipulated that "women shall enjoy equal rights with men in political, economic, cultural, educational, and social life."[38] In spite of this, the percentage of women entering higher education grew only slowly over this period, from an estimated 17.9 percent in 1947 to 24.6 percent in 1956.[39] A look at female participation in general secondary education, the main channel of access to higher education, gives an indication of the reason for this slow advance. Between 1950 and 1956, women's attendance at general secondary schools rose only from 26.5 percent in 1950 to 29.3 percent in 1956.[40] Unfortunately, we do not have separate figures for upper secondary schooling, but it is almost certain that female percentages were even lower at that level.[41]

For urban girls, access to general secondary schools was less difficult than for rural girls, and some provincial-level girls' schools of good academic quality, that had been set up in the Nationalist period, continued to function in the early 1950s.[42] Most were made coeducational either in the Great Leap Forward period or the Cultural Revolution. While there was a certain amount of gender imbalance in the distribution of women by field of study, with relatively higher representation in medicine, teaching, foreign languages, and social sciences,[43] women were also encouraged to enter engineering and other scientific programs. The general emphasis on applied sciences in enrollments meant that a considerable number of women engineers and scientists were trained.

On graduation, the national job assignment system ensured women relatively equal employment opportunities to those enjoyed by men, with full provision of maternity benefits by the employing unit. The main constraint on an increase in women entrants to higher education up to the Cultural Revolution period was access to general secondary education and to the national unified entrance examinations. It was even more important for young women than men to have urban connections and substantial familial support if they were to aspire to professional careers.

Generally, under the Soviet-style patterns, a great deal had been achieved, particularly in terms of the adaptation of the system to immediate economic development needs.[44] However, deep-seated concerns on both the political and the cultural side festered under the surface. From a political perspective, higher education had not effected the kinds of social transformation desired by Mao and other radicals, in terms of producing a new generation of professionals from working-class and peasant backgrounds. Rural youth continued to be excluded,[45] with higher education enrollments dominated by the children of the old intellectual class and the new political elite. Through the new patterns of party control at every level on the campus, the latter were able to gain privileged job assignments and other special benefits within the system,[46] while the former struggled through thought-reform campaigns and sought to make themselves acceptable to the regime.

There was considerable cynicism and hypocrisy in the supposed loyalty of the new elite to the working class and peasantry, which sometimes manifested itself in actions such as the punishment of highly qualified entrants to the system from bourgeois backgrounds by sending them to an agricultural university in a geographically unfavored area, rather than to Qinghua or Beida.[47] Generally, however, both groups tried to be loyal to the task of socialist construction, and made an important contribution to the economic success of the period up to 1957.

On the cultural level, I would argue, the conflicts went even deeper. On the one end, the Soviet patterns had reinforced the tendencies toward the centralization of knowledge and uniformity of thought that characterized the imperial examination system, with a new bureaucracy developing strong patterns of social stratification. These were exacerbated by the absolutist authority of the new ideology, with its claim to scientific status, and by the narrowly specialist patterns of knowledge regimentation, which were bound to stimulate a reactive response from the nonformal, socially critical pole that had always had a balancing role. Thus the events of the Hundred Flowers Movement and the Great Leap Forward, later of the Cultural Revolution, need to be understood both as a cultural and a political backlash. It is the cultural dimension of conflict underlying these movements that I would like to highlight.

THE HUNDRED FLOWERS CAMPAIGN AND ACADEMIC FREEDOM

In 1956, Zhou Enlai made an important speech concerning the intellectuals, in which he indicated that the regime felt most had reformed their thinking adequately, and were now loyal to socialism. In order for their knowledge and skill to be fully utilized in the next stage of development, following a newly drafted twelve-year plan for scientific development, they should be given improved living and working conditions.[48] Later in the year, Mao invited the intellectuals to express their comments and criticisms on both their own working conditions and wider social issues freely, in the call made public by Lu Dingyi that "a hundred flowers should bloom, a hundred schools of thought contend."[49]

It was a year before the intellectuals gained courage to respond to this call, first with strongly expressed criticism of the patterns imposed in education, then with broader criticisms of the overall sociopolitical system. In terms of the education system, there were bitter complaints about the mechanical copying from the Soviet Union, the narrowness of programs of teaching, the neglect and repression of the social sciences, and the fact that Marxism-Leninism was upheld as orthodox doctrine, to be accepted unquestioningly rather than being critically assimilated.[50] Wider social criticism focused on the authoritarian role of the party in all decision making, the increasing gulf between party and nonparty professionals, and the various abuses of privilege of the new political elite.

It is not possible in the scope of this chapter to go into detail on the range of issues raised, but two points may be of particular interest in terms of the university and the issue of academic as against intellectual freedom. The first relates to the fact that the most intense and bitter criticisms were expressed at People's University, which was described by some of its young faculty as "a great beehive of doctrinairism." This criticism went far beyond academic issues to threats of a violent reaction against party authoritarianism.[51] Here we see in microcosm the kind of polarization that seems to be a deep-rooted part of the Chinese knowledge tradition. The extremes of Soviet-style centralism called forth an extreme reaction in terms of forms of locally-inspired rebellion. There was no place for tolerating differences on the theoretical level that could be debated vigorously, yet prevented from spilling over into social and political conflict. The Cultural Revolution, one decade later, exemplified this tendency perhaps more powerfully than any other episode in modern Chinese history.

The second point can be illustrated by reference to the position taken by Ma Yinchu, the distinguished economist and president of Peking University at this period. His words and actions showed the persistence of the ethos of academic freedom introduced to Beida by Cai Yuanpei thirty years earlier and modified through the Nationalist period by integration within an ethic of social responsibility. Ma used the brief period of liberalization in May 1957 to publish his new population theory, which had been criticized in 1955 and so failed to be presented at the second session of the National People's Congress (NPC) as planned. As a result, he was subjected to a series of attacks, culminating in his forced resignation from the presidency of Beida in March 1960. Under enormous pressure to retract his statement of defense, entitled "My Philosophical Thought and Economic Theories," he refused to do so, even at the persuasion of Zhou Enlai. His reason was that he considered the issue to be academic rather than political.[52] His resignation from Beida and subsequent exile might be compared with Cai's resignation in 1919, in protest against the ways in which students were stepping outside their academic responsibility to involve themselves in direct political activism. Both scholars had internalized enough of the Western ethos of academic freedom to persist in seeking for a space between academic dissent and political action.

There is a particular poignancy in Ma's case, since it became increasingly evident in the decades to follow that China could have been spared some of its most wrenching trauma, if sensible population control policies had been initiated at this time instead of fifteen to twenty years later. As it was, the collective knowledge and wisdom of the whole generation of distinguished scholars nurtured within the Nationalist universities was to be lost for two decades, as they were, almost to a person, condemned to exile in the anti-rightist campaign initiated in June 1957.[53] Mao Zedong's speech of February 1957, "On contradictions," had initially suggested that within socialist society these were normally non-antagonistic and could be worked out among the people. In June, it was amended before publication to give a clear warning to the intellectuals that they had gone too far in their criticisms.[54] As noted earlier, in his speeches at the Rectification Campaign of 1944, the integral link between knowledge and social practice that was a part of the Chinese epistemological tradition, made social conflict the inevitable result of what might have been academic debate in a Western university setting.

The anti-rightist campaign effectively silenced the voices of scholars who had been associated with the Nationalist universities. It was not, however, the end of cultural conflict between Soviet patterns of knowledge, and impulses coming from the nonformal pole of the Chinese knowledge tradition. In the restructuring of higher education that accompanied the Great Leap Forward, it is possible to see a reassertion of elements of this tradition underlying the political radicalism of the period.

THE GREAT LEAP FORWARD AND HIGHER EDUCATION, 1958–1966

The Great Leap Forward of 1958–1959 represented a firm move away from the Soviet model in terms of political and economic development, though in education, the new emphasis on links to productive labor reflected reforms being introduced by Nikita Khrushchev in the Soviet Union at the same period.[55] A rapid move to full communism in China was to be achieved through the organization of people's communes in the countryside, and the further collectivization of urban industry. The focus moved from heavy industry to agriculture and light industry, also to a popularization of technology and the encouragement of grass-roots initiatives in industrial development. The main lines of the political struggle between Mao Zedong and the radical wing of the party, and moderates within the party who wished to continue following the Soviet model, are well known, and will not be discussed here.[56]

Almost all of the discussion on new educational policies and developments in this period has been placed within the context of this political struggle, with an emphasis on issues such as the class character of educational participation at all levels, its implications for social stratification, and the ideological and practical content of the curriculum.[57] What I would like to do is to explore more generic cultural foundations of the changes that took place, linking them in turn to certain characteristics of the populist, nonformal pole of Chinese higher education traditions that asserted itself quite strongly in this period. It was a kind of counterbalancing force to the highly formalized bureaucratic Soviet patterns that had transformed a Confucian-style bureaucracy into a gigantic machine.

It may be helpful at this point to go back to the early part of the century and compare the two situations. The last imperial government had erected, in its legislation, a vast structure of specialized institutions, to be headed by a Confucian academy responsible for thought control. In reality, however, most educational development was to be carried out by local efforts and forces, which were rooted in the nonformal *shuyuan* tradition and its impulses. Thus the actual curriculum development of institutions in that period had been far more broad and integrated than the structures suggested in legislation. There had also been a growing concern for the education of the masses, beyond a narrow interest in the education of an official elite.[58]

In the early 1950s, the new Communist government had built a structure of institutions that was hierarchical, narrowly segmented by specialist definitions of knowledge, and entirely controlled from one center at the top. Similar to the higher education system of late Qing legislation, it was elitist and directly oriented to statist ends. It had fair success in the project of forming a new political elite to replace the banished elite of the old bourgeois classes. However, it had moved too far to one pole of China's cultural tradition, introducing elements that exacerbated the tendencies to hierarchy and autocracy already there, and so stimulated a response from the other pole.

The decentralization of education in 1958, with the abolition of the Ministry of Higher Education and the placing of many institutions under provincial-level control, had an important political dimension in terms of a struggle from below against the faction of the party that held a tight grip on the whole system through macro-planning, also a strengthening of party control within institutions. Suzanne Pepper gives a masterly review of this policy struggle and its outcomes in the *Cambridge History of China*.[59]

Here, I'd like to reflect more from a cultural perspective, on the nature and pattern of the changes that took place in higher education. In the absence of the scholars who had carried forward the university traditions of the Nationalist period, the cultural patterns that reasserted themselves went back to an earlier period, I would argue. All of them, in one way or another, expressed some movement toward an integrative view of knowledge in the curriculum, as against the mechanistic and functional one that had been put in place under Soviet influence. To use Bernstein's terminology, it could be described as a movement toward weaker classification and much weaker framing. There was also an impulse toward geographical participation and inclusiveness that went closer to the grass roots than the Soviet patterns had done. While Soviet-style planning had created new hierarchies, emanating from centers of concentration in each of the six regions and mirroring the central hierarchy at a regional level, the focus was now on localities creating their own distinctive new institutions, rather than waiting for them to be "sent down" from above.

One striking initiative was the establishment of colleges of traditional Chinese medicine, a field that had had little legitimacy since the acceptance of Western medicine in the late Qing[60] and that had survived largely through traditional master-disciple relationships. Between 1956 and 1960, nearly every province and autonomous region set up a college of traditional Chinese medicine, Mongolian medicine in the case of Inner Mongolia.[61] These were separate from the regular medical colleges, which had a mixture of European and Soviet curricular patterns. In addition, classes in traditional Chinese medicine were added to the curriculum of the regular system, leading to an approach to medical education in which the two scientific streams—that from China and from Europe—were to develop side by side and exercise mutual influence on one another.[62] Without political support, of course, this would have been impossible, and it reflected Mao's determination to bring stronger indigenous elements to bear in higher learning. It was also part of broader efforts to develop a health system that would be widely accessible, in rural as well as urban areas, at this time.[63]

A second interesting new development in higher education was the founding of new universities that taught basic sciences and technology, areas that had been institutionally separated under the Soviet model. The Chinese University of Science and Technology was set up under the Chinese Academy of Sciences in Beijing, and a similar institution was established in Shanghai. The integration of basic and applied science was seen as important for technological innovation. The model seems to have been that of American polytechnical institutions, even though this was a period of extreme political distance from the U.S.[64] Greater research initiative was encouraged in universities, and new links were forged between the higher education system and the Chinese Academy of Sciences.

There was considerable extravagance and hyperbole in some of the research initiatives undertaken at this time, with a strong emphasis on students having active participation, and often unrealistic ideas of how quickly young people could catch up with and overtake seasoned scientists and researchers in their work.[65] However, there was also a determination to maintain and develop basic theoretical work as the foundation for all fields, and it was at this time that the principle of identifying priority or "keypoint" institutions was formally introduced as a mechanism for fostering excellence and concentrating resources on a certain number of leading institutions.[66] In a sense, this was an essential part of a vision that intended to catch up within a decade with the production levels of European nations. While it has been criticized as a betrayal of the egalitarianism that marked most other aspects of development in the period,[67] it might also be seen as a manifestation of a Chinese tendency always to seek a balance between two poles. Along with egalitarianism and an emphasis on access, there needed to be measures to promote excellence.

A third aspect of educational change was the vigorous growth in locally-supported institutions. The preferred model for most provinces was to establish a new provincial comprehensive university, sometimes on the basis of several specialized institutes or colleges, in other cases entirely new. This integrated type of institution was favored over specialist institutions at the provincial level, and it was expected to exercise cultural and intellectual leadership in the locality. It is interesting to note how some institutions that had been established and controlled from Beijing became absorbed into new provincial universities in what might be seen as a cultural backlash to the mechanistic patterns that had been imposed from above.

A few examples from different regions may serve to illustrate this. In Wuhan, the Central South Institute of Finance and Economics, and the Institute of Political Science and Law were both closed down, and their programs were integrated within Hubei University, a newly established provincial comprehensive university.[68] In Shanghai, the Shanghai Institute of Finance and Economics and the East China Institute of Political Science and Law were closed, and some of their programs and faculty moved to the newly established Shanghai Academy of Social Sciences, others to Fudan University.[69] In Liaoning province, Liaoning University was established as a provincial comprehensive university in 1958 on the basis of the Northeast Institute of Finance and Economics, with the Liaoning Teachers College and a specialist college for the Russian language combined with it.[70] In Harbin, Heilongjiang University was established on the basis of a former Russian language college.

The point of interest from a cultural perspective was the move toward the creation of local centers with a broad and integrated set of knowledge fields, in place of the highly specialized institutions in the social sciences and other fields that had been managed and controlled from the center. This was combined with a strong movement to develop more local curricular content, and to encourage universities to set up small factories and involve themselves in local productive activities. Students contributed to the writing of new textbooks and to research projects, and there was generally a surge of local participation and a diversification of the curriculum, which allowed regional differences to find expression.

This new impulse toward geographical distribution was based less on the kind of macro-planning and centralized regimentation of the "reorganization of colleges and departments" described earlier, than on energetic local initiative. Every province and autonomous region put forward strenuous efforts to establish their own higher learning institutions, with the result that provinces and autonomous regions such as Qinghai, Inner Mongolia, and Ningxia, which had had no higher education institutions up to that period, now established their own. These new institutions were staffed with enthusiastic graduates of some of the best national universities. For example, a large number of students from the graduating class of Beijing Normal University volunteered to go to Qinghai Normal University in Xining in 1958. In the same year, a group of faculty and graduates of the Sichuan Medical College in Chengdu went to help establish the Qinghai Medical College, and a group of Qinghua graduates went to develop the Inner Mongolia Engineering College in Hohhot. Many parallel stories could be told.[71] At a somewhat higher level, quite a few mature faculty from institutions in Shanghai, Beijing, and other coastal cities volunteered to serve as department chairs in the provincial institutions that were set up in 1958.[72] There were also many who were exiled to these regions for political reasons, yet who were able to contribute their knowledge and experience to these new local institutions.[73]

While this was a period of severe trial for those who had been labeled rightists, and of a strong radical tendency in terms of political ideology, many elements of the changes that took place can be understood from a cultural perspective as a reassertion of indigenous views of knowledge and a process of reconnecting the vast hierarchical machine of Soviet specialism to the realities of the Chinese cultural landscape. Concerns about the linking of theory and practice, local content in the curriculum, the active involvement of students in pedagogical processes and curricular reform, all resonated with dimensions of the populist pole of the Chinese tradition, and with aspects of the *shuyuan* tradition.

Over the period from 1957 to 1960 the expansion in the number of higher education institutions and in enrollments was phenomenal. The number of institutions grew from 229 to 1,289, and enrollments from 441,000 to a peak of 961,000 in 1960.[74] This was more than the number of students enrolled in Japanese universities in the same year, although around 60 percent of all Japanese students were in private fee-paying institutions. In addition to the many new provincial-level institutions, factories and communes established their own institutions, mostly small in scale and offering short-cycle programs of two or three years. Short-cycle enrollments quadrupled over the period, while regular enrollments nearly doubled. In terms of class participation, there was a reported rise from 36.3 percent to 49 percent in the enrollment of students from working-class and peasant backgrounds.[75]

As the devastating effects of the famine and economic failure of the Great Leap Forward made themselves felt in higher education, the outcome of the enthusiastic efforts of the period were to be retrenchment to 434 institutions and enrollments of 674,436 by 1965.[76] In the first instance, there had been the expectation that this massive expansion could be achieved without the loss of academic standards, and that graduates could all have the status and perquisites of state cadres, with appropriate jobs at different levels assigned to them. With the economic failure of the Great Leap, it soon became clear that the state could not easily absorb such a large number of new cadres. In the revived pragmatism of the early 1960s, academic standards were invoked for limiting both the number of institutions and the size of enrollments in the formal system.

Nevertheless, the commitment to wider popular access remained a concern, and it is interesting to note the growth of a nonformal or adult system of higher education both through correspondence and evening courses at regular universities, and through the continued development of spare-time universities attached to state enterprises or rural communes.[77] In the early years there had been a negligible number of students in this type of program—only 16,000 in 1955. This was to expand to 64,000 in 1956, 150,000 in 1958, 300,000 in 1959, and to remain at just over 400,000 between 1962 and 1965. The bulge in formal higher enrollments was thus moved over to this nonformal part of the system, where the state had far less responsibility. Entry requirements were flexible, and though completion of secondary schooling was expected, participation in the national college entry examinations was not.

There was thus a two-track system of higher education, with the main distinction between the formal and nonformal systems lying in the fact that only those in the regular system participated in the highly formalized life-pattern on Chinese campuses described above, and were then inducted into the bureaucracy as state cadres. Those in the nonformal system studied similar materials in a more flexible way, and had to depend on their own efforts to find employment or improve their promotion prospects. Due to the deeply ingrained expectation of higher education leading to an official position in Chinese tradition, there was little prestige attached to these nonformal institutions.[78] However, both culturally and politically, they were rooted in a long-standing indigenous tradition.

With the failure of the Great Leap Forward, there was a reassertion of more pragmatist politics, and a restoration of centralized, state-coordinated efforts toward economic development. At the same time, China's leaders faced a complex situation internationally with Khrushchev's trip to the United States and a degree of detente that the Chinese side regarded as a capitulation to capitalism. Events in Indonesia, Laos, and Tibet were also seen as setbacks to the Communist cause. By the summer of 1960, China's refusal to align itself with the Soviet Union had erupted into an open rift between the two countries, and the withdrawal of all Soviet experts, as well as the cancellation of a large number of contracts and projects.[79] Over the years that followed, the Chinese came to see the Soviets as "social imperialists," and one whole dimension of the lead-up to the Cultural Revolution was a concerted research effort critiquing the different aspects of the Soviet patterns that had been bequeathed to China.[80]

In higher education, an important new policy document, the Sixty Articles, was promulgated. It might be seen as an effort to integrate the two approaches to curriculum and development that have been described. Many of the nationally-controlled institutions, such as the institutes of finance and economics, law, and political science, were restored, yet at the same time the new local institutions were also affirmed and developed. They operated as second-echelon institutions, with their graduates being assigned jobs within the provincial bureaucracy or sent down to the prefectural or county level.

The Sixty Articles called for a strengthening of the academic content of teaching, and limited the amount of time students were to spend in productive labor on farms or in university factories to one and a half months. The document emphasized maintaining strength in basic theoretical teaching, as well as applied and practical fields, yet indicated that there should not be a restoration of the overly narrow program definitions and texts of the Soviet period. Research was to be maintained as an integral part of the university's responsibility and faculty were expected to be able to spend five-sixths of their time in teaching, research, and other professional activity, and only one-sixth on political or productive work.[81]

This period saw the beginning of a new international orientation for Chinese universities. While the only outlet for their students in the 1950s had been the Soviet Union or Eastern Europe, and an estimated 8,000 had been sent for training in countries of the Soviet bloc,[82] at this time, students and faculty were sent to several European countries for advanced education.[83] Also, there was a diversification in the teaching of foreign languages away from an exclusive focus on Russian to include English, French, German, and other European languages.[84]

This might have been a time in which a new balance was struck between the two poles of the Chinese cultural tradition, with eclectic foreign cultural influences contributing to a new synthesis, as had begun to happen in the Nationalist period. Instead, it was to culminate in the outbreak of the Cultural Revolution in 1966, and the destruction of the new system of higher education, which had been built up with such high hopes.

THE CULTURAL REVOLUTION DECADE, 1966–1976

A very rich literature exists on the political, economic, and educational dimensions of the Cultural Revolution. In terms of higher education, conflicts over the class background of participants, the differing prestige attached to different levels of the system, and to formal and nonformal institutions, reached a head. Clearly, factional politics, and the struggle between those who supported two different agendas within the Communist party, provide the most convincing explanatory framework for understanding this period. Educational policies and practices can best be understood with reference to the supremacy of the radical faction under Mao Zedong, and the complete overthrow of those who had supported the pragmatist, Soviet-inspired road to socialist construction. The intention was for the nonformal track of education to take over from the formal, for all elitism and selectivity to be abolished in favor of open access to education for the broad masses of peasants and workers, and for successful economic and political development to be engineered from below, by grass-roots activism, rather than from above, by technological expertise and macro-planning.

As a result secondary education over this period saw phenomenal growth in enrollments and the near popularization of a nine-year common school, five years at the primary level, and four years at the secondary level. The intention was to remove distinctions among different types of secondary schools, with a practical curriculum oriented toward production, and intensive political education pervading the whole program. In 1966, there had been 9 million students in general academic secondary schools, in addition to 4.4 million in agricultural and vocational schools, the "second track" that had developed in the 1960s, and 550,000 in specialized secondary schools.[85] The latter institutions had had high prestige, since they assured access to the lowest level of cadre appointment in urban enterprises and to primary school teaching positions. General secondary schools were the essential channel for higher education entry, while agricultural and vocational schools assured neither employment nor further education opportunities for their graduates.

Female enrollments in these three types of institution give some interesting insight into the gender patterns of the system. For the specialized secondary schools, which were mainly in urban areas, females represented 48.6 percent of those in teacher training and 37.9 percent of those in other kinds of technical training in 1966.[86] For general academic schools, mainly in cities and county towns, females represented 32.2 percent of enrollments.[87] For agricultural and vocational schools, most of which were in the countryside, females represented only 23.6 percent of enrollments.[88]

These distinctions among types of school were abolished during the Cultural Revolution, in name at least, and enrollments grew to a remarkable 58 million in 1976, or more than four times the 1965 total.[89] Female participation increased from 32.2 percent to 40.4 percent overall, probably reflecting the greater participation of rural women. There were obviously tremendous costs to this drastic expansion, in terms of the quality of education, but it was to fundamentally change the education system from this time forward, contributing to a general upgrading of the educational level of the whole population.[90]

In higher education, the Cultural Revolution had the opposite effect, with a drastic drop in enrollments from the high point of 961,000 at the height of the Great Leap Forward. For three years, between 1966 and 1969, there were no new enrollments in the formal system, although there were many short-term training classes, which largely focused on political mobilization. When regular enrollments were restored, they began with 47,815 in 1970, and gradually grew to 564,715 by 1976. The entrance examination had been discontinued from 1967, and entrance was based on recommendation, which meant political criteria were very important, and all high school graduates had to have work experience before they could be recommended.

Various studies have shown that the declared intention of opening up the universities to students from worker and peasant backgrounds actually led in practice to an almost exclusive dominance of young people from cadre families at all levels.[91] There may well have been greater rural participation, as many came from the families of rural cadres, though it is difficult to distinguish them from the large numbers of urban young people who had settled in the countryside under rustification campaigns, which reached a high point over this time.[92] Some of these urban youth were recommended for higher education entry, after being reclassified as peasants.

Women students benefited from these changes, and their participation in higher education rose from 26.9 percent in 1965 to 33.6 percent in 1975, probably including more rural women than ever before, and reflecting the opening up of secondary education to women noted above.[93] However, none of the studies of the Cultural Revolution period have focused on women, or tried to explain what may have been particular to gender in the experience. It would be extremely interesting to link up the attack on hierarchy in the system and theoretical abstraction in the curriculum and embrace of integrative holistic approaches to knowledge in this period with aspects of the feminist critique of knowledge and education in the Western context.

Many dimensions of the educational struggle during this period are worth exploring, but the focus here is on the cultural dimension. What, in fact, was cultural about the Cultural Revolution? What happened to the idea of the university that had been modified and adapted to Chinese cultural patterns under the Nationalists, reinstated in an authoritarian Soviet form in the 1950s, and once more adjusted to Chinese conditions in the Great Leap Forward and the early 1960s? My own sense is that its basic values were completely rejected in this period, as a populist and critical approach to knowledge arose from roots in China's nonformal traditions, and took shape within Maoist epistemology. It emphasized social practice, was deeply suspicious of all forms of specialization, and sought the total integration of intellectual life into the struggle for production and for social transformation.

Mao's comments on the aims of education, first expressed in the Great Leap Forward period, now became central to a new kind of higher education, which was precisely opposite to the Soviet emphasis on expertise and specialization: "Our educational policy must enable everyone who gets an education to develop morally, intellectually, and physically and become cultured, socialist-minded workers."[94] In an interesting sociological analysis of this period, and the earlier Great Leap Forward, Chan Hoiman has suggested that it was a matter of the education system being totally reabsorbed into society as a whole in a utopian quest for unity and integration, with revolution as a kind of anti-system or antidote to the specialisms of the Soviet model.[95]

From the cultural perspective, one of the most interesting documents of the period is that delineating the struggle between two lines, the Maoist and the revisionist or Soviet line, which was published in 1967. In this document there is a detailed description of the process whereby Soviet patterns had been introduced and come to shape the system, with a vigorous critique of its academicism, its orientation toward narrow specialization, the dogmatism encouraged in teaching, and the ways in which the power and privileges of a small elite of graduates from the most prestigious universities had been maintained. The two institutions that had been designated centers of Soviet influence, People's University and Harbin Polytechnical University, were particularly held up for criticism.[96]

It may be helpful at this point to return to Bernstein's ideas of classification and framing, as they illumine the ways in which changes in curricular knowledge are related to changes in power relations within and beyond the school. There was a drastic change in this period from the collection code, which had been restored in the early 1960s, with very strong classification and framing, to an integrated code, where both classification and framing were weak. Bernstein noted how a move from collection to integrated codes may well bring about a disturbance in the structure and distribution of power, and in existing educational identities. At the cultural level, Bernstein noted, it involves a shift of the keeping of categories pure to the mixing of categories.

In the Chinese context, it was a kind of total rejection of the artificial boundaries among subjects and knowledge areas that had been first introduced as curricular categories early in the century, and that had become fixed in a particularly rigid way in the 1950s. Distinctions among the large and growing number of specializations, between pure and applied knowledge, academic and everyday life knowledge, were to be abolished, and forms of pedagogy that emphasized the authority of the teacher and the text were to be replaced by activist student participation in the teaching process and the writing of texts.

This was less a mixing of categories than a return to an integrative and organic view of knowledge, based on Mao's monist and dialectical views, whereby knowledge arose directly from social and productive practice, and was in turn refined through further practice.[97] Both the higher and the secondary curriculum were redesigned toward what could be defined as an integrated code. For higher education, the first model to be upheld emphasized the integral link between higher education and production. It was a training school attached to the Shanghai Machine Tools Plant, which was held up as a model in July 1968,[98] not long after the army and teams of workers had been used to restore order on Chinese campuses after two years of violent struggle.[99] This was the period when most university faculty, along with cadres in other organizations and institutions, were sent to be reformed through labor in "May 7th cadre schools." These were located in rural areas and named after Mao's directive of May 7, 1966, which had emphasized "learning about industry, agriculture, and the military, as well as book knowledge."[100] A second model of that period illustrated how a major national university, Tongji in Shanghai, reorganized itself as part of a commune attached to a local architectural firm. Teaching and research were patterned around urban and rural construction tasks in an integrative way.[101]

On July 21, 1968, Mao had stated that "it is still necessary to have universities, here I refer mainly to colleges of science and engineering."[102] He went on to indicate that the period of study should be shortened, students should be chosen from workers and peasants with practical experience, and that the model of the Shanghai Machine Tools Plant School should be followed. Two years later, on July 21, 1970, *Red Flag* published an article entitled "Strive to Build a Socialist University of Science and Technology," which described how Qinghua University had been reorganized with the help of the teams of workers and soldiers, in preparation for the restoration of formal enrollments that autumn. It focused on campus factories, and a reorganization of scientific and technological education around high-level technological production.[103]

While technological education, emphasizing polytechnic principles and integrated with broad political education, was a main focus of the period, there was also interesting discussion around the teaching of humanities and social sciences. Here the integrative notion was that of taking the whole society as a factory and studying ongoing revolutionary processes in a holistic way, while contributing to them through writing and oratory. Fudan University, with its close links to the Gang of Four and its influential journal, *Study and Criticism,* was taken as a model here.[104]

Clearly the expectation was that a new and revolutionary knowledge system could be fostered, with the disciplines and specializations of the Western and Soviet university superseded for once and for all. The autonomy and academic freedom associated with these approaches to knowledge had been subsumed under a new intellectual authority and monopoly of power in the name of expertise that arose from a combination of persisting Confucian values and the Soviet version of Marxism-Leninism. Maoism was now drawing on impulses from the other pole of China's cultural tradition to overthrow these patterns and empower ordinary people to redesign both education and society.

The struggle was to lead to tragedy. No viable educational alternative emerged, only anarchy, violence, and chaos. Much was destroyed, and little was built to take its place. A look at what happened in terms of the knowledge map and the geographical map over this decade gives some sense of the dimensions of the tragedy. Those institutions that had been directly identified with Soviet social sciences, People's University and the regional institutes of finance, economics, political science, and law, were closed for a decade. All agricultural universities were forced to move to rural areas, and their campuses were taken over for use by the army, a situation that was common on other campuses as well. All faculty were required to spend time at May 7th cadre schools in rural areas, often staying there for several years. When regular programs were reinstated from the early 1970s, they were all short-cycle three-year programs, with much of the teaching having to be done at a secondary school level[105] due to the low academic requirements at entry point and the fact that library resources and laboratory equipment had been damaged or destroyed.

In spite of brave efforts to link study requirements with social practice in factories, in the case of students of the humanities, and with productive practice in the case of science students, it is not easy to find actual examples that elaborate a new cultural identity. The student body represented an even more restricted elite than in the period before 1966. It was common knowledge that most entrants were the children of cadres, who had the power to manipulate the political criteria that had replaced academic entrance criteria.[106] Enrollment size in the formal system remained highly restrictive, in spite of the rhetoric about opening up universities to the masses.

The nonformal system was supposed to take a leading role, and vigorous efforts were made to develop institutions called "July 21st universities," after Mao's directive of July 21, 1968. These were in reality small training schools associated with factories and communes. Enrollments at these institutions were reported to have expanded from 16,582 in 1972, to 213,736 students at 10,836 institutions in 1974. By 1976, there were reported to be 46,810 institutions with 2.6 million students. The content of study at these institutions was heavily ideological, as well as including basic technical training. Clearly, they had little connection with the idea of a university, or with the historical university system that had developed in China over a hundred-year period.

Meanwhile, the regular universities were struggling to recover from what had doubtless been the most traumatic phase of their entire history. The experience of two institutions over this period will perhaps serve to illustrate the situation they faced. Both were polytechnical universities that had been established under the Communist regime and thus should have been in a better situation than institutions of the humanities or social sciences, given the explicit focus of the July 21 directive on science and technology. The Huazhong University of Science and Technology (HUST) in Wuhan had been established in 1952 as the leading polytechnical university of the Central South region, while the Chinese University of Science and Technology had been set up under the Chinese Academy of Sciences in Beijing in 1958.

In a moving recollective account, Zhu Jiusi, then party secretary and vice president of HUST, described conditions on his campus in 1970, when most of the faculty had already spent two years in a May 7th cadre school in the countryside, and he himself had returned to reflect on the university's present and future. The campus was largely abandoned, with a small number of workers and staff living there and growing vegetables for subsistence. Since it was a highly attractive site, his expectation, and that of many of the faculty, was that it would probably be taken over by a central government ministry, and their rural exile would become permanent.

In this situation, it was a tremendous relief when *Red Flag* published the article on "socialist universities of science and technology" in July 1970, reaffirming Mao's statement of 1968 that "it is still necessary to have universities," and indicating that regular institutions would now be reopened. Zhu described the feeling of elation that came with this knowledge that the Chinese university might have a future after all, and his own determination to build his university into a new type of institution.

To do this, Zhu focused first on improving the faculty's grounding in basic theory, particularly mathematics, and also on exposing them to foreign language study, with a focus on English, which he saw as the most important language for science and technology. He also put great emphasis on library development and the restoration and development of the university's scientific and technological equipment. A further significant element of his vision for the future was the fostering of related social science areas such as journalism, industrial management, the philosophy of science, and higher education in a university that had originally been limited to an applied scientific curriculum.

Perhaps Zhu's boldest and most interesting move over the years between 1970 and 1976 was the effort he made to recruit excellent scholars in a range of knowledge areas, who were still exiled in remote rural regions and had little hope of returning to their own universities. Altogether, he brought 600 new faculty members to the university in this way, building its reputation with such success that it was one of the first group of universities approved to establish a graduate school in 1984. His own status and prestige as a revolutionary intellectual who had been at Yan'an enabled him to take initiatives that other university leaders might not have dared to consider in that period.[107]

The general climate was one of fear, and a sense of the worthlessness of academic knowledge, as can be seen in the experience of the Chinese University of Science and Technology over this same period. It was slated to be "moved down" from the national capital to a local region in 1970 and it had some difficulty in finding a home. The first location considered was Zhengzhou, the capital of Henan province, but conservative officials there saw its coming as problematic and refused to authorize the move. This behavior is now bitterly regretted in a province where engineering education remains weak.[108] It is fully understandable, however, as an expression of the general mood of the early 1970s, and the prevalent attitude on the part of local government toward intellectual institutions. In the end, the institution moved to Hefei, capital of Anhui province, with the help of Wan Li, and its subsequent development as a leading scientific institution has done much to raise the academic profile of that province.

In terms of the geographical map, we thus see a situation in the Cultural Revolution that was unlike either the large-scale mechanistic planning of the early 1950s, or the enthusiastic local mobilization of resources for higher education in the late 1950s. Intense political struggle, which had focused on universities and the educational hierarchy, left intellectuals nervous and exhausted. Local government personnel were also cautious and lacked motivation to support higher education. Zhu Jiusi was a rare figure in his ability to look ahead to a new future for the Chinese university during this difficult period.

Overall, the period is now seen as one of overwhelming tragedy in terms of China's modern history, a tragedy that resulted mainly from extreme political factionalism and the ruthless tyranny of a small group on the far left who took over Mao's agenda. From the perspective of higher education and culture, it might be seen as a swing of the pendulum from the highly authoritarian academic centralism that represented a kind of melding of state Confucianism with Soviet/European academicism to an opposite extreme of populism and integration into society that ended up close to nihilism. Not only was there no place for the university, in any of the forms or adaptations that had been the subject of experiment for more than a century, but locally oriented, populist learning institutions failed to develop an effective alternative to the university. The Yan'an model had had a vital role in the Liberation struggle, but it could not provide an adequate set of institutional and curricular patterns for the needs of this period.

With the death of Mao in 1976, and the subsequent fall of the Gang of Four, the moderate faction of the party regained power, under the leadership of Deng Xiaoping, and initiated a whole new phase in China's development in the 1980s. The next chapter will explore what happened to the idea of the university, and to Chinese values of higher learning in a new synthesis that was achieved over this decade.

1. John Gittings notes a lack of attention to this point in a recent review of Vols. 14 and 15 of the *Cambridge History of China*. See *China Quarterly*, no. 133, March 1993, p. 159. I was interested to note the use of the word "tragedy" by Jonathan Spence in commenting on the reasons for the Chinese decision toward all-out Sovietization, as against its original espousal of a "new democracy." See J. Spence, *The Search for Modern China* (London: W.W. Norton, 1990), p. 533.

2. Hu Shi Ming and Eli Seifman, *Toward a New World Outlook: A Documentary History of Education in the People's Republic of China, 1949–1976* (New York: Ams Press, 1976). See pp. 9–11 for an English translation of the Common Program. This volume includes translations of many important educational documents for the period dealt with in this chapter.

3. Ma Xulun's academic and administrative career is summarized in Boorman's *Biographical Dictionary of Republican China* (New York: Columbia University Press, 1968), Vol. 2, pp. 465–468.

4. *Renmin ribao*, June 14, 1950, in Hu and Seifman, *Toward a New World Outlook*, p. 13.

5. The mandate and setting up of these committees is described in some detail in Mao Lirui and Shen Guanjun, *Zhongguo jiaoyu tongshi* (Jinan: Shandong jiaoyu chubanshe, 1988), pp. 60–66. Details can also be found in *Zhongguo jiaoyu nianjian 1949–1981* (Beijing: Zhongguo dabaike quanshu chubanshe, 1984), pp. 250ff.

6. A document describing these principles was published in *Renmin ribao*, August 3, 1950, and can be found in translation in Hu and Seifman, *Toward a New World Outlook*, pp. 16–17.

7. A laudatory article on the reformed higher education system entitled "Higher Education Takes a New Path" by Qian Duansheng can be found in *China Reconstructs*, September–October 1953. For Ma Yinchu's views, see Ronald Hsia, "The Intellectual and Public Life of Ma Yin-ch'u," in *China Quarterly*, no. 6, April–June 1961, pp. 53–63.

8. In a series of talks given by Professor Zhu Jiusi, former president of Huazhong University of Science and Technology in Wuhan in May 1992, Professor Zhu expressed his own deeply felt regret at what had happened to China's nationalist universities in 1952. He had personally been associated with Wuhan University, where he studied philosophy in the 1930s, and Zhejiang University, where he had worked in a clerical position for two years, before going to Yan'an in 1937. For a fuller discussion of this point see R. Hayhoe, "Chinese Universities and the Social Sciences," in *Minerva*, Vol. XXXI, no. 4, Winter 1993, pp. 500–503.

9. See Ronald Price, *Marxism and Education in China and Russia* (London: Croom Helm, 1977) for a detailed discussion of Marxist principles of polytechnical education, which Price feels were never well understood in the Chinese context.

10. Leo A. Orleans, *Professional Manpower and Education in Communist China* (Washington, D.C.: National Science Foundation, 1960). Chapter 6 of this volume describes the science system established in the 1950s, with the Chinese Academy of Sciences as the most important institution. In 1957, the academy had a budget of 90 million yuan for research, contrasting with 10 million yuan provided to universities for research. (See p. 114.)

11. Department of Planning, Ministry of Education, PRC, *Achievement of Education in China: Statistics, 1949–1983* (Beijing: People's Education Press, 1984), p. 53.

12. I was first alerted to this early conflict over higher curriculum in a discussion with Zhao Andong of the Shanghai Higher Education Research Institute, who had himself been intimately involved in the early higher education reform process. In an article entitled "Jianguo chuqi gaodeng jiaoyu gaige," [Higher Education Reform in the Early Period of Socialist Construction] in Yu Li (ed.), *Xiandai jiaoyu sixiang*

yanlun [Introductory Discussions on Contemporary Educational Thought] (Shanghai: Huadong shifan daxue chubanshe, 1986) he describes the concerns of the time over the Sovietization of the curriculum.

13. Mao Lirui and Shen Guanjun, *Zhongguo jiaoyu tongshi*, pp. 89–113, gives a detailed description of the Soviet presence, followed by an evaluative discussion of its impact.

14. Frederick Teiwes, "Establishment and Consolidation of the New Regime," in J.K. Fairbank and Dennis Twitchett (eds.), *The Cambridge History of China*, Vol. 14, (Cambridge: Cambridge University Press, 1987), pp. 79–83.

15. See Mao and Shen, *Zhongguo jiaoyu tongshi*, pp. 72–82, for a detailed depiction of this reorganization process.

16. Xiaoshi bianxiezu, (ed.), *Huazhong ligong daxue de sishi nian* [The Forty Years of Central China University of Science and Technology] (Wuhan: Huazhong ligong daxue chubanshe, 1993).

17. This move is described in detail in the university's history, *Jiaotong daxue xiaoshi, 1896–1949* (Institutional History of Jiaotong University 1896–1949) (Shanghai: Shanghai renmin chubanshe, 1986).

18. Mao Lirui and Shen Guanjun, *Zhongguo jiaoyu tongshi*, pp. 82–83.

19. An English translation of Liu Shaoqi's speech can be found in the *Collected Works of Liu Shao-ch'i, 1945–57*, Vol. 2, (Hong Kong: Union Research Institute, 1969), pp. 235–254. Two volumes in Chinese on the history of People's University have appeared. The first by veteran Communist Cheng Fangwu, who was vice president and subsequently president of the university after Liberation, describes its various main forerunner, Shaanbei gongxue, and the transition to People's University in 1950. Cheng Fangwu, *Zhanhuo zhong de daxue* [A University Under Fire] (Beijing: Renmin jiaoyu chubanshe, 1982). The second gives a chronology running from 1937 to 1992: *Zhongguo renmin daxue dashiji* [A Chronology of Events at China People's University, July 1937 to February 1992] (Beijing: Zhongguo renmin daxue gaodeng jiaoyu yanjiushi and xiaoshi bianxiezu, 1992).

20. A detailed description of the development of these new institutions is given in the *Zhongguo jiaoyu nianjian, 1949–1981*, pp. 265–270.

21. Full details on the reorganization of normal education in the 1950s can be found in an excellent collection of documents from the period that has been recently published. See *Dangdai Zhongguo gaodeng shifan jiaoyu ziliao xuan* [Selected Materials on Contemporary Chinese Higher Normal Education] (Shanghai: Huadong shida chubanshe, 1986). Anita Chan, *Children of Mao* (London: Macmillan, 1985), gives a vivid picture of the authoritarian personality type fostered by this new pedagogy.

22. Ibid., pp. 88–110.

23. *Zhonghua renmin gongheguo jiaoyu dashiji 1949–1982* [A Record of Educational Events in the PR China, 1949–1982] (Beijing: Jiaoyu kexue chubanshe, 1983), p. 132.

24. *Achievement of Education in China: Statistics, 1949–1983* (Beijing: People's Education Press, 1985), p. 183.

25. Susan Shirk, *Competitive Comrades: Career Incentives and Student Strategies in China* (Berkeley: University of California Press, 1982), p. 27.

26. Julia Kwong, *Chinese Education in Transition: Prelude to the Cultural Revolution* (Montreal: McGill-Queens University Press, 1979), p. 70.

27. Suzanne Pepper, *China's Education Reform in the 1980s: Policies, Issues, and Historical Perspectives* (Berkeley: University of California Institute of East Asian Studies, 1990), p. 43.

28. Ibid., An excellent discussion of the various dimensions of this tradition can be found in chapter 1, "The Anti-establishment Backlash," of Pepper's volume, especially pp. 14–15.

29. See, for example, Marianne Bastid, "L'argument économique dans les

réformes de l'enseignement en Chine au XXe siècle," in *Interchange*, Vol. 19, nos. 3/ 4, Fall/Winter, 1988, pp. 19–31, and R. Hayhoe, "Lessons from the Republican Era," in R. Hayhoe (ed.), *Education and Modernization: The Chinese Experience* (Oxford: Pergamon, 1992), pp. 58–60.

30. H.C. Barnard, *Education and the French Revolution* (Cambridge: Cambridge University Press, 1969), p. 216.

31. Ibid., p. 218.

32. William Johnson, *Russia's Educational Heritage* (Pittsburgh, Pa.: Carnegie Press, 1950), chapter 3.

33. Alexander Korol, *Soviet Education for Science and Technology* (Cambridge, Mass.: M.I.T. Press, 1957). This volume gives a very detailed depiction of the Soviet system as it functioned in the early 1950s. "Soviet civilian institutions of higher education include two general types: the universities, of which there were thirty-four in 1956, and the institutes, a general category embracing more than 700 schools (729 as of January 1955). The distinction between the two types rests mainly on the fact that courses at the university are organized more or less horizontally around a given major field, . . . whereas those in all other types of schools (institutes) are geared to the specific requirements of a particular industry or a well-defined vocation . . . it is only in the university that each basic science, such as physics, chemistry, or mathematics, constitutes a field of study."(p. 135). See Sheila Fitzpatrick, *Education and Social Mobility in the Soviet Union, 1921–1934* (Cambridge: Cambridge University Press, 1979), especially chapter 9, "The Making of a Proletarian Intelligentsia," for a discussion of how these patterns were put in place.

34. Basil Bernstein, "On the Classification and Framing of Educational Knowledge," in Michael Young (ed.), *Knowledge and Control* (London: Collier Macmillan, 1971).

35. Nicholas Lardy, "Economic Recovery and the First Five-Year Plan," *Cambridge History of China*, Vol. 14, chapter 3.

36. A vivid depiction of how this system worked at Beijing University in the early 1950s can be found in Maria Yen, *The Umbrella Garden: A Picture of Student Life in Red China* (New York: Macmillan, 1954). See also Chao Chung and Yang I-fan, *Students in Mainland China* (Kowloon, Hong Kong: Union Research Institute, 1962). This situation is described and commented on in relation to the beginnings of the Cultural Revolution activism by Julia Kwong, *Cultural Revolution in China's Schools* (Stanford, Calif.: Hoover Institution Press, 1988), p. 10.

37. The following comments were made on my analysis by Dr. Nina Borevskaya, a specialist on Chinese literature and education at the Institute of East Asian studies at the Russian Academy of Sciences in Moscow: "I've found your core assumption about the cultural conflict between the Soviet-Western academicism, scientism, and centralism on one side, and the opposition from the populist ideas rooted in Chinese reality during the Nationalist government period as very productive. . . . My assumption is that the Chinese challenge to the Soviet pattern of modernization during the Great Leap, as well as in the Cultural Revolution, was about the extent of centralization and industrialization. It was intrinsically the internal Chinese conflict between the centripetal and centrifugal tendencies. Decentralized American patterns couldn't work in China, but an overcentralized Soviet model was rejected by Chinese local authorities. But the crucial point was that of industrialization. Higher education was perfectly adjusted to the needs of the latter, but I see the core problem in the conflict between the Maoist vision of modernization (his populist version for the rural countryside), and the urban model suggested by the USSR. In general, I agree that 'the connection of the new elaborately structured system to China's own cultural context was very tenuous.' I like your assumption that the response to the Soviet pattern that had reinforced the tendencies toward the centralization of knowledge and uniformity of thought came from the nonformal, socially critical pole that had always had a balancing role." (Personal communication, November 29, 1994.)

38. Hu and Seifman, *Toward a New World Outlook*, p. 10. This is article six of the Common Program.

39. *Achievement of Education in China Statistics 1949–1981*, p. 106.

40. Ibid., p. 202.

41. Julia Kwong, *Chinese Education in Transition*, pp. 70–72, 105, discusses the persisting disadvantages of rural youth in the period up to 1956, and how it proved easier to change this situation for men than women (p. 105). See also Grace Mak, "The People's Republic of China," in Gail Kelly (ed.), *The International Handbook of Women's Education* (Westport, Conn.: Greenwood Press, 1988), pp. 109–133.

42. In interviews done with thirty-eight women faculty in Northwestern universities in May 1993, a significant number, around half of those aged over fifty, reported that they had attended an all-girls secondary school in the 1950s, and that this experience had been extremely significant in creating a basis for their subsequent academic careers.

43. Unfortunately, up to the present there are no accurate Chinese statistics on gender representation by field of study in higher education. However, regional statistics which I have collected (see, for example, the tables in chapters 5 and 6) clearly indicate certain general trends.

44. Zhou Ju, "Mei Su gaodeng jiaoyu jingyan yu woguo gaodeng jiaoyu gaige," [The American and Soviet Experience of Higher Education and Higher Educational Reform in Our Country], in *Zhongguo shehui kexue* [Social Sciences in China], no. 3, 1984, pp. 3–20. In this article, Zhou Ju, a Soviet-education scholar, affirms the important contribution to China's industrialization made by the cohorts educated under the Soviet model between 1952 and 1957. However, she notes that China copied Soviet patterns of the 1930s and paid little attention to reforms going on in the Soviet Union in the 1950s. She identifies the following five problems with the model that was borrowed: 1) the separation of engineering and agriculture from the basic sciences; 2) the overly narrow definition of some engineering specializations, which were too closely linked to product lines, resulting in graduates being unable to adapt to new areas; 3) a one-sided emphasis on Russian in foreign language teaching; 4) an overly heavy load of courses for students that inhibited their creative participation in learning; and 5) an unfortunate dispersal of personnel and programs from some of the distinguished universities established in the Nationalist period.

45. Jonathan Unger, *Education under Mao: Class and Competition in Canton Schools, 1960–1980* (New York: Columbia University Press, 1982). Chapters 1 and 2 give a detailed picture of how the system worked to exclude rural students from higher education, even during the expansion of the Great Leap Forward period.

46. One important channel of opportunity for undergraduates with mediocre academic records but good political qualifications was entry into the army of political study tutors and political education instructors on each university campus. Appointments to these positions were made virtually every year, and provided a comfortable and relatively prestigious professional environment for those who were politically acceptable and well connected.

47. In my extensive interviews with faculty who have returned from abroad in Chinese universities, I have often heard stories of the career development of particular individuals whose family background was "unfavourable" and who were therefore relegated to study or work at an agricultural university. Susan Shirk, *Competitive Comrades,* develops an interesting theory around the character of virtuosity, and the difficulty of establishing firm standards of political orientation, to explain this cynicism.

48. A translation of this speech and of the science plan is found in Stewart Fraser, *Chinese Communist Education: Records of the First Decade* (Nashville, Tenn.: Vanderbilt University Press, 1965), pp. 222–229, and 235–245.

49. Ibid., pp. 229–234.

50. Theodore Chen, *The Thought Reform of Chinese Intellectuals* (Westport,

Conn.: Hyperion Press, 1958). See especially chapter 15.

51. Ibid., pp. 164–65; Roderick MacFarquhar, *The Hundred Flowers and the Chinese Intellectuals* (New York: Octagon Books, 1974). See especially pp. 86–89.

52. For sources on Ma Yinchu, see the biography in Boorman's *Biographical Dictionary of Republican China* (New York: Columbia University Press, 1968), Vol. 2, p. 478, also Roland Hsia, "The Intellectual and Cultural Life of Mao Yin-ch'u," in *China Quarterly*, no. 6, April–June 1961, pp. 53–63. See also Rene Goldman, "The Rectification Campaign at Peking University May–June 1957," in *China Quarterly*, no. 12, October–December 1964, pp. 138–153. For a discussion of his ideas for the Second Five-Year Plan, which were to be swept aside by the Great Leap Forward, see N. Lardy, "Economic Recovery and the First Five-Year Plan."

53. Mao Lirui and Shen Guanjun, *Zhongguo jiaoyu tongshi*, p. 126, gives the figure of 17,769 university faculty, or 6.5 percent of the total, who were labeled as rightists in 1957.

54. Spence, *The Search for Modern China*, p. 572.

55. Suzanne Pepper, "New Directions in Education," *Cambridge History of China*, Vol. 14, pp. 398–399.

56. Kenneth Lieberthal, "The Great Leap Forward and the Split in the Yenan Leadership," in *Cambridge History of China*, Vol. 14, pp. 293–320.

57. Julia Kwong, *Chinese Education in Transition: Prelude to the Cultural Revolution*; Suzanne Pepper, *China's Education Reform in the 1980s: Policies, Issues and Historical Perspectives*.

58. Marianne Bastid, *Educational Reform in Early Twentieth-Century China* (Ann Arbor: Center for Chinese Studies, 1988); Paul Bailey, *Reform the People: Changing Attitudes Towards Popular Education in Early Twentieth-Century China* (Edinburgh: Edinburgh University Press, 1990).

59. Pepper, "New Directions," pp. 400–431.

60. Ma Kanwen, "Chinese Medicine and the West," in R. Hayhoe (ed.), *Knowledge Across Cultures: Universities East and West* (Toronto: OISE Press, Wuhan: Hubei Education Press, 1994), pp. 154–181.

61. Brief histories of all these colleges of traditional medicine can be found in *Chinese Universities and Colleges: A Guide to Institutions of Higher Education in China* (Beijing: Higher Education Press, 1989).

62. Ralph Croizier, "Traditional Medicine in Modern China," in Guenter B. Risse (ed.), *Modern China and Traditional Chinese Medicine* (Springfield, Ill.: Charles C. Thomas, 1973, pp. 40–41.) See also Maryann Burris, "To Serve China: Medical School and Modernization in the People's Republic of China," unpublished Ph.D. dissertation, Stanford University, 1990. This dissertation gives detailed insight into how the Western-style medical curriculum in China has been affected by persisting value patterns from Chinese traditional medicine, as well as describing the movement to restore institutions of traditional Chinese medicine from 1954.

63. AnElissa Lucas, *Chinese Medical Modernization: Comparative Policy Continuities, 1930s–1980s* (New York: Praeger, 1982, pp. 108–110; David Lampton, *Health, Conflict, and the Chinese Political System* (Ann Arbor: Center for Chinese Studies, 1974), pp. 49–78.

64. Tsang Chiu-sam, *Society, Schools, and Progress in China* (London: Pergamon, 1968), p. 208.

65. Mikhail A. Klochko, *A Soviet Scientist in Red China* (New York: Praeger, 1964). See Suzanne Pepper's helpful summary of Klochko's comments in the *Cambridge History of China*, Vol. 14, pp. 410, 414–415.

66. Mao Lirui and Shen Guanqun, *Zhongguo jiaoyu tongshi*, p. 117.

67. Suzanne Pepper, *China's Education Reform in the 1980s*, pp. 57–58, takes particular care in tracing the keypoint idea back to the central schools in Yan'an, and in criticizing it. See also the *Cambridge History of China*, Vol. 14, pp. 420–429. According to the *Zhongguo jiaoyu nianjian 1949–1981*, p. 329, the first keypoint uni-

versities were People's University, Beijing University and Harbin Engineering University, selected in 1954, while the sixteen selected in 1959 were a second group, and another sixty-four were selected in 1960. When this designation was revived after the Cultural Revolution, there were ninety-eight institutions in the formal higher education system that were designated as keypoint.

68. The story of this merger is told in *Zhongnan caijing daxue xiaoshi 1948–1988* [An Institutional History of the Central South University of Finance and Economics] (Wuhan: Zhongnan caijing daxue chubanshe, 1988), pp. 51–69.

69. I gained firsthand information about these episodes from personal visits to the two institutions in 1987. See R. Hayhoe, "Shanghai as a Mediator of the Educational Open Door," in *Pacific Affairs*, Vol. 61, no. 2, Summer 1988, pp. 261–262.

70. This information comes from a visit to Liaoning University in September 1985. See also *Liaoning gaodeng xuexiao yange* [The Evolution of Higher Education in Liaoning], (Shenyang: Liaoning renmin chubanshe, 1983), pp. 293–311.

71. This information comes from personal visits to Inner Mongolia Engineering College in May 1989, and to Qinghai Normal University in May 1993. The story of the development of the Northwest will be told in more detail in chapter 6.

72. Quite a few went from Shanghai universities, as noted in R. Hayhoe, "Shanghai as a Mediator of the Educational Open Door."

73. In my visits to universities in peripheral regions, I have come across many such individuals. The one who comes most vividly to mind is an older professor sent from Beijing Foreign Languages Institute to Inner Mongolia University in the 1950s as a kind of punishment. Fluent in both French and English, and a highly cultivated individual, he has built up an excellent department of foreign languages and literatures over the years, and most recently provided dynamic leadership for a newly developing Canadian studies center.

74. *Achievement of Education in China: Statistics*, p. 50.

75. Julia Kwong, *Chinese Education in Transition*, p. 105.

76. *Achievement of Education in China: Statistics*, p. 50.

77. Jonathan Unger, *Education Under Mao*, pp. 48–65 gives a detailed depiction of the parallel movement at the secondary level, which led to a kind of second track of nonformal secondary schools located mainly in rural areas.

78. In the early 1980s, the distinction between these two tracks or systems was further formalized with the development of a separate national entry examination for adult education, and the vigorous development of television universities and other new approaches to the nonformal system.

79. John Gittings, *Survey of the Sino-Soviet Dispute* (London: Oxford University Press, 1968); Alan Whiting, "The Sino-Soviet Split," in the *Cambridge History of China*, Vol. 14, pp. 478–525.

80. Johann Galtung, "Conflict on a Global Scale: Social Imperialism and Subimperialism—Continuities in the Structural Theory of Imperialism," in *World Development*, Vol. 4, no. 3, March 1976, pp. 153–165.

81. Theodore Hsi-en Chen, *Chinese Education Since 1949: Academic and Revolutionary Models* (New York: Pergamon, 1981), pp. 182–185.

82. Ibid., p. 39.

83. *Achievement of Education in China*, lists a small number for Switzerland and Italy in this period, but we know a few were also sent to England and France. For those in France, see Roland Depierre, "Maoism in French Educational Thought and Action," in Hayhoe and Bastid (eds.), *China's Education and the Industrialized World*, pp. 200–204. These students were recalled due to the Cultural Revolution, and it was not until the early 1970s that students were again sent abroad.

84. Heidi Ross, *China Learns English: Language Learning and Social Change in the People's Republic* (New Haven and London: Yale University Press, 1993), pp. 42–47.

85. *Achievement of Education in China*, pp. 146, 183, 207.

86. Ibid., p. 175.

87. Ibid., p. 202.

88. Ibid., p. 210.

89. Ibid., p. 183, 202.

90. In the 1980s, enrollments dropped considerably, with many rural secondary schools shut down or combined, but secondary participation never dropped below 40 million, in contrast to the 14 million of the pre-Cultural Revolution period. The elitism now took the form of a multi-track, rather than a two-track system, with a restoration of strong differentials in quality and prestige among different types of schools, and particularly between rural and urban schools.

91. Both Unger, *Education Under Mao*, and Shirk, *Competitive Comrades*, emphasize this point.

92. Thomas Bernstein, *Up to the Mountains and Down to the Villages: The Transfer of Youth from Urban to Rural China* (New Haven: Yale University Press, 1977).

93. Stanley Rosen, "Women, Education, and Modernization," in R. Hayhoe, *Education and Modernization: The Chinese Experience*, pp. 263–269, indicates the lasting effects of women's opportunities over this time in the gender patterns of scientists and professionals educated during the period.

94. Mao Zedong, "On Contradiction," in C.T. Hu, *Chinese Communist Education* (New York: Teachers College, Columbia University, 1962), p. 82.

95. Chan Hoiman, "Modernity and Revolution: Toward an Analytic Agenda of the Great Leap Forward and the Cultural Revolution," in R. Hayhoe, *Education and Modernization*, pp. 73–102.

96. "Chronology of the Two-road Struggle on the Education Front in the Past Seventeen Years," in *Jiaoyu geming* [Educational Revolution], May 6, 1967, translation in Peter Seybolt, *Revolutionary Education in China: Documents and Commentary* (New York: International Arts and Sciences Press, 1973), pp. 5–60.

97. Mao Zedong, "On Practice," in *Selected Works of Mao Tse-Tung* (Peking: Foreign Languages Press, 1975), Vol. 1, pp. 295–310. See Peter Seybolt, *Revolutionary Education in China*, "Introduction," for a good discussion of Maoist pedagogy.

98. "The Way to Train Engineering and Technical Personnel as Viewed from the Shanghai Machine-tool Plant," in *Renmin ribao* [People's Daily], July 22, 1968.

99. A vivid description of this struggle at one important campus, that of Qinghua University, is given by William Hinton in *Hundred-Day War* (New York: Monthly Review Press, 1972). Julia Kwong, *Cultural Revolution in China's Schools*, p. 131, notes that 136 campuses were taken over by workers in a similar manner.

100. "The 'May 7th' Cadre School," in *Peking Review*, Vol. 12, no. 19, 1972.

101. *Renmin ribao* [People's Daily], November 3, 1967; *Peking Review*, Vol. 11, no. 20, May 17, 1968.

102. *Renmin ribao* [People's Daily], July 22, 1968.

103. "Strive to Build a Socialist University of Science and Engineering," in *Hong Qi* [Red Flag], no. 8, July 21, 1970, translation in Seybolt, *Revolutionary Education in China*, pp. 272–300.

104. "Liberal Arts Universities Must Carry Out Revolutionary Mass Criticism," in *Hong Qi* [Red Flag], no. 1, January 1970; "Reform Liberal Arts Universities through Revolutionary Mass Criticism," in *Hong Qi* [Red Flag], June 1, 1971, translations in Seybolt, *Revolutionary Education in China*, pp. 303–330. See also John Gardner, "Study and Criticism: The Voice of Shanghai Radicals," in Christopher Howe (ed.), *Shanghai: Revolution and Development in an Asian Metropolis* (Cambridge: Cambridge University Press, 1981), pp. 326–347.

105. Unger, *Education Under Mao*, p. 201.

106. Ibid., pp. 191–196.

107. Ruth Hayhoe, "Chinese Universities and the Social Sciences," pp. 501–503.

108. This information comes from discussions with the provincial education commission in Zhengzhou, May 30, 1992.

4 THE STORY OF THE REFORM DECADE, 1978–1990

The reform decade is usually seen as beginning in 1977–1978 when Deng Xiaoping returned to power after the death of Mao in 1976, and initiated a series of changes under the rubric of "four modernizations." In the late 1970s and early 1980s, the most important area of reforms was in agriculture, with the dissolution of the communes, and the development of an agricultural responsibility system, allowing a degree of autonomy in rural areas unknown since the mid-1950s. This was followed by reforms in industry, initiated around 1984, and culminating in the emergence of a dynamic collective and township enterprise sector of the economy, and a small private sector. By the end of the decade, the collective sector was challenging the large state enterprises that had dominated the urban economy since the 1950s.

There are many excellent analyses of the reform decade, from its early promise to its denouement in the major political crisis of 1989. One common way of interpreting it is to see it as a case of remarkable economic success, in both agricultural and industrial sectors, which was hindered by the unwillingness or inability of the political system to reform itself. This approach identifies a growing civil society, as increasing numbers of people found employment outside of the state sector, and made demands for a more rapid pace of democratic reform than the political leadership was prepared to respond to. The demands that began with intellectuals and professionals in the mid-1980s had spread to workers and urbanites by the late 1980s, and it was when workers' autonomous unions and academic professional groups joined forces in May 1989 that the resultant threat to the political system elicited a violent response.[1]

Another analysis suggests that it was more the failure of economic reform than its success that led to a series of protests against governmental corruption, which was seen as responsible for escalating economic problems. In this view, the demands for political reform are better understood in relation to traditional Chinese patterns of intellectual-state relations than a movement for democracy and pluralism in the Western sense. Intellectuals, students, and urbanites were calling for people of quality to be given positions of power, people whom they could relate to and advise,[2] not for a Western-style democratic process. Probably the truth lies somewhere between these two positions, and Merle Goldman's recent volume, *Sowing the Seeds of Democracy in China: Political Reform in the Deng Xiaoping Era,* provides a detailed and helpful analysis of the political change process, focusing on the struggle between the democratic elite and the political reformers they supported on one hand, and the conservative party elders and their propagandists on the other.[3]

My intention in this chapter is to put the ongoing story of China's universities into this wider framework of political, economic, and social change, with an emphasis on understanding underlying patterns in the culture. Let me begin by recapitulating the argument so far.

The book began with a consideration of the central values and patterns of the European university tradition, which were summed up in the concepts of university autonomy and academic freedom. The persistence of these values was traced through the various versions of the university that emerged in Europe, America, and the Soviet Union in the nineteenth- and early twentieth-century experience of nation-building. Set against these Western patterns were the core values and patterns of the Chinese higher education tradition, which are related in a kind of polar opposition, a Daoist dialect between two extremes, necessary to one another, yet never synthesized. At one pole were the institutions associated with the civil service examinations, which might be characterized by reference to the intellectual authority and academic monopoly enjoyed by scholarly institutions within the traditional bureaucracy. At the other were local institutions such as the *shuyuan,* which enjoyed radical intellectual freedom and a fragile local autonomy in certain periods, but were constantly subject to either cooptation or closure by the state.

It was my argument in earlier chapters of this book that in the period up to 1911, the "modern" higher institutions that came into being may have borrowed from Western patterns in their forms, but they remained untouched by the values of academic freedom and university autonomy as understood in the West. While the last Qing government established an Imperial University in 1898, which was given a leading position over the whole education system in legislation of 1903, this so-called university functioned in a way very similar to that of traditional bureaucratic institutions. Meanwhile, much of the actual higher education development of this period took place in local colleges, founded by scholar-gentry, missionaries, or revolutionary activists, which had resemblances and linkages to the traditional *shuyuan*.

Only with the efforts of Cai Yuanpei, first briefly as minister of education in 1912, then as chancellor of Beijing University from 1917, was there a systematic and conscious effort to introduce patterns of university autonomy, and values associated with academic freedom. In the subsequent period, there was a rich variety of interactions between newly developing Chinese universities and Western counterparts, which gradually led to the emergence of a Chinese university identity characterized by values that lay somewhere between a broad intellectual freedom and a more narrowly defined academic freedom. During this time, the Chinese university gained considerable autonomy due to the political chaos of the warlord period and the subsequent inability of the Nationalist government to exert the degree of control and direction that it strived for. This freedom was exercised in a remarkable demonstration of social responsibility that included both substantial efforts to support economic and military modernization, as well as a continuous watchdog role over governmental inaction and corruption.

All of the learning and maturing of this period in terms of the university's modern development, however, was to be lost in the 1950s, when the universities of the Nationalist period were dismembered in the reorganization of 1952, and their most distinguished intellectuals were exiled in the anti-rightist movement of 1957. What emerged under Soviet influence was a system made up of a few comprehensive and polytechnical universities and many specialized higher institutions. The leading comprehensive institution, People's University, operated as a kind of central ideological body, giving direction to the whole system. This configuration might be viewed as a realization of the model promoted in detailed legislation of the late Qing period, but never implemented. Set against this highly centralized system, which had been carefully tailored to serve specific sectoral development needs within a macro-plan, were forces rooted in China's traditions of nonformal education, and the particular form they had taken during the Yan'an period. Between these two poles there were no real intermediaries, none of the diverse foreign influences, which had combined with Chinese traditions in different constellations during the late Qing and the early Republican period.

The one moment of opportunity, when it seemed some balancing of the two poles might be achieved, came in the early 1960s, when a reform agenda that included tentative engagement with a diversity of foreign countries was initiated.[4] However, the radical pole was to triumph, as the country became engulfed in the Cultural Revolution. This experience might be seen as another cycle in the long-standing pattern of historic rebellions against centralized autocracy and forms of political control that could no longer be tolerated. One dimension of the tragedy of the Cultural Revolution lay in the fact that the pure nativist patterns of the Yan'an period in higher education proved unable to offer a workable alternative to the universities, which had combined authoritarian, Soviet-derived patterns with state Confucianist values. Only after Deng Xiaoping launched the modernization movement in the late 1970s were Chinese universities again allowed some degree of autonomy and the opportunity to develop their own institutional identities. For this reason, the experience of the Nationalist period is of particular interest as a point of reflection and comparison for the reform decade.

Let me begin with a kind of characterization of the most important moments for higher education over the decade. The reform period began with a major national education conference in April 1978, which abandoned the Cultural Revolution goals of class struggle and adopted modernization as the main goal for educational development. This was accompanied by the restoration of unified national entry examinations for higher education in 1977–1978, and a remarkable new era of rapid expansion for higher education. In the formal system, national institutions expanded enrollments and diversified their programs. Provincial institutions also increased in both size and number, and a new layer of institutions was created at the local level as municipalities established vocational universities offering two- to three-year short-cycle programs intended to train mid-level professionals for their own urban localities. By 1990, 39 percent of all enrollments in the formal higher education system were at the short-cycle level. Between 1978 and 1985, the formal system more than doubled its capacity, with enrollments growing from 625,319 in 1977, to 1,703,115 in 1985.

Over the same period, a renewed adult higher education system was built upon the heritage of the nonformal sector, which had been so central to Cultural Revolution efforts. Its total enrollments reached 1,725,039 in 1985. In the early 1980s, national unified entry examinations were set for the system of adult higher education, and a whole range of institutions, including television and radio universities, urban adult institutions associated with large enterprises, and colleges of adult education in major national universities began to thrive. Although entry requirements were lower than those of the formal system, great efforts were made to set good standards for curricular development, and often texts used in the formal system were adopted. As national universities joined the adult education movement, there was the possibility of some integration between the two systems.

There was no lack of adult students up to about 1985, since a large number of cadres who had been promoted during the Cultural Revolution were threatened with the loss of their positions if they did not achieve at least a short-cycle higher education qualification. The adult higher education system thus carried out a massive reeducation program, which enabled the old revolutionary elite to fit themselves to the new modernization goals.

Other important dimensions of change over this first half of the decade included revived programs of educational exchange with many Western countries, the initiation of programs of development aid by most Organization for Economic Cooperation and Development (OECD) countries in China, which opened up further opportunities for study abroad, and the launching of a whole series of major World Bank projects that supported faculty training abroad in about 180 higher institutions. The majority of those who went abroad for study were middle-aged faculty members, who typically went as visiting scholars for a two-year period in a foreign university, where they could familiarize themselves with international developments in their fields. Most had returned by the mid-1980s and many took up leadership positions in their own universities. By the late 1980s, it was common for many department deans, vice presidents, and even presidents to be a part of this group.

While it is hard to identify figures among these returnees who might be compared with a Cai Yuanpei, many of them were scholars of considerable stature who were prepared to struggle for greater autonomy and academic direction within their institutions. With the educational reform document of 1985, universities were promised a degree of autonomy never experienced before in the period after 1949, at a time when there was a new generation of academic leaders who could give thought and effort to forming a modern Chinese university ethos. The reform document stated that universities were to be centers of both teaching and research, unlike the sole mandate for teaching or professional training that had characterized the Soviet model, and that they were to have control over the content of their programs and the selection of textbooks to be used. Considerable autonomy was promised in other areas as well, with a commitment to phasing in a presidential responsibility system, which would give the president final decision-making power in all areas except those specifically defined as political, and thus the responsibility of the university party secretary.[5]

Overall, this first half of the decade was one of expanding hope and promise for most universities. The new programs that emerged were guided by a desire to raise standards of knowledge and connect them to an international world of scholarship. Graduates were largely content with the opportunities available to them in national and provincial bureaucracies, due to the existing gap in professional personnel left by the ten-year hiatus of the Cultural Revolution.

In the second half of the decade, however, universities experienced many disappointments and discouragements that paralleled in certain ways the faltering of economic and political reforms. After 1985, job prospects for graduates were less and less favorable, as succeeding cohorts of an expanded system filled all available professional and bureaucratic openings. Added to this were complaints about the way in which graduates of urban vocational universities monopolized openings in municipal-level institutions that were coveted by graduates of national and provincial institutions that had higher academic standing.

The adult higher education system also changed radically over this period, creating new strains in terms of the employment of graduates. By about 1986, the retraining needs of the Cultural Revolution generation had been met, and the system had to look elsewhere for entrants. Young people in positions as workers or technicians were not necessarily interested in entry to the adult higher system, since there was little hope of advancement to cadre status on the basis of its credentials. Therefore, the system began to cater more and more to the large number of young secondary school graduates who failed to reach the standards required in the unified national entry examinations for entry to the formal higher education system. It became a kind of second track of higher education. These students had aspirations for professional employment as strong as those in the formal system, and they constituted further competition for popular job openings. Some had personal connections that enabled them to capture positions that might otherwise have gone to graduates of the formal system.

Between 1985 and 1990, expansion slowed in the formal system, with the enrollment growing from 1.7 to 2.04 million, while a reduction in enrollments took place in the adult system, from 1.7 million to 1.4 million. Graduates in the formal system still expected to receive the status and perquisites of state cadres, as had been the case for all graduates since the early 1950s. Gradual efforts to dismantle the national job assignment system, beginning in 1986, and culminating in plans for the majority of graduates to seek their own employment opportunities by the early 1990s, left young people confused and disturbed. Many felt this was likely to lead to rampant nepotism, and make it impossible for those who had gained good qualifications through honest effort to find appropriate positions.[6]

This situation made increasing opportunities for graduate study abroad more and more attractive to the most ambitious young graduates, and the whole study abroad movement changed in nature over this period. It came to be dominated by recent graduates who had just begun their teaching careers, and who gained access to graduate programs in Western countries, sometimes under private auspices. Many of them had little intention of returning to China on graduation.[7] The events of Tiananmen merely cemented a tendency already evident in the slow return of the young generation of faculty. These young people left behind gaps in the faculty contingent in many universities, where their positions were held open in the hope that they would eventually return, and there was a general mood of discouragement over the failure of reforms that had once held such promise.

Add to this the increasing economic pressures that universities experienced in the late 1980s, as inflation eroded the modest salaries of faculty and led to a situation where government funding covered only the basic salary requirements of keeping institutions open, leaving little or nothing for library and program development, equipment acquisition, and general maintenance. Universities found themselves forced into seeking new sources of income, in some cases on the basis of genuine academic expertise in teaching and research, in other cases not. The term "creating an income" (*chuangshou*) came to cover a variety of profit-making activities entered into by individuals, academic departments, and whole institutions.[8] Naturally, some individuals and departments were much more able than others to devise money-making schemes, resulting in great differences in income among faculty in different departments and fields. Similar gaps appeared among institutions, as those in fields of engineering, finance, foreign languages, and management were able to develop substantial independent incomes, while normal universities and agricultural universities fell more and more behind.[9]

The second half of the 1980s thus saw many problems develop, as Chinese universities sought to establish a new identity, yet found themselves engulfed by broader forces of change largely outside of their control. The evolution of the intellectual protest movement can be seen in relation to this general picture. The early protests in 1985 were high-minded and principled, relating to a perception that the political leadership was courting Japan and acceding to a new economic imperialism. By 1986 and 1987, the protests were more strongly grounded in local discontent, both discontent with management within the university community, and with the way in which local elections for people's congresses were being manipulated by party authorities. By 1989, there was considerable pessimism in the university community over the outcomes of both economic and political reform, with a sense that the problems of economic reform had to be understood in relation to increasingly evident political corruption and nepotism. This was one of the main themes of the democracy movement in April and May 1989.[10]

What surprised most observers in the aftermath of the Tiananmen tragedy, however, was the rapidity with which economic change continued, after a brief period of retrenchment, and in spite of little movement in terms of political reform. The new challenges this has created for universities will be dealt with in the final chapter of this volume.

This chapter will cover the same three themes that have informed earlier chapters: issues of curriculum and research, or the knowledge map; issues relating to the regional distribution of higher education, or the geographical map; and issues of female participation in higher education, or the gender map. In addition, there will be a consideration of the various external influences that affected this period. Since knowledge is at the heart of the university's identity, I will begin with a consideration of the main changes that took place in the university curriculum and the research role of the university over the 1980s.

CURRICULUM AND RESEARCH

Chinese higher institutions had been divided by sector and regimented according to centrally-devised curricular programs that had an almost law-like authority after 1952. Added to this was the fact that most major state projects of research were carried out either in institutes under the Chinese Academy of Sciences or under various state bureaus. Consequently there were few channels whereby new knowledge coming from research could exercise a continuing influence for revitalization over curricular content. The curriculum tended to be narrowly defined, almost canonical, and the dissemination of specialized knowledge was supervised by an army of political instructors who were to ensure that it never posed any threat to the legitimacy of the regime.

Two vital changes made it possible for universities with a measure of autonomy and some capacity for self-renewal to reemerge in the early 1980s. One was a new freedom over the content of programs and the latitude to establish new programs; the other was the restoration of research as a central mission and responsibility of the university. As noted earlier, these two changes was given formal expression in the reform document of 1985,[11] but by the early 1980s they had already become evident. With the increased autonomy experienced by university leaders in this period, a whole series of curricular changes was rapidly introduced. All of them represented a move away from narrow specialization, toward more integrative and comprehensive approaches to knowledge.

Comprehensive universities, which had been allowed only pure disciplines of the sciences and arts in 1952, developed a whole series of applied disciplines, as well as restoring such social sciences areas as sociology and anthropology, banned since the early 1950s. Polytechnical universities, with only applied engineering fields under the Soviet model, established departments of mathematics and basic sciences, as well as developing related social sciences such as management, scientific journalism, and demography. Specialized institutions in medicine and agriculture set up new programs in biology, medical sociology, agricultural management, and other related areas.

Most striking of all were the changes in political education. A new generation of young political instructors began to develop innovative teaching materials that used some of the new ideas emerging in the social sciences to redesign what had traditionally been highly didactic and rigid texts. For the first time, there seemed to be a possibility that political study could enter into a relationship of dialogue and mutual transformation with other fields of knowledge, rather than functioning as a kind of watchdog over the boundaries of specialized professional knowledge.[12]

Many changes also took place in the internal management of the curriculum, including the development of a modified credit system, whereby students were encouraged to choose courses both in areas related to their major fields and in areas of general cultural interest. Also, double major programs were organized for excellent students, and major/minor programs were arranged for students wishing to develop a second area of professional expertise. In some universities, colleges were established in order to group together related departments and foster cooperation in teaching and research across disciplines.

There were also changes in the macro-structure of the curriculum in terms of enrollment emphasis, with a considerable increase in the applied social sciences and in engineering. Between 1980 and 1990, enrollments in finance and economics grew from 3 percent to 13 percent of the total, law from 1 percent to 2 percent, and engineering from 34 percent to 37 percent. By contrast, agriculture dropped from 7 percent to 5 percent, medicine from 12 percent to 9 percent, education from 30 percent to 24 percent, and basic sciences from 7 percent to 4 percent. Humanities, a category that also includes such basic social sciences as history, philosophy, sociology, and anthropology, remained at 6 percent. These changes initially represented a balanced reassessment of professional employment needs, as well as a growing recognition of the importance of "soft sciences" in the change process. Lately, however, they reflected a kind of market response to student demand that had some disturbing dimensions.

Overall, it was a decade of considerable curricular experimentation, in which universities made choices in the development of new programs and the reform of old ones that were based both on academic concerns and on changing professional training needs arising from the economic reforms. In many cases, one of the stimuli for change came from a restored interest in their historical legacy, particularly that of the Nationalist period. In my book, *China's Universities and the Open Door*, which was written in 1987–1988, and based largely on interviews done in 1985, there is a detailed analysis of the overall patterns of curricular change, as well as examples drawn from particular institutions. The volume reflects the spirit of hope and optimism that was so evident at the time the research was done, though it had waned by the time the book was published early in 1989.

If the freedom to carry out curricular change was one of the essential conditions for the reemergence of university identities in China, the other was the reintroduction of research into the university community. This brought with it a different attitude toward knowledge, as something tentative, subject to constant questioning and change, rather than something canonical and absolute, to be accepted without discussion or question. Under the relaxed conditions of the early 1980s, many universities developed or restored research institutes on their campuses, and struggled to gain permission for new appointments to these institutes, where the main responsibility was for research. It became a general expectation that all faculty should spend about two-thirds of their time on teaching and one-third on research, while those in research institutes were expected to spend two-thirds of their time on research, one-third on teaching.

In the initial period, the main stimuli for research development were a concern to raise academic standards, aspirations to develop particular areas of strength that would enhance the unique identity of each university, and a degree of academic curiosity. What made possible a real flowering of university research was the availability of new funding sources distributed on the basis of the academic merit of proposals as judged by a panel of peers. This was a well-enough-known process in the West, but it was new to China, when the National Natural Sciences Foundation (NNSF) was established in 1986, modeled to some degree after the National Science and Engineering Research Council of Canada (NSERCC). In the same year, another very important source of funding became available for university researchers, and that was the High Technology Foundation, called the 86/3 Fund, due to the fact that it was approved by the state council in March 1986. It had higher levels of funding than the NNSF.

By 1990, universities had succeeded in capturing 70 percent of all funds distributed by the NNSF[13] and 36.7 percent of all funding for high-technology research dispensed by the 86/3 Fund,[14] a remarkable achievement in face of stiff competition with research institutes that had long been used to substantial state funding under successive five-year plans.[15] Universities also gained a considerable amount of research funding through application to other state sources, which continued to be dispensed by various ministries on the basis of the national or provincial agenda laid out in five-year plans. Peer review procedures were gradually adopted in decisions over the distribution of these funds as well.

New sources for funding of social science research were slower in coming, but in 1987, a national social sciences research foundation was established under the auspices of the Chinese Academy of Social Sciences (CASS). It also encouraged a free competition for funds, with projects judged on the basis of peer review, though its funds were limited compared to those for research in basic and applied sciences. In the aftermath of the Tiananmen events, when social science teaching and research fell under a cloud, this fund was transferred to the control of the Ministry of Propaganda, and tight political control was asserted. However, this phase was surprisingly short, as the importance of social research for ongoing economic change became more and more evident. By 1994, there were calls for an integration of the funding mechanisms for social and natural science research.[16]

Under these conditions for teaching and research, universities had taken on a new vitality by the mid-1980s, with each seeking to establish a particular knowledge and research identity, and to bring together in a new synthesis the fragmented dimensions of its past experience. While academic aspirations were strong, especially in national-level institutions, there was also a spirit of social responsibility, with interesting initiatives in adult education, projects in support of rural development, and twinnings with hinterland regions and institutions. In 1987, I did a study of Shanghai institutions that illustrated their efforts to balance ties to the international scholarly community with a continuing commitment to social and economic development in China.[17]

The combination of a new autonomy over curricular development and research and an ongoing yet increasingly independent mission of social responsibility was part of the background to the student democratic movement. Interesting comparisons might be made with Cai Yuanpei's curricular reforms at Beijing University, which had created conditions for the May 4th Movement in 1919. The many salons organized to discuss issues of social, cultural, and political change, and the creation of new adult education institutions like the Chinese Culture Academy, which reached 30,000 correspondent students with the new ideas being discussed in the university community,[18] all contributed to the movement.

However, as economic reform became more and more tenuous, and political non-reform more and more evident by the late 1980s, both curricular change and research development faced serious problems in Chinese universities. In place of the early enthusiasm for kinds of curricular innovation and integration that were based on scholarly considerations, a commercialization of the curriculum set in, with universities desperately seeking approval for new programs that would be likely to attract large numbers of self-paying students and so enhance university income. Whether they had the appropriate resources or not, most universities tried to set up programs in areas such as international trade, management, and foreign languages, which looked economically promising in the short term. Likewise, research was more and more oriented toward pragmatic links with enterprises, so-called "horizontal projects," that might have little academic value but could turn a quick profit. Sophisticated equipment purchased with World Bank funding in order to make possible high-quality basic research was often made available to commercial users at high prices in order to pay for its maintenance and bring in further income, leaving scholars who wished to use it for academic purposes waiting for access.

The political campaign that followed the Tiananmen events compounded these economic pressures, with new political restrictions on innovative work in teaching and research. The social sciences were particularly vulnerable, and both teaching and research were subject to campaigns of investigation carried out by party secretaries, many of whom were newly appointed to major national campuses in order to restore order and control. Teaching materials and course outlines in the humanities and social sciences were systematically investigated for traces of "bourgeois liberalism," and graduate theses and academic articles were subject to the same treatment.[19] New enrollments in the humanities and basic social sciences were also drastically cut in 1989, 1990, and 1991, with employment difficulties for graduates in these fields providing a useful excuse.[20] By contrast, programs in finance, management, and economics, which were seen as supportive of economic reform yet politically non-threatening, were allowed to flourish.

The new conservatism that followed the Tiananmen events was expressed in educational projections for the Eighth Five-Year Plan (1991–1995). They announced a strict limit on enrollment expansion in higher education, allowed for a greatly reduced number of self-paying students, and kept a particularly tight rein on enrollments in the basic social sciences.[21] However, what was perhaps most surprising about the aftermath of the Tiananmen events was the relative brevity of the period of increased political conservatism and control, and the speed with which economic change took off, beginning with Deng Xiaoping's journey to Shenzhen in February 1992.

By the summer of 1992, it was already evident that economic change demanded a rapid expansion in some areas of professional training, and there were enormous pressures from the provinces for enrollment expansion. The center soon gave in, and policy discussions moved to issues of how rapid expansion should be, and what correlation with yearly percentages of economic growth was appropriate. These issues will be dealt with in chapter 7, which looks at the Chinese university in the 1990s, and the choices that face it as it stands on the brink of a move toward mass higher education.

THE GEOGRAPHICAL MAP OF CHINESE HIGHER EDUCATION IN THE 1980S

We have noted earlier the long-standing concern among Chinese educators and politicians that modern higher education should be distributed evenly throughout the country, and should root itself effectively in the different regions of China. In many ways, it could be said that this concern was antithetical to the values of autonomy and academic freedom, which had meant that universities tended to establish themselves in major coastal cities, and remain aloof from the vast hinterland. By the Sino-Japanese War period, however, a level of maturity had been reached that enabled many nationalist universities to relocate to the hinterland under conditions where they continued to exercise considerable autonomy, and were also able to make linkages in teaching and research that gave them a definitive Chinese identity.

By contrast, the geographical reorganization of 1952 was a rather mechanistic affair, with institutional hierarchies set up in each of the six major regions that imitated the national hierarchy, and left universities with little possibility for independent initiative. Local initiatives in the Great Leap Forward period, which drew on dimensions of China's own progressive traditions, did much to change this, but the tenuous balance that emerged in the early 1960s was soon to be destroyed by the Cultural Revolution. Here, geography was used as a kind of punishment, with whole institutions banned to hinterland regions and remote rural areas where there simply were not the conditions for any genuine intellectual work to be done. The achievements of the 1950s, in ensuring a fair geographic distribution of the modern system of higher education, thus had rather frail and tenuous foundations.

Chapters 5 and 6 will explore two contrasting regions, the Central South and the Northwest, and the detailed picture they give of higher education and economic change over the reform decade indicates that the patterns of the 1950s did take root, in spite of the rigidities of the Soviet model. Where large gaps are now emerging is in the two new types of higher education that developed in response to economic change during the 1980s: the new vocational universities at the municipal level, and adult education institutions. Both of these depend on local economic resources, and it is not surprising to find great differences between their level of development in the Central South and the Northwest. Thus, of the 114 new vocational universities, forty-three are in East China, another twenty-nine in the Central South, and only eight in the Northwest.[22] Likewise, the development of adult higher education is far behind in the Northwest. Of the 1,256 adult higher institutions in existence in 1990, 325 (26 percent) were in East China, 249 (20 percent) in the Central South, and 101 (8 percent) in the Northwest.[23]

Other aspects of geographical disparity that are part of the story of the 1980s are the increasing gap between rural and urban students in terms of higher education entry. While rural students have maintained a relatively high rate of participation, they tend to be clustered in prefectural institutions serving their own regions, or in provincial and national institutions whose subject areas hold little appeal for urban youth: agriculture, teacher education, mining, and heavy industrial fields. Meanwhile, urban youth dominate enrollments in foreign languages, finance and trade, civil engineering, law, and political science, which have become more and more popular under the economic change process. These patterns are clear in the detailed statistics by region and institution presented in chapters 5 and 6. With the introduction of a larger and larger number of places for self-paying students in the 1990s, rural students in remote areas are likely to be more and more disadvantaged, although those in prosperous areas where successful industrialization is underway may benefit.

Perhaps the most significant change in terms of the geographical distribution of higher education over the reform decade has been the beginnings of greater freedom for graduates in seeking work, and also for university faculty in transferring within the university community or in leaving for jobs in other sectors. From about 1985, changes were initiated in the national unified job assignment system. Universities were given increasing opportunity to participate in decisions over the employment of their graduates though national conferences that brought together student affairs officers, officials of the State Education Commission (SEdC) and representatives of employing agencies.[24] The system that emerged was called one of "mutual selection," meaning that the university, acting on behalf of and sometimes in consultation with its students, recommended candidates for positions, while employing agencies chose those they wished. This innovation applied mainly to national institutions under the SEdC, while national ministry institutions continued to distribute the majority of their graduates according to sectoral plans. At provincial and local levels, graduates were almost always expected to return to the place they had come from, though they were sometimes able to move to a slightly better location or situation.

After the Tiananmen events, there was a tightening up of graduate job assignment for a brief period, ostensibly to ensure that the best graduates were protected and the use of back doors did not run rampant, and also to make possible the punishment of student activists through unfavorable job assignments, a practice that has had a long tradition under the socialist system. Students themselves have been ambivalent about the changes, as many feared greater choice would also mean greater freedom for some to take advantage of personal connections, and the marginalization of those who depended entirely on their professional qualifications for satisfactory jobs. The new freedoms have created particular problems for women graduates, and this will be discussed in the next section.[25]

In the reform document of 1993, which delineates the main directions for education in the 1990s and beyond, it is clearly stated that the state will no longer be responsible for the employment of all university graduates, but will select only a small number for positions in state organs at all levels. The rest will be expected to seek their own employment.[26] No statement is made about the issue of the residential permit, which constitutes the main constraint on university graduates seeking employment independently, and it is unclear how this problem will be dealt with. It seems likely that there will be much greater freedom for graduates of national institutions than for those at other levels, who will be expected to find employment in their own localities. Perhaps the greatest challenge of the market reforms and greater mobility of professional personnel will be that of geography. Chapters 5 and 6 show the problems already arising due to the outflow of graduates from peripheral provinces and regions. It seems unlikely that the state will allow the massive influx of professional talent from hinterland and rural areas into major coastal cities that would be likely to result from a complete lifting of restraints on geographical mobility at all levels of the higher education system. However, it will not be easy to restrain this, given the increasing reliance on market forces.

By the late 1980s, the mobility of university faculty had also become a concern. We have already noted the tendency for young faculty in major urban centers to go abroad for graduate study, with very few intending to return. Compounding this by the late 1980s was the attraction of joint venture and other new commercial opportunities for university teachers. There are no accurate statistics, but it is well known that a considerable number have either moved or changed careers.[27] The pattern that seems to be emerging is one where coastal institutions are losing faculty to new careers in business, then seeking to replace them by arranging transfers for faculty from hinterland institutions. This group is eager to improve its geographical location, and is attracted to the large coastal cities. The situation leaves hinterland institutions suffering a severe brain drain, particularly in areas like engineering, management, and economics.[28] As we will see in chapter 6, many institutions in the Northwest reported in 1993 that they were unsuccessful even in employing their own graduate students as young faculty in these areas, since the opportunities elsewhere were so compelling.

In addition, hinterland institutions face a situation where their backbone faculty contingent is now reaching retirement age. These were the heroic youth who volunteered to go to the hinterland and serve in newly developing institutions in the mid-1950s, a part of the story told in chapter 3. As they prepare for retirement, many of them plan to return to the coastal areas, and in many cases their children have preceded them in this return migration.

A further twist on this geographical shift that is taking place lies in the fact that it is men, far more than women, who are leaving the hinterland regions, and also leaving the university for other careers. The result is an increasingly high percentage of women among younger faculty ranks. It is also true that a far larger number of men have gone abroad for further study than women, due to various kinds of discrimination that make it more difficult for women professionals to pursue such opportunities.

To conclude these comments on the geographical map in the 1980s, perhaps we could say that the formal higher education system has proven itself reasonably well, in terms of continued geographical representation. This will become evident in chapters 5 and 6, which give a detailed picture of the Central South and the Northwest, and some insights into the situation facing centers and peripheries within these two regions. However, newly developing kinds of higher education, both vocational universities and adult institutions, are dependent on the local economy, and thus reflect increasing geographical imbalances.[29] Compounding this is a kind of ongoing internal brain drain, with large numbers of graduates and faculty leaving hinterland areas for opportunities in coastal regions.

THE GENDER MAP

The situation for women faculty and students in higher education over the reform decade in many ways reflects the overall mood of change that has been described earlier. Up to the middle 1980s, women's participation in formal higher education improved rapidly, from 24 percent in the year that national entry examinations were reinstated, to 30 percent by 1985, and subsequently to 33.7 percent in 1990.[30] At the graduate level, women student participation rose from 9.9 percent in 1980, to 23 percent in 1990, but at the doctoral level, they represented only 10.6 percent of students enrolled in 1990.[31] Unfortunately, we do not have national statistics for female participation in adult higher education.

Women faculty have increased their representation in the total faculty contingent from 25 percent to 29.1 percent over the reform decade, and there is increasing evidence of a higher and higher female representation among younger faculty, 37 percent of those under thirty, and 30 percent of those between thirty-one and forty in 1991.[32] This reflects the tendency for a larger number of male faculty to go abroad, and to be attracted into new careers in business in the late 1980s and early 1990s. Women thus seem to have won their greater representation in faculty ranks as much by default as by active struggle. Their future career development in the university context is threatened by the fact that relatively few of them have master's and doctoral degrees, compared to their male counterparts. They are in a situation where they will be expected to take on heavy teaching loads, and be responsible for routine administration at the lowest level, instead of being able to compete on an equal basis with male colleagues for promotion. The fact that promotion rules in the university now stress formal graduate degrees and research publication puts women at a particular disadvantage.

Since the mid-1980s, women graduates have faced increasing discrimination in employment, as the centralized job allocation system has been modified to allow for greater and greater autonomy on the part of employing agencies over the recruitment process. Given the fact that there exists no national health system (health and maternity provision is the responsibility of the employing unit), and all productive units are under increasing pressure to raise their profit level, naturally there is a strong preference for employing male graduates. Even state institutions in the areas of health, education, and other social areas tend to prefer male graduates on the grounds that there will be fewer disruptions in their professional work and they can be more easily sent on out-of-town assignments, among other reasons.[33]

A new law protecting women's rights was passed by the National People's Congress (NPC) in 1992, which specified that "schools and pertinent departments should ensure that females and males are treated equally when it comes to starting school, progressing from a lower-level school to a higher one, assigning jobs on graduation, awarding academic degrees, and selecting people for overseas study."[34] In a sense, this particular clause was outdated before the law was even passed, as schools have less and less con-

trol over the employment of their graduates. Another section of the law speci-
fies that "Except for certain work categories or positions that are unfit for
women, no unit should refuse to hire women, or set a higher threshold for
hiring women on the sheer basis of sex."[35] The problem with this clause is
both the loopholes it contains, and the fact that there are no organs to ensure the implementation of the law.[36]

While young university graduates are in a particularly vulnerable situation, women faculty also face considerable difficulties. As their profession
becomes feminized, with higher education teaching being one of the areas
that is most accessible to women graduates, their status is at risk. While an
increasing percentage of the faculty under thirty are women, few of them
have the qualifications needed for promotion through the ranks. The rem-
edy being adopted by faculty development offices at universities is to arrange
a program of inservice training for their young faculty that enables them to
take a certain number of graduate courses without doing a thesis or achieving a graduate degree. This basic graduate qualification is a minimal requirement for promotion to the position of lecturer, but further promotion up
the ranks to associate or full professor requires a graduate degree.[37] Thus a
whole category of young faculty is taking shape, the majority of them
women, who will carry heavy teaching and administration loads, while lacking the opportunity for career development.

Meanwhile, women make up only 9.2 percent of the national contingent of 17,087 full professors,[38] and the likelihood of a rapid improvement in representation at this level is slight. Fewer women have graduate
degrees, either from China or from abroad. Far fewer have gone abroad than
men, and fewer still have returned. Among those who have returned, many
are unwilling to accept responsibility for administrative leadership,[39] so this
road to promotion is not promising.

A considerable literature has developed by and about Chinese women,
which indicates that the problems they face may come not only from new
barriers to participation emerging with the market reforms, but also from a
certain lack of resolve within themselves, and a degree of eagerness to take
up feminine roles, earlier denied to them, under the greater personal freedom of the reform era. Chinese feminists such as Li Xiaozhang at Zhengzhou
University are struggling to define and develop a vision for Chinese professional women that will stimulate them to struggle for equal participation.
Li affirms the remarkable advances women made under socialism since the
1950s, but believes that women themselves have never identified fully with
the changes made by the state on their behalf. It was as if the state took over
from the patriarchal family in determining women's lot.[40] Only in the 1980s

did Chinese women themselves begin to define their problems and work toward solutions.[41]

Li is a professor in a provincial university and the founder of a women's college and museum, while at the same time being an activist in many areas relating to women's rights. She is thus squarely in the tradition of the Chinese intellectual, blending the desire for intellectual freedom, a space in which women can develop their own perspectives, with a strong sense of social responsibility. In the preparation for the U.N. Conference on Women, held in Beijing in September 1995, there was considerable tension between professional women such as Li, who were seeking an independent voice, and women who continued to function largely as mouthpieces of the state in its pronouncements on women's issues. The issues of autonomy and academic freedom thus have a particular relevance for the women's movement that is taking shape in newly established research institutes in a few major universities.

Minority women face some particular challenges as both students and faculty. Given that they are officially allowed more than one child, and therefore need longer maternity leave time, they are likely to experience even greater discrimination than women from the majority Han nationality in the professional employment market. Both faculty and students also face greater hurdles when seeking opportunities for graduate study or study abroad, since proficiency in English or another international language is usually required for graduate school entry in China, and it is essential for study abroad. Given that they already have had to learn Chinese, in addition to their own language, and that Chinese is usually the only medium through which they can learn English or another foreign language, the demands on their linguistic ability are considerable.

Some attention is given to minority issues in chapter 6, the regional study of higher education in Northwest China, where there is a large minority population. From a geographical perspective, one fascinating point of difference between minority and Han students and faculty is that they are less likely to be attracted to coastal areas. Thus, opportunities for minority students and faculty in institutions in their own areas are increasing by a kind of default, with the escalating brain drain of faculty and students to coastal areas underway. There are interesting parallels here with the women's situation. Vigorous self-assertion on the part of women and minority professionals seems to be called for.

CHINESE UNIVERSITIES AND THE INTERNATIONAL MILIEU

An important part of the reemerging identity of Chinese universities in the

1980s was the role they played in helping China reconnect to an international milieu after a decade of isolation during the Cultural Revolution. Perhaps one of the important reasons that considerable support was given to higher education, enabling it to expand rapidly and gain a growing autonomy in certain areas, was the leadership's realization of a need for people who could build bridges to the world outside. Together with this realization, of course, was a continuing determination to maintain political control, often justified in terms of cultural autonomy and national pride. As in the late Qing and under the Soviet patterns, there was a continuing impulse to limit higher education to the creation of a technical intelligentsia, which would be instrumentally useful. There was little tolerance for the broader kinds of cultural and social critique that emerged as Chinese intellectuals introduced new ideas and opened up a many-faceted dialogue with members of an international community of universities. One dimension of the tensions that exploded in the Tiananmen events of 1989 had doubtless been built up through intensive international involvement.

It will not be possible in this section to do justice to the full range of international activities entered into by universities over the reform decade, but an overview of various types and categories of activity, and some reflections on their importance in relation to the newly emerging identities of universities, may be useful. A general distinction between multilateral and bilateral types of interaction is helpful, with multilateral relating mainly to institutions associated with the United Nations, and bilateral to national level linkages, that have distinctive cultural, economic, and geopolitical implications in each case. My focus will be on those interactions that have had the most significant impact, and also to an extent on those with which I have some personal familiarity.

In terms of multilateral international institutions, a distinction needs to be made between such United Nations organizations as UNESCO, UNDP, UNFPA on the one hand, and the World Bank on the other. The former reflect the broad U.N. constituency, with every country having a vote, large or small, and a situation where countries of the "South" have succeeded in asserting themselves more and more in terms of economic and cultural perspectives through campaigns such as the New International Economic Order in the 1970s and the New World Information Order in the 1980s.[42] By contrast, the World Bank is directed by a board of governors representing the major industrialized countries that donate to the Bank, with the president always being American. The World Bank's relation to China is thus embedded in a different and less reciprocal set of relations than that of other U.N. agencies.[43]

In spite of this reality of international power relations, the Chinese government has succeeded in asserting a relatively high degree of control over decisions concerning World Bank projects in China, and has even had some impact in shaping the direction of World Bank lending more widely.[44] This is particularly the case with regard to higher education. Whereas the bank had emphasized support for basic education and some secondary technical education in its loans up to the early 1980s,[45] the Chinese were successful in persuading it to give a primary focus to higher education in loans to China over the decade. Subsequently, higher education in other developing countries gained increasing support through World Bank loans, while in China the focus of World Bank educational aid gradually shifted to lower levels within the education hierarchy.

Total World Bank loans to Chinese education have amounted to about 1.2 billion U.S. dollars over the decade.[46] Given the scale of this input, it has naturally been managed in a rather bureaucratic way, with the Ministry of Finance having overall supervision, a loan office in the State Education Commission overseeing the disbursement of loans to all institutions at the national level, and similar offices in provincial education commissions responsible for the oversight of projects at the provincial level. In my 1989 study, I mapped both the geographical and sectoral distribution of the first eight major World Bank projects in education, all of which dealt with higher institutions. It was fascinating to see how the system managed a fairly equitable distribution of resources by sector and region, with national comprehensive and polytechnic universities getting in on the first project, agricultural universities on the second, municipal and provincial vocational and television universities on the third, sectoral institutions in the areas of medicine and agriculture next, followed by sectoral institutions in engineering, finance, and law, then provincial universities.[47] Clearly, the opening of a door to the World Bank had set in motion an intense lobbying process at all levels and in all sectors of the system, with each asserting its right to a share.

Subsequent to these eight projects, which I have already documented in detail, there have been another five projects, which have mainly focused on the grass-roots level. Two that were approved in 1989 provided assistance for the improvement of textbooks and for vocational and technical education at the secondary level. A third, approved in 1992, supported integrated educational development at all levels for a defined group of poor provinces, including Guizhou, Hubei, Hunan, Shaanxi, Shanxi, and Yunnan. At the level of higher education, it encouraged the amalgamation of small and often specialized local colleges into larger and more comprehensive higher institutions. A fourth, entitled "Effective Teaching Services," and approved in 1993, provided extensive support to the lowest level within the Chinese higher education system, the prefectural teacher training colleges that train teachers for rural secondary schools. Altogether, 124 institutions in fifteen provinces, as well as provincial and county education bureaus, have been involved.[48]

While the main emphasis in the projects of the late 1980s and early 1990s has been on developmental aspects of education, universities managed to gain continued support through a project entitled "key studies," which provided funds for centers of excellence in scientific disciplines in universities and research institutes under the Chinese Academy of Sciences (CAS) across the country. A total of 133 laboratories located in forty-four universities and twenty-two institutes of CAS gained support for the purchase of equipment, library resources, and assistance in management. Many of these laboratories are open, with international scholars, as well as scholars from other parts of China, involved in their projects, and they have a particularly important role in doctoral and post-doctoral training. They have also been intended to provide good working conditions for young scholars returning from abroad with doctoral degrees and seeking a suitable environment for high-level scientific research.

In some ways, World Bank projects in higher education have been closely supervised and subject to highly bureaucratic processes of implementation. In other ways, however, there has been considerable freedom for international initiatives by participating universities, with most projects providing for a considerable number of faculty and staff to spend time studying and doing research abroad, and for a large number of international specialists to visit and support curricular and research development. While the latter activity was often supervised by international advisory panels mandated to ensure that well-qualified international scholars would be appointed to visit project universities, there was a great deal of latitude in each institution to decide on whom it would send abroad, where they would go, and what kind of activities they would undertake. This has had some unfortunate consequences, particularly with regard to the large number of younger faculty who went abroad and did not return, but on the positive side it allowed universities considerable autonomy in the emphasis they placed on particular fields, the countries chosen for study visits, and the range of contacts and networks that were set up.

It would be difficult in a few sentences to summarize the substantial contribution made to Chinese universities by these World Bank projects. However, much of the curricular innovation that has been described earlier in the chapter would not have been possible without a considerable input from scholars who had been abroad under various bank-supported projects. In addition, each project had a substantial component for library development that has been crucial to the development of more flexible teaching methods and also of graduate thesis work. On the research side, it is almost certain that Chinese universities could not have been so successful in competing for important national projects and sources of funding, if they had not benefited from the purchase of significant amounts of scientific research equipment, computer systems, and testing and analysis laboratories under bank projects. Also, for the first time, Chinese scientific publications have achieved a modest visibility in the international scholarly literature, second only to India among Third World countries.[49]

In contrast to World Bank projects, cooperative projects funded by agencies such as UNESCO, UNDP, UNFPA and UNICEF[50] in China have been small in scale and focused on particular developmental goals related to their area of responsibility. These agencies have a fairly diffuse presence within many different governmental offices and provide a wide range of opportunities for university scholars to participate in regional or international projects of mutual learning and enhancement. Universities have been active in these projects, and in many cases have become involved in linkages with an Asian developmental community that differs considerably from those to the developed industrial world that dominate both World Bank projects and bilateral developmental projects. In areas such as population study, agricultural reform, and women's issues, China is regarded as having valuable experience and its scholars may take leadership roles in these U.N. projects. To a certain degree, China has been able to build upon some dimensions of a reputation for independence, self-reliance, and cultural autonomy, which was built up during the Cultural Revolution, in these relationships.[51]

If we turn now to bilateral projects, it may be useful to divide them into two broad categories also. On the one hand are projects of educational, cultural, and academic exchange, often organized under the terms of cooperation agreements between two governments, and usually expressing in identifiable ways both the cultural patterns and the foreign policy objectives of the country in question. On the other side are developmental projects, under the auspices of the overseas development aid programs that most major industrialized nations have adopted, and that often serve economic and trade aims quite directly, as well as being subordinate to foreign policy objectives. These tend to have higher levels of funding, but less autonomy in terms of field and subject area than educational exchange programs. Most of the major industrialized nations engage in both types of interaction with China, with the exception of the United States, which has a large number of educational and cultural exchange agreements, but so far has not included China in the activities of the United States Agency for International Development (AID). These two types of project provide different kinds of opportunity and different constraints for Chinese universities.

Through participating in activities arranged under national cultural and educational agreements, Chinese universities become involved in a complex and fascinating set of cultural dynamics, which often express some continuity with historical precedents, making possible the creative use of scholarly communities in China that have long historic links with particular foreign countries. Perhaps the most striking example of this is found in the restoration of relations between Germany and China. Tongji University, which was founded by German industrialists early in the century, quickly became a major actor in this process, and developed an identity shaped to a considerable degree by these connections. Somewhat more muted continuities can be seen in institutions with historic links to the American missionary movement, in spite of the systematic dismantling of missionary institutions carried out in 1952.

Most countries involved in bilateral agreements of exchange needed either a disciplinary or a geographic focus, given the limited nature of the resources that they could dedicate. Some countries have supported diffuse interactions, encouraging a multitude of institutional-level linkages; others have preferred a more centralized approach, providing substantial support to one or several centers that, in turn, reached out to their communities. The French strategy of comprehensive cooperation with one center, Wuhan University, as a primary focus, is described in more detail in chapter 5. By contrast, the British have set up a number of regional centers, with a mandate for educating teachers of English language, linguistics, literature, and culture in major Chinese universities. The Canadian approach has been even more diffuse, supporting small Canadian studies centers in many universities all over the country, and providing multiple opportunities for university scholars to make research visits to Canada.[52]

My interest in watching these projects over the years has been in reflecting on how and in what ways they have supported Chinese universities in the forging of a new identity. Perhaps one of the most important ways has been in making it possible for scholars to enter into kinds of cooperation aimed at long-term cultural and social understanding, rather than specific and often short-term economic development concerns. This has been diverse and varied, involving translations, historical, literary, and sociological research, the teaching of new courses with the sponsorship of specific countries, and a planned infusion of appropriate books and audiovisual materials, etc. The kinds of cultural understanding fostered by these projects has almost certainly contributed to the lively atmosphere of social and cultural criticism that characterized the salons organized by students and teachers to discuss reform issues in the late 1980s.

This aspect of cultural exchange therefore came to be perceived as a direct threat by Chinese authorities after the Tiananmen events.[53] However, its importance for fostering a genuine cultural autonomy can hardly be overemphasized. It has made possible some critical reflection on the cultural, educational, and social patterns that have been an integral part of economic and political development in the West.[54] A thorough understanding of these interconnections is the essential foundation for adapting knowledge from the West to the Chinese context. A major difficulty of the Chinese environment in this regard has been the way in which the principle of cultural autonomy has been held up by political authorities for purposes of legitimating their own power base. This has made it difficult for the intellectual community to envision a genuine cultural autonomy and open themselves seriously to the critical literature on Western experience.

Western scholars are usually the most convincing critics of their own societies, as illustrated in the work of Max Weber, Juergen Habermas, and others from the Frankfurt school. Yet it has not been easy for the Chinese scholarly community to gain access to this kind of literature, due both to the constraints imposed by their own government, and the narrow developmental intentions of much foreign aid. Bilateral educational and cultural exchanges provide the best opportunity for this kind of interaction.[55] I have argued elsewhere that Habermas's notion of communicative action might be applied to international educational relations. His distinction among three important arenas of knowledge, instrumental-technical, aesthetic-practical, and moral-practical and their respective validity claims could be used to create an evaluative framework for processes of knowledge transfer that would measure the degree to which all three realms were represented, and the extent to which mutual enhancement of understanding resulted.[56]

Finally, let me turn briefly to the various kinds of bilateral development project that have involved Chinese universities in one way or another over the decade. While the cultural arm of foreign policy is often subtle and indirect, development aid projects that act as a kind of economic arm of foreign policy are often more direct and self-interested. They also tend to reflect the economic health of the donor nation to a certain degree. Thus the economic slowdown experienced by OECD nations in the late 1980s was expressed in aid projects to China in the form of an increasing emphasis on areas of likely mutual economic benefit in terms of trade and investment.

Japan has been one of the largest donor nations, with a wide range of projects supported by the Japan International Cooperation Agency (JICA). These have focused on technical training, usually in work experience programs in Japan, and on management training, with a large center set up in Tianjin in cooperation with the State Economic Commission. There have also been many large infrastructural projects related to the modernization of railways, port facilities, energy, and telecommunications. Projects in health have focused on the Friendship Hospital built by the Japanese in Beijing. Neither Japanese nor Chinese universities have been offered the opportunity for extensive participation in these aid projects, perhaps because of the type of development undertaken in China, and the fact that there are few links between the university community and JICA in Japan itself. However, a large number of educational exchange projects, generously supported by other agencies within the Japanese government and involving extensive university level links, cooperative research projects, and a range of opportunities for Chinese scholars to study in Japan, might be seen as complementary to these aid projects.[57]

The Canadian case provides an interesting contrast to the Japanese. Here there has been much greater cooperation between the university community and many aspects of developmental aid projects, with one of the core emphases of projects under the Canadian International Development Agency (CIDA) being on the development of human resources through a range of training programs. With CIDA support, Canadian universities and colleges entered into three extensive university linkage network projects during the 1980s, one providing for cooperation in a diverse set of disciplinary areas from engineering to the social sciences, a second focusing on management education, and a third bringing together Canadian community colleges and Chinese vocational and technical universities in parallel regions within the two countries. Altogether, more than a hundred universities and colleges in both countries became involved.[58] While each project was required to have a specific and well-defined set of developmental goals, this did not preclude a considerable amount of intellectually stimulating interaction around areas of shared academic interest.[59]

European policies have also encouraged considerable university involvement in various developmental projects, with Britain perhaps being the best example. In addition to the British studies centers and English-language training for university teachers that receive ongoing support in major national universities in China, provision is made for about 400 Chinese scholars to do graduate study in Britain every year.[60] About half of the funds for this come from overseas development assistance budgets, though they are administered by the British Council alongside of their own scholarship program and various other academic linkage programs. Similar patterns can be found in France and Germany, though they also have extensive developmental assistance programs that operate outside of the university community as well. Other European countries, Australia, and New Zealand also have a diverse set of development projects with China that involve universities, and a few examples will appear in chapters 5 and 6.

The challenge for Chinese universities in their participation in these developmental projects is to find ways in which they can make use of the research and training opportunities both in China and abroad to build their own renewed identities and strengthen their capacity to contribute in an independent yet socially responsible way to Chinese society. An interesting focal point for the evaluation of these projects, I would suggest, is the degree to which they offer opportunities for broader social and cultural understanding in addition to the specific developmental goals that are a given in this kind of cooperation.

In the wake of the Tiananmen events, many of the diverse interactions with universities abroad that had become a vital part of the process of forging new identities in Chinese universities came under threat. In some cases, the Chinese government took action in protest against what they felt to be unwelcome influences from Western countries in Chinese university programs. The cessation of the Fulbright scholarship program with the United States for the year 1989–1990 was an example of this.[61] In most cases, it was a matter of foreign governments' deciding to express their disapproval of the Chinese government's conduct toward students and citizens through the suspension of various programs. Cultural programs were often a less costly sacrifice than economic or developmental ones. Probably France took the strongest stand in terms of cultural and educational relations, providing for 3,000 Chinese scholars already in France to stay long-term, and suspending most of their normal exchange activities.[62] The Canadian government took a different approach, maintaining and increasing educational and cultural exchange programs, while canceling a certain number of CIDA projects that might have military or police applications, and delaying the renewal of favorable financing arrangements for economic projects.

As cultural attaché in the Canadian embassy over the two years following the Tiananmen events, I had a unique opportunity to visit universities and discuss aspects of international academic cooperation. In many quiet discussions with scholars over the Tiananmen events, it was interesting to note a deep ambivalence. On the one hand, they were greatly concerned at the possible consequences of a renewed isolation, as universities came under tight political surveillance and many international projects were suspended.[63] They were particularly appreciative of Canadian efforts to increase academic cooperation and university-level linkages. On the other hand, they sensed the symbolic importance of the strong stand taken by French authorities in their condemnation of the Chinese leadership and their suspension of most educational exchange activity. They were glad that one high-profile Western country had chosen this particular response to the situation.

Perhaps this ambivalence in itself is indicative of the central issue that I am trying to explore in this account of Chinese universities, the fact that the ethos of Chinese universities must find its own expression and identity in the modern period. This is likely to lie somewhere between the autonomy and academic freedom that have been the ideal for universities linked to the European tradition on the one hand, and the values that have been identified earlier as defining patterns of the Chinese tradition.

It is unlikely, if not impossible, that Chinese scholars will fully embrace the notion of academic freedom for the same reason that gave Cai Yuanpei such difficulty in introducing the concept to Beijing University in 1917. The tradition of an integrated view of knowledge that emphasizes practical social and political action, and also of intellectual authority and scholarly participation in government, precludes a commitment to academic freedom with the connotations of the neutrality of theoretical knowledge and a detachment from direct political and social involvement that characterized the concept in European history.

What Chinese scholars and Chinese universities are seeking, I would argue, is the possibility of an intellectual freedom, integrally linked to social responsibility, along some kind of continuum that affirms a nexus of connections among academic, social, and political spheres. In place of university autonomy, in the clear-cut sense in which it has found political and legal protection within Western societies, they are looking for something that allows both more involvement in the affairs of state,[64] and the possibility of a more comprehensive critical oversight of the polity.

The vivid and detailed account of the Tiananmen events provided by George Black and Robin Munro in their account of the lives of Chen Zimin and Wang Juntao provides an illustration of the difficult dilemma facing Chinese intellectuals in the social sciences up to the present.[65] Trusted at one point to manage a correspondence program that involved more than 200,000 students in the adult higher education sector,[66] these two scholars made a striking contribution to the most sensitive intellectual field of all, that of political science, in the Chinese context. The large number of translations of classic Western volumes on the subject, combined with commentary and discussion that attempted to make connections with the Chinese context, was one important aspect of their work. Another was the extensive survey work that provided path-breaking insights into changing political and social attitudes in the Chinese population.

Perhaps the most poignant part of this story of two scholars who ended up being labeled the "black hands" behind the student movement is that depicting the difficult choice they had to make in the final days before the movement ended in tragedy. Should they throw their support behind the students on the square or not? Aware of the volatility and immaturity of the student leadership, also that an open identification with the demands of the students would compromise permanently the project of independent social research they had worked so hard to develop, they nevertheless felt there was no alternative. Scholars facing a similar dilemma in the West might well have made a different choice. The difference, I would argue, could be at least partially due to the differing scholarly traditions of Europe and China. I thus tend to agree with the view presented in the opening section of this chapter, which sees the problems and achievements of Chinese intellectuals in the 1980s in the context of particularities of China's intellectual and political tradition.

The modern Chinese university is seeking to forge an identity and role that has its own unique constellation of social, cultural, economic, and political relations. In the final chapter of this volume I will try to anticipate both the possibilities that may be particular to its scholarly culture, and the problems that could beset its future development. Meanwhile, we turn to portraits of two contrasting regions during the reform decade, the Central South and the Northwest. These chapters are intended to provide details that complement and illustrate the rather broad lines of analysis offered in this chapter, and they contain information that will be of particular interest to the specialist in Chinese education and society. Readers who are interested mainly in the general picture may wish to move directly to chapter 7 at this point.

NOTES

1. Tony Saich, "The Reform Decade in China: The Limits to Revolution from Above," in Tony Saich and Marta Dassu (eds.), *The Reform Decade* (London: Kegan Paul International, 1992), pp. 10–73.

2. Marie Claire Bergère, "Tiananmen 1989: Background and Consequences," in Saich and Dassu (eds.), *The Reform Decade*, pp. 132–150.

3. Merle Goldman, *Sowing the Seeds of Democracy in China: Political Reform in the Deng Xiaoping Era* (Cambridge, Mass.: Harvard University Press, 1994).

4. There is considerable evidence in the university community of the importance of Zhou Enlai's diplomatic vision in this period. For example, it was an important time for the development of foreign language institutes, with the Guangzhou Institute of Foreign Languages set up in 1964, and students were sent to various countries of both Western and Eastern Europe. Another interesting initiative was the establishment of centers for research on various Western countries. For example, Wuhan University was given direct encouragement by Zhou Enlai to set up a research institute on the North American economy in the early 1960s, and it has continued up to the present.

5. Shirin Rai, *Resistance and Reaction: University Politics in Post-Mao China* (Hemel Hempstead: Harvester Wheatsheaf and St. Martin's Press, 1991), pp. 65–70, has an interesting discussion of this, the main problem being what is defined as "political," and the fact that all important decisions tend to have a political element in the Chinese context.

6. A survey of university students in fifteen higher institutions in the central city of Wuhan, made in 1990, indicates considerable anxiety on the part of students over how far ability and achievement will determine their employment prospects in the wake of these reforms. See Tian Jinghai, Gong Yizhou, and Peng Jun, "Daxue biyesheng de xintai diaocha fenxi," [Analysis of a Survey of University Graduates' State of Mind] in *Gaodeng shifan jiaoyu yanjiu* [Higher Normal Education Research] 2 (Feb., 1992): 41–48; also in *Gaodeng jiaoyu* [Higher Education] (People's University Abstracting Service, September 1992): 61–68.

7. A particularly large number were in the United States. See Leo A. Orleans, *Chinese Students in America: Policies, Issues, and Numbers* (Washington, D.C.: National Academy Press, 1988).

8. For an excellent analysis of the effects of this commercialization of the system, see Yin Qiping and Gordon White, "The 'Marketization' of Chinese Higher Education: A Critical Assessment," in *Comparative Education*, Vol. 30, no. 3, 1994, pp. 217–237.

9. See Rai, *Resistance and Reaction*, pp. 75–78, for a useful discussion of these developments.

10. Ruth Cherrington, *China's Students: The Struggle for Democracy* (London: Routledge and Kegan Paul, 1991), provides a useful overview of the successive sets of demonstrations from the students' perspective.

11. "Decision of the Communist Party of China Central Committee on the Reform of the Education System," May 27, 1985, in *FBIS*, no. 104, May 30, 1985, p. K7.

12. I came to this conclusion after reviewing a large number of political education texts developed in the mid- to late 1980s. See R. Hayhoe, "Political Texts in Chinese Universities Before and After Tiananmen," in *Pacific Affairs*, Vol. 66, no. 1 (Spring 1993).

13. *Zhongguo jiaoyubao*, February 3, 1990, p. 1.

14. Beijing *Xinhua* in English, September 30, 1991, *FBIS*, no. 191, October 2, 1991.

15. For a fuller discussion of university research, see R. Hayhoe, "China's Universities Since Tiananmen: A Critical Assessment," in *China Quarterly*, no. 134 (June 1993): 302–308.

16. See Hu Yicheng, "Qiantan woguo shehui kexue yanjiu tizhi gaige," [A Preliminary Discussion of Reforms to the System of Social Science Research in China], in *Zhongguo jiaoyubao*, October 19, 1994, p. 3.

17. R. Hayhoe, "Shanghai as a Mediator of the Educational Open Door," in *Pacific Affairs*, Vol. 61, no. 2 (June 1988).

18. I visited the Chinese Cultural Academy in the autumn of 1989, while working at the embassy, and had a good talk with Professor Tang Yijie and his assistants, who gave me a full set of the books and journals produced by the academy in its hey-

day of influence. These ranged over comparative culture, literature, history, law, and society. In the spring I met Liang Congjie, who was trying to revive aspects of the work of the academy, and was responsible for a project to create a video record of some of China's well-known older scholars. They had been successful in making videos of both Liang Shuming and Feng Yulan shortly before their deaths.

19. Si Hua, "Renzhen qingli zichan jieji ziyouhua sichao zai xueke lingyu de yingxiang," [Thoroughly Purge the Influences of the Tide of Bourgeois Liberalism over Academic Fields," in *Zhongguo gaodeng jiaoyu* [Chinese Higher Education], no. 11 (1991): 26–27.

20. R. Hayhoe, "The Context of Educational Reform," in *China Exchange News*, Vol. 20, no. 1, March 1992, pp. 3–9.

21. R. Hayhoe, "China's Universities Since Tiananmen," pp. 291–296.

22. Department of Planning and Construction, State Education Commission, P.R.C., *Educational Statistics Yearbook of China, 1990* (Beijing: People's Education Press, 1991), p. 132.

23. Ibid., pp. 294–5.

24. For a detailed analysis of changes in the job assignment system for university graduates, see R. Hayhoe, "Student Enrollment and Job Assignment Issues," *China News Analysis*, no. 1481, March 15, 1993.

25. For an excellent discussion of the post-Tiananmen situation, see Shirin Rai, *Resistance and Reaction*, pp. 175–184.

26. "State Issues New Development Program," Beijing *Xinhua Domestic Service in Chinese* in *FBIS*, no. 40 (March 3, 1993): 17–32.

27. Bai Zhou, "Guanyu dangqian gaodeng xuexiao shizi duiwu xianzhuang de diaocha baogao," [Report on a Survey Concerning the Contemporary Situation of the Faculty Contingent in Higher Institutions], in *Zhongguo gaodeng jiaoyu*, no. 12, 1993:21–22. This survey covered 121 higher institutions in twenty-two provinces, and indicates an overall loss of faculty due to all causes, including retirement, as 16.5 percent between 1990 and 1992. New appointments were at 15.6 percent over the same period. While 61 percent of graduate students went into faculty positions in 1990, and 68 percent in 1992, many subsequently left their university for other jobs, 9.8 percent for joint ventures, 12.4 percent for positions in government bureaus, 19.6 percent for positions in state enterprises, and 57.6 percent to move to other higher institutions. On the geographical side, 75 percent remained in their own region, 18.2 percent moved from hinterland to coastal areas, and 6.1 percent moved from coastal areas inland. This information makes possible a considerable nuancing of the trends as perceived by worried university administrators.

28. Bao Changhai, Chen Qiang, and Liu Yuecheng, "Liaozhu lei de huiyi" [Recollections that Cause Tears to Flow], in *Zhongguo jiaoyu bao*, October 20, 1994, p. 3. This article reports the situation at Jiamusi Engineering College in Heilongjiang, where 97.5 percent of younger faculty who had been supported by the college in gaining master's degrees had already left.

29. Wang Ruilan, Zhang Hui, and Jiang Bo, "Gaodeng jiaoyu fei junheng fazhan de xianshi sikao" [Realistic Reflections on the Uneven Development of Higher Education] in *Jiaoyu yanjiu* [Educational Research], no. 4, 1993, pp. 46–48, 59. This article offers a justification for unequal geographical development in the future, based on the personnel needs of the more rapid economic development taking place in coastal areas, and also the need to have a certain number of institutions, around 100, which reach international standards of scholarship.

30. Unfortunately, we do not have national statistics for female participation by field, but statistics for Sichuan province show the rapid increase in social science enrollments, relative to the whole, favored women's participation, while there continued also to be high female participation in such areas as medicine and the basic sciences. See Sheng Shihan, Zheng Xinrong, Liu Huizhen, and Xu Xuedong, "Participation of Women in Higher Education in China," in Regional Co-

Operative Programme in Higher Education for Development in Asia and the Pacific (ed.), *Women's Participation in Higher Education: China, Nepal, and the Philippines* (Bangkok: UNESCO Principal Regional Office for Asia and the Pacific, 1991), p. 53.

31. All statistics on participation are drawn from the educational statistic yearbooks that have been put out by the State Education Commission every year since 1985, in addition to earlier compilations covering 1949–1983, then 1980 to 1985. An increasingly detailed breakdown of female participation has been provided for in these statistics, though there are still many gaps.

32. *Educational Statistics Yearbook of China, 1991–1992*, pp. 32–33.

33. Jiang Naiyong, "The Plight of Job Placement for Female College Graduates," in *Chinese Education*, Vol. 25, no. 1 (Spring 1992): 48–52.

34. "Law Protecting Women's Rights, Interests," Beijing *Xinhua* Domestic Service in Chinese, April 7, 1991, in *FBIS*, no. 92 (April 14, 1992): 18.

35. Ibid., p. 18.

36. In a lengthy speech made on March 27, 1992, presenting the draft law to the NPC, Zou Yu, vice chairman of the NPC's Internal and Judicial Affairs Committee, admitted serious implementation problems and suggested governmental committees to be set up at all levels to handle implementation. See "Explanation of Law on Women's Rights, Interests," Beijing *Xinhua* Domestic Service in Chinese, April 6, 1992, in *FBIS*, no. 92 (April 15, 1992): 37–41.

37. For promotion to associate professor a master's degree is required, and for promotion to full professor a doctorate is expected.

38. Wu Haiqing, "The Current Status of Women Professors in China," in *Chinese Education*, Vol. 25, no. 1 (Spring 1992): 53–55. This is divided as follows by discipline: 20 percent of the national total in medical science, 11 percent in agronomy, 7.6 percent in basic sciences, 8.2 percent in art and literature, 7.6 percent in education, 4.8 percent in economics, 4.4 percent in history, 3.6 percent in philosophy, 3.3 percent in engineering, and 1.6 percent in law. The relatively high representation in the sciences stands in contrast to most other countries, but it remains a question whether this will be maintained in the future.

39. We discovered this fact in our interviews with thirty-eight women scholars who had returned from abroad in the Northwest. More details are reported in chapter 6 of this volume.

40. Li Xiaozhang visited the Ontario Institute for Studies in Education (OISE) and the Joint Center for Asia Pacific Studies, University of Toronto, York University, in March 1994. In two lectures given at OISE on March 30, this was the main theme she addressed. Of course, Western feminists have gone farther than this, seeing a deliberate intention on the part of the new revolutionary elite to subordinate women's liberation to the broader process of socialist transformation. See, for example, Judith Stacey, *Patriarchy and Socialist Revolution in China* (Berkeley: University of California Press, 1983).

41. Tan Shen, "A Study of Women and Social Change," in *Social Sciences in China*, Vol. 15, no. 2, Summer 1994, pp. 65–73. This article has been translated from the *Shehuixue nianjian 1992* [Yearbook of Sociology 1992], and provides an informative overview of the development of women's studies in China, including a discussion of the leading role played by Li Xiaozhang.

42. A sympathetic overview and analysis of this process can be found in Samuel Kim, *The Quest for a Just World Order*, (Boulder, Colo.: Westview Press, 1984).

43. Earl Drake, "World Bank Transfer of Technology and Ideas to India and China," in R. Hayhoe et al. (eds.), *Knowledge Across Cultures: Universities East and West* (Toronto: OISE Press; Wuhan: Hubei Education Press, 1994), pp. 237–254.

44. Harold K. Jacobsen and Michel Oksenberg, *China's Participation in the IMF, the World Bank, and GATT: Toward a Global Economic Order* (Ann Arbor: The University of Michigan Press, 1990), pp. 109–121, provides an excellent over-

view of the evolution of the bank's China projects in the wider context of bank activities and policies.

45. Wadi Haddad et al., *Education and Development: Evidence of New Priorities* (Washington, D.C.: World Bank, 1990).

46. Nasir Jalil, "A Note on Bank Assistance for the Education Sector in China (first draft)," internal World Bank document.

47. R. Hayhoe, *China's Universities and the Open Door* (Toronto: OISE Press, N.Y. M.E. Shampe, 1989), chapter 7.

48. Information on these projects came from interviews with World Bank representatives in February and May 1994.

49. Ruth Hayhoe and Wenhui Zhong, "Chinese Universities and Chinese Science: A New Visibility in the World Community," in *Higher Education Policy*, Vol. 6, no. 2, 1993, pp. 37–41. For a detailed study of this topic, see Wenhui Zhong, "China's Participation in the World Community: A Study of Chinese Scholarly Communication," University of Toronto Ed.D. thesis, 1992.

50. An example of the type of approach taken by these organizations can be found in the study, *Children and Women of China: A UNICEF Situation Analysis* (Beijing: United Nations Children's Fund, 1989), which concludes with guiding principles for UNICEF projects in China drawn both from an assessment of China's needs and priorities and UNICEF's overall policies, global objectives, and criteria for cooperation. There is an intention to focus projects on the financing and management of social services at the local level, and the needs of remote, rural, and mountainous areas, as export-led rapid economic growth threatens the welfare of children (see pp. 169–172).

51. See, for example, Samuel Kim, *China, the U.N., and World Order* (Princeton, N.J.: Princeton University Press, 1979).

52. In *China's Universities and the Open Door*, chapter 6, I provided some detailed examples of these various kinds of cultural cooperation, and while there have been new initiatives, the patterns have not changed greatly.

53. In a political textbook entitled *Guoqing yu rensheng* [National Conditions and Life Issues] written by Jin Binghua and Yi Jizuo (Shanghai: Renmin chubanshe, 1990) for university political classes after the Tiananmen events, there is a chapter on class struggle under commodity socialism that specifically mentions the provision of Western books and academic journals as part of a campaign for supporting a "peaceful evolution" toward capitalism.

54. Xu Qingyu, "Luetan shishi '2/1/1 gongcheng' de ruogan xiangguan yinsu" [A Brief Discussion of Various Related Factors in Carrying Out the 211 Engineering Project] in *Jiaoyu yanjiu* [Educational Research], no. 3, 1994, pp. 42–45. This article provides an interesting example of this kind of reflection, as it is mainly a comparative historical discussion of state policies towards universities in Germany and France during the nineteenth century. The author argues that the great success of the Germany university, both at home and abroad, resulted from the degree of autonomy it was allowed from the state.

55. R. Hayhoe, *China's Universities and the Open Door*, chapter 5, provides a detailed overview of cultural and educational exchange policies of representative OECD countries toward China. While there have been many new initiatives, the patterns and approaches have not changed greatly.

56. R. Hayhoe, "China's Universities in the World Community," in *Higher Education*, no. 17, March 1988, pp. 121–138.

57. R. Hayhoe, *China's Universities and the Open Door*, pp. 102–109.

58. Information on these projects has been gained through extensive personal involvement with CIDA in both research and project management.

59. Song Yijun, "A Comparative Study of the Aid Policies of the World Bank and the Canadian International Development Agency in Chinese Higher Education: A Synthesis of Different Perspectives," University of Toronto Ed.D. thesis, 1994.

60. Ibid., pp. 119–123. See Dru Findley, "The Impact of Recent Events in China on International Professional and Academic Exchanges and Related Development Activities," The Ford Foundation, Beijing Office, August 31, 1989, pp. 20–23, which indicates that the overall profile of British programs had continued pretty close to these original patterns.

61. Dru Findley, "The Impact of Recent Events in China on International Professional and Academic Exchanges," pp. 23–26.

62. Ibid., pp. 9–12.

63. This was not only my observation, but also that of my doctoral student, Zhong Wenhui, who interviewed 85 scholars in the spring of 1990 as part of his doctoral research. See Zhong Wenhui, "China's Participation in the World Community: A Study of Chinese Scholarly Communication," Ed.D. thesis, University of Toronto, 1992.

64. Timothy Cheek has developed the concept of "establishment intellectuals" to capture this characteristic in the Chinese intellectual community. See, for example, Carol Lee Hamrin and Timothy Cheek, *China's Establishment Intellectuals* (New York and London: M.E. Sharpe, 1986).

65. George Black and Robin Munro, *Black Hands of Beijing: Lives of Defiance in China's Democracy Movement* (New York: John Wiley and Sons, 1993).

66. Ibid., pp. 89–90.

5 PERSPECTIVES FROM THE CENTRAL SOUTH REGION

This chapter provides a kind of snapshot of the Central South region, taken in the spring of 1992, not long after Deng Xiaoping's celebrated visit to Shenzhen in February of that year, amid the economic ferment that resulted from it. The region contains the provinces of Henan, Hubei, Hunan, Guangdong, and the Guangxi Zhuang autonomous region. Hainan Island was separated from Guangdong and given provincial status in 1988. The center of the region is the major industrial city of Wuhan, with a concentration of national-level universities in that city reflecting the planning priorities of the 1950s. The dynamic southern coastal part of China, which had historically been both economically open and politically radical, seems to have been purposely marginalized in this administrative division of territory. While Guangdong and the Guangxi Zhuang autonomous region were made part of the Central South region under the leadership of Wuhan, Fujian province was made part of East China, whose center is in Shanghai.

With the reforms of the 1980s, a new approach to regional territorial lines was adopted based on the dynamics of economic change. Three zones were defined in economic terms—the developed eastern coastal region, which contained around 40 percent of the population and produced 57 percent of the gross agricultural-industrial product in the mid-1980s, the developing central region, which contained 37 percent of the population and produced 29 percent of the gross product, and the underdeveloped western region, which contained 23 percent of the population and produced 14 percent of the gross product. (See Figure 5.1) The Seventh Five-year Plan, promulgated in 1986, gave its official blessing to this perspective and laid out development plans that would give differential responsibilities and opportunities to each region, and encourage greater lateral economic ties based on the respective strengths of each.[1]

In the Central South region, three provinces belong to the develop-

FIGURE 5.1 The Central South Region in Relation to Three Economic Zones

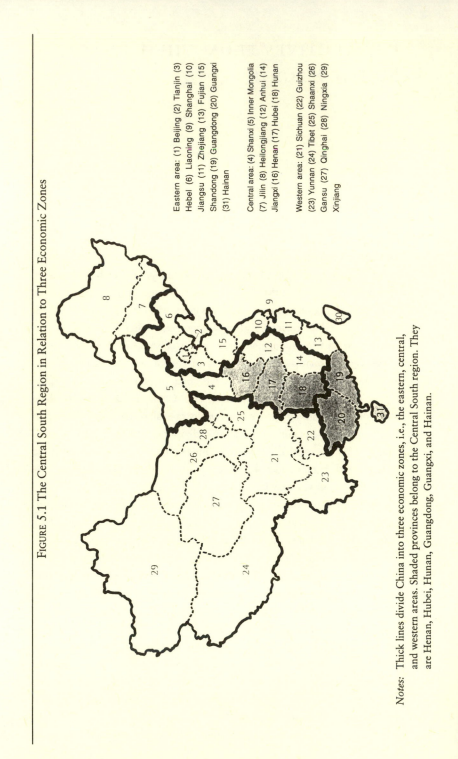

Eastern area: (1) Beijing (2) Tianjin (3) Hebei (6) Liaoning (9) Shanghai (10) Jiangsu (11) Zhejiang (13) Fujian (15) Shandong (19) Guangdong (20) Guangxi (31) Hainan

Central area: (4) Shanxi (5) Inner Mongolia (7) Jilin (8) Heilongjiang (12) Anhui (14) Jiangxi (16) Henan (17) Hubei (18) Hunan

Western area: (21) Sichuan (22) Guizhou (23) Yunnan (24) Tibet (25) Shaanxi (26) Gansu (27) Qinghai (28) Ningxia (29) Xinjiang

Notes: Thick lines divide China into three economic zones, i.e., the eastern, central, and western areas. Shaded provinces belong to the Central South region. They are Henan, Hubei, Hunan, Guangdong, Guangxi, and Hainan.

ing central region—Henan, Hubei, and Hunan, while three belong to the developed eastern coastal region—Guangdong, the Guangxi Zhuang autonomous region, and Hainan Island. Table 5.1 provides a developmental profile of the region over the period from 1982 to 1990. Overall, it contains 27.5 percent of China's total population, with somewhat different population growth trends in different provinces and regions. Guangdong province leads the region economically, with growth between 1982 and 1990 at a rate that is much higher than the national average in both agricultural and industrial production. By contrast, Hubei province, the administrative and political center of the region, has fallen behind national growth rates in industry, as has Hunan province in both industry and agriculture. Henan province is slightly ahead of the national rate, yet it is still one of the poorest provinces of the region, with a 7.6 percent share of national population, a 4.3 percent share of industrial product, and a 6.6 percent share of agricultural product. The Guangxi Zhuang autonomous region was included in the eastern coastal region in the official schematization adopted for the Seventh Five-Year Plan,[2] yet it remains a relatively poor province whose participation in national industrial development lags far behind its population ratio.[3]

GEOGRAPHY AND GENDER IN HIGHER EDUCATION

Higher education provision in the Central South region reflects the patterns of the 1950s, with the city of Wuhan dominating the region. Table 5.2 shows how Hubei was the only province where the percentage of higher institutions and enrollments was considerably higher than its percentage share in national population in 1991. Its share of adult higher education enrollments had an even higher profile, which may be related to the fact that more and more adult higher education in recent years has been carried on by burgeoning adult education colleges in prestigious national universities. Hubei's high concentration of formal higher education institutions at the national level has thus given the province an added advantage in adult higher education.

By contrast, Henan and the Guangxi Zhuang autonomous region were obviously in the periphery, showing the lowest levels of enrollment in both formal and nonformal education in relation to their share of national population. Hunan was an interesting case in that it appeared to have offset its somewhat low ratio of enrollment in formal higher education by relatively high enrollments in adult education. Guangdong's figures indicated that in spite of its economic prosperity, both formal and nonformal higher education provision still lagged behind its share of national population. However, this was a far less serious problem for Guangdong than for Henan and Guangxi, since Guangdong could attract excellent graduates from all over the nation.

TABLE 5.1 A Developmental Profile of the Central South Region, 1982–1990

	Population (millions)			Industrial Product (billion yuan)			Agricultural Product (billion yuan)		
	1982	1990	% up	1982	1990	% up	1982	1990	% up
China	1,008	1,133	1.12	581.1	2,392.4	4.12	248.3	766.2	3.09
Henan	74.4	85.5	1.14	24.63	103.67	4.21	15.11	50.2	3.32
	(7.4%)	(7.5%)		(4.2%)	(4.3%)		(6.1%)	(6.6%)	
Hubei	47.8	53.97	1.13	28.35	75.82	2.67	12.62	41.2	3.26
	(4.7%)	(4.8%)		(4.8%)	(3.2%)		(5.1%)	(5.4%)	
Hunan	54.0	60.6	1.12	20.58	71.27	3.46	14.27	39.74	2.78
	(5.4%)	(5.3%)		(3.5%)	(2.9%)		(5.7%)	(5.2%)	
Guangdong*	53.6	62.8	1.17	25.86	190.2	7.35	12.06	58.95	4.89
	(5.3%)	(5.5%)		(4.45%)	(8.0%)		(4.85%)	(7.7%)	
Guangxi	36.4	42.2	1.16	9.27	35.34	3.81	8.82	25.22	2.86
	(3.6%)	(3.7%)		(1.6%)	(1.5%)		(3.55%)	(3.3%)	
Hainan*	5.67	6.56	1.16	0.75	4.39	5.85	1.75	6.22	3.55
	(.56%)	(.58%)		(.12%)	(.18%)		(.7%)	(.81%)	

* Hainan figures are for 1985 rather than 1982, and these have been subtracted from Guangdong's 1982 figures. This may exaggerate Guangdong's growth profile slightly, but we do not have disaggregated figures for Hainan for 1982, before it was an independent province.

Sources of the figures are from the following materials:

China Population Statistics Yearbook, 1991; *Guangxi tongji nianjian*, 1992; *Hainan tongji nianjian*, 1992; *Zhongguo gongye tongji nianjian*, 1992; *Hubei tongji nianjian*, 1992; *Henan jingji tongji nianjian*, 1991; *Guangdong tongji nianjian*, 1991; *Hunan tongji nianjian*, 1992; *Zhongguo tongji nianjian*, 1993; (Beijing: Zhongguo tongji chubanshe).

TABLE 5.2 A Higher Education Profile of the Central South Region, 1990–1991

	Population (millions)	No. of Higher Inst's	Undergrad. Students	% Female	% Rural	Grad. Students	% Female	Adult Ed. Students
China	1,143	1,075	2,043,662	33.3	n.a.	88,128	23.0	1,476,021
Henan	86.5	49	80,100	30.8	70	940	25	76,000
	(7.6%)	(4.6%)	(3.9%)			(1%)		(4.5%)
Hubei	54.4	62	130,000	26.1*	n.a.	7,000	14	135,000
	(4.8%)	(5.8%)	(6.3%)			(7.5%)		(8.1%)
Hunan	61.3	46	90,000	27.1*	60	2,000	8	106,000
	(5.4%)	(4.3%)	(4.4%)			(2.2%)		(6.4%)
Guangdong	63.5	42	94,000	32.6*	50	3,000	n.a.	80,000
	(5.6%)	(4.1%)	(4.6%)			(3.2%)		(4.8%)
Guangxi	42.6	33	37,800	31.7*	n.a.	n.a.	n.a.	28,500
	(3.7%)	(3%)	(1.8%)					(1.7%)
Hainan	6.63	4	9,500	22.7*	n.a.	n.a.	n.a.	3,700
	(.58%)	(.37%)	(.46%)					(.22%)

* These figures are taken from *The Education Statistics Yearbook*, China, 1991–92, published in December 1992. The figures given to me by provincial officials were quite different—33 percent for Hubei, 20 percent for Hunan, and 25 percent for Guangdong. I believe the yearbook statistics are more likely to be reliable. These discrepancies show how little importance is given to the issue by provincial education officials, most of whom are male.

The statistics in Table 5.2 show that the patterns put in place in the 1950s, with Wuhan as the intellectual center of the region, continued to be reflected in provincial higher education profiles, even though the decade of the 1980s has seen a remarkable growth in higher education for each province. The intention had been that national-level institutions in each province would serve both the Central South region and broader national needs, with annual student intakes and graduate job assignments tightly controlled by central planning mechanisms. One of the guiding conceptions of the Soviet model was that intellectual resources should be concentrated in major comprehensive and polytechnical universities (under the national education ministry) that would serve the general scientific and professional personnel needs of the nation, and also in specialized institutions that would serve particular sectors of the national economy.

Thus Wuhan was allowed to have three major national universities under the Ministry of Education: Wuhan University, Huazhong Normal University, and the Huazhong University of Science and Technology (HUST), as well as the largest concentration of national-level institutions under sectoral ministries anywhere in the region. As a result, in 1992, it had the capacity for an enrollment of 7,000 graduate students. Guangdong, as a kind of secondary intellectual center, had been allowed two national universities under the Ministry of Education: Zhongshan University and the Huanan University of Technology, as well as about half the number of national ministry universities, and it had a total of 3,000 graduate students enrolled in 1992. Hunan had seen its comprehensive university reduced to a provincial normal university in the reorganization of 1952, but had several excellent national ministry institutions, including the National University of Defense Technology, and so was able to provide for 2,000 graduate students in 1992. There were no national universities under the State Education Commission in the provinces of Henan and Hainan, nor in the Guangxi Zhuang autonomous region, though there were a certain number of national ministry institutions. As a result, the capacity for establishing graduate programs in these provinces/regions has been limited.

These differences among provinces were beginning to have serious effects by the late 1980s, due to the relaxation of national planning over student enrollments and job assignments, with students at national-level institutions gaining considerable freedom to choose where they would work on graduation, both in terms of geography and professional area. The effects could be seen in the inflow and outflow of students to national universities for each province.

Over the late 1980s and early 1990s, Hubei province had a pattern of sending about 8,000 of its best students to national universities in other provinces, yet its own national institutions were able to enroll about the same number from around the country. In the employment of these top graduates, Hubei's strengths as an intellectual center enabled it to attract into the province as many qualified graduates as it sent out to other regions. The greatest threat to the province in 1992 was the powerful and growing attraction of Guangdong on its graduates, especially those in the applied sciences.

Henan province was in a much more difficult situation. Its provincial officials greatly regretted the fact that Shandong University had failed to move there in 1957, as originally planned, and that subsequently, political conservatism had prevented them from welcoming the National University of Science and Technology to the province in 1970, when it was forced to leave Beijing, and finally relocated in Hefei, the capital of Anhui province. As they had no national comprehensive or polytechnical institutions in the province, they were trying to raise their major provincial comprehensive university, Zhengzhou University, to priority status and enhance its engineering and technological programs. Overall, the province attracted very few students from other parts of China, yet each year 10,000 to 12,000 of their most talented high school graduates went to national universities around the country, and only 6,000 returned to their home province on graduation. Of the 800 local students who went into graduate programs in other parts of the country, fewer than 200 returned to their own province. There was thus a net outflow of talented young people from the province each year.

Hunan province saw an outflow of 10,000 students to universities around the nation each year, with only about 4,000 returning to work in the province. However, the fact that it had some national institutions, including the National University of Defense Technology, something of a superpower, and a higher graduate training profile than Henan meant it was not as severely affected by the regional brain drain as Henan.

Guangdong province was in the most favorable position in terms of attracting graduating students, due to its economic dynamism. Over recent years, all of Guangdong's 6,000 students that were enrolled annually in national universities around the country had wished to return to their home province on graduation. In addition, 70 percent of the 3,000 students that came to Guangdong from other provinces were allowed to remain in Guangdong on graduation. There was thus a net inflow of young professionals each year. It was also able to attract professionals at higher levels. For example, Shenzhen University claimed to have a list of more than 10,000 highly qualified academics from all regions of China who wished to come and teach in Shenzhen, and was in a position to choose the very best from a national pool of scholars. Shenzhen enterprises were also able to attract highly qualified engineering and management personnel from around the country, and many had begun to limit intake to persons with graduate degrees from major national universities by the early 1990s.[4]

Table 5.2 gives some indication of female participation in higher education by province, showing the more conservative inland provinces of Hubei and Hunan falling considerably below national averages, while the coastal provinces of Guangdong and Guangxi were close to the national average. Henan's participation rate was surprisingly high, considering that 70 percent of its university students came from rural areas, and rural women have tended to be highly disadvantaged in terms of access to higher education. Henan, Hubei, and Hunan all reported a policy of adding two to four extra marks to the scores of women candidates in the national college entry examinations as a form of positive discrimination. Officials in Guangdong, however, insisted that this was not necessary. They noted market demands for male graduates and the unwillingness of many employing agencies to pay maternity costs for women. It was significant to find less resistance to this new form of gender discrimination in Guangdong than in the inland provinces where socialist norms remained somewhat stronger.

On the issue of rural participation in higher education, the figures in Table 5.2 are rough and incomplete. They were given by provincial education officials in three of the four provinces visited, and referred to young people whose families lived in rural areas below the level of the county seat. Henan province, with its huge agricultural population, reported that 70 percent of the province's undergraduate enrollments were from rural areas, while most of those selected to study in national institutions outside of the province were from urban areas. A similar pattern could be detected in Hunan province. In contrast, Guangdong province reported only 50 percent of its enrollments coming from rural areas. This may have been due to the considerable number of national institutions and the rapid rate at which the countryside was being industrialized. No figures were available for Hubei province, but the situation may well have been similar to that of Guangdong, given the even larger number of national institutions attracting the best urban students from around the country.

Overall, the degree of rural participation in higher education was surprisingly strong, and there was a general perception that rural students tended to be more hard working and goal oriented than urban students because they regarded higher education as their only means of social mobility. Even though many of them entered higher education under "directed enrollment programs" that required them to return and serve in the region they had come from, they usually returned to a slightly better location, with the status and perquisites of a state cadre.

Developmental and support links among provinces of the region, and with the underdeveloped Western region, which had been set up in the 1950s, continued to be active in the early 1990s. It was interesting to note that Hubei province, long the center of the region, had the most notable sense of mission in this regard. We were informed about its special responsibility to train students for Guangxi and Hainan in the Central South region, its activities in supporting the training of oil technicians for Xinjiang, and the work of two of its local universities, Hubei University and Hubei Normal University, in educating teachers and cadres for Tibet and Xinjiang.

Through the national enrollment planning process, all national institutions enroled students from outside their own province, and most tended to give some priority in numbers either to other provinces of the Central South region, or more generally to southern China. Adult education programs in major national universities did quite a lot of contract training of personnel at the short-cycle level for other provinces in their regions. This was particularly true for Hubei province, with its national priority institutions being in a good position to compete for such contracts with other provinces, and making considerable income in the process. Here there was evidence of a transition from vertical cooperation, based on administrative responsibility, to horizontal cooperation, based on mutual economic benefit.

REFORM POLICIES AT THE PROVINCIAL LEVEL
Programs

Provincial higher education officials interviewed in this region in the spring of 1992 were preoccupied with the central question of how education could contribute to local economic development. The topics they emphasized in the interviews included the adaptation of higher education programs to new economic demands, the rate of expansion of enrollment in formal and nonformal programs, the ways in which higher institutions could engage in research that had direct relevance for local economic development needs, and possibilities for international projects that would support provincial higher institutions, as well as national ones.

In the area of program development, several concerns came to the fore. One was encouraging greater curricular breadth and more applied curricular content in provincial-level institutions in order to ensure that graduates could adapt flexibly to the changing job market. An example of this was in the province of Guangdong, where newly developed vocational universities with a focus on applied fields were being combined with prefectural normal colleges to create local-level comprehensive institutions. A second was adjusting the structure of programs to correct imbalances that were the legacy of the planning system of the 1950s. In Guangdong and Henan provinces, for example, there was a severe shortage of engineering personnel. A third concern was the development of programs in new areas of high technology and management that could stimulate, as well as reflect, industrial changes in the province. At the same time, institutions training personnel for rural teaching and agricultural work were to foster practical skills and a knowledge of the economic structure of their own counties that would enable them to be effective as local intellectuals, contributing to rural economic development in their home counties.

Generally, in the area of program development, there was a concern with improving quality, both meeting the requirements of national-level standards and setting up their own evaluation procedures. At the same time, the emphasis was on the expansion of short-cycle programs in provincial institutions. In most cases, these made up 60–70 percent of their programs, and it was the rapid development of this level that had made possible the fulfillment of national objectives, set in 1985, for a formal higher education structure in which at least half of all enrollments were short-cycle.[5] In adult education programs, more than 90 percent of all students were enrolled in short-cycle programs, and most of the initiative for this work was at the provincial level.[6]

Enrollments

On the issue of the enrollment size in regular higher education, strong disagreement between provincial and national authorities was evident in the spring of 1992. The Eighth Five-Year Plan (1991–1995), set in motion shortly after the Tiananmen events, had emphasized raising the quality of formal higher education and restricting enrollment growth. The projected national intake for 1995, the last year of the plan, was 650,000,[7] lower than the 669,000 enrolled in 1988,[8] the last year before the Tiananmen events. Justification was couched in terms of quality control, as well as the manpower needs of an economic development process that had slowed down somewhat in the latter part of 1989 and 1990, under policies of economic retrenchment. Clearly, this agenda had political as well as economic motives behind it, with an evident fear that graduates who were unable to find positions that suited their ambitions might congregate in the large cities and become a source of political disturbance, rather than accepting job assignments to regional and local-level units.

From the perspective of provincial governments, however, this fear, and the resultant policy of retrenchment, was unwarranted. They were convinced an economic upsurge was on the way in the spring of 1992, which would lead to escalating manpower needs at all levels. Most provincial governments told us that institutions in their provinces had the capacity to handle 20 percent or 30 percent more enrollments than were allowed to them under national planning, and there was a strong demand for graduates. They particularly resented the restriction imposed on the enrollment of self-paying students in 1990 and 1991, which limited this group to 3 percent of the total. They felt higher institutions should have the autonomy to respond to social demand, where self-paying students could meet slightly lowered entrance requirements on the national examination, and that the local economy could well absorb these extra graduates.

The case of Hunan province was particularly interesting in this regard. In the year when controls over enrollment numbers were least restrictive, 1988, they had enrolled 8,500 self-paying students in institutions throughout the province, nearly one-third of their total intake. This was an increase on the 5,400 enrolled in 1987, and the 3,100 enrolled in 1986. While the self-paying students were not assured job assignments, the provincial bureau undertook to assist them in finding suitable positions over a period of one and one-half years after they had graduated. The official in charge reported to us that by May 1992, all had found positions, and generally they were far more satisfied with their professional work than graduates who were assigned to work units directly on graduation through the state plan.

Guangdong province was also strongly opposed to these national restrictions on enrollment numbers. Through a special document approved in May 1988 by the State Education Commission, they had been given greater autonomy than other provinces in twelve areas, in recognition of the economic requirements of the province. However, the June 4th events prevented them from the experimentation they had planned. Only in 1992 were they near to negotiating permission for an extra 30 percent above the enrollment quota under the form of contract training, much of which would be in the form of contracts with individuals, requiring them to pay the full price of their higher education. On the basis of this agreement, they projected 36,000 entrants to formal higher education programs for September 1992, up from 32,000 in 1991, and 30,000 in 1990.

In adult education, the problem of expansion was somewhat different. Here there had been fewer national restrictions on the number of entrants, although most students had to pass national adult education entrance examinations and were enrolled according to plan in all programs that led to diplomas or degrees. The problem facing adult higher education programs was that most potential students who were already in cadre positions and had missed higher education during the Cultural Revolution decade had by this time received the needed qualifications. Therefore higher institutions doing only adult education could no longer attract students as easily as in the past. They now depended for their main enrollments on urban secondary school graduates who had failed to make it into the formal higher education system, yet many of these preferred enrollment in the adult education college of a prestigious national university rather than in a local adult institution. Although there were few restrictions on enrollment growth in adult higher education, except for a limit on the number of nonemployed youth they were supposed to enroll, the fact that its diplomas and degrees did not assure entry into the national bureaucracy made these programs far less attractive to young people than regular programs.

In spite of these constraints, provincial governments were trying to encourage the expansion of the relatively inexpensive places in adult higher education. Guangdong had enough burgeoning new enterprises to employ educated young people, no matter what type of qualification they held. For example, the Guangzhou Foreign Languages Institute had full-time adult programs in foreign languages for 1,500 young people, more than their total regular enrollment. Since most of these students had not passed the adult higher education entrance examination, a state-approved short-cycle diploma was not available on graduation. Still, graduates of these programs had no difficulty finding employment. Meanwhile, the income brought to the institution by these students made it possible to double faculty salaries.

Research

We have noted in chapter 4 the emerging research profile of universities at the national level. At the provincial level, it has been more difficult for universities to develop strong research programs due to the more limited resources available to provincial institutions and the generally lower quality of their faculty. However, provincial educational commissions in the Central South were putting great emphasis on encouraging research in their institutions, in most cases focusing their research support on a small number of relatively strong provincial institutions. Provincial funds were also available to national universities in each province. So-called "horizontal research," which was oriented toward development needs and based on support gained from enterprises and government bureaus responsible for various areas of production, had also become an important resource for universities, and provincial institutions with a strong practical orientation were often successful in attracting this kind of funding.

A few figures from provincial education commissions give some interesting indications. Hubei province reported that half of all its local research projects were done in universities, even though only 20 percent of the province's research personnel were located in universities, indicating the relative efficiency of university research. In Guangdong province, 70 percent of all research projects were done in universities, probably a reflection of the small number of research institutes (compared to Wuhan) that had been established there under the planning of the 1950s. To a degree, the lack of a large entrenched research infrastructure in some provinces was a benefit, since research institutes established by the state under government bureaus or the Academies of Science and Social Science have tended to hold a monopoly over research funding, whether or not they could compete with educational institutions in terms of quality.

Research resources differed greatly by province, with Hubei reporting a research budget under the provincial education commission of 100 million yuan, half of which came through "horizontal" contracts, Guangdong reporting a budget of 50 million, two-fifths of which came through horizontal contracts, and Henan province reporting a budget of only 12 million, little of which came through horizontal contracts. Provincial research funds were available to national universities in the province, as well as local ones, but efforts were made to ensure that local institutions got a share appropriate to their capacity. Henan's low budget reflects, in part, the low research profile and capacity of its higher institutions.

In all four provincial bureaus, there was considerable enthusiasm and support for the application of research to new product development, what was popularly called technological innovation (*keji kaifa*). Provincial commissions strongly encouraged their institutions to seek ways in which their scientific research results could be directly applied to regional economic development needs, both in agriculture and industry. Universities were encouraged to set up factories for product development and to cooperate actively with local enterprises. Provincial officials responsible for these activities in the education commission were closely involved in helping universities under their jurisdiction to get started in this process, and they elaborated on a whole range of new products under development. Their most serious problem was a lack of capital for initial investment in projects that promised to contribute to local economic development. Only the Guangdong Education Commission was able to give direct financial support to this sort of activity, with a loan fund set up specifically for universities to apply for funds to develop productive activities. It had started at 1 million yuan in the first year, but had reached 10 million yuan by 1992.

Another creative way in which provincial education and science commissions were linking universities to local economic development was through participation in the national "Spark" program, which provided funding to ensure that each county had a "high-tech vice-county head." This was a professor appointed to the position for a two- to three-year term from one of the national or local universities. Those provinces with national priority universities, such as Hubei and Guangdong, were able to recruit faculty from the top level to this kind of activity. Most institutions that had some research profile were involved, with five to ten faculty located for periods of two or three years in counties specifically linked to that university. This made it possible for the university community to become familiar with local economic needs, and it was an important channel for the dissemination of research results and new technology to the grass-roots level. In some cases, with more prosperous counties, the county itself bore some of the cost. There were also a few cases where cooperative ventures between county enterprises and universities developed.

Higher institutions thus had a multi-level network. There were links to the center in terms of national research projects, graduate programs, and the selection of top students through college entry exams; there were regional connections in terms of adult education programs attracting students from the region, and research oriented to regional needs; and there was local-level involvement, with increasingly active linkages being formed with county-level institutions.

International Activities

The provinces also aspired to a more active international role in higher education, and provincial officials actively tried to ensure that their institutions participated in some international activities. However, the only linkages where they enjoyed a substantial and growing share of support were those with the World Bank. The first World Bank project directly involving provincial institutions was the polytechnic and television university project, launched in 1983, which assisted seventeen vocational universities across the nation, including several in the Central South region, as well as television universities in each province.[9] The second was the Provincial Universities Project, launched in 1986, which assisted two institutions in each province, usually one comprehensive and one normal university. More recently, World Bank assistance had been increasingly focused at the local level, with projects for secondary vocational education and teacher upgrading, the improvement of normal training colleges at the prefectural level, and comprehensive support for education at all levels in selected poor counties, including some in Henan, Hunan, and Hubei. These projects were greatly valued by provincial commissions.

By contrast, they found it difficult to compete for participation in bilateral aid projects, and only a few cases of cooperation were cited in the four provinces visited. One was a joint venture secondary school with Germany in Hubei province for training young people in beer making and food processing. It was supported by the successful Zhongde (China-Germany) Beer Company. Another was a series of projects supported by the Canadian International Development Agency in Hunan province involving two vocational universities, Changsha and Yueyang, and also Hunan Agricultural University.

One way provincial education officials could bring their institutions into the orbit of international activity was through the hiring of foreign teachers. Officials in Henan province indicated they had employed a total of 300 foreign teachers since the early 1980s, and had forty-eight teaching in eighteen provincial colleges in 1992. Hunan province had seventy foreign teachers in thirty-one provincial colleges. Due to very limited budgets, they tended to rely on voluntary organizations such as Britain's Voluntary Service Overseas (VSO), and the American-based English Language Institute, an Evangelical Christian organization sending only Christian teachers, which made the cost relatively low.

At the higher level, provincial governments hoped to see their better universities able to participate more fully in opportunities for study and research abroad. However, provinces received only a small quota from the State Education Commission each year for participation in national programs. They might have ten places to be shared among all provincial institutions, while one national university might be allocated fifteen or twenty places in a year for its faculty. Thus Henan province had only been able to send a total of 480 scholars abroad for extended periods since 1978, in contrast to 800 or more sent from such national universities as the Huazhong University of Science and Technology and Zhongshan University.

World Bank projects had opened up some opportunities for scholars at local institutions to study abroad, yet serious problems had been encountered. The non-return rate was so high in the case of the provincial universities project, that the universities had changed their approach midway through the project, arranging for teams of three or four mature scholars to go together for short periods, rather than sending younger faculty for longer periods. The vocational universities project had been one of the first to begin, yet these institutions lacked contact with the outside world and it was only in the late 1980s that they were able to arrange suitable placements for their faculty abroad. Many of these young people did not return, due to the special opportunities for permanent residence abroad that opened up in the wake of the Tiananmen events.

There were thus many obstacles to developing an international program at the provincial level. Some arose from a centralizing tendency in Chinese policy, resulting in the assumption that national-level institutions should lead the way in international linkages, and pass the benefits down through the system. Others arose from a variety of practical problems and constraints.

UNIVERSITIES OF THE CENTRAL SOUTH: A SERIES OF CASE STUDIES

Altogether, twenty universities in the Central South were visited in the spring of 1992, and Table 5.3 gives an overview of the student population at these institutions. They have been listed according to their level within the overall higher education system, as it is this that determines the scope and nature of their contribution to national, provincial, or local development. The three institutions at Level I, Huazhong University of Science and Technology, Zhongshan University, and Guangzhou Foreign Languages Institute, are administered directly by the State Education Commission, and tend to have the highest prestige, recruiting students nationwide and offering job opportunities at the national level on graduation. Because of their status and the kinds of career opportunities they give entry to, they are highly attractive to the best urban secondary graduates. It is interesting to note that a considerable percentage of rural students still managed to find their way into Zhongshan University and the Huazhong University of Science and Technology. However, very few could meet the entry standards of the Guangzhou Foreign Language Institute, due to the fact that rural schools are particularly disadvantaged when it comes to foreign language teaching.

The five institutions at Level II are administered by national ministries other than the State Education Commission, serve specific sectors of the country, and are oriented toward the Central South region in their enrollments. Striking differences are evident in Table 5.3 in the character of their student populations. Agriculture and metallurgy are notably unpopular fields for urban students, so that 80 percent of the students at these national institutions come from rural areas. In contrast, programs in medicine, civil engineering, and finance and economics are popular choices for urban students, with a lower representation of rural students at Zhongnan University of Finance and Economics, Hunan University, and Zhongshan Medical University.

The four provincial universities at Level III are typically leading in-

TABLE 5.3 A Profile of Twenty Higher Institutions in the Central South Region

	Regular Undergrad Students	% Female	% Rural	% Directed	% Contract	% Self-paying	Adult Educ. Students
I. National SEdC							
*Huazhong-P	9,429	23	40	.5	2.4	2.5	3,600
*Zhongshan-U	5,592	25	35	1	5.4	5.4	3,321
Guangzhou-L	1,200	54	15	–	2.1	.8	1,500
II. National Ministry							
*Wuhan-S	2,900	24	80	5	9.6	2.4	2,500
*Huazhong-Ag	2,900	22	80	11	7	1.4	n.a.
Zhongnan-F	4,000	35	40	1.5	8	1	3,700
Hunan-E	4,987	30	35	1.2	n.a.	3	1,500
*Zhongshan-M	2,532	45	15	2	5.5	2	700
III. Provincial							
Henan-U	5,973	30	80	12	9.2	–	7,670
Zhengzhou-U	4,800	30	60	6	1.1	2	n.a.
Hunan-N	7,200	44	60	15	–	3	n.a.
*Hunan-Ag	3,500	14	70	15	–	–	1,500
IV. Municipal							
Shenzhen-U	3,078	40.7	10	–	12	9	3,000
Jianghan-V	3,406	40.6	30	30	–	–	1,363
*Changsha-V	1,200	50	0	–	–	–	400
*Wuhan-Ad	2,000	55	25	–	–	–	974
V. Prefectural							
Xiaogan-N	1,770	23.5	95	85	10	5	750
Lingling-N	1,586	29.5	75	90	n.a.	n.a.	812
Hengyang-N	2,182	34.7	86.9	85	n.a.	7	n.a.
Huizhou-N	2,000	32.3	56	70	15	15	763

Key: P—Polytechnical; U—(Comprehensive) University; L—(Foreign) Language; S—(Iron and) Steel; Ag—Agricultural; F—Finance and Economics; E—Engineering; M—Medical; N—Normal; V—Vocational; Ad—Adult.

All data in Tables 5.3–5.7, 6.4–6.11 were supplied by the institutions at the time of our visit.

* Institutions having CIDA projects.

stitutions within their provinces that are given special support and consideration by the provincial education commission. This is particularly the case for Henan and Hunan provinces, since they have no national-level comprehensive, polytechnic, or normal universities. Their student populations are strongly rural and many will return to work in rural areas on graduation, usually at the level of the prefectural seat or county town. These institutions have to compete with urban vocational universities for good urban students, even though their programs are academically superior, as career opportunities on graduation are a main consideration in student choice. An interesting example of this comes from Jianghan Vocational University in Wuhan, which reported that there were 700 students competing for twenty-five places in its English program in 1991, while Hubei University, a provincial comprehensive institution, could not fill its quota for English students in that same year. The difference was simply that graduation from Jianghan assured a position in Wuhan city, while graduation from Hubei University would lead to a job assignment in a prefectural town, or even a county seat.

The four urban institutions at Level IV represent a new echelon of higher education that has emerged in the reform decade, with the major financial resources for these institutions coming from urban governments. Jianghan and Changsha Vocational Universities are typical of the new-style urban vocational universities, which operate mainly at the short-cycle, non-degree level. As members of the group of seventeen institutions selected for support in the second World Bank higher education project in 1983, they are virtual priority institutions with a national profile. Their student intake was almost exclusively urban in 1992, with the exception of some teacher education students at Jianghan who were recruited from counties attached to Wuhan and returned there to teach on graduation. The close links these institutions enjoyed with urban governments meant their graduates sometimes even had priority over the graduates of national institutions in the urban job market, making their programs extremely attractive to urban youth seeking to retain their urban residential permits. Shenzhen's remarkable prosperity and position nationally as a special economic zone enabled it to create a regular comprehensive university with four-year degree programs, which recruited 70 percent of its student body locally and another 30 percent from other parts of Guangdong province. Only 10 percent of its entrants were rural in 1992, and all of its graduates were expected to stay in Shenzhen for employment.

The prefectural-level normal colleges at Level V were funded mainly by provincial governments and represented the lowest echelon within the provincial higher education system. Their situation was precisely opposite to the urban vocational university, in terms of high rural enrollments, as can be seen in column 3 of Table 5.3. Just as provinces such as Henan and Hunan lost their best urban secondary graduates to national institutions, prefectural towns tended to lose their most talented secondary graduates to institutions in the provincial capital. This was really the only way these students could be assured of job assignments within their own prefectural seat, or at an equivalent level. Meanwhile, prefectural institutions took in rural students, who had to return on graduation to rural areas for employment. Most of those considered "non-rural" at these institutions came from county towns or from cadre families at the grass-roots level.

Prefectural institutions served the real grass roots and faced the challenging task of training enough rural teachers to make possible the popularization of lower secondary education in the rural areas in the 1990s, a task already achieved in most urban areas. These colleges also had significant potential for supporting the industrialization of the countryside through the contribution their graduates made to township and village enterprises. Huizhou Normal College in Guangdong province indicated possible future directions at this level. Because the whole region of southern Guangdong province, where it is located, was rapidly industrializing, already 44 percent of its entering students held non-rural residential permits in 1992.

Overall, we can see a highly stratified hierarchy, allowing very different degrees of mobility to students who found their way into its different levels. The fact that marks on the national unified university entry examinations decided the level at which a student could be accepted into the system made the great disparities in the opportunities allotted to different categories of students seem "fair." Every young person and his or her family would make the fullest possible use of the opportunity to seek whatever degree of mobility was possible.

CURRICULAR IDENTITIES

The curricular identities of the twenty universities are varied, and continue to reflect, to some degree, the patterns of the 1950s, especially in the case of the national-level institutions. Without doubt, the leading institution of the Central South region is Wuhan University, a national comprehensive university with a history going back to 1912. Its arts and basic sciences were strengthened by the addition of similar departments that were transferred there from other institutions in the region in 1952, while its colleges of agriculture, medicine, and engineering became the foundation for such new universities as the Huazhong University of Agriculture, the Huazhong University of Science and Technology and Tongji Medical University in 1952.

In the early 1980s, Wuhan University entered into a comprehensive project of cooperation with France, under the influence of a visionary vice president and subsequent president, Liu Daoyu, who did much to reinvigorate the university over the reform decade.[10] New programs in applied sciences, applied arts, and social sciences were developed. However, Liu was attacked as a "bourgeois liberal" by conservative forces within the State Education Commission and forced to resign even before the 1989 student movement. After the Tiananmen events, social science and humanities programs at Wuhan University fell under a cloud, with a new party secretary seeking to remold all scholars of the arts and social sciences into orthodox teachers of politics, and to ensure that all published scholarship in these areas served the propaganda purposes of the state.[11] Our request to spend two days doing interviews there in May 1992 was turned down. Apparently, the outline of questions proposed for discussion was regarded as too sensitive. We were allowed only to have a brief interview with the head of the foreign affairs program to discuss the university's international activities. That is why Wuhan University does not appear on Table 5.2.

The other major comprehensive university of the region, Zhongshan University, appeared to be somewhat more open in 1992, probably due to its location in a coastal area and its extensive contact with Hong Kong and with overseas organizations. It had originally been a kind of flagship institution for the Guomindang party in the 1930s.[12] After the reorganization of 1952, it was left with eight departments, reflecting the traditional orientation of the Soviet-style comprehensive university: mathematics, physics, chemistry, biology, geography, Chinese, foreign languages, and history. Over the reform decade of the 1980s, it had expanded to twenty-three departments, with new social science departments in anthropology, sociology, law, library science, management, politics and administration, economics, accounting, and philosophy, and also new science departments in such applied areas as electronics, computer science, atmospheric sciences, mechanics, and geology.

The Huazhong (Central China) University of Science and Technology (HUST) in Wuhan was one of the most interesting of the institutions under the State Education Commission in the region, in terms of recent curricular reforms. As a polytechnical university, newly created after 1949, it had been less prey to suspicions of "bourgeois liberalism" than comprehensive universities with strong programs in the arts and social sciences, and traditions going back to a period before the Communist regime. Founded in 1952 through the amalgamation of some of the best engineering departments in institutions throughout the Central South region, it developed up to the Cultural Revolution decade as a polytechnical university, with a range of engineering sciences but no other programs. It benefited from a long period of leadership under Zhu Jiusi, a veteran Communist with experience in Yan'an, who had also been considerably influenced by a liberal academic education in some of China's best Nationalist institutions, including

Yangzhou Secondary School, Zhejiang University, and Wuhan University.[13]

The story of this institution during the Cultural Revolution has already been told in chapter 3, but it bears repeating here. At a time when all universities were under a cloud and uncertain if they had any future in a new radical China, Zhu took vigorous steps to bring in new faculty and lay the foundation for new programs in mathematics and basic sciences, in journalism and the arts, in management and various social science areas. Between 1971 and 1976, he succeeded in recruiting about 600 scholars from some of China's best universities who had been driven down to the countryside and felt they had little hope of returning to their own institutions. As a result, the university's engineering programs were strengthened with a more systematic and integrated basic science program to support them, and it became a leader in such new areas as the philosophy and history of science, higher education theory and practice, and scientific journalism. When the first group of graduate schools were approved in 1984, HUST was among the twenty-two institutions chosen on the basis of the quantity and quality of doctoral and master's programs already in place.[14]

The Guangzhou Foreign Languages Institute also had a national profile, but its very small size and the specialized nature of its curriculum limited the scope of its development. Founded in 1965, just before the Cultural Revolution decade, out of foreign language departments from Zhongshan University, Jinan University, and the Guangzhou Foreign Trade Institute, it had recruited only one class before the convulsions of the Cultural Revolution.[15] In the reform climate of the 1980s, its programs became extremely popular. From a focus on languages, linguistics, and literature, it moved to develop new programs in tourism, international diplomacy, secretarial studies, and international trade. It also set up interdisciplinary teaching programs in areas such as British studies, American studies, and Canadian studies.

The national sectoral institutions at Level II in the system differed considerably according to the sector they served. The two engineering universities, Wuhan University of Iron and Steel under the Ministry of Metallurgy, and Hunan University under the Ministry of Machine Building experienced some shared constraints and problems. Both were originally well funded by these important ministries, but the decentralization of state enterprise control under the economic reforms left these ministries mainly with a policy role. The fact that they had far less control of funding in their sector meant less ability to support their higher education systems. Hunan University leaders noted that they had been used to receiving at least 10 million a year in basic construction fees from the ministry, but by 1992 were receiving less than 3 million, and Wuhan Steel University mentioned similar cutbacks. Both universities continue to train personnel for sectoral needs, and so had limited freedom for curricular innovation.

Hunan University had succeeded with new programs in the basic sciences, industrial design, environmental engineering, management, and foreign languages. It was also struggling to develop some research and teaching on cultural topics related to remarkable classical cultural institutions on its campus, the 1,000-year-old Yuelu Academy and adjacent Confucian temple, which had been restored by the architecture department. Wuhan Iron and Steel University reported great difficulty with curricular innovation, partly due to its somewhat lowly position within the hierarchy of institutions under the Ministry of Metallurgy. In addition to its basic programs in metallurgy, chemical engineering, electronics, and materials sciences, it had tried to develop new departments in social sciences and management. However, it was never able to attract students for the social science program, due to its obvious political content and purpose, and graduates of its management program had great difficulties in finding jobs, since the rather traditional steel sector wanted only engineers and felt new graduates could not be given managerial responsibilities. The university's response was to rename the management program "quality control," a popular catchword in industrial circles in China, which enabled them to find suitable positions for graduates, even though they had not yet gained official permission for the new program.

Zhongnan (Central South) University of Finance and Economics had probably seen the most severe convulsions in its history, due to the fact that its orthodox Soviet-defined social sciences came under attack in both the radicalism of the Great Leap Forward movement of 1958 and in the Cultural Revolution decade, a point that has been discussed in chapter 3. Its origins went back to Zhongyuan University, created by the Communist party in 1948, and from 1953 it had been called the Central South Institute of Finance and Economics, and exercised a role similar to that of People's University at the regional level. With the movement towards decentralization and local control of 1958 it was combined with the Central South Institute of Political Science and Law and the Law Department of Wuhan University to form Hubei Provincial Comprehensive University. During the Cultural Revolution, it was separated from Hubei University to become a short-cycle training college for economic cadres.[16] Restored to the national Ministry of Finance in 1975, it had developed new programs in economic information, investment economics, international trade, and international law after 1978. As a participant in the second World Bank project in support of national-level institutions under various national ministries other than education, it had helped to develop and introduce eleven core courses in economics, reflecting Western and international standards in the field. Its administrators hoped to develop a broad curriculum, with a common first year for all students, but they faced the demands of employing units under the Ministry of Finance for graduates who were narrowly trained to suit specific needs.

Huazhong (Central China) Agricultural University had started the reform decade with departments that reflected Soviet patterns very closely—agronomy, veterinary science, agricultural machinery, agro-economics, and horticulture. Since agriculture was the sector in which economic reforms had their beginnings, innovation began relatively early, including such fields as food sciences, biological engineering, crop genetics, land management, agricultural sociology, and agricultural trade. It had extensive involvement with Japanese- and Chinese-American scientists in the food science area, and had a joint doctoral program with the University of Manitoba, Canada, which was supported by CIDA.

Zhongshan Medical University had quite a remarkable curricular openness going back to 1958 when its faculty first experimented with the American-derived "body systems" approach to curricular organization, and the early 1980s when they became familiar with McMaster University's "problem approach." In the end, they kept the Soviet legacy of a curriculum mainly structured around academic disciplines, but introduced modifications that drew on both of these alternatives, and found this compromise worked well. They were also actively developing new areas, such as an innovative program in clinical nutrition that gained support from both CIDA and the Canadian-based International Development Research Center (IDRC).

As noted in chapter 3, provincial institutions mostly traced their history back to the Great Leap Forward period, around 1957, when there was a major move to decentralize the administration of higher education. The exceptions in this region were those institutions such as Henan University and Hunan Normal University, which had inherited parts of national institutions from the period before 1949. Generally, provincial institutions have tended to be more comprehensive in their curriculum patterns than national institutions, and also to have a more applied and locally-oriented approach to knowledge. However, they too have been constrained by national patterns to some degree.

Zhengzhou University had been established in 1957 on a campus originally intended to receive Shandong University, which had been mandated to move to Zhengzhou from Qingdao at the same time that so many Shanghai institutions had been moved inland. Provincial authorities in Shandong objected to the loss of one of their proudest institutions, and in the end it moved to the provincial capital of Jinan. Henan officials were left to establish their own provincial comprehensive university, Zhengzhou University, and these aspirations for a national comprehensive university meant that it had tended for years to emulate such national institutions as Beijing, Fudan, Wuhan, and Nankai Universities. In the reform decade, however, it had broadened its curriculum with the development of ten new engineering fields linked to its original basic science departments, and new applied arts and social science programs in the areas of editing, arts management, secretarial studies, statistics, banking, and accounting. It had gained a national profile for curriculum reform through an innovative approach to programming in the late 1980s. In order to enable its students to have a second major field, it had added a short six-week term to the normal pattern of two longer terms, exclusively for elective courses. Students were then able to shape a second major that was complementary to their main field of specialization.[17]

Henan University in Kaifeng was an example of those that suffered most in the reorganization of 1952. It had a history going back to 1912, when it had started as a preparatory school for study in Europe and America; subsequently it had developed into a tertiary college in its own right, and by the 1930s had become a comprehensive university with colleges of arts, sciences, law, engineering, and agriculture, the pride of the province. It had its own heroic story of resistance and movement to rural areas during the Anti-Japanese War, and had managed to become recognized as a national university in 1942.[18] In 1952, however, it had been almost totally dismembered. Its agricultural and medical colleges became independent provincial institutions, while its college of sciences moved to the city of Xinxiang to form a new normal university. Its engineering college was transferred to the Huazhong University of Science and Technology; its economics and finance program went to Zhongnan University of Finance and Economics; and its hydraulics program was combined into the Wuhan Institute of Hydraulics.[19] Left with only the college of arts and a mandate to do teacher education, it had struggled to survive through many vicissitudes until it gained some autonomy in the reform decade.

Over this period, Henan University developed new programs in the areas of computers, biology, chemical engineering, civil engineering, accounting, taxation, opera arts, secretarial studies, law, environmental aesthetics, arts and crafts, etc. It also promoted research relating to the rich cultural resources of the area, which had been the imperial capital during the Song dynasty. Programs in areas such as comparative biblical and Chinese classical literature and local folk literature had gained financial support from the

National Social Sciences Foundation. Henan University also had a large cooperative research project with Nankai and Jilin Universities in new materials, involving eight returned doctoral students and supported by funding from the National Natural Sciences Foundation (NNSF). Its experience illustrated how older institutions could revive aspects of their traditional ethos under the new reform conditions.[20]

Hunan Normal University was probably the strongest of the provincial-level institutions included in the study, due to the fact that it too had a long academic tradition in what had been National Hunan Normal College and National Hunan University before Liberation. Hunan University had lost many of its most vital departments to the "center" of the Central South region in 1952, with electronics and mechanical engineering being moved to the Huazhong University of Science and Technology, law to Zhongnan University of Political Science and Law, and humanities departments to Zhongshan University in Guangzhou. Its science and social science departments were then combined with those of the National Normal University to form Hunan Normal University in 1952, which operated under provincial jurisdiction.[21] It received particularly strong provincial support due to the absence of a national comprehensive or normal university in the province. It had an excellent teaching and research profile in the humanities and social sciences, and also in some basic science areas. In addition, it had succeeded in developing a large number of new applied fields, as well as taking leadership in the training of teachers for vocational secondary schools in the province.[22]

Municipal universities at Level IV on Table 5.3 had the greatest freedom in curricular development over the reform decade, being farthest removed from the constraining curricular patterns of the 1950s. All had been founded in the early 1980s, and most of their programs, with the exception of Shenzhen University, were at the short-cycle level. Provincial governments had gained the right to approve the establishment of new short-cycle programs after the reform document of 1985. These urban institutions had created programs in the arts, social sciences, and applied sciences in direct response to urban employment needs. There was a distinction between long-term programs rooted in academic disciplines and maintained at a basic level, no matter what the employment market was like, and programs established for limited time periods in response to specific employment needs.

Jianghan University, one of the earliest and most famous of the vocational universities, founded in 1980, had a total of fourteen departments covering the areas of arts, law, economics, engineering, sciences, teacher education, and agriculture. Changsha University had a somewhat more limited range of programs, focusing on new areas that reflected the economic changes going on in the city—electronics, interior decorating, fashion, textiles, finance and economics, and tourism. It required all students to develop strong skills in basic areas such as computer literacy, Chinese composition and writing skills, and foreign languages. Interestingly, Cantonese was an important "foreign language," as well as Japanese and English, reflecting a conscious effort to compete with Guangdong province.

Prefectural normal colleges at Level V were responsible mainly for the formation of rural teachers so that their programs reflected the structure of the secondary curriculum, including mathematics, physics, chemistry, biology, history, Chinese, politics, and English. Because many rural teachers had to teach more than one subject, many of their students enroll in combination fields such as Chinese and politics, and physics and chemistry. They were also broadening their curricula to include technical and agricultural subjects that would enable their graduates to contribute to rural development in practical ways, as local intellectuals.

The most striking example of this was Lingling Normal College in a mountainous region in southwestern Hunan. It had won national recognition for curricular reforms that made it possible for each student to select one agricultural and one technical area of study in addition to his or her academic and educational subjects. The school had an experimental farm, with opportunities for students to study fruit trees, vegetable growing, fish cultivation, the raising of pigs and ducks—in short, the main areas that had contributed to agricultural prosperity in many rural regions. They were expected to introduce new seed types and assist rural farmers in improving productivity. The school also had workshops in areas such as the maintenance and repair of electronic equipment, sewing, and fashion design, which were intended to foster skills supportive of rural industry.[23]

Types and Categories of Student

The story of student enrollment and the employment of graduates is an important one for each of our twenty universities and for the region more generally. It can be seen from the perspective of the state, adopting new policies to solve a series of problems that arose in the reform process, and also from the perspective of young people, seeking to achieve as much social and geographical mobility as possible through the higher education system. The twenty universities visited in this study found themselves caught between these two, often conflicting, sets of concerns.

The state had been attempting to reform student selection and job assignment policies in ways that would strengthen ongoing economic reform processes, seeing the professional and technical level of the labor force and its flexibility and adaptability to changing needs as a very important issue.[24] Under the old patterns, whereby young people were selected from all over the nation and trained at national universities in accordance with their level of talent, there had been a large annual outflow of talent from the Central South region to the Southwest, the Northwest, and the Northeast. Within the region, less favorable locations were also assured of qualified graduates. With the greater expectations for individual freedom and choice that had been allowed to develop in the reform decade, however, this kind of macro-planning was no longer possible. The only way in which the state could assure adequate professional talent to the various sectors and regions of the country, especially those that had little to attract, was to adopt a policy of non-mobility in terms of geography.

Thus by the late 1980s, most students expected a job posting on graduation in the same geographical region where they had come from, although a few would succeed in improving the geographical location of their residential permits through entering graduate school or gaining exceptional recognition as outstanding students. Student affairs offices at Level I and Level II institutions, which had taken over much of the detailed decision making on job assignments after 1985,[25] took into careful account the professional opportunities and needs of each province and of various state units when they made up their enrollment plan. Even before students were given entry to university, the problem of finding suitable jobs for them on graduation, in geographical as well as professional terms, had been carefully considered.

A second important issue from the state's perspective was that of enrollment expansion. The State Education Commission continued to hold a strict control over the numbers enrolled in the national plan each year up to 1992, yet the reform decade had seen a dramatic rise from around 281,000 entrants in 1980 to a high of 669,000 in 1988. Questions of political stability and of the size of national and provincial bureaucracies were main considerations.[26] Since Liberation, all university graduates had had the right to be treated as state cadres and had come to expect appropriate status and remuneration. By the late 1980s, however, many graduates had to expect job assignments at provincial or local levels, often outside of the major cities, due to the fact that favored urban positions were already filled. Some graduates simply refused to accept these job assignments and remained in their home city, a situation that was disturbing from the state's perspective.

The best way to expand enrollments in this situation was to link them to the identified needs of geographical regions and professional fields. Regions in need of professional personnel were thus favored, on the understanding that their candidates would return home on graduation. Enterprises and units that had particular difficulty in attracting graduates could enter into direct contracts with universities for the training of young people who were committed from the beginning to working in that particular enterprise. These students were allowed to enter with somewhat lower marks on the national entry examination. In the years between 1985 and 1988, quite a large number of students were trained by contract, and university budgets benefited from the flow of funds that came to them in this way, including contributions to building and equipment, as well as training fees.[27] With the economic slowdown of 1989, however, enterprise managers became more reluctant to spend money on training, as most had little difficulty getting graduates trained at state expense.

Thus we can see in Table 5.3 that the percentage of students enrolled under contract arrangements was quite low in 1992, except in a small number of institutions. Shenzhen University had 12 percent, which is not surprising given its special economic circumstances, while the nearby Huizhou Normal College had 15 percent, also reflecting the prosperity of the region. Some national ministry institutions such as Wuhan Steel University, Huazhong Agricultural University, and Zhongnan University of Finance and Economics were still able to gain a certain number of training contracts, but they reported that numbers were considerably down from earlier years. State policy allowed for 10–15 percent of all enrollments to be on contract, with permission to lower entry marks to twenty below the normal standard on the national college entry examination.

Another new initiative of the state was to allow for a certain number of self-paying students, which was essentially a response to growing social demand for entry to higher education. From 1985, a limited number of students were allowed entry with somewhat lower marks on the national entry examinations, and expected to pay for their education at around the same level as the payments made by employing units for contract students. On graduation they were free to find their own jobs, but their residential permit was not moved into the university, so practically they had to find jobs in the place they had come from. This policy was popular, especially with newly prosperous individual households, also with urban intellectuals whose children had not been able to pass the national entry examinations. In 1989, the State Education Commission put strict limitations on this category of enrollment, allowing no more than 3 percent, except in the province of Guangdong. This is evident in column 6 of Table 5.3, and we have noted earlier the strong dissatisfaction of provincial education commissions with this policy.

These two categories of contract and self-paying students did not solve the serious problem of how to assure professional talent to rural schools, rural agro-technical stations, and rural medical units. This was addressed by the introduction of a category entitled "directed" (*dingxiang*) enrollment, which allowed entry at up to twenty to thirty marks below the normal standard to young people from rural or hardship areas, on the condition that they promised to return to their own area on graduation. There was generally a two-stage job assignment process, as the college or university sent them back, after graduation, to the prefectural or county unit that had nominated them, and there they were assigned a position by the prefectural or county authorities, usually in the same place they had come from, sometimes in a slightly more favorable location, always with the new status and privileges of a state cadre.

Table 5.3 indicates that this type of enrollment dominated prefectural teachers colleges in 1992. While provincial agricultural and teacher training colleges had only about 15 percent of their enrollments in this category in the sense of a lower entry mark, in fact, about 80–90 percent of all their students were in directed programs in the sense of being expected to return to their own prefecture or county to work on graduation. At the national level, however, directed study constituted only a very small percentage of enrollments, a little higher for agricultural and steel institutions with high rural enrollments overall. It was not used at all in municipal institutions, with the exception of Jianghan University, where it covered only the teacher education program preparing teachers for rural counties under the administration of Wuhan city.

The state's key concerns found different expression in different levels and types of institution. In major national universities, especially those under the State Education Commission, the trend was toward greater and greater student involvement in the choice of work unit and career, within the constraints of maintaining some geographic balance in the distribution of professional talent and meeting the needs of important state units. This was called a policy of "mutual choice" (*shuangxiang xuanze*). For specialist ministry institutions, the policy of mutual choice between the work unit and the individual was still unrealistic, as macro-planning continued to dominate the work of sectoral ministries, especially with reference to students trained in specializations directly linked to ministry needs. In new specializations such as management, social sciences, and some high-technology areas, however, there was greater potential for student choice.

The crucial question at Levels I and II was how to ensure that graduating students made choices that would meet the economic development needs of the state and at the same time ensure the fullest possible use of their talents and professional knowledge. One of the most serious problems of the old planning system was the fact that graduates had been mechanistically slotted into places that often did not suit either their inclinations or their educational background. There had been a tremendous waste of professional talent. In the more open situation of the late 1980s, students tended to choose their preferred geographic region first, the level and type of employing unit second, and only lastly consider professional career development. Due to the rigidity of the system, this choice was the most important of their lives, and family pressures, as well as current fads such as the fascination with joint ventures and opportunities in Guangdong, tended to play a large role. For example, the Huazhong University of Science and Technology reported that half of all its graduates had gone to the east coast in a search of high-paying jobs in 1988, regardless of the fact that many might have found more satisfying long-term careers in research and teaching environments or in public service. Clearly, it was not easy to create conditions for the best use of professional talent from the perspectives either of the state or of the individual.

To turn to the perspective of young people themselves, higher education offered them one of the few opportunities for social mobility in China. For rural youth, the only other possibilities for "escaping the countryside" were the army, usually available only to those with good political connections, or the occasional chance for the recruitment of low-level urban labor on a contract basis, which did not provide urban residential permits. Urban youth also often found themselves unemployed for long periods after secondary school graduation, depending on the state of the urban job market for workers and clerical personnel. Entry to the lowest level of position within the state bureaucracy was only available to those who graduated from secondary technical or normal schools (*zhongzhuan*), and the expansion of enrollments in these institutions was strictly regulated, while vocational and agricultural secondary schools that gave no entry to state jobs had proliferated over the 1980s.

What were the strategies, then, of rural and urban youth seeking to use the higher education system as a means of enhancing their life chances? Everything depended on the level of their marks in the national unified entrance examinations. Thus, in filling in their application forms and stating their preferences in terms of field of study and institution, a delicate balance between the possible and the ideal was required. The very best students had the widest choice, and were aware that certain fields and certain institutions offered them preferable career opportunities. Students less certain of high marks, whether from urban or rural areas, would weigh the possibilities of a national-level institution in a relatively unpopular field, such as agriculture, steel, or teacher education, against those of a provincial or local-level institution in a preferable field. Those with the lowest level of marks would have to be satisfied with entry to a provincial or prefectural institution, often under directed training programs, which allowed for lower entry marks and required a commitment to return to one's place of origin.

Generally, the greatest mobility and choice was available to those who entered national institutions, and this was almost certain to assure urban job postings to rural students, though they could be anywhere throughout the nation, a consideration that often gave pause to urban students. On the whole, there was some certainty of a good job opportunity at one level lower than the level of institution entered. Thus, graduates of national universities, who did not make it into the national bureaucracy, were almost sure to be able to return to a job assignment in their provincial capital or a main provincial city, whereas graduates of provincial institutions would probably have to accept job postings at the prefectural or county town level. Graduates of prefectural institutions would almost certainly have to return to grass-roots units, as desirable positions in county and prefectural towns were held for graduates of provincial-level institutions.

The level of one's institution was all important in terms of career prospects. Students in urban vocational universities probably faced the least anxiety, as they were likely to get jobs in their own urban area. Professional field was usually a secondary consideration in the early 1980s. By the late 1980s and early 1990s, however, more and more students became interested in new business opportunities and saw the need to have a competitive advantage in terms of expertise in certain fields. Table 5.3 illustrates the preference of urban youth for fields such as management, finance, foreign languages, medicine, civil and electronic engineering, and general arts and science subjects. This left less favored opportunities in programs of agriculture, teacher training, and such engineering areas as steel, mining, and petroleum to rural students, who tended to have lower marks due to the disadvantages they suffer in rural secondary school programs.

Women Students

Table 5.3 gives evidence of great differentials in female participation by level and field. Generally, high female levels of participation were correlated with high urban enrollments. For example, Changsha Vocational University had no rural students and a 50 percent female participation, while Guangzhou Foreign Languages Institute had an 85 percent urban enrollment and a 54 percent female participation. By contrast, those institutions with high rural enrollments tended to have lower percentages of female participation, the most obvious cases being the two agricultural universities, Wuhan Steel University, and some of the prefectural normal colleges. These figures reflected a situation in rural lower secondary schools where girls were not encouraged by their families to enter upper secondary schools, and where many dropped out due to the pressures of family needs. Most rural families had several children, and boys were almost certain to receive greater family support for higher education than girls. The highest aspiration of most rural families for their daughters was entry to a professional or normal school at the upper secondary level, which assured a state job in the locality on graduation. In 1991, 45.5 percent of enrollments in these institutions were female.[28]

Prejudice against female graduates was a problem that reached serious proportions during the reform decade,[29] and that was beginning to affect enrollment policies at institutions that feared having too many female graduates with problems seeking employment. While three of the four provinces visited had a policy allowing entry to women at two to four marks below the standard, some universities demanded higher entry scores for women than men, in order to ensure a "balanced" enrollment. This was particularly the case for programs that were popular with women students. For example, Guangzhou Foreign Languages Institute reported that it tried to ensure that female enrollment did not go above 50 percent, which meant offering places to male applicants with much lower marks on the national college entry examinations than those required of female applicants. Qualified female entrants had little recourse, in this situation, except to accept an entry offer to a less desirable institution.[30]

Adult Students

Some of the problems facing adult higher education in the late 1980s have been discussed both in chapter 4 and earlier in this chapter. Table 5.3 indicates that many of the twenty universities visited under this project had large enrollments of adult students. Regular higher institutions in the formal sector were often more easily able to attract these students than local adult institutions, given the greater prestige of their diplomas. Many of these adult students were actually recent secondary school graduates who had failed to get enough marks for entry to the formal higher education system, and saw the adult system as a kind of second opportunity.

Most regular institutions reported making considerable income through their adult education programs, a needed and valuable addition to their budgets, as well as an important outlet for the talents of their faculty in a situation where teacher-student ratios remained low. The main concern facing university administrators was how far to develop this type of activity, given that the levels of teaching were lower than regular university programs, and an overextension of faculty in this type of activity could have a negative affect on research and professional development.

Institutions specifically devoted to adult higher education, however, faced a much more serious situation. Wuhan Adult Education Institute illustrated the problem well. Integrated with Wuhan city's television university, it served Wuhan and its three outlying city districts and four rural counties. In 1982 and 1983, it recruited totals of 6,285 and 6,705 students per year, whereas by 1987, yearly enrollment intakes had dropped to the level of 2,559, by 1989 to 1,254, and by 1991 to 843. Of the total of 2,974 students enrolled in 1992, 2,000 were full-time undergraduates in short-cycle diploma programs, and only 974 were genuine adult education students. In its search for new students, it clearly faced tough competition from programs at the large number of excellent national universities in the city of Wuhan.

Actually, this problem was nationwide by the early 1990s, and is reflected in national statistics for television and radio universities. While they had been enrolling around 250,000 students per year in 1982 and 1983,[31] by 1991 they registered entrants of only 86,243, with about 20 percent of these being full-time students not yet in the labor market.[32] As a kind of second-rate, or second-choice higher education, adult education was certain to continue losing ground in the 1990s, as expansion was allowed to escalate in the formal higher education system. Nonformal higher institutions clearly needed some rethinking to suit new needs and conditions, an issue that will be considered in chapter 7.

UNIVERSITY RESEARCH AND DEVELOPMENT ACTIVITIES

The development of the research function of higher institutions has been one of the significant achievements of the reform decade and an important aspect of newly emerging university identities. Table 5.4 profiles the research and development activities of the twenty universities included in this study. The national universities under the State Education Commission and other ministries tended to have the highest research profile, while provincial institutions were struggling to develop their research potential. Municipal and prefectural institutions, whose teaching was mainly at the short-cycle level, were not expected to have substantial research activities. Unfortunately, there are some gaps in Table 5.4, which reflect the reluctance of some institutions to reveal sensitive financial statistics, but these figures give an indication, nevertheless, of the importance of research in relation to the broader university budget. They also give an idea of how far universities were succeeding in 1992 in developing independent sources of funding through their own profit-making activities.

Vertical (*zongxiang*) research funding refers to funds gained from national and provincial sources, such as the National Natural Sciences Foundation and state allocations under the national and/or provincial five-year plan. This funding was usually won on the basis of competitive peer review, and tended to go for projects oriented toward basic questions that represented a relatively high academic level. Horizontal (*hengxiang*) funding was gained through contracts with productive units, either enterprises or state bureaus responsible for production. Projects were generally of a lower academic level, as well as being applied in nature. At best, horizontal projects represented interesting applied areas of investigation, as well as making possible funding for equipment and other facilities that could also be used in basic research. At worst, they were little more than routine industrial testing and problem-solving activities that were far below the normal level of research expected of a higher institution.

It is clear from Table 5.4 that the Huazhong University of Science and Technology had by far the strongest research profile, both in terms of the size of its research budget and its relative importance in relation to the overall budget of the university. Its administrators explained a strategy of encouraging researchers to put forward maximum efforts to gain vertical funding, while using horizontal funding possibilities to supplement the more limited levels of funding available through state funds. National ministry institutions such as Hunan University and Wuhan Steel University relied more heavily on horizontal funding. Their specific engineering orientation and their extensive contacts with enterprises within their sector made this kind of funding more easily accessible than it was for other institutions. Social science institutions such as Zhongnan University of Finance and Economics had far less possibility of gaining substantial research funds, and what was available came largely through vertical projects. The same was true for provincial institutions, which gained most of their limited research funding from provincial governments.

The striking point that was evident to us in all the institutions visited that had a research mandate was the significant potential of this research for contributing to local economic development and for providing a basis for new industries that could open up substantial new income sources for the institution and the region. Almost all of the national and provincial universities were participating in the "Spark" program. This was even true of

TABLE 5.4 A Profile of R & D Activities in Twenty Higher Institutions

	Reg.	Students Adult	Grad.	Budget (mil. yuan)	Research (mil. yuan)	% Vertical	% Horizontal	Profits (mil. yuan)
I. National SEdC								
Huazhong-P	9,429	3,600	1,700	45	26.5	68	32	7.5
Zhongshan-U	5,592	3,321	895	n.a.	10	65	40	6.0
Guangzhou-L	1,200	1,500	47	n.a.	n.a.	n.a.	n.a.	3.0
II. National Ministry								
Wuhan-S	2,900	2,000	110	15.4	2.5	30	70	1.8
Huazhong-Ag	2,900	n.a.	228	n.a.	4.0	75	25	n.a.
Zhongnan-F	4,000	3,700	250	10	.7	80	20	–
Hunan-E	4,987	1,500	500	25	7.0	40	60	5.0
Zhongshan-M	2,532	700	475	15*	3.0	30	70	3.0
III. Provincial								
Henan-U	5,973	7,670	250	14	.75	90	10	1.0
Zhengzhou-U	4,800	n.a.	126	20	1.2	90	10	3.0
Hunan-N	7,200	n.a.	200	n.a.	1.4	97	3	1.0
Hunan-Ag	3,500	1,500	100	n.a.	1.0	70	30	n.a.
IV. Municipal								
Shenzhen-U	3,078	6,000	–	31	.3	20	80	12
Jianghan-V	3,406	1,363	–	9	.2	100	–	1.0
Changsha-V	1,200	400	–	3.5	–	–	–	1.7
Wuhan-Ad	2,974	–	–	1.3	.01	100	–	–
V. Prefectural								
Xiaogan-N	1,770	750	–	3.5	.03	100	–	.46
Lingling-N	1,586	812	–	n.a.	n.a.	n.a.	n.a.	n.a.
Hengyang-N	2,182	n.a.	–	n.a.	.02	100	–	–
Huizhou-N	2,000	763	–	n.a.	.24	17	83	–

Key: For key to descriptions see Table 5.3.

* This is the educational budget and does not include a budget of 14 million yuan for the university's six teaching hospitals.

Zhongnan University of Finance and Economics. It assigned a vice-county head each year to one county in Hubei, as well as sending young teachers to work in accounting departments at the county level in the provinces of Henan, Guangxi, and Hunan.

Most universities had their own factories and some had companies that produced and marketed products of various kinds. Some of these factories were part of the heritage of the 1950s, when universities had been encouraged to combine education and production. However, the idea of universities getting involved in joint ventures of various kinds was quite new. Shenzhen was in the lead in these activities, due to its special geographical position, and it reported that 4 of its 12 million yuan in profits in 1991 came from university factories, while the other 8 million came from joint ventures, including a new computer software company formed in cooperation with IBM Canada. In this case a certain percentage of the shares belonged to the university.

Most other universities were in the process of planning new ventures on a more modest level. Many of them related to agriculture, and had some potential for supporting local development. A striking case was a project to produce a fine white flour and clear noodle from sweet potatoes, the main crop of one of the poorest mountainous counties in the province. Others included new types of pesticide entirely based on vegetable products, new forms of animal feed that used up the waste products of rapeseed oil production, electric generators for remote areas that burned only vegetable oil, water treatment and waste management systems, new high-tech medical equipment, new health foods, etc. The final column of Table 5.4 indicates that this kind of profit-making activity still made a very limited contribution to university budgets, except in the case of Shenzhen University. Much of the limited funding in this category actually came from adult education classes.

This kind of development appeared to have both considerable promise and a real potential for harm in Chinese universities. On the positive side, the increased funding could make them less dependent on the state and much more autonomous. Productive activities linked universities directly to the economic change process and ensured that their faculty and staff were not left behind as incomes rose in other sectors. There were also educational possibilities, as creative teachers and researchers could involve their students in all aspects of product development, from applied research and engineering design to market analysis, advertisement, and new product promotion, in a new approach to integrating education, research, and production.

On the negative side, "business fever" on university campuses was beginning to be a serious distraction from academic teaching and research work. It also resulted in great disparities between those departments whose knowledge made a saleable commodity in the form of popular classes and technical consulting, like English and engineering departments, and those that were not easily amenable to this kind of activity, like philosophy, history, literature, and the theoretical social sciences. Thus by the late 1980s the question was whether the great efforts made to develop new university identities, through expanded teaching programs and vigorous new research initiatives, would falter in face of increasing pressures for the commercialization of both teaching and research.

FACULTY AND INTERNATIONAL ACTIVITIES

Table 5.5 gives a picture of faculty numbers at the twenty universities studied in this project, and the extent of their international involvement. In national universities under the SEDC, the percentage of faculty who had spent extended periods abroad was quite high in 1992. Although there was a serious problem of non-returnees at this level, those who had returned made up a substantial part of the overall faculty contingent, 71 percent in the case of Guangzhou Foreign Languages Institute, 30 percent in the case of Zhongshan University, and 16 percent in the case of HUST. Many of these returnees remained in contact with universities where they had done research abroad and participated in international research projects and conferences, thus bringing their institutions into an international orbit. In national ministry institutions, percentages of foreign returned faculty were more modest, yet they nevertheless represented a force within the university community.

At provincial and municipal institutions, the presence of returnees was smaller, yet in some cases it gave an important impetus to specific program areas. This was particularly notable with two institutions with cooperative projects supported by the Canadian International Development Agency. At Changsha Vocational University, ten of the twenty returnees had come back from Canada under a CIDA project and they were working together to bring about program innovations in the areas of fashion, tourism, interior decorating, and computers. In Wuhan Adult Education Institute, seventeen of twenty-two persons sent to Canada under a CIDA project had returned, and they constituted the total body of returnees in the institute. Many of them had science and engineering backgrounds, but their exposure to adult education in Canada enabled them to develop new approaches to teaching, to prepare new textbooks, and to develop research into teaching and learning processes for adults.

The case of Shenzhen University was a special one, which we were not able to reflect in the statistics of Table 5.5. Since the university was founded only in 1983, and started operation in 1984, it had sent very few scholars abroad, and even fewer had yet returned. However, its location enabled it to attract a large number of returnees who had gone abroad from other Chinese institutions, including twenty-five with foreign doctorates, and even more with master's degrees.

Table 5.5 indicates that the proportion of women in the teaching faculty was close to the national average of 29.1 in most institutions, with municipal institutions having a particularly high proportion of women on faculty, as was true for two of the national agricultural and engineering institutions. Prefectural colleges had relatively low female representation on faculty, probably reflecting their rural orientation.

When it came to opportunities for study abroad, however, the percentage of women in those who had been sent was lower than their general representation in the faculty contingent, with one exception. This can be seen by comparing columns 2 and 5 in Table 5.5. The reasons seemed to lie in the fact that women found themselves in the lower echelons of faculty, with less support from both the university and their families for study abroad than their male counterparts. Another interesting statistic evident in comparing columns 5 and 8 is that there were even fewer women represented in the contingent of returnees in all cases but one. There may have been two reasons for this. Women gained opportunities for going abroad somewhat later, so it is natural that fewer should have returned by 1992. Also, it may be harder for them than for their male colleagues to adjust to the social constraints facing them in professional life in China after having become used to greater freedoms in Western countries.

At Shenzhen University we had an interesting discussion with four returnees on this issue. Three had doctoral degrees and had been abroad for very lengthy periods, two in the United States and one in France. The fourth had spent a shorter period of time in Japan. They had originally gone abroad from Changchun, Shanghai, Xi'an, and Harbin, respectively, but all had chosen to come back to Shenzhen because they perceived opportunities for freer social relations and fuller professional growth there. This choice represented a kind of compromise between staying abroad permanently and returning to the perceived social and professional restrictiveness of their home environments. Two of these four were women, one of them single, and the two women particularly emphasized the importance of this more open social environment.[33]

Overall, Table 5.5 shows the considerable contribution that has been made to faculty development by various programs for study and research abroad, in spite of the large gap between the number who went and the number who returned. An interesting example comes from the Huazhong University of Science and Technology, where the whole management program had been shaped through cooperation with Canadian universities under a CIDA project. Even though only twelve of the thirty-eight faculty sent abroad under the project had returned by 1992, the involvement of Canadian fac-

TABLE 5.5 Profile of University Faculty and Their International Activities

	Total Faculty	% Female	Total Sent Abrd. since 1978	% of Total Faculty	% Female	Total Return	% of Total Faculty	% Female	% Grad. Degree
I. National SEdC									
*Huazhong-P	2,311	23.9	810	35	16	370	16	11	10
*Zhongshan-U	1,799	n.a.	800	45	n.a.	536	30	n.a.	n.a.
Guangzhou-L	340	n.a.	300	88	n.a.	240	71	n.a.	n.a.
II. National Ministry									
*Wuhan-S	800	15	53	7	8	28	3.5	n.a.	46
*Huazhong-Ag	693	34	189	27	19	105	15	14	12
Zhongnan-F	800	25	74	9	30	50	6	20	–
Hunan-E	1,218	35	200	16	8	120	10	n.a.	2
*Zhongshan-M	1,500	n.a.	400	26	33	200	13	n.a.	n.a.
III. Provincial									
Henan-U	1,422	37.5	75	5	n.a.	25	1.8	12	–
Zhengzhou-U	1,132	23	60	5	n.a.	41	3.6	7	10
Hunan-N	961	26	124	13	28	42	4.4	31	7
*Hunan-Ag	552	n.a.	40	7	n.a.	18	3.3	n.a.	6
IV. Municipal									
Shenzhen-U	400	33	n.a.	n.a.	n.a.	n.a.	n.a.	n.a.	n.a.
Jianghan-V	500	30	47	9	15	30	6	7	–
*Changsha-V	320	n.a.	37	12	n.a.	20	6	n.a.	–
*Wuhan-Ad	130	33	22	17	n.a.	17	13	29	–
V. Prefectural									
Xiaogan-N	250	n.a.	5	2	n.a.	5	2	n.a.	–
Lingling-N	178	15.1	–	–	–	–	–	–	–
Hengyang-N	238	23	4	2	n.a.	4	2	n.a.	–
Huizhou-N	223	25	6	3	n.a.	6	3	n.a.	–

Key: For key to descriptions, see Table 5.3.

* Institutions having CIDA projects.

ulty in teaching, research, and curricular development, combined with the ongoing efforts of the returnees, had made a lasting impact.

Two international projects may illustrate how universities could sometimes become a conduit for a specific external influence that reached into a wider Chinese society. Wuhan Iron and Steel University had a large-scale cooperative project with Australia, which was supported by the Australian International Development Assistance Bureau. It was one of two major adult education projects carried out under a national agreement between the two countries, with a focus on the steel industry that reflected strong trade relations between the two countries.

The purpose of the project was to train 1,900 personnel throughout China's national steel industry in management, technology, and computing. The Australian side had invested 10.5 million Australian dollars in the project, with matching funds of 10.5 million yuan from the Chinese Ministry of Metallurgical Industry. There were ten Australian teachers in residence, including an Australian director and co-director of the project, both of whom had some expertise in the Chinese language and the Chinese economy. They worked closely with Chinese faculty from Wuhan Steel University, who were being given the opportunity for some training in Australia. Overall, the project demonstrated how a sectoral university could play a significant role in shaping new directions for a major national industry, as the conduit for new ideas in management, and new skills in computing and high-technology areas.[34]

The other interesting case was that of Wuhan University, which had had an ongoing project of cooperation with the French government since 1978. A department of French language and literature had been established, which made it possible for about one-third of the university's students to learn French as their first foreign language, and many others as a second foreign language. There was also a special program in mathematics education, whereby a certain number of classes had done their whole undergraduate program in French, and the best graduates had gone to France for doctoral training. Seventeen young Chinese scholars of mathematics with French doctorates were teaching in the mathematics department by 1992, and there was a center for mathematics research and doctoral training supported jointly by both sides. There had also been considerable cooperation in the training of students in French literature, economics, and management up to the pre-doctoral level. This was one of the rare international projects that had a broad knowledge base, with a strong emphasis on theoretical teaching and research. It was also unusual in the fact that there had been between ten and fifteen French professors in mathematics, language, literature, and economics teaching there on a regular basis over the decade, with support from the French government.[35]

The new initiative that was being planned in 1992 was to set up a university institute of technology on the French model at Wuhan University that would recruit students nationwide, have all its programs taught in

French, and establish national standards for the kind of short-cycle education normally done by vocational universities on the municipal level. The expectation was that the university would be able to make contracts for the training of personnel nationwide, due to the prestige it had as a national comprehensive university and its special connection with France.[36] This was an ambitious project, and one that might well exert a broad national influence in the area of technical education, as well as bring considerable income to the university. It somehow exemplified a European preference for a highly visible, centralized approach to educational cooperation that stood in contrast to the more diffuse patterns of local cooperation that characterized CIDA's institutional linkage projects.

REFLECTIONS FROM THE RETURNED SCHOLARS

While most of the information so far in this chapter came from interviews with university administrators, this last section presents the views of scholars who had returned from abroad. Individual interviews were held with thirty-nine returned scholars at twelve of the universities visited. These were arranged for us through the foreign affairs office, and it is likely that those considered most competent professionally and most positive in their attitudes were selected to meet with us. We asked to interview as many women as possible, yet only four of the thirty-nine selected were women.

Table 5.6 gives a profile by field and by family background of the thirty-nine scholars. Though this was not a representative sample, it is interesting to note that 26 percent came from peasant backgrounds, and many of these were faculty in the agricultural and steel universities. Another 38 percent were from intellectual families, 13 percent from working-class families, and 10 percent from cadre families. The "other" category mainly referred to older scholars who had grown up in families having small businesses before 1949.

Table 5.7 indicates the countries where these scholars were trained and the level of study. Only seven had taken graduate degrees, five at the master's level and two at the doctoral level, while all the rest had been visiting scholars. This made the group fairly representative of the overall returnee population, as the final column of Table 5.5 indicates the low percentage of degree holders among returnees overall. The main countries of study were Canada and the United States, but there were also returnees from England, Japan, Germany, and Australia.

Generally, the scholars were positive and enthusiastic about their period of study abroad. Many indicated that this had been a significant turning point in their professional lives, and had opened up areas of research and teaching that would otherwise have been impossible. A small number expressed severe frustration that they had not been able to undertake graduate degree work—in some cases to complete graduate degrees that had been initiated—due to financial or other constraints. This was a crucial issue for younger faculty, who returned to an environment in which graduate degrees had become all-important in promotion decisions.

When asked their reason for returning, most responded that the main one was a sense of the possibilities for further professional development and for putting to use the new areas of knowledge acquired abroad. This outweighed family or patriotic considerations, and indicated how important an ongoing reform climate in Chinese universities was in attracting faculty back from abroad.

We asked each of the thirty-nine scholars interviewed to tell us about his or her work in teaching, research, and administration after returning from abroad, and to comment on how the balance of responsibility had changed. In almost all cases, they reported an enhanced participation in research as a result of being abroad. Some scholars who had only done teaching in the past were able to initiate research projects as a result of their time abroad. As for administration, there was considerable difference of view. Some felt that it was a waste of time for them to take on administrative work and made every effort to guard their time for research and teaching. Others saw real possibility for having a wider impact in the reform process by undertaking administrative responsibility at the level of the academic department or higher.

Almost all returned scholars reported that their experience abroad had had a definite impact on their teaching style and course content. Most had initiated new courses, using material they had collected abroad and one of the serious problems they faced was the lack of appropriate textbooks or teaching materials. In addition to their involvement in starting new courses in their own institutions, a considerable number were also serving on curriculum development committees at the provincial or national level.

Teaching methods had changed quite a lot, most reported, yet they were frustrated by constraints within their own university environment that prevented them from going as far as they would have liked with experimentation in teaching. Older faculty often gave little support to such efforts, and students tended to be conservative, resisting innovative approaches that might call for greater independent effort and more initiative on their part. The mood and atmosphere among university students was a real concern. Many commented on their lack of serious commitment to study, their restlessness, and a general malaise that seemed to reflect both the political

	Family Background	Worker	Peasant	Intellectual	Cadre	Other
6	Agriculture (15.5%)	1	2	1	–	2
5	Steel (13%)	–	3 (1F)	1	–	1
7	Education (18%)	1 (F)	–	6 (1F)	–	–
4	Management/ Economics (10%)	–	2	–	2	–
5	Math/Science (13%)	1	1	3	–	–
4	Engineering (10%)	1	–	2	1	–
6	Foreign Languages (15.5%)	1	1	1	1 (F)	2
2	Medicine (5%)	–	1	1	–	–
	Total: 39	5	10	15	4	5
	(100%)	(13%)	(26%)	(38%)	(10%)	(13%)

Women: Only four (10%) of total interviewed.

TABLE 5.7 A Profile of Returnees by Country and Level of Study

Country	Visiting Scholar	Doctoral	Masters
Canada 11	9	–	2
USA 10	10	–	–
England 7	4	1	2
Japan 3	3	–	–
Germany 3	2	1	–
Australia 3	2	–	1
Sweden 1	1	–	–
Ukraine 1	1	–	–
Total: 39	32	2	5

stresses of the post-Tiananmen period and the profound value changes associated with the burgeoning commodity economy. The mood among graduate students also affected the research of returned faculty. Many reported that one of the most serious constraints they faced in their research work was the lack of reliable graduate student assistants. Many had entered graduate school with the hope of going abroad, rather than ambitions to enter university research and teaching positions in China.

Nevertheless, the majority of returnees, except those in municipal institutions, were very active in research. Those in natural and applied sciences had considerable success in gaining research funding, although this depended to a large degree on their status. Younger scholars, at the level of lecturer or below, had much greater difficulty. There was a kind of vicious circle at work, in that it was hard for them to get the publications needed for promotion without solid research funding, yet funding was mainly awarded to those with the status of associate professor or above.

Younger returnees who had doctoral degrees, whether they had been gained abroad or in China, were in the best position to launch good research projects. There were several striking cases of young professors who had been rapidly promoted and who were engaged in research in areas on a leading edge. For example, a thirty-three-year-old full professor at Huazhong Agricultural University, who had a British doctorate and was working on aspects of genetic engineering related to agriculture, regularly spent three months of every year in Britain. He had gained support from the Rockefeller Foundation, and had ongoing research, as well as joint doctoral training, with several professors in Britain. This young man came from a peasant family, in a small village, and both of his parents were illiterate.

Generally, most returnees felt themselves to be part of an international milieu. Although it was rare for them to have the opportunity for attending conferences abroad, they were able to attend international conferences held in China and this was of the greatest importance for enabling them to keep in touch. They were often frustrated by the slowness of their library systems, and the lack of an adequate and timely information flow in their specialist areas of research. Thus they were most eager for ongoing research cooperation that would keep them in direct contact with colleagues abroad in their field, and they were enthusiastic about the possibility of doing some teaching in cooperation with colleagues from abroad.

CONCLUSION

This picture of the Central South provides some details that may serve to fill out the broad lines of change over the reform decade sketched out in chapter 4. In curricular terms, we have seen examples of the way in which many different types of university have moved toward a more comprehensive and integrated curriculum, in many cases under the stimulus of active participation in diverse programs of international academic exchange and cooperation. While most of the curricular reforms have been positive, by the late 1980s, there was a disturbing commercialization of knowledge underway.

In geographical terms, the Central South was a favored area that benefited both from the policies of the 1950s, emphasizing the development of a strong industrial base around Wuhan, and the reforms of the 1980s, giving Guangdong a leading role in stimulating the economy. While Wuhan continued to benefit from the large concentration of universities and colleges it inherited from the 1950s, Guangdong was able to attract the very best graduates and faculty from all over China in a vigorous expansion program. By contrast, the heavily rural province of Henan, and the Guangxi Zhuang autonomous region with its large minority population, remained relatively underdeveloped in terms of higher education. They were likely to become increasingly disadvantaged with the greater freedom given to graduates of national institutions in seeking employment.

Under the market system, the strong were becoming stronger and the weak weaker. This pattern could also be seen in adult education, where prestigious national institutions were able to develop vigorous programs on the basis of their academic excellence and the attraction of their reputation, while nonformal adult institutions were becoming increasingly marginalized. Some sort of integration of these two tracks of higher education, which would make good use of the faculty and resources of both seemed to be called for.

In spite of these increasing imbalances, peripheral provinces and cities within the region were taking vigorous action to see that their institutions were not left too far behind. There was a pragmatism in their determination to ensure their contribution to local economic development, and also a pride and vision in their efforts to provide channels for them to participate in a wider international community.

Overall, therefore, a fairly hopeful picture was captured in this snapshot taken in May 1992. The vision and energy with which universities and colleges at all levels were revitalizing their teaching programs, embracing new research opportunities, and connecting to their past, to future opportunities, and to the particular communities they served was remarkable. The compromises being made between state demands and expectations of students, and the space for them to pursue their own interests and ambitions was also promising. Chapter 6 continues the story with a picture of the Northwest region taken one year later in the spring of 1993.

NOTES

1. "Plan Sets Target for Three Economic Belts," *Beijing Review*, April 21, 1986, pp. 8–9; "Economic Growth in Different Regions," *Beijing Review*, December 6, 1986, pp. 21–24.

2. An alternative schematization developed by economists put Guangxi in the Western region, which reflects its economic profile more accurately. See Li Shiyi and Wu Ming, "China Prepares a Major Program of Economic Development of Its Central Areas—First Forum for Strategies for Economic and Social Development in Central China held in Wuhan," in Hong Kong—*Liaowang Overseas Edition in Chinese*,

no. 5, February 3 , 1986, *(FBIS)*, no. 32, February 18, 1986, p. K6.

3. Most of the information in this chapter is derived from visits to the four provinces of Henan, Hubei, Hunan, and Guangdong in May and June 1992. Unfortunately, we were not able to visit Guangxi or Hainan, only to use sources of statistical information to represent their situation. Special thanks is due to CIDA for funding this research, and to the Higher Education Research Institute of Huazhong University of Science and Technology (HUST) for making all arrangements. The visits and interviews were carried out in partnership with Professor Chen Changgui of HUST.

4. Unfortunately, we are not able to give parallel information for Guangxi and Hainan, as they were not included in our visits. However, it is likely that Hainan finds itself in a situation similar to Guangdong, while Guangxi probably faces even greater difficulty than Henan.

5. *Essential Statistics of Education in China for 1992* (Department of Planning and Construction, State Education Commission, P.R.C., March 1993) indicates that 349,847 students were enrolled in four-year academic programs that year, and 404,345 in short-cycle vocationally oriented programs. This can be contrasted with 1980, when 204,142 were admitted to four-year programs, but only 77,088 to short-cycle programs.

6. Ibid., p. 53.

7. *Zhongguo jiaoyu bao*, February 18, 1992, p. 2.

8. R. Hayhoe, "The Context of Educational Exchanges: Challenges for China and the West," *China Exchange News*, Vol. 20, no. 1, Spring 1992, p. 4.

9. R. Hayhoe, *China's Universities and the Open Door*, pp. 174–176.

10. Interview with Liu Daoyu, Shanghai, October 24, 1985.

11. "Wuda jiehe wenke jiaoxue pipan zichan jieji ziyouhua," [Wuhan University Combines Teaching in the Humanities with the Criticism of Bourgeois Liberalization], in *Zhongguo jiaoyu bao*, February 2, 1991, p. 1; Ren Xinlian, "Jianchi jiaoxue lingyu de shehui kexue fangxiang, pipan zichan jieji ziyouhua sichao," [Hold Firm to Social Science Orientations in Educational Circles, and Criticize the Wave of Bourgeois Liberalization] *Zhongguo gaodeng jiaoyu*, no. 5, 1991, p. 18.

12. Yeh Wen-hsin, *The Alienated Academy*, pp. 173–176. Liang Shan, Li Xian, and Zhang Kemo, *Zhongshan daxue xiaoshi 1924–1949* [A History of Zhongshan University, 1924–1949] (Shanghai: Shanghai jiaoyu chubanshe, 1983).

13. Interviews with Zhu Jiusi, Wuhan, May 14, 15, 16, 1993. See also R. Hayhoe, "Chinese Universities and the Social Sciences," *Minerva*, Vol. XXXI, no. 4, 1993, pp. 500–503.

14. Yao Qihe et al. (eds.), *Huazhong Ligong Daxue de sishi nian* [The Forty Years of Huazhong University of Science and Technology] (Wuhan: Huazhong Ligong Daxue chubanshe, 1993), p. 209.

15. For an illuminating overview of the role and development of foreign language institutes in China, see Heidi Ross, *China Learns English: Language Learning and Social Change in the People's Republic* (New Haven and London: Yale University Press, 1993), especially chapter 2, and chapter 3, pp. 42–47.

16. *Zhongnan caijing daxue xiaoshi* [An Institutional History of the Central South University of Finance and Economics] (Wuhan: Zhongnan caijing daxue chubanshe, 1988). This volume gives a detailed account of the university's development, with proud reflections on its early revolutionary role, and details on each phase of its torturous history. One wry comment made about the Cultural Revolution was that, of the eighteen institutes of finance and economics established in 1952–1953, only one and a half managed to remain open. As a short-cycle college, it was the "half," while the "one" was Liaoning Institute of Finance and Economics in Dalian.

17. This new approach was described in detail in our visit to Zhengzhou University, June 2, 1992. It was also featured in the national press. See *Zhongguo jiaoyu bao*, May 18, 1991, p. 2.

18. *Henan daxue xiaoshi 1912–1984* [Henan University Institutional History,

1912–1984], (informal publication, May 1985), p. 41–53.

19. Ibid., pp. 82–92.

20. Visit to Henan University, June 1, 1992.

21. *Hunan shifan daxue wushi nian* [Hunan Normal University Over Fifty Years] (Changsha: Hunan jiaoyu chubanshe, 1988).

22. Visit to Hunan Normal University, June 6, 1992.

23. Visit to Lingling Normal College, June 9, 1992. In the enthusiasm around the success of these reforms, the school had edited a special issue of its journal with articles describing all aspects of these initiatives. It is titled *Jiaoyu gaige shiyan ziliao huibian* [A Compilation of Materials on Educational Reform Experiments], edited and published by Lingling shifan zhuanke xuexiao, August 1990.

24. For an excellent analysis of the character of China's professional labor force, see Huang Shiqi, "Non-formal Education and Modernization," in R. Hayhoe (ed.), *Education and Modernization: The Chinese Experience* (Toronto: OISE Press, Oxford: Pergamon, 1991), pp. 141–146.

25. "Student Enrollment and Job Assignment Issues," *China News Analysis*, No. 1481, March 1993.

26. For a discussion of the retrenchment in enrollment growth initiated in 1989, and the initial projections of the Eighth Five-year Plan (1991–1995), see R. Hayhoe, "China's Universities Since Tiananmen," *China Quarterly*, no. 134, June 1993, pp. 293–296.

27. For an excellent discussion of enrollment innovations, such as contract training and oriented enrollments, see Vilma Seeberg, "Access to Higher Education: Targeted Recruitment Reform Under Economic Development Plans in the People's Republic of China," in *Higher Education*, Vol. 25, no. 3, March 1993.

28. Department of Planning and Construction, State Education Commission, P.R.C., *Educational Statistics Yearbook of China, 1991/2*, pp. 50–52.

29. Stanley Rosen, "Women, Education, and Modernization," in R. Hayhoe (ed.), *Education and Modernization: the Chinese Experience* (Oxford: Pergamon, Toronto: OISE Press, 1992), pp. 155–184.

30. For a detailed description of how this process worked in the Shanghai context, see Ross, *China Learns English*, pp. 180–185.

31. *Achievement of Education in China: Statistics, 1949–1983* (Beijing: Renmin jiaoyu chubanshe, 1984), pp. 240–241.

32. *Educational Statistics Yearbook, 1991/2*, pp. 98–9.

33. Interview at Shenzhen University, June 17, 1992.

34. Interview with John Sullivan, Australian director of the project, May 21, 1992.

35. R. Hayhoe, *China's Universities and the Open Door*, pp. 140–142.

36. Interview with members of the Foreign Affairs Office, Wuhan University, May 28, 1992.

6 PERSPECTIVES FROM THE NORTHWEST REGION

Chapter 6 provides a kind of snapshot of the Northwest region taken in the spring of 1993, which can be contrasted with the picture of the Central South in chapter 5. The region contains three provinces—Shaanxi, Gansu, and Qinghai—and two autonomous regions—Ningxia and Xinjiang. The economic and cultural center is Shaanxi province and the city of Xi'an, while Lanzhou in Gansu province has the role of a kind of secondary center. There is a large concentration of universities and scientific research institutes in these two cities, also a strong military presence, with eleven military colleges and 20,000 students in Xi'an alone.

Qinghai was separated from Gansu and became a province in 1929, and has retained that status to the present. Due to its huge size and strategic location, it has considerable importance for military reasons, and has also been known as a place of exile, with a number of prison camps and sites for reform through labor. However, it has never enjoyed the degree of economic subsidy from the central government that goes to autonomous regions with large minority populations. Although 34 percent of its population is minority, mainly Tibetan and Hui, special status already belongs to the Tibet and Hui autonomous regions.

Ningxia was separated out from Gansu as a province in 1932, but in 1954 it was rejoined to Gansu. In 1958, at the time of the Great Leap Forward, it was reduced in size, with parts going to Inner Mongolia, and established as an autonomous region for the Hui nationality. A large number of Hui minority cadres came there from all over the country at that time. Also, a considerable number of Han intellectuals and cadres from coastal areas were sent there, in some cases as patriots, in other cases as political exiles. By 1989, the minority population in the region constituted 34.3 percent of the total, mainly Hui.

Xinjiang, the largest and most remote region, had a minority population making up 62 percent of the total in 1989, with the Uighur nationality being the largest at 42 percent, next the Kazak at 7.4 percent and a total of forty-eight other nationalities. Han people made up only 38 percent of the population and were themselves a minority in the region, which had been delineated a Uighur autonomous region after 1949. Wang Zhen had led the People's Liberation Army in to liberate the region in 1949 and many of the military personnel who took part in this activity remained in Xinjiang to form large agricultural collectives (*bingtuan*), which were to lead agricultural development in the region. Due to Wang Zhen's influential position in the party and his ongoing interest in the region up to his death in 1993, it gained considerable attention from Beijing as a site for massive oil and gas development projects, and other heavy industrial projects. It also had special links with Shanghai, due to the large number of Shanghainese sent there over long periods.[1] However, it has had no national-level institutions of higher learning under the State Education Commission, as is the case also for Ningxia and Qinghai. These are all concentrated in the cities of Lanzhou and Xi'an, a pattern similar to that already noted in the Central South.

Figure 6.1 shows the Northwest region in relation to the Central South and to the country as a whole. It constitutes the upper half of the economically underdeveloped western region, as defined in the Sixth Five-year Plan. Its landmass constitutes 31.4 percent of the nation's total, while its population represents only 6.9 percent of the total, a density lower than any other part of the country, including the Southwest.

Table 6.1 gives a developmental profile of the region over the decade of the 1980s. The relative size of the industrial product lagged far behind the population ratio, a lag that increased slightly over the decade, notably in the important provinces of Shaanxi and Gansu. This may reflect the disadvantages they experienced as hinterland provinces under economic policies that favored the coastal region. There was a somewhat better record for agricultural development during the 1980s. The overall growth ratio of the region, 3.14 percent, outpaced the national level of 2.83 percent, and Xinjiang and Gansu did particularly well.

The most striking characteristic of the region is its large minority population, which increased from 32 percent of the total in 1982 to 33.8 percent in 1989. While the overall population growth for the region was just .1 percent above the national level of 1.10 percent, over the decade of the 1980s, the population growth for minorities was 1.17 percent. This reflects a national policy of far less restrictive birth control for minority populations, and is resulting in minorities gaining ground in each province/region, with the gain most dramatic in Qinghai, from 26 percent to 33.4 percent of the

FIGURE 6.1 The Northwest Region in Relation to Three Economic Zones

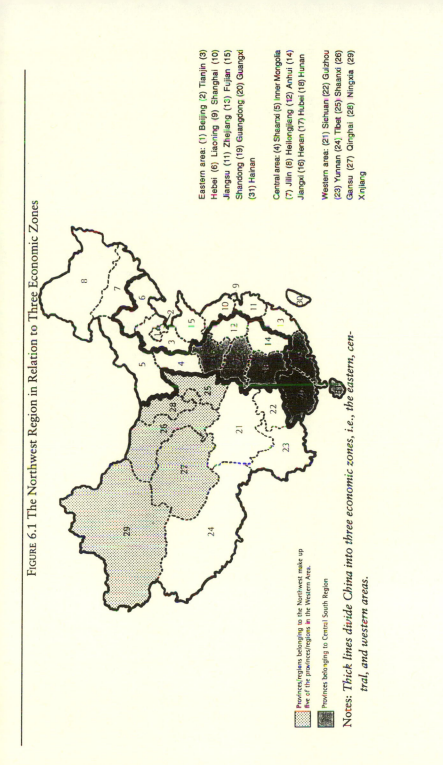

Eastern area: (1) Beijing (2) Tianjin (3) Hebei (6) Liaoning (9) Shanghai (10) Jiangsu (11) Zhejiang (13) Fujian (15) Shandong (19) Guangdong (20) Guangxi (31) Hainan

Central area: (4) Shaanxi (5) Inner Mongolia (7) Jilin (8) Heilongjiang (12) Anhui (14) Jiangxi (16) Henan (17) Hubei (18) Hunan

Western area: (21) Sichuan (22) Guizhou (23) Yunnan (24) Tibet (25) Shaanxi (26) Gansu (27) Qinghai (28) Ningxia (29) Xinjiang

Provinces/regions belonging to the Northwest make up five of the provinces/regions in the Western Area.

Provinces belonging to Central South Region

Notes: *Thick lines divide China into three economic zones, i.e., the eastern, central, and western areas.*

Table 6.1 A Development Profile of the Northwest Region

	Size (1,000 km2)	Population (million)					Industrial Product (billion yuan)			Agricultural Product (billion yuan)		
		1982 Total	1982 Minority	1989 Total	1989 Minority	% up	1984	1989	% up	1981	1989	% up
National	9,600	1,015	6.7%	1,112	8.0%	1.10	703.0	2,201.7	4.25	218.1	653.47	2.83
Shaanxi	190 (2.0%)	28.90 (2.9%)	(0.46%)	31.91 (2.9%)	n.a.	1.10	14.5 (2.0%)	40.67 (1.8%)	3.87	5.0 (2.2%)	14.78 (2.3%)	2.96
Gansu	390 (4.1%)	19.75 (1.95%)	1.2 (6.2%)	21.72 (1.95%)	1.4 (6.2%)	1.10 / 1.15	9.8 (1.4%)	24.83 (1.13%)	3.36	2.8 (1.2%)	8.91 (1.4%)	3.18
Qinghai	720 (7.5%)	3.89 (.39%)	1.04 (26%)	4.55 (.41%)	1.52 (33.4%)	1.16 / 1.46	1.6 (.23%)	5.42 (.25%)	4.52	.8 (.35%)	2.16 (.33%)	2.7
Ningxia	66 (.69%)	3.93 (.39%)	1.24 (31.6%)	4.40 (.40%)	1.51 (34.3%)	1.12 / 1.21	1.8 (.23%)	5.85 (.27%)	4.88	.8 (.35%)	2.14 (.327%)	2.68
Xinjiang	1,650 (17.5%)	13.16 (1.3%)	7.80 (59.2%)	14.54 (1.3%)	9.01 (62%)	1.10 / 1.16	6.0 (.85%)	18.74 (.85%)	4.57	3.4 (1.47%)	12.15 (1.86%)	3.57
Regional Total	3,016 (31.4%)	69.81 (6.9%)	22.31 (32.0%)	77.15 (6.9%)	26.06 (33.8%)	1.11 / 1.17	33.7 (4.7%)	95.51 (4.43%)	3.91	12.8 (5.54%)	40.14 (6.14%)	3.14

Sources: Zhongguo tongji nianjian, 1983, p. 106; 1990, p. 91; 1985, p. 30; 1981, p. 19; 1990, p. 30.

total population. When this trend is combined with the outflow of the Han population in response to the economic pull of the coastal regions, it has important implications for the future of the region.

A. Doak Barnett gives a vivid description of the region in his recent volume, *China's Far West*, contrasting the conditions he found on an extended research visit made in 1988, with those of forty years earlier, when he had visited the region in 1948. Overall, the degree of development and integration into modern patterns of life over that period were remarkable, from his perspective, and he had much to say that was positive about the policies of the Communist government. An important means for this transformation had been the influx of Han professionals and bureaucrats sent from other parts of the country, and this forms an important part of the higher education story for the region. However, the degree to which minority populations have been given access to education and the opportunity for leadership is also noted in Barnett's account of political development, and this too has been a vital aspect of educational policy in the region.[2] It may turn out to be crucial in the future, as the educated Han population is increasingly drawn back to other regions by new opportunities under the market.

A HISTORICAL OVERVIEW OF HIGHER EDUCATION IN THE REGION

There were four distinctive periods or movements that helped to build a foundation for modern higher education and scientific research in the Northwest. The first was the Sino-Japanese War of 1937–1945, when many coastal universities moved to the hinterland to escape Japanese occupation and to contribute to the war effort, and when the Communist party set up its fledgling revolutionary colleges in the liberated areas. In 1937, as a result of the Japanese invasion of the northeast reaching Beijing, major national institutions in Beijing, Tianjin, and Shanghai began their move westward.

Three important national institutions moved to Xi'an in 1937: Beiyang Engineering University, China's first modern university, founded in 1895 in Tianjin; Beiping University, which had been founded by the Francophile scholar, Li Shizeng, by bringing together several specialized institutions in 1928 as part of the movement to adopt a university district system modeled on France; and Beijing Normal University, which had a history going back to 1897, when the first government normal training college had been established. There they combined with Northwest (*Xibei*) University, an institution that dated back to 1912, but had had a weak and interrupted development up to that time,[3] and formed the Northwest United University (*Xibei lianda*).

In 1938, this university divided into several parts—a comprehensive university, an engineering college, an agricultural college, and a normal college, and was dispersed around the south of the province due to Nationalist government concerns about the potential influence of the Yan'an revolutionary base, in the north of the province, on its students.[4] In 1939, the normal college moved to Lanzhou, forming the foundation for Northwest Normal University.[5] In 1942, Gansu College, a provincial institution that had developed from a small college of law and politics, was made a national institution, and in 1946, it was renamed National Lanzhou University.[6] Over the same period considerable support was given to the development of Xinjiang University, which had been established in 1935.

The main foundations for higher education in the Northwest were thus laid in this wartime period, with many distinguished faculty from the best eastern universities contributing to this development. By 1949, there were eight universities, Xinjiang University in Urumchi, Northwest Normal and Lanzhou Universities in Lanzhou, and five universities in Shaanxi, including Northwest University and the Communist party's own Yan'an University.

The second great period of development for higher education in the Northwest took place in the 1950s. With the reorganization of the whole higher education system on a Soviet model in 1952, particular attention was given to ensuring a rational geographic distribution of higher institutions throughout the country, and systematic efforts were made to build up hinterland areas, as we have seen in chapter 3. One of the major projects of the First Five-year Plan was to build a medical university on the model of Leningrad Medical University in Xinjiang, and Xinjiang Medical University remains a strong center of medical training and research to this day. Its campus and buildings still carry an architectural flavor of Leningrad, and its development was also assisted by the transfer of faculty and resources from Shanghai No. 1 Medical University, China Medical University in Shenyang, and Shandong Medical University.

In the area of engineering, several important coastal institutions were transferred to Xi'an to build its capacity for the support of heavy industry in the whole region. The most striking case was the move of China's most famous engineering university, Jiaotong (Communications) University, founded in 1896, from Shanghai to Xi'an in 1956, under the personal supervision of Zhou Enlai. In the same year, the East China Aeronautics University in Nanjing was moved to Xi'an and combined with Northwest Engineering University, which had its roots in the engineering departments that had moved to Xi'an in the wartime period. It was administered by the powerful Ministry of Aeronautics and Astronautics Industry. In 1958, a major institution of communications technology, which had roots in the revolutionary base areas and was located in Zhang Jiakou, Hebei province, was moved to Xi'an and named the Northwest Institute of Telecommunications Engineering. It had absorbed the communications department of Dalian Institute of Technology in 1952, and had become a priority institution under the Ministry of Machine Building and Electronics.

These efforts to build a strong foundation in national-level institutions were complemented in 1958 with the creation of major provincial-level institutions in each province/region. Ningxia University and Qinghai Normal University were both created at this time, and a large contingent of the best graduates of Beijing Normal University were assigned to both places as young faculty on graduation. Qinghai Medical College was set up in 1958 with the help of a group of twenty key faculty from the West China Union University's medical school in Chengdu, originally a Canadian missionary school.[7] Also, the Lanzhou Railway Institute was set up in 1958, as the final institution in the network of railway colleges throughout the country. Its faculty came mainly from Northern Jiaotong University in Beijing and the railway college in Tangshan.

The final period in which Northwest higher education gained some support from eastern regions was the Cultural Revolution decade, when several institutions and numerous individuals were transferred there. Northwest Light Industry College was established in Xianyang, Shaanxi, in 1970, on the basis of a college of light industry that was moved from Beijing, where it had been set up in 1958. It remained under the administration of the Ministry of Light Industry. In 1972, the Beijing College of Mechanical Engineering was combined with the Shaanxi University of Technology, which had been founded in 1960 in Xi'an, and the new Shaanxi Institute of Mechanical Engineering was located in Hanzhong as part of the attempt to send institutions down to the grass roots. After the Cultural Revolution, it moved back to Xi'an, and it has remained under the administration of the Ministry of Machine Building and Electronics.

Throughout the period from the mid-1950s to the Cultural Revolution decade, large numbers of intellectuals and cadres who fell into disfavor under the various political/ideological movements that were launched also found themselves exiled to the great Northwest, especially to regions such as Qinghai, Ningxia, and Xinjiang. Many of these ended up teaching secondary school and establishing remarkably high standards for secondary education in such remote locations as the agricultural collectives (*bingtuan*) under the military in Xinjiang.

This historical sketch gives us a picture of a region whose educational and scientific strength, in terms of both quantity and quality of higher institutions and their faculty, definitely outpaced its economic strength, in spite of considerable potential in terms of natural resources, heavy industry, and agriculture. It was, in a sense, a triumph of the socialist planning system, and it will be interesting to see how far it is possible in future to preserve and build further on this base under the conditions of a market economy.

By 1982, there were seventy-one institutions in the region, and by 1989 the number had increased to ninety-nine. Table 6.2 shows how the percentage of formal higher institutions and enrollments in 1982 was considerably higher than the region's share of population, 8.6 percent as against 6.9 percent. Very little ground was lost over the 1980s, with an 8.5 percent figure in 1989. By contrast, adult higher education had developed more slowly than in other regions of China, with enrollment levels in 1989 that made up only 4.8 percent of the national adult student population.

Table 6.2 also gives an interesting picture of the role given to various parts of the region. Shaanxi was clearly the superpower, with 99,000 students, 4.5 percent of the national total, as against a population ratio of 2.9 percent. It also had 6,000 graduate students, 6.5 percent of the national total, and held a role similar to Wuhan as the main center for graduate education for the region. By contrast, Gansu, Ningxia, and Qinghai had a low ratio of higher education participation in comparison to their population ratios, and Ningxia and Qinghai had lost some ground over the 1980s. The gap here was even greater than the one noted between peripheral and central provinces of the Central South. By contrast, Xinjiang had increased its percentage share of both higher institutions and enrollments over the 1980s, indicating vigorous local initiatives.

Secondary education is the essential basis for a higher education system, and Table 6.3 indicates that regular secondary enrollments in academic programs remained strong throughout the decade, increasing from 8.0 percent to 8.2 percent of national totals. However, vocational and technical secondary education, a major area of development nationwide, fell back from a 9.5 percent level to a 5.4 percent level in the nation's share over the decade. This probably indicates a lack of the kind of economic stimulus that has supported the rapid development of vocational/technical education in other regions.

Generally, the picture for the 1980s was one of a strong commitment to mainstream academic forms of education at secondary and tertiary levels, based on traditional patterns, with a rather slow development of new types of education that could respond to economic change. Interestingly, the participation of women and minority students in both academic secondary

TABLE 6.2 A Higher Education Profile of the Northwest Region

	% Population (1989)		# of Higher Ed. Institutions		# of Students (thousands)			Adult Higher Ed. (1989)		Graduate Students (1990)
	Of Nat. Total	Minority in Region	1982	1989	1982	1989	1989 % Female	Institutions	Enrollment (Thousand)	
			715	1075	1,154	2,082	33.7	1,333	1,032	93,018
Shaanxi	2.9	n.a.	33 (4.6%)	48 (4.4%)	56 (4.8%)	99 (4.8%)	30.5	42	36.5 (2.1%)	6,000 (6.5%)
Gansu	1.95	6.5	13 (1.8%)	18 (1.7%)	17 (1.5%)	33 (1.6%)	30.3	24	13.7 (.79%)	1,000 (1.1%)
Qinghai	.41	33.4	7 (.98%)	7 (.65%)	5 (.43%)	6 (.28%)	43.3	8	2.9 (1.6%)	42 (.05%)
Ningxia	.40	34.3	6 (.84%)	6 (.56%)	5 (.43%)	8 (.38%)	38.8	5	6.4 (.36%)	60 (.06%)
Xinjiang	1.31	62	12 (1.68%)	20 (1.85%)	16 (1.4%)	32 (1.5%)	44.7	29	23.8 (1.37%)	258 (.3%)
Regional Total	6.9	33.8	71 (9.9%)	99 (9.8%)	99 (8.6%)	178 (8.5%)	33.8	108 (8.1%)	83.2 (4.8%)	7,129 (7.7%)

Sources: *Zhongguo jiaoyu tongji nianjian, 1982–84; 1989*; (Beijing: Renmin jiaoyu chubanshe).

TABLE 6.3 A Secondary Education Profile of the Northwest Region (in thousands)

	Pop. (%) [1989]	Technical and Professional Secondary Enrollment			Regular Secondary Enrollment		
		1982	1989	% Female	1982	1989	% Female
		1,039	5,525	17.9	45,285	45,554	41.4
Shaanxi	2.9	38 (3.7%)	98 (1.8%)	25	1,575.8 (3.4%)	1,356 (3.0%)	43.4
Gansu	1.95	21 (2.0%)	82 (1.5%)	22.7	827 (1.8%)	995 (2.2%)	36.7
Qinghai	.41	8 (.08%)	18.4 (.03%)	27	192 (.42%)	219 (.48%)	44.8
Ningxia	.40	7 (.07%)	19.2 (.03%)	26.6	200.8 (.44%)	277 (.61%)	42.7
Xinjiang	1.31	25 (.24%)	78.6 (.14%)	29.3	842.8 (1.9%)	893 (2.0%)	49
Regional Total	6.9	99 (9.5%)	296.2 (5.4%)	25.7	3,638.4 (8.0%)	3,740 (8.2%)	43

Sources: Zhongguo tongji nianjian, 1990, p. 233; Zhongguo jiaoyu tongji nianjian, 1982–84 (Changsha: Hunan jiaoyu chubanshe, 1985).

TABLE 6.4 1992 Student Intake by Province/Region

	Regular Enrollment	% Female	% Rural	% Minority	Adult Student Enrollment	% Female	% Minority	Graduate Students	% Female	% Minority
National	619,874	33.7	n.a.	6.9	465,529	n.a.	n.a.	29,679	25	n.a.
Shaanxi	25,480 [+5,000]	35.5	64	1	29,857	47.4	.08	1990	26	2.2
Gansu	10,418 [+6,000]	30	50	n.a.	7,947	20	n.a.	423	10	n.a.
Qinghai	2,335 [+2,300]	40.2	28.6	36.4/24%*	581	24.5	13.5	4	–	–
Ningxia	3,500 [+2,400]	43.1	36	23.8/18%*	3,500	43.2	n.a.	12	40	n.a.
Xinjiang	8,800 [+6,500]	44	40	56/n.a.*	8,000	38	n.a.	100	20	20

* The first % indicates the minority share in enrollments within the region. The second % indicates their share in total enrollments, which is much lower, as fewer minorities are able to gain entrance to national institutions.
Bracketed figures indicate the number of additional students selected to go to national institutions throughout the country. See note 8, p. 247.

and regular tertiary education was above that of national ratios, reflecting the persistence of socialist values that was evident also in the more conservative parts of the Central South region.

GEOGRAPHICAL PATTERNS IN NORTHWEST HIGHER EDUCATION

Table 6.4 provides a picture of student intakes in each part of the region in the autumn of 1992.[8] The main figures represent intakes to institutions within the province/region while the bracketed figures indicate the number selected to go to national institutions throughout the country. Until recently, about 70 percent of these students returned to their own province/region on graduation. However, provincial/regional authorities in each place reported to us that this figure was now being eroded every year, with the increasing freedom of career choice open to these graduates. Thus only half of Shaanxi's 5,000 students studying elsewhere returned in 1992, only one-third of Gansu's 6,000, 40 percent of Qinghai's 2,300, 60 percent of Ningxia's 2,400, and around 60 percent of Xinjiang's 6,500. In all cases, the percentage of returnees was expected to be reduced much further in 1993 and subsequent years.

A further problem associated with these internal returnees is the fact that most who came back did so because they were unable to compete in the job market, and thus were either less academically able, or had been trained in areas not in great demand under the economic reform impetus. Very few graduates in engineering returned to the Northwest, for example. This was particularly problematic for provincial authorities, since provincial institutions had been required, under the plan, to focus on teacher training, agriculture, and medicine. Their responsibility had been to meet basic social needs in their province/region, while expertise in engineering and other areas was to be provided through national-level training and the job assignment of graduates according to plan.

For Shaanxi and Gansu this situation was not too serious, since their own national-level institutions attracted students from throughout the country. Some of these graduates were willing to stay in the province on graduation. For example, national institutions in Shaanxi province enrolled 5,000 students from all parts of the country, one-fifth being from the Northwest region, and those in Gansu enrolled 3,500. Many of these students came from less favored provinces or regions, in a geographical pecking order that is clearly established in the minds of students and their families in China. For these students, professional career development in Xi'an or Lanzhou was likely to be preferable to returning to their own region, and about one-third of these external students stayed on after graduation. In Qinghai, Ningxia, and Xinjiang, however, there were few national-level institutions, and very few students from outside their own region. The exception was a minority college in Ningxia that recruited students of minority backgrounds from the whole Northwest, and two agricultural institutions under the Ministry of Agriculture in Xinjiang.

These regions were thus particularly disadvantaged, as they faced a permanent loss of their own most talented young people to better career prospects in other parts of the country. In addition, they reported an increasing outflow of graduates of their own local higher institutions each year, particularly those in engineering, who were able to find attractive positions in economically dynamic areas, and also those whose parents had reached retirement age and decided to return to the regions they came from in the great migrations of the 1950s and 1960s. While Shaanxi and Gansu were able to replenish their human resources by attracting young people from somewhat less advantaged areas in the Northwest or elsewhere, there were few places lower in the geographical pecking order than Ningxia, Qinghai, and Xinjiang. Their main hope lay in their minority populations, who had deeper attachments to the region than many of the Han.

A Chinese phrase that we heard constantly during this visit to the Northwest was "The peacock is flying eastward and southward, and now the sparrow has also joined the southeast flight."[9] There was a certain wry humor with which this phrase was repeated—everyone understood the attraction. Most families were involved in one way or another with trying to send their children out of the region, yet there was also an affectionate regard for all that had been achieved and some belief in a future for those who chose not to fly.

MINORITY PARTICIPATION IN NORTHWEST HIGHER EDUCATION

Quite remarkable policies of affirmative action had been put in place in the 1950s to ensure the training of minority personnel for leadership positions. As a result, Xinjiang had reached a level of 56 percent of all students in higher education in the region being minority, as against a 62 percent ratio of minority peoples within the population. Only a few specialized institutions in areas such as oil development did not have quotas that matched the population ratio for entering students, and marks were lowered by as much as 200 points on the national entrance examinations to ensure this level of representation. Most institutions provided an extra year of study as a kind of compensatory education for minority entrants. In addition, about 800 of the very best minority students were selected every year for higher education programs in prestigious national universities throughout the country.

There were thus more than 3,000 minority students from Xinjiang at any one time at national universities throughout the country, with a large concentration in Beijing and Shanghai. Almost all of these students were expected to return on graduation to take up positions within the region.

Ningxia was somewhat behind this level of affirmative action, with 23.8 percent of all students enrolled in local institutions in 1992 being minority, in contrast to a 34.3 percent minority ratio in the population. If the total contingent going on to higher education nationally as well as locally was counted, minority representation dropped to 18 percent. The regional education commission had adopted a policy in 1992 whereby this percentage was to be increased by one point each year, until parity with the population ratio was reached. Like Xinjiang, Ningxia also had the opportunity to send a certain number of its best minority students to special programs at national universities throughout the country. For example, Shanghai International Studies University, a prestigious national institution, had been selecting a certain number of minority students from Ningxia each year for English language training. Returnees from this program were playing a valuable role in international liaison in the region.

Qinghai had reached a level of 36.4 percent of all students enrolled in local institutions being minority in 1992, outpacing the 33.4 percent population ratio of minorities in the region. The minority percentage in the total student population going into higher education, including national institutions, was 24 percent. This reflected both vigorous affirmative action policies for minority students and the special conditions of a province where the Han population seemed ill at ease, and the attraction of the south and east was strongest. Higher education opportunities for local young people in other parts of the country constituted an important and valued channel for the Han outflow. As an increasing number of places for self-paying students at a somewhat lower level of marks in the national entry examinations opened up in national institutions, provincial institutions in Qinghai were having a more and more difficult time recruiting quality students among the local Han.

WOMEN STUDENTS IN THE NORTHWEST

In the picture of student intakes to all regular and adult higher education in 1992, given in Table 6.4, one of the most striking statistics was the high proportion of female students. It was consistently above national levels, except in the province of Gansu. While in Shaanxi province only 30.5 percent of all students enrolled in higher education were women in 1989, by the 1992 intake this percentage had risen to 35.5 percent, above the national figure of 33.7 percent, though still considerably lower than those of Xinjiang, Ningxia, and Qinghai.[10]

This relatively high female participation in higher education was not a matter of policy, as was the case for minority students. While there were policies that gave a slight advantage to women applicants in the national selection process reported in the Central South in 1992, we were told in the Northwest that no special consideration was given to women candidates. Their high participation simply reflected their excellent standing in the national entry examinations.

Much questioning and discussion around this issue did not lead to any clear explanation for its causes. We wondered whether one explanation might be that more men than women found their way into national institutions in other regions.[11] This would explain why Shaanxi and Gansu, which had their own national institutions, were at a level closer to the national average. We also wondered whether the high female participation in Ningxia, Qinghai, and Xinjiang might have reflected historical conditions, especially the large number of urban intellectuals and cadres who had gone there either voluntarily or under political duress in the 1950s and 1960s. These people greatly valued higher education for their children, and were as likely to encourage daughters as sons to go into higher education. The relatively low level of rural participation in higher education in the region seems to confirm this.

With minority people, there were some special conditions. A larger size of family was common, and in some cases there were religious strictures against coeducation for girls. For Hui and Sala Muslim girls, coeducation was frowned upon, but Uighur Muslims had no problem with it. Other fascinating angles included the fact that young men in the Hui, Sala, and Tibetan nationalities were often expected to take up productive activities in herding or farming at an early age, as well as a certain number being encouraged to enter religious training as lamas, in the case of Tibetans, or imams, in the case of the Hui and Sala. This meant that girls were sometimes encouraged to continue with secular education to a higher level. Unfortunately, we do not have disaggregated figures for male and female minority students in higher education.

While female participation in higher education was remarkably high overall, this was not maintained at the graduate level, with only 26 percent of graduate students in the major center, Shaanxi, being women, and 10 percent of graduate students in Gansu. The number of graduate students in Xinjiang, Ningxia, and Qinghai was low and on the decline. The main explanation given for the low levels of female participation in graduate education related to difficulties facing young women graduate students in establishing a family, due to social conservatism and the preference of men for marriage partners with lower levels of education. This was the case throughout China, but possibly more severe in this region, and certainly an even more serious barrier to minority women, who had difficulty enough, as regular university graduates, in finding husbands.

In addition, both minority men and women were highly disadvantaged in applying to enter graduate school, due to the foreign language requirement. It was not easy for them to reach an adequate level in a foreign language, when they had already had to master Chinese in addition to their own language, and normally had to learn the foreign language through the medium of Chinese. Nor was there much evidence of affirmative action for minority students at the graduate level.

Another problem with regard to women's participation in higher education was the fact that the strict age requirements of the system tended to work against women at both undergraduate and graduate levels. We wondered whether opportunities for adult higher education provided an alternative that women could take advantage of. The figures in Table 6.4 give a mixed response to this question, with relatively high female participation in adult education in Shaanxi, Ningxia, and Xinjiang, but rather low participation in Gansu and Qinghai. It seemed clear that women with young families in urban areas, were able to improve their qualifications in this way, but these opportunities did not extend to rural women. Generally, adult higher education was far less developed in this region than in other parts of China.

Table 6.5 gives a picture of the teaching force in higher education institutions in the Northwest in 1992. It is interesting to note that the percentage of women faculty was above the national average in Qinghai, Ningxia, and Xinjiang. This seemed to reflect both the relatively high female enrollments, and the fact that male faculty were more prone than female to leave teaching for opportunities in other sectors, and also to depart for coastal areas. Minority faculty represented substantial percentages of the total in Xinjiang and Qinghai, less so in Ningxia in 1992, but there was still a long way to go before they came near their representation within the population.

Over the decade of the 1980s, considerable effort was put into faculty development. Table 6.5 shows the numbers sent abroad and returned over the decade. It is notable that almost 10 percent of all faculty in Shaanxi belong to this group, though the levels are much lower elsewhere in the region. The main avenue for faculty development was graduate training in other parts of China. In each of the provinces/regions in the Northwest, provincial officials described to us the efforts they had made along these lines. The faculty who

TABLE 6.5 A Faculty Profile for the Northwest

	Total Teaching Faculty	% Female	% Minority	No. Sent Abroad since 1978	Total Returned since 1978	Estimated Brain Drain to Coastal Region in 1992
National	390,771	29.6	1.9	n.a.	n.a.	n.a.
Shaanxi	19,384	27.3	n.a.	3,500 (18%)*	1,900 (9.8%)*	1,000 (5%)*
Gansu	6,000	26.4	n.a.	600 (10%)*	200 (3.3%)*	300 (5%)*
Qinghai	1,400	32	25	60 (4.3%)*	29 (2.1%)*	100 (7.1%)*
Ningxia	1,703	29.8	12	107 (6.3%)*	38 (2.2%)*	100 (5.8%)*
Xinjiang	7,269	33.8	36.8	400 (5.5%)*	160 (2.2%)*	160 (2.2%)*

* = % of total faculty. Source: See note 8, p. 247.

gained degrees through these programs had had all expenses paid by the province/region, a considerable outlay from their perspective, and most had returned to teach for a few years on graduation. However, provincial officials and university administrators told us that few had stayed long term. After having experienced the professional and intellectual opportunities of coastal regions, these young faculty often found the urge to leave irresistible. Most had developed a network of contacts, which enabled them to arrange a transfer to a more favored region and institution. This movement constituted an increasing annual brain drain of the best qualified younger faculty. In addition, many of the older faculty who had been the core force in the development of programs since the 1950s were reaching retirement age by the early 1990s, and many were preparing to return to their home regions.

There were no exact figures on the scale of the brain drain underway, but column 6 of Table 6.5 provides the best estimate we were able to get. It is a very conservative one, since most of the authorities we talked with were reluctant to provide precise information, though they did not underestimate the seriousness of the crisis. In many cases, particular institutions told us they were losing up to fifty faculty a year, and the new appointments they were able to make from among their own graduates or other qualified personnel could only fill about half of the positions being vacated.

We have noted in chapter 5 the struggle that was going on between provincial education commissions and Beijing over the issue of enrollment expansion in the spring of 1992. By the spring of 1993, there was considerably greater latitude for provincial authorities, and various deals were being made by provinces such as Shandong and Guangdong to gain permission for high enrollments of self-paying students on the basis of local economic growth and employment needs. Even in the Northwest, where economic growth did not provide such a ready rationale for expansion, there was considerable potential for provincial initiative. It was interesting, therefore, to see the different approaches taken.

Ningxia was allowing 31 percent of students enrolled in 1993 to be self-funded or funded by enterprises on contract, with all of these extra funds going directly into university budgets, enabling them to raise faculty salaries and improve conditions. However, enrollment growth was still to be modest, with the larger number of self-paying places resulting in a reduced number of places for government-sponsored students within the plan. This policy was likely to favor young people from cities and prosperous regions.

Xinjiang was taking a bolder stance on the position of self-paying students, with a plan to increase its student intake from 8,800 in 1992 to 20,000 in 1993. Of these 20,000 students, 13,500 were expected to be self-paying, a staggering increase from the 2,300 self-paying students in 1992. The figure of 6,500 enrolled under the plan was to be held at the same level as in the past. All self-paying students were responsible for finding their own jobs, but the regional government would continue to bear responsibility for the employment of graduates who had been recruited within the plan.

These might be seen as two contrasting policies in face of the problems facing the Northwest, one a vigorous affirmation of the market reforms and a fearless move into market-driven higher education, without undue concern about problems of graduate unemployment, the other a more cautious and controlled approach to change. An important question was whether to allow social demand to be the main determinant of enrollment expansion or to restrain growth in order to avoid graduate unemployment and a large inflow of rural youth to the cities. The experience of the late 1950s, when a massive expansion of higher education had been undertaken in the Great Leap Forward, followed by a severe retrenchment, had left a particularly strong impression in Qinghai province, where officials were hesitant about rapid expansion, as they feared the kinds of losses that had been experienced in the province in the early 1960s, when newly established institutions had been closed or recombined with old ones, and there had been a considerable outflow of professional personnel from the province.

A related issue for all provinces and regions in the Northwest, and one that reflected the interface between new and older views of higher education, was that of the rural/urban balance in enrollments. Under the plan, higher education had always been a key channel for geographical and social mobility, with rural participants who entered national universities being able to gain entrance to major urban professional postings and others able to move upward into county or prefectural seats, and also to gain the advantages of urban residential permits. New market pressures, however, were working against rural students, especially those in the Northwest, where there were few county enterprises and even fewer individual entrepreneurs (*geti hu*), and so little possibility of personal or family support for the costs of higher education. As an increasing proportion of places were going to self-paying students, urban young people tended to benefit. On graduation, however, these urban youth were almost certain to be unwilling to work outside of the cities where they had come from, unless they could move to a more advantageous region.

Thus the danger of a floating urban population of unemployed graduates was a more serious one in the Northwest than in other parts of the country. One policy response to this situation was to maintain restrictions on enrollment growth, also to organize a certain percentage of students under "directed enrollment programs," meaning that students from rural areas were targeted and allowed entrance at somewhat lower academic levels on condition that they agreed to return and serve in their own rural areas on graduation. This approach belonged to the planning mentality of the past, and it was not clear how long it could be maintained under new market conditions. At the same time, without such measures, it seemed likely that the gap between rural and urban levels of prosperity in the Northwest would widen, even as the gap between hinterland and coastal areas was widening. Table 6.4 gives an indication of rural percentages in student intakes in 1992, showing relatively low levels for Qinghai, Ningxia, and Xinjiang, somewhat higher for Shaanxi and Gansu. These figures might be compared with those of the Central South region, where overall rural participation had been considerably higher one year earlier.

If provincial authorities remained ambivalent about these tensions between planning and market models of higher education, some institutions were eager to adopt a market approach. Ningxia University was an interesting case in point. It had succeeded in attracting 400 students from all over China in 1992, entirely on a self-paying basis, while still serving the normal size of local student population. The combination of good academic standards and an excellent study environment, with low living costs, made their programs attractive. University officials felt these students from outside the region brought a new dynamism to the campus. This in turn made it easier for them to keep their younger faculty engaged and interested. However, they were strongly reprimanded by provincial authorities and required to stick closely to the allowed quota for 1993. Otherwise they were threatened with losing the extra income from approved self-paying students recruited locally.

Clearly, provincial authorities were not comfortable with the notion of a higher education that responded broadly to social demand and the market, nor did they see how the locality could benefit from students attracted from other parts of the country. Yet, with aggressive programs of expansion for self-paying students in other parts of the country drawing away some of the best students from the Northwest region, the initiative taken by Ningxia University seemed worthy of more thoughtful attention. One wondered whether there might not be a place for the Northwest to attract self-paying students from around the nation on the basis of some of its academic strengths and special qualities of the region. This issue is discussed further in chapter 7.

In terms of program emphasis, there was perhaps a greater readiness on the part of provincial officials to adapt to social demand and market needs. Their main handicap lay in the fact that, under the plan, they had been called on to be responsible only for fields such as health, teacher training, and agriculture, in order to meet local employment needs in these areas. Specialized personnel in fields such as engineering, basic sciences, economics, and management were to be formed in national institutions, and then allocated to them under the plan. Now that universities of engineering and economics/finance had become the most attractive to students in terms of social demand and market opportunities, provincial/regional institutions were at a considerable disadvantage. Provincial commissions were trying to help them deal with this challenge.

All institutions were being encouraged to become more comprehensive, including new programs in areas such as economics, trade, and foreign languages. Also, new technological programs were being developed in connection with the basic sciences, which had always been strong in local comprehensive and normal universities. In humanities and social science areas, there was a new emphasis on programs such as administration, archives management, information and library science, business relations, etc. The greatest constraint on the growth of new types of programs lay in the fact that the economic environment remained far less dynamic than in eastern and southern regions, thus making it difficult to provide adequate funding for new initiatives.

Crucial policy concerns of the Northwest region were how to maintain and develop teaching faculty in conditions of greater professional mobility and, where institutions in coastal areas were actively recruiting good faculty from the hinterland, how to replace faculty in their institutions who had failed to return from abroad or moved out of academic life into new business opportunities. Northwestern administrators recognized the fact that they could no longer hope to gain new personnel either through the plan or through heroic mobilization campaigns, as in the past, but must find ways to attract their own graduates and give support to all professionals who elected to stay.

This support involved two important elements—one was the opportunity for professional career development in terms of both teaching and research; the other was adequate salaries and living conditions. In many ways the second was of lesser importance than the first. Chinese professionals tend not to make high demands in terms of living standards, so long as they are given the opportunity for professional advancement.[12]

In most of the five provinces/regions of the Northwest, there were fairly dynamic policies to attract and keep faculty. One was provincial support for "key studies," areas of academic excellence that gained special funding for the enhancement of both teaching and research programs. A second was assistance given to local institutions in applications for research funding both to provincial/regional authorities and national bodies, such as the National Natural Sciences Fund. A third was efforts to encourage international programs, including competition for participation in national programs for study abroad, and efforts to develop their own local linkages with other countries.

For Xinjiang, one of the most lively new areas of international cooperation was with Kazakhstan, a huge new country next door, whose legacy from the Soviet Union included some excellent higher education and research institutions. For Qinghai, Japan had been one of the most supportive international partners, with a scholarship program that had sent quite a few young faculty there, and a new center for Japanese and English language training at the provincial level, supported by a Japanese business foundation. The return rate for faculty in these regions was surprisingly high, as evident in Tables 6.5 and 6.8, making the vigorous development of international linkages of cooperation a viable and significant way of improving the professional development opportunities of faculty, and so of keeping them in the region.

On the side of salaries and living conditions, all universities in China were struggling to raise faculty salaries through income they could generate by recruiting self-paying students, undertaking research contracts with enterprises, and developing school-based factories and enterprises. In the Northwest, this was more difficult than other regions, due to the slower pace of economic development. Nevertheless, provincial/regional authorities were making an effort to offer support. One means was through a loan program to assist school factories and businesses. Shaanxi provincial authorities had helped to negotiate 140 million yuan in loans for university business development activities in 1992, and Xinjiang had a loan program of about 5 million yuan per year for its universities. Provincial authorities were also actively encouraging their institutions in the recruitment of self-paying students, as noted earlier, and this was a significant source of funding for improving faculty salaries.

UNIVERSITIES OF THE NORTHWEST: A SERIES OF CASE STUDIES

Altogether, sixteen institutions were visited under this research project, and they are listed in Table 6.6. Their level and place within the overall system, and their curricular emphases, are their most important distinguishing features. A cursory look at their student bodies indicates a relatively high rural participation in national institutions and at other levels, and also less clear patterns of coordination between urban and female participation than in the Central South.

The first three institutions were administered by the State Education Commission, and thus held the highest prestige. They represented the three main types of institution created under the Soviet model of the 1950s at this level: a national comprehensive university—Lanzhou, traditionally responsible for high-level academic programs in basic science and humanities—a national polytechnic university—Xi'an Jiaotong, having programs in a wide range of engineering fields—and a national normal university—Shaanxi Normal, having programs in basic sciences and humanities, with the addition of a faculty of education and a special responsibility for training higher-level teachers. These three universities recruited students from across the nation, with a particular emphasis on the Northwest.

Each had a different base from which to start in academic program reforms. Thus Xi'an Jiaotong had a very strong foundation in the engineering sciences. It had added new departments in basic sciences over the decade in order to create a better foundation for further high-technology development, and to correct the distortions of the Soviet model, which had separated basic and applied sciences. It had also vigorously developed new programs in such applied social sciences as management and information science.

Lanzhou University had moved somewhat in the opposite direction,

TABLE 6.6 1992 Enrollments at Sixteen Higher Institutions in the Northwest

	Total Student Body			Reg.	% Female	% Min.	% Rural	% Dir.	% Self-paying/ Contract	Grad.	% Female	% Min.	% Dir.
	Reg.	Adult	Grad.										
I. National SEdC													
Shaanxi-N	7,000	n.a.	353	1,630	42	11	40	2	10	104	36	16	41
Xi'an Jiaotong-P	9,990	2,300	1,722	3,318	23	2	44	–	44	573	24	14	34
Lanzhou-U	5,656	1,000	588	1,544	30	4	48	–	16	189	32	–	26
II. National Ministry													
Shaanxi-F	3,421	n.a.	140	1,113	49	4	41	5	37	47	32	–	21
Northwest-P/L	2,495	2,400	75	756	27	11	41	–	25	28	21	–	25
Northwest-Ag	3,250	n.a.	288	1,000	25	10	75	20	30	96	29	–	23
Lanzhou-R	3,800	500	36	1,215	28	4	36	–	34	14	21	7	21
Northwest-Min.	3,000	500	18	890	44	95	n.a.	n.a.	10	6	17	100	n.a.
III. Provincial													
Northwest-N	5,413	n.a.	91	1,827	41	15	39	–	13	32	19	1	31
Ningxia-U	3,569	346	40	917	36	18	60	–	44	–	–	–	–
Qinghai-N	1,800	300	–	427	49	18	51	–	22	–	–	–	–
Qinghai-Min.	1,427	–	4	303	42	98	53	10	10	–	–	–	–
Xinjiang-U	5,917	1,019	90	1,240	47	45	47	–	28	23	50	50	18
Xinjiang Medical	2,100	708	80	611	57	60	30	12	27	40	34	10	n.a.
IV. Local													
Yinchuan-N	n.a.	n.a.	–	356	57	7	39	3	11	–	–	–	–
Urumchi-Prof.	n.a.	n.a.	–	1,600	65	30	30	–	100	–	–	–	–

Key: U—(Comprehensive) University; P—Polytechnical; F—Finance and Economics; Prof.—Professional; N—Normal; R—Railroad; Ag—Agriculture; Min.Minority; P/L—Politics and Law; Reg.—Regular; Grad.—Graduate Student; Dir.—Directed enrollment. Source: See note 8, p. 247.

building new engineering and applied science fields on its strong foundation in basic fields such as chemistry, physics, biology, and geography. On the humanities side, it had developed two new programs in law and philosophy, fields where it had excelled before Liberation, but had not been allowed to develop in the restrictive conditions of the 1950s and 1960s. It had also initiated a large number of applied social science programs in fields such as economic planning, marketing, and administration.

Shaanxi Normal University probably suffered the greatest constraints in program development, due to the fact that its mandate called for a focus on the training of teachers, and the teaching profession had continued to lose prestige as the pace of economic change continued. It had just begun to capitalize on its strengths in basic fields of both the natural and social sciences to develop a large number of new applied programs, many at the short-cycle level, for young people going into areas other than teaching. This was one of the few means available for it to bring in funding to support its major academic emphasis on basic fields and education.

The second level in Table 6.6 constitutes national universities managed by ministries other than the State Education Commission, in each case part of a nationwide sectoral system of higher education. These systems were facing very different opportunities and conditions by the early 1990s, and the five included in this study illustrated these differences rather well.

Institutes of finance and economics under the Ministry of Finance or the People's Bank were once part of a highly restrictive network for training economic planners and managers, but they had now become extremely popular institutions as they expanded and reoriented their programs in response to economic change. Shaanxi University of Finance and Economics had moved vigorously into developing a wide range of new programs, from an original six programs in the old Soviet-derived patterns for macro-economic management, to twenty programs that included many new areas suited to the market economy. While these programs were highly diverse, they made use of the eleven core economics courses developed under cooperation between the State Education Commission and international experts through a major World Bank project. Basic courses in political economy and Marxism also remained a part of the curriculum, and we were told that considerable struggle went on between differing perspectives on the economic change process.

As the lead institution for economics and finance in the Northwest, Shaanxi University of Finance and Economics had an important regional role and had been responsible for training faculty for two new institutions in the field, one in Lanzhou and another in Urumchi. It was able to attract excellent students whose marks in the unified college entrance examinations were next only to those of Xi'an Jiaotong students, the most prestigious university in the region. Its further expansion was somewhat of a threat to universities in less popular areas, such as teacher training and agriculture, since it was likely to monopolize an ever larger share of students with high marks on the national examinations.

The Northwest Institute of Political Science and Law was under the jurisdiction of the Ministry of Justice, and was also in transition from being part of a highly restrictive network for the training of a small number of specialists in law under Soviet patterns to a much more diverse institution in terms of its programs. From one program in legal theory, which had been its mandate under Soviet patterns, it had developed ten new programs covering areas such as economic law, administrative law, commercial law, international trade law, and procuratorial practice. The economic reforms, and a huge amount of new economic legislation, had stimulated a tremendous need for legally trained people, making this institution nearly as popular with students as the finance and economics institute.

The third university managed by a central ministry in our study was Northwest Agricultural University in Xianyang, about 100 kilometers from Xi'an. It was facing a more difficult situation, with agriculture being one of the least popular areas for students entering higher education. In response to this, the university had developed a vigorous policy of recruiting students who made agriculture their first choice, even if their marks were somewhat below normal entry standards on the national entrance examination, as well as attracting students with some work experience from the countryside. Its programs remained focused on core agricultural areas, with the addition of new courses and programs in fields such as food science, land planning, and agricultural finance.

Lanzhou Railway Institute was one of seven in a network of institutions specifically designed to serve the railway system. Because of the prestige, security, and excellent career prospects of the railway system, it was able to attract excellent students, especially in the Northwest, where this type of career remained more popular than in coastal regions. Its program changes had been modest, focusing on new high-tech areas relevant to railway development such as automated information systems, electronic equipment, and financial and economic management. It has taken a leading role in the development of computer science in the region, and in its application to systems management.

Northwest Minorities Institute was a priority university under the State Minorities Commission, and it mainly served the large minority populations in the Northwest. Traditionally, its role has been to educate minority peoples for positions of leadership as cadres throughout the Northwest, and its programs had focused on areas such as politics, history, literature, and languages, with some attention also to such practical fields as animal husbandry and medicine. However, at this time there were new demands among minority students for economically relevant programs in areas such as finance, food engineering, and management, since the administrative patterns that had ensured affirmative action in the employment of graduates were now breaking down, and minority graduates were finding it difficult to compete with Han youth for attractive jobs.

The next level of institution—those managed by provincial/autonomous region education authorities—had traditionally had the responsibility of educating young people for the prefectural towns and county seats, right down to the grass-roots level. Under socialist planning, the main areas of concern for provincial higher education were the training of teachers, medical practitioners, agricultural specialists, and cadres for political/administrative leadership. The six institutions in this group were leading institutions for each province/area.

Northwest Normal University in Lanzhou had lost its status as a national-level institution to Shaanxi Normal in 1978, and so recruited students only from Gansu province. Teacher training for the tertiary and upper secondary levels remained its main focus, and its graduates had staffed the five prefectural-level teachers colleges in Gansu province that trained teachers for rural secondary schools. However, it had started to develop programs in areas other than teacher training. Building on its strong basic science programs, it had developed thirteen new programs in applied engineering areas related to economic reform needs. All of them were at the non-degree level and designed to attract self-paying students. While their main justification was revenue for the university, these new programs also contributed to the improvement of training programs for vocational teachers.

An anecdote at this point might illustrate how universities are being affected by these market-oriented initiatives. We stayed at Northwest Normal University in May 1993, during our visit to various institutions in Lanzhou, since we had a particularly close link to the institute for educational research through a cooperative project supported by CIDA. We had hoped to visit the institute, but instead, all our meetings with colleagues were held in the international guesthouse. It turned out that a main profit-making activity of the institute was the renting out of its office space as dormitories for self-paying students! This situation illustrated, rather poignantly, the particular difficulty faced by social scientists when called on to bring in funds for the university.

Ningxia University was the major higher institution in the Ningxia Hui autonomous region. It had a main responsibility for teacher training for the region, and most of its graduates went into schools. However, in the 1980s, it had added new departments of economics and geography that were oriented to training for a wider range of fields, and more recently it had developed sixteen new programs in economically-oriented areas such as accounting, finance, management, and a range of high-technology subjects.

Of all of the five provinces/regions, we found Qinghai authorities to be the most cautious in terms of enrollment expansion and new program development, and this was reflected in both of the priority provincial institutions there. Qinghai Normal University maintained an exclusive focus on the training of teachers for the region, its mandate since it was founded in 1958, although its administrators mentioned efforts underway to ensure that the teachers trained had broader knowledge and capabilities, beyond their specialist area. All required courses for each program were covered in the first two years, and in the third and fourth years, students were encouraged to choose a second area of knowledge, to gain good practical skills in areas like computer use, and to foster creative interests in music and the arts that would help to liven their classroom environments.

A project of particular interest in Qinghai Normal University was the development of a full set of science teaching materials at the university level in the Tibetan language. This was seen as an essential step in training science teachers for Tibetan schools who would be able to teach secondary students science subjects in their own language. The commitment to this kind of long-term program seemed to be typical of the strong academic ethos of this institution.

The Qinghai Minorities Institute was the oldest higher institution in the province, and the only one going back to 1949. Like Northwest Minorities Institute, its main responsibility had been for the training of minority cadres, and so its programs were mainly in areas such as political education, Han and minority language and literatures, as well as mathematics and chemistry. It had responded vigorously to the new economic climate, with new programs in accounting, economic law, and secretarial studies. It was also most eager to develop new programs in chemical engineering areas, but was being held back by provincial authorities who felt this prerogative should go to the local engineering college. Another of its initiatives had been a program in the Arabic language and trade, in preparation for future cooperation with Middle Eastern countries, which were already providing some support for Muslim communities in the region. However, this program had not yet been able to gain provincial approval.

The two Xinjiang universities included in the study exemplified a duality between a vigorous response to new opportunities arising from economic reforms, particularly evident in Xinjiang University, and a stubborn commitment to maintaining and enhancing academic standards that had been established at great cost and effort, most notable at Xinjiang Medical University. Both qualities seemed to be important for the future of the region.

Xinjiang Medical University had excellent standards due to its historical links to Shanghai No. 1 Medical University and Leningrad Medical University, and it was continuing with fairly traditional medical programs and a strong emphasis on graduate training and research. While it could have attracted students nationwide for its graduate programs, it was not willing to do so unless they made a commitment to subsequent professional service in Xinjiang, indicating a traditional view of their service role. They were very proud, however, of their many master's graduates who went on to doctoral work throughout the country, few of whom returned.

Xinjiang University, by contrast, was responding vigorously to new opportunities related to economic reform. Originally a traditional comprehensive university with programs only in basic humanities and science areas, it had developed nine new degree programs over the 1980s in areas such as law, journalism, computer applications, applied mathematics, physics and chemistry, electronics, and information systems. In the early 1990s, in response to new opportunities for training self-paying students at the short-cycle level, it had designed twenty-two new programs in areas such as urban planning, economic law, secretarial studies, etc. Its administrators made the point that, in the past, new program development had been heavily constrained by political considerations, while at this time the main constraint was an economic one—the lack of funds for adequate program development in the many new areas of popular interest.

Finally, two institutions visited were operative mainly at the local level. Yinchuan Normal College was responsible for teacher training programs at the lower secondary level in the northern half of Ningxia autonomous region, the southern half being served by another local normal college. It had retained a rather traditional role in its programs, with the one main area of innovation being in developing training for pre-education or nursery-level childcare workers. Its administrators saw a great need for programs to train vocational teachers, but lacked funding for this kind of program development. They faced an increasing difficulty in placing their graduates, since all openings at the county level and above had been filled, leaving only village schools where young graduates were reluctant to work.

Urumchi Professional College in Xinjiang, an institution newly established during the reform decade, represented the opposite end of the spectrum from the normal college. Its students were entirely self-paying, its programs oriented toward changing social and economic demand, with five departments indicating broad areas of emphasis—science and engineering, English, business relations, economics, and applied arts. Its students were mainly from the city of Urumchi, but about 30 percent came from nearby rural areas. With very low faculty and logistical costs, due to the fact that many faculty were cross appointed from other institutions and only a small proportion of students lived on campus, it was well situated for program innovation, and was trying at the time to develop programs of excellence in English, accounting, and decorating—three extremely popular areas.

TYPES AND CATEGORIES OF STUDENTS

There had been two striking changes in policy toward students between spring of 1992, when the study of the Central South was done, and spring of 1993, when we visited the Northwest. One was the decision to allow large numbers of self-paying students, and the second was a further move to dismantle the job assignment system and allow graduates to seek their own employment on graduation.

Table 6.6 gives a picture of student enrollment patterns for the sixteen universities in the Northwest in 1992. In the figures provided for the Central South in chapter 5, there were two distinct categories of fee-paying students, those under contract, where the work unit paid all costs, and self-paying students. By 1993, these two categories had been combined into one, since it had become difficult to distinguish between contracts made with individuals and with employing units. Generally, factories were less prepared than they had been to pay for the training of personnel in this way, unless it would benefit the children of their employees, or special arrangements were made so that families actually absorbed the cost. This was called contract training in name, but self-payment in reality.[13] Most of the funds coming into the university in this category were thus from students' families.

Column 9 of Table 6.6 indicates the growing importance of these self-paying students within the system. At Xi'an Jiaotong University, 44 percent of all students were self-paying in 1992, as were 37 percent of all students at Shaanxi Finance and Economics University. Engineering and economics were the two areas with the best employment prospects and so had the highest level of enrollment in this category. However, almost all of the institutions included in the study were actively recruiting self-paying students, and most had designed programs intended to attract them. This was a striking contrast to the situation in the Central South one year earlier, when there were strict controls over the number of self-paying students allowed. The institutions that were least able to attract self-paying students were the two institutes for minority students, and the local normal college. In the case of the minority institutes, they were seeking permission to enroll Han students from urban backgrounds on a self-paying basis as a source of income, but so far had not been allowed, since their mandate was to serve minority communities. In the case of the normal college, its orientation toward rural areas and toward the field of education made it difficult to attract self-paying students.

This brings us to the question of how the new emphasis on self-paying students was affecting student participation. Most institutions informed us that the proportion of rural students in their intake had dropped in recent years, and that the emphasis on self-paying students was likely to reinforce this trend. Few rural and minority young people in the Northwest would be able to pay for higher education. It seemed inevitable, therefore, that some of the gains of affirmative action over the years would be eroded, particularly for rural students. Minority students were still protected to some degree by quotas, and the determination noted earlier among provincial officials to ensure their fuller participation.

As for women students, those in urban areas seemed to be able to benefit from the new conditions, with female participation being particularly high in the finance and economics institute (49 percent), the normal universities (41–49 percent), and the medical university (57 percent). Engineering, agriculture, and political science/law had notably lower female enrollments. Overall, however, women's participation was higher than in any other part of China, and the increasing urban bias in enrollments was likely to reinforce this.

Where the market reforms were likely to affect women and minorities most seriously was in the gradual abolition of the job assignment system. In the past, all employing agencies had been required to accept the graduates assigned to them by the plan, but they were at this time participating in a process of "mutual selection," choosing the personnel they needed from those recommended by the universities. In future, they would have no obligation to employ any graduate who did not suit their precise needs.

With employing agencies of all kinds concerned with the immediate profitability and efficiency of their operations, this meant a considerable change of view toward the employment of graduates. In the past, they had often hired far more than were needed, "storing up" qualified personnel for possible future needs. However, this was no longer regarded as affordable with rising salary costs. Employers wanted graduates immediately able to provide useful service in specific areas. This had led to openly stated preferences for men over women in all parts of China, and for Han over minorities in the Northwest. In the case of women graduates, the reasons given were a reluctance to take responsibility for maternity leave (a double burden in the case of minority women), and a perception that women graduates were less likely to be able to travel and take on difficult assignments. In the case of minorities, it seemed to be a matter of racial prejudice and a belief that minority graduates had a lower academic standing due to the special conditions under which many were enrolled.

While women and minority students continued to do relatively well in terms of opportunities to enter higher education, they were increasingly disadvantaged in their access to the job market on graduation. An interesting example of this situation was provided by Xinjiang University, where the student affairs officer reported that 274 of the 1993 graduating class of 1,030 had already found suitable positions through the "mutual selection" process several months before their graduation. Of these, 178 (65 percent) were male Han, forty (15 percent) were female Han, and the remaining fifty-six (20 percent) were minority. This was a university where 47 percent of the entering class had been women in 1992, and 45 percent were minority students, as indicated in Table 6.6.

The category of "directed enrollments" was losing ground in comparison to figures for 1992 in the Central South, as can be seen by comparing Tables 5.3 and 6.6. This allowed rural students to enter higher education with relatively low marks on the college entrance examination, if they promised to return and work in their own locality on graduation. Only three institutions of those visited in the Northwest had significant programs of this kind at the undergraduate level.

Northwest Agricultural University had 20 percent of its student body under a directed enrollment policy, with these students being rural youth who had had some work experience in their own locality after secondary school graduation and who were selected by a special examination prepared by the university rather than the national unified entry examination. While these young people had lower academic levels than urban youth, who selected agricultural university entrance as a last resort, their high motivation and practical experience made up for this. An innovative approach to program development at Northwest Agricultural University had led to new patterns whereby these students spent three years in the university, then were given a pre-graduation work assignment of one year as a kind of internship in the unit that was to employ them, then returned to the university for a final year in which they concentrated on research and skill-development relevant to their future job.

The other two institutions that continue this type of program at a significant level are Xinjiang Medical University, with 12 percent of its student body coming under directed enrollment programs and expected to return and serve at the local level, and Qinghai Minorities Institute, with 10 percent. Both of these institutions had relatively large minority student bodies, and minorities were generally more willing than Han students to return to their own regions.

At the graduate level there continued to be a high proportion of students enrolled under directed programs, as a result of a State Education Commission policy that required graduate programs for students from the hinterland regions to emphasize this category in order to ensure that graduates would serve in areas of need. This might be seen as a kind of damming up of the flow of qualified personnel to eastern and southern regions, one that seemed likely to work in the short-term but would probably be difficult to maintain over the long term. A greater emphasis on affirmative action to encourage minority participation in graduate education might have been a more worthwhile approach.

UNIVERSITY RESEARCH AND DEVELOPMENT ACTIVITIES

In the first half of the 1980s, universities were encouraged to develop an active role in research, as well as teaching, as has been discussed in chapter 4. By the late 1980s, this new research role was becoming an important resource in order to raise funds outside of state allocations, which were becoming increasingly inadequate. Table 6.7 profiles the budgets of the sixteen northwestern universities included in this study, indicating funds won by competition for basic research from national and provincial-level agencies, and funds brought in through research contracts with industry, often called "horizontal" projects. A further important category in all budgets was that of self-generated income, including research and development contracts, adult education classes, profits from factories, and joint venture companies. While the figures given in Table 6.7 are rough,[14] they do give an indication of the great differences among different institutions.

One of the comments made by administrators in many institutions was that state allocations had increased substantially in the decade since the early 1980s, yet these increases simply did not keep up with the pace of inflation, and the rising costs of salaries. Most reported that 80–90 percent of their state allocations were now used simply to cover personnel costs, a figure that had been closer to 40–50 percent in the early 1980s. This meant

TABLE 6.7 A Financial Profile of Sixteen Institutions in the Northwest

	Total Students			Total Budget (million yuan)			Research Budget (million yuan)			Total Self-generated Income (million yuan)	% from Student Fees	% Research Contracts	% Factories	% Other
	Reg.	Grad	Adult	Total	% from State	% Self-generated	Total	State %	Contract %					
I. National SEdC														
Shaanxi-N	7,000	353	n.a.	31.3	70	30	3.3	40	60	9.4	31	20	10	39
Xi'an Jiaotong-P	9,990	1,722	2,300	120	50	50	52	38	62	60	12	54	13	21
Lanzhou-U	5,656	588	1,000	37.6	70	30	8.4	68	32	11.3	38	20	20	22
II. National Ministry														
Shaanxi-F	3,421	140	n.a.	10	90	10	.2	50	50	1	95	5	-	-
Northwest-P/L	2,495	75	2,400	8.5	98	2	.1	90	10	.17	53	6	-	41
Northwest-Ag	3,250	288	n.a.	15	90	10	n.a.	n.a.	n.a	1.5	50	n.a.	n.a.	n.a.
Lanzhou-R	3,800	500	56	13.6	80	20	2.15	14	86	2.8	n.a.	n.a.	n.a.	n.a.
Northwest-Min.	3,000	500	18	10	98	2	.4	100	-	.2	100	-	-	-
III. Provincial														
Northwest-N	5,413	91	n.a.	17	90	10	.4	95	5	1.7	53	1	41	5
Ningxia-U	3,569	40	346	8.5	82	18	.23	65	35	1.5	60	-	40	-
Qinghai-N	1,800	-	300	4.5	83	17	.08	100	-	.73	100	-	-	-
Qinghai-Min.	1,427	4	-	5.7	94	6	.06	100	-	.35	100	-	-	-
Xinjiang-U	5,917	90	1,019	13	90	10	1.5	70	30	1.3	50	41	-	9
Xinjiang Medical	2,100	80	708	n.a.	n.a.	n.a.	.44	77	23	n.a.	n.a.	n.a.	n.a.	n.a.
IV. Local														
Yinchuan-N	1,118	-	1,280	3.2	94	6	.01	100	-	.2	100	-		
Urumchi-Prof.	4,900	-	-	3	1	99	-	-	-	3	60	-	40	-

Key: For key to descriptions see Table 6.6.

there was minimal funding available for program development, library acquisitions, and the replenishment of basic educational supplies.

Therefore, their relative success in developing alternative sources of income was crucial to preserving the quality of teaching and research, in terms of books, equipment, and teaching resources. It also determined the degree to which they were able to raise faculty salaries and improve housing conditions, a crucial factor for keeping their faculty from migrating elsewhere.

As can be seen from Table 6.7, national institutions under the State Education Commission were the most successful in developing alternative sources of funding, with Xi'an Jiaotong generating half of its large budget through contract research for industry. Lanzhou University and Shaanxi Normal were able to generate 30 percent of their budgets from non-state sources, with both teaching and research, as well as school-based factories, playing a role. Lanzhou Railway Institute was also able to generate 20 percent of its income from outside sources, mainly through contract research for industry. However, national universities in social science areas, such as the finance and law universities and the minorities institute, had minimal research budgets and were only able to generate extra income through self-paying students. Even this income source was limited for minority institutes, since they were not allowed to recruit local Han students for some of their new economically oriented programs, an initiative they were pressing for.

Institutions at the provincial level faced even greater difficulties in generating significant income outside of state allocations, with the recruitment of self-paying students being the only possibility for most, although Northwest Normal and Ningxia Universities both had significant income from school-based factories. Finally, the two local institutions represented opposite ends of a spectrum, one entirely relying on student fees and various local fund-raising efforts, the other fully dependent on state allocations. The difference was that one mainly served a rural population with teacher training programs, while the other served a largely urban population in economically attractive areas, and so could depend on student fees.

Generally, university administrators in the Northwest were energetic in seeking ways to develop alternative funding bases, though they faced many difficulties. When it came to contract research, even administrators at engineering universities such as Lanzhou Railway Institute remarked that it was far more difficult to get contracts in the Northwest than other regions due to the fact there was little county enterprise development, and the major heavy industrial enterprises either had their own in-house research staffs, or were accustomed to making contracts with research institutions in coastal cities for work they needed done.

Other problems faced by these institutions in research were their distance from Beijing and the major funding agencies, and also the persistence of traditional bureaucratic practices in distributing research funding by local authorities. National institutions did fairly well in winning substantial research funding from such organizations as the National Natural Science Foundation, as column 8 indicates, and one provincial-level university, Xinjiang University, also had been quite successful. For scholars in these institutions, however, the costs of travel and liaison were much greater than for researchers in coastal areas.

At the provincial level there was a different kind of problem with winning research funds. Administrators of research programs in provincial/regional universities all commented on the difficulty experienced by their institutions in getting a significant share of provincial/regional research budgets because the traditional mentality of allocating funds according to plan favored inefficient research units attached to governmental offices.

The development of school-based factories was difficult for the same reasons that contract research for industry was difficult. There was simply not the kind of economic environment needed to encourage this activity. However, loan programs had been launched by provincial commissions to provide some capital, and a few institutions had been able to augment their income significantly in this way. Northwest Normal University and Ningxia University had been quite successful, for example, in building up factories that had originally been established in the Great Leap Forward period.

The one source of funding that was becoming more and more vital for all institutions was that of student fees. By 1993, all students were required to pay fees at a modest level, including even those in the formerly protected areas of normal education, agriculture, and minority education. These fees were low for students recruited under the plan, but increasing each year. The more significant student-fee income came from self-paying students, whose fees were between 2,500 and 4,000 yuan per year, and who were recruited outside of the regular enrollment intake. Column 11 of Table 6.7 indicates that student fees were the major source of self-generated income for all institutions except the three under the SEdC.

FACULTY AND INTERNATIONAL ISSUES

Table 6.8 gives a picture of the faculty contingent in the sixteen institutions visited under the project. Column 2 shows that quite vigorous programs of faculty development had been carried out over the 1980s and early 1990s, with the result that many younger faculty had graduate degrees, mostly acquired within China. However, after Deng Xiaoping's trip to Shenzhen in the spring of 1992, and the reinvigoration of the economic reforms, these programs were threatened by a large outflow of some of the most talented younger faculty, many with graduate degrees, to coastal areas. This was such a sensitive topic that not all university administrators were prepared to discuss it, but the figures in the last two columns of Table 6.8 give a partial picture. The two universities that were most frank about the problem, Lanzhou University and Qinghai Normal, indicated that twice as many faculty had departed in 1992, as they had been able to appoint replacements for in 1993. Many of these were highly qualified younger people. Ningxia University also reported that only one-third of the young faculty whom they had trained to graduate level remained at the university, and most of these were trying to leave.

Administrators at Shaanxi Finance and Economics University and Northwest University of Law also indicated severe losses of faculty due to the popularity of their fields under conditions of the market reforms. Furthermore, they indicated that it was impossible to persuade any of their graduate students to stay on as faculty, and difficult even to keep promising undergraduates, since the employment prospects were so much more attractive in the business or public affairs arena.

The only university that seemed to be holding its own in terms of new appointments over departures was Xi'an Jiaotong University, the one real superpower of the region. However, it had problems with certain fields. The university found it easy enough to attract good younger faculty in basic sciences, social sciences, and some technological areas, but extremely difficult to find good people for the teaching of management and certain technological areas. All of their management graduates were in high demand throughout the country.

Administrators in most of these institutions felt that the vigorous development of graduate programs in their institutions was crucial to ongoing faculty development. This would give the faculty already in place the opportunity to take part in graduate training, as well as making it possible for them to train younger teachers through inservice graduate study programs. They were fully aware that they would not be assigned new faculty from other regions, nor could they be sure even of attracting local graduate students.

Their second concern was to develop more active and viable projects of international cooperation so that faculty would be able to feel themselves part of a wider world, and avoid being isolated. Column 6 of Table 6.8, indicates the percentage of total faculty who had had the opportunity for study

TABLE 6.8 A Profile of Faculty Development at Sixteen Institutions in the Northwest

	Total	% with Grad. Degree	% F.	% Min.	Total Sent Abroad since 1978	% of Total Faculty	% F.	% Min.	Total Returned since 1978	% of Faculty	% F.	% Min.	% with Grad. Degree	No. Who Left in 1992	No. of New Appointments in 1992
I. National SEdC															
Shaanxi-N	1,397	33	30	3	252	18	n.a.	n.a.	144	10	35	–	15	n.a.	n.a.
Xi'an Jiaotong-P	2,124	40	21	1	634	31	n.a.	n.a.	336	16	14	–	17	44	100
Lanzhou-U	1,319	30	24	2	390	30	12	3	176	13	12	6	4	60	30
II. National Ministry															
Shaanxi-F	450	5	40	1.3	25	6	n.a.	n.a.	9	2	n.a.	n.a.	n.a.	35	n.a.
Northwest-P/L	352	6	30	.5	26	7	38	–	10	3	40	–	–	18	n.a.
Northwest-Ag	781	n.a.	24	n.a.	n.a.	n.a.	n.a.	n.a.	126	16	6	.7	9	n.a.	n.a.
Lanzhou-R	658	30	38	3	51	8	21	n.a.	30	5	23	n.a.	–	30	30
Northwest-Min.	460	n.a.	40	n.a.	7	1.5	57	43	6	1.3	50	50	–	n.a.	n.a.
III. Provincial															
Northwest-N	1,101	27	23	1.5	84	8	24	n.a.	50	5	26	n.a.	–	n.a.	n.a.
Ningxia-U	500	27	20	10	38	8	18	n.a.	16	3	19	n.a.	–	30	–
Qinghai-N	491	14	37	7	n.a.	n.a.	n.a.	n.a.	6	1	33	n.a.	–	40	20
Qinghai-Min.	294	30	27	43	6	2	n.a.	67	3	1	n.a.	n.a.	–	15	5
Xinjiang-U	1,165	n.a.	30	46	170	15	30	n.a.	45	4	20	65	27	n.a.	n.a.
Xinjiang Medical	423	n.a.	44	32	49	12	16	31	32	8	16	16	–	4	n.a.
IV. Local															
Yinchuan-N	253	4	n.a.	n.a.	8	3	25	n.a.	3	1.2	–	–	–	12	n.a.
Urumchi-Prof.	550	n.a.	–	–	–	–	–	–	–	–	–	–	–	–	–

Key: For key to descriptions see Table 6.6. F.=Female.

abroad, a somewhat lower percentage than in parallel institutions in the Central South for the most part, but still substantial for national institutions under the State Education Commission. It was interesting to note that several provincial-level institutions, notably Xinjiang University and Xinjiang Medical University, also Northwest Normal and Ningxia, had ratios as high as or higher than the national ministry institutions, indicating the result of vigorous policies at the provincial level to support international cooperation. The percentage of faculty having the opportunity for study abroad was a very important indicator as it affected the perception of young faculty concerning their opportunities for professional development.

Column 9 indicates the number of faculty who were returnees from abroad, and it is surprisingly high, given the difficult conditions of the region generally. There was also reasonably good female participation in these programs, in several cases approaching or even exceeding the percentage of women on faculty. In the last section of this chapter, special attention is given to the women returnees. Overall, the ability of this group to use what they had learned abroad and exercise leadership in teaching, research, and administration was a significant factor in the participation of northwestern universities in an international milieu.

Generally, these universities had a rather limited number of international projects, and were eager for more international cooperation. The interest was not only in direct training opportunities for faculty, but also in opportunities for cooperative research and development activities. While their financial resources were limited, there were very rich cultural, linguistic, human, and natural resources in their region, and university administrators hoped these might be an attraction.

Not surprisingly, the university with the most striking record in international activity was Xi'an Jiaotong, which had a wide range of projects with Germany, France, the United States, and Canada, also with such U.N. agencies as the UNFPA. Its research quality was such that it was able to attract doctoral and postdoctoral students from Europe and Southeast Asia. Most of its cooperation was in high-technology areas such as heat transfer and boiler technology, and some was linked to the work of multinational companies.

The other strikingly active university in terms of international cooperation was Northwest Agricultural University. On the day we visited, they were busy with guests from the Ukraine, Japan, and Russia. Also, many of their key administrators and faculty were away on local or international projects. They had active cooperative research with institutions in the Ukraine, Tashkent, Kazakstan, the United States, Canada, and Japan, and a special project with the U.N.'s Food and Agriculture Organization that ensured that all U.N. agricultural documents were added to their library collection.

Lanzhou University and Shaanxi Normal University also had substantial projects of international cooperation in various areas of research related to natural and social features of the Northwest region. However, few of the institutions at other levels had much international activity. All saw this as an important aim for the future, and of particular significance in providing opportunities for the professional development of their faculty.

There were four projects supported by CIDA in Northwest universities. A project in management education at Xi'an Jiaotong University made it a center for the training of doctoral students in a national network of polytechnical universities that included universities such as Qinghua in Beijing, Huazhong in Wuhan, and Jiaotong in Shanghai. However, it was not clear if any of the first class of fifteen doctoral graduates, who had not yet completed their program, would be willing to accept teaching positions there. Of the thirty-eight graduates of their CIDA-supported M.B.A. program, only five had accepted faculty appointments there, while twelve had gone to Shenzhen for business openings, ten were teaching in institutions in coastal regions, and the rest were working for banks or government organizations.

A second CIDA project linked the department of agricultural economics at Northwest Agricultural University and the University of Manitoba. The main focus of this project was faculty development, and already two members of faculty had gone to Canada as visiting scholars for brief periods. One of the returnees was a woman economist who had also spent time in the Ukraine in recent years. She described how visits to eighteen Canadian farms under the project had enabled her to grasp concepts of planning in a market situation that had been mere abstract ideas in American textbooks before her visit. She had initiated a new graduate course in comparative agricultural management on her return from Canada, and was actively involved in research on comprehensive economic development at the village level in China. In addition to faculty development, the project also involved cooperation in organizing an international conference on the subject of crop insurance, which involved other Chinese agencies such as the China National Insurance Company.

A third CIDA project was between Lanzhou Railway Institute and Ryerson Technical University in Toronto. It focused on cooperation in developing programs for computer-aided management in the railway system in Northwest China. Rail links were of great importance in the economic development of the region, and new lines within the region, and toward Russia and Europe, were being rapidly developed, giving this project particular significance. The university was being assisted through visiting Canadian specialists to arrange a series of six-week classes for railway personnel from the whole Northwest region. In addition, the project had a research component relating to the continuing education of women engineers within the system, and there had been an international conference on the subject of the career development of women engineers in Canada and China.

The fourth CIDA project in northwestern universities was the Canada-China Joint Doctoral Program in Education, which involved both Northwest Normal University in Lanzhou and Shaanxi Normal University in Xi'an, as well as five universities in other regions of the country. The main focus of the project was on the training of doctoral students from both China and Canada, as well as opportunities for new course development and research for young faculty on the Chinese side. These two northwestern universities were among the most active and committed participants in the project. An international conference, held in conjunction with the project in May 1993, focused on aspects of psycholinguistics and special education, and brought together researchers and scholars on both sides, as well as some international participants. By 1994, three doctoral students and four faculty had returned to the two universities after spending six months at the Ontario Institute for Studies in Education in Canada, and plans were underway for a cooperative research project that would look at issues common to Canada and China in the curriculum at all levels.

These CIDA projects were relatively small in scale and geographically diffuse, but they had considerable importance as channels whereby institutions in the region could participate directly in an international milieu. However, it was becoming increasingly difficult to gain such opportunities, as the development programs of OECD countries became increasingly trade related, and the possibilities of cooperation with economically dynamic coastal regions became more and more attractive.

WOMEN'S PERSPECTIVES FROM THE NORTHWEST

While statistics on percentages of women students and faculty in different provinces/regions and institutions have been discussed earlier, these don't indicate how women themselves viewed the situation. To get this kind of picture, interviews were held with as many women faculty who had returned from study abroad as we were able to contact. Their experience abroad gave them a comparative vantage point in reflecting on women's issues, and they were able to comment on both their own professional development as women faculty, and their observations of women students.

A total of thirty-eight women faculty, located in all of the provinces/

TABLE 6.9 A Profile of Thirty-Eight Returnees by Family Background and Field of Study

	Worker	Peasant	Intell.	Cadre	Other	Total
History				1 (M)		1
Education				1		1
Law			1	1		2
Foreign Language	1	1(M)	3	1	4(2M)	10
Library Science			1			1
Sciences	1	1	5	2	2	11
Engineering			2	2	3	7
Agriculture			1		1	2
Medicine			1	1	1	3
Total	2	2	14	9	11	38

Sciences: 23   Humanities: 15

Other indicates accountants, clerks, and small business people, mainly from the pre-Liberation period.

(M) indicates the four minority women returnees: one Manchu, one Mongolian, and two Uighurs. Source: See note 8, p. 247.

regions except Ningxia,[15] were interviewed. Table 6.9 provides a profile of these women faculty in terms of their field of expertise and family background. They had a broad disciplinary representation, with ten in foreign languages, five in social sciences, eleven in basic sciences, seven in engineering, three in medicine, and two in agriculture. Four of the thirty-eight were minority women, with three being in foreign language teaching, one in history. Three spoke excellent English, the fourth was Mongolian and had spent time as a researcher of Mongolian and Tibetan literature in the Republic of Mongolia.

Only two of these 38 women came from workers' families, and another two from peasant families—just over 10 percent of the total. While this was by no means a representative sample, it is still interesting to note the difference between this group and that interviewed in the Central South one year earlier, which had been almost entirely male. There, thirty-nine percent had come from peasant and worker families. Here the majority were from intellectual or cadre families, with a significant number of older women whose fathers had been engaged in small business activities or clerical work before 1949. All of the women had a story to tell, often related to their parents' political history, as to how and why they had found their way to the

Northwest, or came to be born in the region. Many were the children of parents who had migrated there either for patriotic reasons, or under conditions of political exile.

One had followed her father in the building of the Northwest railway, reaching the western part of Gansu province by the time she was ready to take examinations for college entrance. Another had been the daughter of a Shanghai intellectual who was labeled a rightist in 1958. Due to her family background, she was refused entry to Qinghua University, in spite of having very high marks in the unified entry examinations. She was sent to Northwest Agricultural University as a kind of punishment, indicating the cynicism of Communist authorities even in that early period. It was touching to hear her describe how interested she had become in agrochemistry and how she had refused later opportunities to return to Shanghai because she was so absorbed in her professional work at Northwest Agricultural University.

Perhaps the most remarkable story of all came from another Shanghai woman, whose mother had been illiterate, but as an "amah" in the home of foreign business women in Shanghai, had given her daughter the opportunity of speaking English from an early age. As a young secondary school graduate in 1956, this woman had been sent to Xinjiang with a large group of intellectual youth, and settled down first to a factory job in Urumchi. When the factory closed in the hard times of the early 1960s, she and her husband went to a much more remote part of the region, where he found employment but she was unable to do so. After bringing up several children, she persuaded the leadership of a local secondary school to let her teach English on a part-time basis, and did this for some years, yet she was treated poorly and experienced frustration over the fact that her fluency in the language and teaching abilities were neither understood nor appreciated. Finally, in the early 1980s, she wrote a letter to the dean of foreign languages at Xinjiang University, offering her services to teach English there. He was so amazed to receive a letter in excellent English from a remote part of the region that he immediately telegrammed her to come for an interview, and she was appointed to the faculty. Now a full professor, she was responsible for setting up English-language training programs for faculty going abroad from various universities in Urumchi and became a heroine in the region.

Table 6.10 shows the age and type of study of the women. The majority were aged between forty-six and fifty-five, but there were nine between thirty-six and forty-five, and another five under thirty-five. Four had gained master's degrees abroad, while the rest had all gone as visiting scholars. Almost all told us that the main reason they had returned was because they felt they could make a professional contribution in their own institution, which they would not be able to do abroad. In the case of the younger ones, some had been disappointed and found themselves facing considerable obstacles to their careers on return.

	25–35	36–45	46–55	Over 55	Total
TABLE 6.10 A Profile of Thirty-Eight Returnees by Age and Type of Study					
Master's Program	1	3			4
Visiting Scholar	4	6	18	6	34
Total	5	9	18	6	38

We were particularly interested in the degree to which returnees took up administrative responsibilities, beyond their specific research and teaching activities, on return. Table 6.11 indicates the level of administrative responsibility undertaken on return, as well as all the countries of study represented by the group. A full half had been unwilling to undertake any administrative responsibility, as they wished to focus entirely on teaching and research. Only two were department chairs, while four were vice-chairs, and thirteen held positions of leadership in the research and teaching unit, which involved management of the teaching and research process only.

Individual interviews were held with each woman, first eliciting general information on her family background, experience studying abroad, and career development, then asking her to comment in some detail on her achievements in teaching, research, and administration after returning to China. In addition to these individual interviews, there were group discussions with all of the women faculty who participated in the study at each institution. These provided the opportunity for interesting observations more generally on the situation of women students and women professionals in the university. Most of the women remarked that they had never gotten together with colleagues to discuss common concerns of women before. The comments that follow are based on both the individual interviews and the group discussions that were held.

Nearly all of these thirty-eight women returnees were strongly committed to teaching. For those in foreign languages, often 70–100 percent of their time was occupied with teaching, and in other social sciences/humanities areas about 50–60 percent. Those doing high-level scientific research, about five to six in the group, taught mainly at the graduate level, usually giving only 20–30 percent of their time to teaching. Those in applied sci-

	No Admin. Responsibility	Vice-head of TR Unit	Head of TR Unit	Vice-chair of Dept.	Chair of Dept.	Total
Canada	3			1		4
USA	7	1		2		10
England	1	2			2	5
Australia/ New Zealand	1	1				2
France	1					1
Germany	1		1			2
Switzerland			1			1
Finland	1					1
Russia		2	2	1		5
Yugoslavia	1					1
Ukraine			1			1
Mongolia			1			1
Japan	2		1			3
Hong Kong	1					1
Total	19	6	7	4	2	38

Note: About five had been to two to three countries: England/USA, Russia/USA, USA/ Japan, USA/Canada/England, Canada/Switzerland.

TR=Teaching and Research Unit. Source: See note 8, p. 247.

ences, however, especially at institutions of applied study such as the railway college or normal institutions, gave a substantial amount of their time to undergraduate teaching.

Most were very enthusiastic about their teaching work and gave meticulous attention to making improvements. About two-thirds had started new courses after return from abroad (in some cases two or three courses), and most were enthusiastic about trying out new approaches to teaching and encouraging more active student participation. Several talked of having started up seminar-style classes, which were fairly new in the Chinese context.

The main limitations and problems experienced were a lack of funds for new course development, a lack of reference material, and in the case of scientific courses, a lack of adequate equipment. On the whole, we sensed that these women were making significant innovations in their teaching, and serving to link their students to a wider international community, at both undergraduate and graduate levels.

In terms of research, there was great variation among the women interviewed. A significant number, around ten, were clearly excellent researchers, able to win substantial research funding from national agencies and carry forward their own projects with confidence and vigor. These were all in fields of science, engineering, and agriculture. One minority scholar was doing fascinating research in Mongolian and Tibetan literature, which was well funded and extremely productive in terms of research publications.

There were also many who were experiencing great frustration over research. Science scholars working at provincial-level institutions had great difficulty in getting research funding. Almost all scholars in the social sciences and humanities lacked research funding, though some were still able to be productive. Those scholars working in foreign language teaching felt there was no encouragement for research, and it was useless even to try, though a certain amount of translation was being done.

The greatest problems experienced by the returned scholars in terms of research was a lack of up-to-date information. Other serious problems were the lack of research assistance and the potential for cooperation. Graduate students and younger scholars were preoccupied with finding an opportunity to go abroad, and few young scholars had returned. This meant older ones often had to work very much on their own. A further complication was the great distances between cities and universities in the Northwest region, and between the region and the coastal cities. Many felt isolated even from the scholarly community in their field within China. To attend a conference in Beijing or Shanghai cost far more than it would for scholars in southern and eastern areas. For those who had research money, much of it got used up with trips to Beijing to keep in touch with the main funding agencies and ensure future opportunities.

In terms of international cooperation, most said they had not been able to continue significant cooperation with colleagues in the country where they had studied. Even attendance at international conferences held within China was difficult due to the distances involved. One woman mentioned her despair over the fact that her university, a provincial-level comprehensive university, had not even been able to provide living expenses for the Ukrainian professor she had worked for who was planning to come for a visit to initiate research cooperation.

There were a few scholars, however, in the top national institutions who continued in regular contact with colleagues abroad, and were able to attend international conferences and take part in international research projects. They were all in engineering or natural sciences, and clearly had a high research profile and good research funding from national bodies.

We have noted already that fully half of the thirty-eight scholars had no administrative responsibilities. In almost all cases, they emphasized the fact that they did not wish such responsibilities, since they felt they could not change the system, and that they would be more useful as teachers or researchers. Quite a few of those who were either head or vice-head of the teaching and research group spoke positively of this role, in terms of what they could do to improve teaching conditions and support younger faculty. Most were reluctant to consider responsibilities as a department chair, or vice-chair, as they felt there were too many complexities in the personnel system to be effective in this role. However, among the few who had undertaken this responsibility, there were two or three who were obviously using it to introduce sound academic principles in department management.

Overall, this group of women did not feel that their own careers had been significantly hampered due to gender. While they had been through harrowing struggles in the Cultural Revolution decade, these were related to their political or social backgrounds. Most felt their career development, in terms of promotion through the ranks, had been relatively smooth in the period since 1978, when the academic ranking system was restored. Two or three of the younger ones, however, felt strongly that they were being held back for promotion due to jealousies and misunderstandings around their special status as "returnees from abroad."

As we have noted earlier, most of the group made teaching a priority and were meticulous in class preparation and new course development. Heavy teaching loads, combined with household responsibilities, hindered their achievements in writing and publishing, and so affected promotion prospects. Generally, they felt that men in the same ranks, including their own spouses in some cases, tended to be promoted first, partly because they had more time for research and writing, and partly due to a general bias in favor of male faculty.

Housing was also a matter of dissatisfaction, as women faculty were only provided with housing on their own campus when they had reached the level of associate professor, whereas men were given accommodation as teaching assistants. The expectation had been that professional women would be provided with housing through their husbands, and this often meant long distances to travel from the husband's work unit to their own, and complex childcare arrangements. It also meant that it made sense for an academic couple to concentrate on the husband's career development, as his promotion would improve housing conditions, while the wife's promotion did not carry this condition. As for single women, they were expected to live in dormitory accommodations, and there was little tolerance or understanding for the kind of contribution they might make.

Generally, however, the life experience of this group of women faculty reflected the values of China's socialist academic system, which had supported women in science and engineering and provided more or less equal remuneration and equal career development opportunities for both sexes. Most had very little sense of having suffered gender discrimination, and none were involved in any kind of feminist activity. In many cases, they had never before even discussed the issues that were raised in these informal meetings.

When asked about the situation of women students, they noted that, with the new market conditions, contemporary women students faced greater difficulties than they themselves had done. Most serious of all, they faced an unfair situation in terms of employment due to the preference of many work units for male graduates. If they wished to go on to graduate school, they would likely face difficulties in finding a spouse due to the revival of traditional social values that encouraged men to select wives who were less qualified than themselves and who would make sacrifices for their careers. The socialist slogan about "women holding up half the sky" was no longer heard, and the main influences on young women students came from television advertisements and popular images that suggested that the best strategy for a young women was to make herself attractive and find a well-to-do husband. Several of these women faculty felt that women students were beginning to behave in ways reminiscent of their idea of Japanese girls' colleges, a kind of finishing school ethos where the main concern was over social connections and prestigious marriages rather than professional development. Many women students did not seem to have a strong orientation toward professional work, but were simply anxious to secure a comfortable urban job that would make few demands on them on graduation. This was a kind of passive, even negative, response to the economic environment around them.

However, a minority of women students had been stung into action by their awareness of the discrimination they faced in employment and other areas. This group was determined to ensure that their qualifications were better than those of the men they would have to compete with. Some of them went on to graduate school, and many of the women faculty noted the excellent academic quality of their women graduate students. An interesting point was the difference noted by quite a few of these women faculty between rural and urban women. For rural women, education was the only hope to improve their condition, and thus they tended to be more serious about their academic work. On graduation, they could not count on urban parents to solve their employment problems, and for this reason many opted for graduate study to improve their chances for professional career development.

The problems faced by women at all levels seemed to be linked to two mutually reinforcing social forces: On the one hand there was a concern for short-term economic efficiency in employing agencies of all types, including governmental, which made them unwilling to support women professionals in their child-bearing role. On the other hand, there was a revival of traditional attitudes toward women that served these short-term economic interests. This conservatism was perhaps more evident in hinterland regions.

One impressive woman faculty member, head of the political education department at Ningxia University, had not been abroad, but was interested in our research. She made the point that the whole economic change process had to be seen in terms of a kind of "systems engineering." Many complex factors had to be taken into account in the change process. Thus women were doing relatively well in university entrance and performance, but suffering in employment and career development opportunities. Research around the transition from employment arrangements made by the state to greater freedom of choice for both the employing unit and the young professional needed to consider social policy and legislation that might take the place of the administrative mechanisms that had protected women and minorities, in her view.

CONCLUSION

This snapshot of the Northwest gives us some different angles on the changes going on in higher education over the 1980s, while at the same time illustrating many of the general trends identified in chapters 4 and 5. We definitely see more autonomous universities emerging in the early 1980s, with the initial emphasis in curricular change being on a move toward more comprehensive patterns. Thus Lanzhou University restored law and philosophy to its programs, while also developing some applied natural and social sciences. Xi'an Jiaotong developed strong basic science programs, and certain social science fields to complement its engineering sciences. Provincial-level institutions emphasized new practical and applied programs. In the case of national universities, particularly, there was a variety of programs of scholarly exchange and cooperation with various countries that made possible some mutual dialogue.

By the late 1980s and early 1990s, as the possibilities of attracting self-paying students were expanded, most universities moved vigorously to establish new programs in economically popular areas. This appeared to be essential for their financial health, but it represented a very different force at work in curricular change than the academic one that had been in evidence earlier. There was a real danger of a kind of commercialization of knowledge, as every institution tried to set up programs in subjects such as international trade, foreign languages, and finance that often had little academic basis.

The new emphasis on encouraging self-paying students was also beginning to erode opportunities for rural students, and even bring into question how long the special protection for minority students could be maintained. Minority institutions themselves were seeking permission to enroll self-paying urban students who were non-minorities. We have noted the differential views of different institutions and provinces/regions over how far to embrace a market philosophy in student enrollment, and how far to maintain and build upon the older socialist patterns.

Whatever compromise was likely to be reached, there was little doubt that regional gaps were being widened, both within the region, and between it and the more prosperous coastal regions. Peripheral provinces/regions within the Northwest, such as Qinghai, Ningxia, and Xinjiang, were no longer able to get personnel assigned to them from elsewhere, and were increasingly losing their own best graduates, both from local and national institutions. Xinjiang seemed to be making the most vigorous efforts to counter this by encouraging excellence in its own institutions through research and international contacts.

Shaanxi and Gansu were in a somewhat better situation, as the centers of the region, since they had a considerable number of national institutions and were able to attract and keep personnel from less favored areas, even as they lost some of their own. Their prestigious national institutions continued to attract students from around the nation and they could capitalize, to a certain degree, on the concentration of resources they had inherited from the socialist past. However, they were not in a position to compete with parallel institutions in the Central South, and they were experiencing increasing difficulty in keeping their best faculty, and attracting young faculty, even among their own graduate students.

The contrast between Lanzhou University and Zhongshan University in Guangzhou might be taken as an illustration. Whereas both were excellent comprehensive universities under the State Education Commission, Lanzhou had traditionally had the edge in terms of scholarship. Four of its faculty were members of the prestigious national academic committee (*xuebu weiyuanwei*), while there was only one such member in the whole province of Guangdong at the time. Both Lanzhou and Zhongshan established graduate programs in the early 1980s, and in 1986, both had about 1,000 applicants to their programs. By the early 1990s, however, Zhongshan was still able to attract 1,000 applicants, and had 895 graduate students enrolled. By contrast, Lanzhou had only 500 applicants, and an enrollment of 588. This was clearly related to the added attractions of geographical location and professional opportunities in Guangdong, which Lanzhou could not provide. In addition, Lanzhou University administrators told us they feared losing all four of their academic committee members due to the active efforts being made in Guangdong to attract them by high salaries and various perquisites that Northwest institutions could not afford.

Lanzhou University administrators told us that they felt they could not maintain their present academic level for more than five years unless special measures were taken by the State Education Commission to provide extra financing and other kinds of support. The impoverished Gansu provincial government could barely give adequate support to its own institutions and so was not likely to help. By contrast, the Guangdong provincial government was doubling every national grant to Zhongshan University, and by 1994 had put in place a salary subsidy for all higher education institutions in the province, which added about one-third to the national standard.

This brings us to an intriguing question regarding the relationship between scholarship and financial resources. Clearly, Guangdong province was in a position to buy scholarship, and in a visit made to seven provincial institutions in May 1994,[16] we were struck by the vigorous efforts underway to attract the very best scholars from all parts of China with high salaries, good housing, and other benefits. It was laudable that the provincial government was prepared to make this kind of investment in higher education, but university administrators themselves admitted that they were not sure how well it would succeed. They might attract good scholars, but would those scholars find the kind of infrastructure and social attitudes that would support and stimulate their further scholarly development and enhance the academic quality of the institutions they had come to? Or would they use the opportunity to move to Guangdong for other purposes, perhaps business opportunities or family matters?

The other side of this coin in the Northwest was whether and how the wealth of scholarly resources and scientific research capacity accumulated in thirty years of socialist planning could be turned to some economic advantage for its institutions. Should it have been taking an aggressive approach to attracting self-paying students from around the country outside of the national plan, making use of a combination of excellent academic resources and relatively low living costs? We have noted that one institution, Ningxia University, had started on this road with some success, but had been reprimanded by provincial officials. Somehow, this seemed too daring a view, too far removed from the patterns of the past to find acceptance, yet there seemed to be little other hope for any kind of balancing of human resources between coastal and hinterland areas.

Women's issues had some interesting dimensions in the Northwest. On the one hand there was greater social conservatism, yet on the other hand both women and minorities were making certain gains in terms of higher education entry and faculty appointments by a kind of default, as male students and faculty were more aggressive about opportunities to move to coastal areas. There seemed a window of opportunity here for both groups to take a proactive position in terms of defining their own vision of future participation in and contribution to China's future. The degree to which the university of the future could become a locale for this kind of envisioning is an important question. Will Chinese women and minorities be able to take the opportunities accruing to them by default, under the present economic change process, and transform them into a platform for their own distinctive perspectives? Such a development could offer an important new dimension in terms of China's scholarly contribution to the international community of scholars, as well being important within a national and local context.

NOTES

1. For example, there has been a long-term cooperation between Shanghai Jiaotong University and Xinjiang University involving faculty training, the provision of books and research equipment, etc.

2. A. Doak Barnett, *China's Far West: Four Decades of Change* (Boulder, Colo.: Westview Press, 1993).

3. Xibei daxue xiaoshi bianxie zu, *Xibei daxue xiaoshi gao* [A Draft History of Northwest University], (Xi'an: Xibei daxue chubanshe, 1987), pp. 24–30.

4. Ibid., pp. 88–94.

5. Wang Minghan and Heng Jun, *Xibei shifan daxue xiaoshi 1939–1989* [A History of Northwest Normal University 1939–1989] (Xining: Qinghai renmin chubanshe, 1989), p. 7

6. Lu Runlin et al. (eds.), *Lanzhou daxue xiaoshi 1909–1989* [An Institutional History of Lanzhou University] (Lanzhou: Lanzhou daxue chubanshe, 1990), pp. 1–75.

7. For a detailed and illuminating history of this Canadian missionary institution, see Karen Minden, *Bamboo Stone: The Evolution of a Chinese Medical Elite* (Toronto: University of Toronto Press, 1994).

8. All of the data presented in Tables 6.4–6.11 was collected through a research visit to the region made between May 1 and June 5, 1993. Special thanks are due to CIDA for funding the research, and to the Northwest Center for Training Educational Administrators at Shaanxi Normal University for arranging all of the visits. Thanks are also due to Professor Qiang Haiyan, vice-dean of education at Shaanxi

Normal University, who cooperated in the research, and Mr. Tian Jianrong, lecturer in education, who assisted. Our small research team had interviews with officials at the educational commissions and bureaus of each province/region, as well as visiting each of the sixteen universities included in the case studies.

9. *Kongque dongnan fei; maque ye dongnan fei.*

10. *Educational Statistics Yearbook of China 1991/1992*, p. 158.

11. Percentages for female participation in Tables 6.2 and 6.3 related only to those students enrolled within the province or region.

12. In the dozens of interviews I have done with Chinese faculty, both in China and abroad, the strongest reason for return to their home institution has always been a sense that they could make a substantial professional contribution, in contrast to a much more dependent situation abroad.

13. *Jia weipei, zhen zifei.*

14. The total budget reflects only operating budget, and does not include special allocations for buildings or other projects that vary from year to year, and in accordance with the relative resources of different administering agencies. For example, while the Ministry of Railways was able to provide quite handsomely for its institution, the State Minorities Commission had far less capacity to support the Minorities Institute.

15. We were able to learn of only one female faculty member who had returned from abroad in Yinchuan, and she could not be reached for an interview!

16. This visit was under the auspices of a World Bank team, doing an overall study of the higher education system, with which I was involved. The study was scheduled for publication by the bank early in 1995.

MASS HIGHER EDUCATION
AND THE CHINESE UNIVERSITY

In this book I have tried to tell the story of China's universities from a cultural perspective, to identify and reflect on patterns in the culture that have shaped the emergence and development of modern universities over a century of dramatic social, political, and economic change. These cultural patterns have been dichotomized at two poles: the authoritarian and centralizing structures of the bureaucratic institutions of higher learning linked with the civil service examinations, and the relatively progressive and flexible style of organization in the *shuyuan* and other nonformal institutions which, historically, provided an important counterbalancing force. We have seen how values associated with both of these poles have shaped the modern higher education system in different ways, and how they have combined with models introduced from the West at different periods. At times, a balance was achieved in the new institutions that emerged; at other times, fierce conflict erupted as an emphasis on one dimension elicited a backlash based on values associated with the other.

While a major purpose of the volume has been to foster a deeper understanding of Chinese higher education, there has also been an explicit normative intent, a commitment to envisioning a preferred future on the basis of points of hope that can be identified. It is a relevant utopia that is sought, a utopia for which there is some basis in the culture.[1]

In this last chapter, I am less interested in predicting what the Chinese university is likely to be in future on the basis of empirical trends than in anticipating what it could be, in visionary terms, if the bases for hope that have been identified in the culture are consciously built upon. The hope is for an institution that may contribute not only to the scientific and technical knowledge needed for rapid economic growth, but also to the social knowledge that could ensure justice with growth, and the cultural knowledge that could root this justice firmly within Chinese civilization. It is also for an institution in which women and minorities are able to participate in a full and equal way.

A contrasting vision could also be conjured up through comparative and historical reflection. Negative dimensions of the cultural tradition could well shape the university of the future toward greater elitism, hierarchy, and a renewed patriarchy. A situation in which little critical cultural reflection was allowed or encouraged, as rapid economic change went forward, could be the result. Campaigns against cultural contamination, spiritual pollution, and bourgeois liberalization over the reform decade have been ostensibly an attempt to prevent the wholesale borrowing of Western ideas by intellectuals and students. In fact, however, they have hampered the very kinds of creative social and cultural research that is essential to the search for cultural authenticity and social justice.

On a deep level, it seems China's political leadership has difficulty in letting go of patterns in the cultural tradition that have enabled them to exercise control over all social knowledge in ways that legitimate their continuing rule. This was noted in the patterns legislated by the Qing government for modern higher education, and in those set in place by the new Communist government with the assistance of Soviet experts in the 1950s. It was also evident in the Nationalist period, though the government was not always able to implement the control it sought through legislation.

At the opposite pole to these patterns for central control, hierarchy, and regimentation have been forces of populism, practical emancipatory knowledge, and critical thought, which have provided an alternative resource for both scholars and politicians. Thus during the 1920s, aspects of the *shuyuan* tradition were consciously emulated by Mao Zedong and other Communist thinkers in designing nonformal universities, and by progressive thinkers such as Cai Yuanpei and Hu Shi in shaping formal universities.[2] Much later, Mao's use of these ideas in launching the Cultural Revolution illustrated their continued force in terms of an effective attack on the Soviet-derived structures of the formal system. Unfortunately, their limitations within the Maoist orthodoxy of the time made them incapable of fostering a viable alternative to what had been destroyed.

What progressive elements in the Chinese cultural tradition might now provide a foundation for China's university of the future? What elements in the patterns that have been introduced from outside over the past century may serve to support and reinforce these progressive elements? What practical policy choices might be taken to move toward the relevant utopia of a university or institution of higher learning that combines scholarly excellence, social justice, and cultural authenticity? These are the main questions which this last chapter will address.

The first point we need to be reminded of as we take up these reflections on the future of Chinese universities is the fact that throughout the whole century of development that has been described, China's universities have been elite institutions, accessible only to a tiny minority of the population. During the Nationalist period, this was largely urban youth from the middle classes, while during the Communist period it was mainly the children of government cadres and intellectuals, though a certain number of working-class and peasant young people found entry at certain periods. Even after a decade of rapid expansion over the reform decade of the 1980s, when enrollments in the formal system tripled, age cohort participation was estimated at about 2 percent in 1990,[3] with another 1.5 percent of young people in the adult higher education system.[4]

Meanwhile, China was being urged by advisors from the World Bank to consider a rapid expansion of the higher education system toward the threshold of mass higher education, which has been identified as 15 percent of the age cohort of young people between eighteen and twenty-two years old. In 1986, the bank suggested three scenarios to China in setting forth expansion goals for the year 2000: a low scenario, which set a goal of 10 percent of the age cohort or 5.2 million enrollments in the formal system and 3.7 in the adult system; a medium scenario, which set a goal of 12.5 percent of the age cohort, or 6 million formal enrollments and 5 million adult enrollments; and a high scenario, which set a goal of 15 percent, or 7.6 million formal enrollments and 5.6 million adult enrollments.[5]

Chinese policy makers resisted moving toward even the lowest scenario up to 1991, when the Eighth Five-year Plan and a ten-year development plan put forward a policy of stabilizing enrollment size and focusing on the improvement of quality.[6] This was partly a reaction to the Tiananmen events, with a concern that further expansion of the higher education system would contribute to greater political unrest. It was also related to fluctuating policy concerning the university graduate job assignment system, which had assured every graduate of the formal system the position of a state cadre since the middle 1950s. Clearly, substantial expansion of enrollments in the formal system would be impossible as long as this practice continued.

The reform document of 1993 made a firm commitment to the abolition of the job assignment system, and called for rapid expansion of both formal and adult higher education systems in response to escalating economic change, and an apparently more stable political situation. We have seen the surge of enrollment growth in the Central South and the Northwest in 1992 to 1993, as an increasing number of self-paying students were enrolled. While the 1993 document did not give exact projections for enrollment expansion, these have been revealed elsewhere. The intention by late 1993 was to expand at a rate of .6 for every percentage of economic growth, reaching 3.5 million enrollments in the formal system and 2.5 million in the adult system by the year 2000, or about 7 percent of the age cohort.[7] While this is still far below the threshold of mass higher education, it is a highly significant change for a nation with China's huge population. The tremendous surge of support for this expansion at the local level, in both the economically dynamic Central South region and the more impoverished Northwest region, suggest that it may in fact be difficult to control the numbers at 6 million, and a somewhat higher enrollment level may well be reached.[8]

A fairly certain feature of the future is thus a greatly expanded higher education system moving toward a mass system as rapid economic growth generates both the resources to support expansion and the jobs to absorb graduates. The question of concern in this chapter is what kind of mass higher education system is likely to emerge, and what transformative values are available in the culture that could shape this system toward greater social justice and cultural authenticity. Some reflections on the comparative literature dealing with the transition to mass higher education may be helpful at this point.

A classic study by George Bereday on the process of transition to mass higher education makes three main points. Firstly, open admission and rapid quantitative expansion need not reduce quality, except possibly in the short term. Secondly, enrollments need not be closely linked to the numbers the economy can absorb, since a continual upgrading of various kinds of position can be expected with the stimulus of mass higher education. Thirdly, the basic principle of mass higher education is one of openness and a belief that all are infinitely educable; it is a compensatory rather than an egalitarian ethos in terms of provision for diverse groups. Bereday's study is particularly interesting as an example of inductive method, with a final chapter that seeks to construct a theory of mass higher education based on common elements in the experience of North America, Japan, and the Soviet Union.[9] It is also interesting to note that these values resonate with aspects of China's own progressive tradition in education.

Around the same period, Martin Trow noted how the movement to mass higher education greatly changes the functions of the university, bringing formal and nonformal higher education closer together.[10] Perhaps the most vivid depiction of the broadened functions of the university in the North American context of mass higher education has been the "multiversity" depicted by Clark Kerr. In *The Uses of the University*, he describes it as "a city of infinite variety," a complex, diverse entity with greatly fractionalized power. Massive in size, it has many levels, serves diverse populations, and feeds into various echelons of society in the employment of its graduates. "As in a city, there are many separate endeavor under a single rule of law."[11]

The emergence and growth of the multiversity has coincided with increasing political and cultural pluralism in North America, and a growing commitment to social equity perceived in terms of equity of outcome, as well as equality of opportunity. The fact that much is left to be done in equity terms, and that recent global economic pressures threaten to undo some of the compensatory programs of the past, does not take away from the ethos of the multiversity as an institution accessible to a wide population and committed to an excellence which is, in principle if not in practice, achievable by most. One of its striking achievements is the equal participation of female students at all levels, if not in all fields of knowledge.[12]

In the Canadian context, the multiversity is fully public, though a modest yet increasing part of the cost is recovered from students and their families.[13] In the United States, publicly funded institutions are responsible for 78 percent of all enrollments, and some major private universities have become multiversities in their own ways. Kerr takes the examples of Harvard and the University of California in his discussion of the idea of the multiversity. A key point here is the belief that openness of access and diversity of level and program can coexist with the highest standards of academic achievement. While a clear hierarchy still exists in both countries, perhaps more evidently in the United States than Canada, a hierarchy that has historic roots and that has not changed greatly over the past century, there is nevertheless considerable fluidity of movement among the different parts of the system.

Graduates of the multiversity constitute an extremely large professional/intellectual class that is critical of its politicians and active in promoting a wide range of autonomous cultural, social, and charitable activities. This autonomy and diversity coexists with an increasingly fractured sense of national identity and an unraveling of the social cohesion derived from traditional familial patterns.

This picture of the multiversity is an idealized one, expressing more the hopes and intentions of mass higher education than its actual achievements. Nevertheless, it may be a helpful reference point in reflecting on China's future. The question of interest at this point is how far there are patterns in Chinese culture and China's socialist experience that might support a future development for the Chinese university toward the lessening of hierarchy, greater democratization in terms of access and the employment of graduates, and an openness in the curriculum that would permit a conscious and critical search for cultural authenticity, rather than the cultural conformity imposed by a leadership trying to buttress the legitimacy of its regime.

We have noted in earlier chapters how hierarchialized have been the patterns of modern Chinese higher education, with the level of institution entered having a determining effect on employment prospects within the bureaucracy, and there being no possibility of upward mobility outside of this tightly constructed framework. There are, in fact, many parallels with the traditional civil service examination system. Efforts to break through these patterns toward greater popular access and curricular openness during the Great Leap Forward had some success, but this could not be sustained due to the economic disasters that followed it. Parallel efforts during the Cultural Revolution ended in the almost total destruction of the university system in favor of short-cycle, nonformal training classes of various kinds. These in turn left a legacy of nonformal higher education that has continued to embody some of the progressive and populist values of China's alternate traditions and of its socialist experiments. However, the subordination of nonformal higher education to the formal system, as a less favored second track, has limited the influence of these values.

We thus see a situation in the early 1990s when there are very real reasons to believe that cultural patterns of the hierarchical, highly centralized civil service examination tradition could well shape the transition to mass higher education. In order to anticipate the form these might take under a mass system, we can look to three major post-Confucian societies of East Asia that made this transition in historical succession—Japan in the 1960s, Taiwan in the 1970s, and South Korea in the 1980s.[14] An interesting feature of these three societies has been the enhancement of hierarchy over the transition period, with an increasing gap between the highest and lowest levels of the system, and each level feeding directly into a specific echelon of the bureaucracy and industry for employment purposes. Japan is the classic example, and Ikuo Amano has noted how "the relative position of particular institutions has scarcely changed since the system's inception in the 1870s . . . in other words, the movement of the system into the mass stage has merely served to reinforce the hierarchy established in the formative period."[15] Studies of Korean higher education in the transition to a mass system indicate a parallel phenomenon to that of Japan.[16] Taiwan has similar patterns as well, though there is an interesting anomaly between the elitism of the higher education system, and the lack of evidence for drastic socioeconomic inequities.[17] In addition to shared cultural patterns, of course, the historical legacy of Japanese colonialism had a lasting influence in both Taiwan and South Korea.[18]

If we reflect on the transition to mass higher education from the perspective of the emergence of civil society, or the activities of a semiautonomous grouping of intellectuals and professionals,[19] it is possible to see how the huge increase taking place in the size of the professional/intellectual class was managed in ways that allowed fairly authoritarian political systems to stay in place in all three societies. It was really only in the mid- to late 1980s that there was some movement toward greater political pluralism, with the end of military rule in Korea, the end of martial law and the development of alternative political parties in Taiwan, and the undermining of a long Liberal party monopoly in Japanese politics. Teruhisa Horio's *Educational Thought and Ideology in Modern Japan*[20] provides a profound critique of the way in which persisting patterns of Confucian hierarchy have stifled ongoing popular demands for education toward human emancipation and democratic participation in Japanese society. In all three societies voices can be heard that express deep frustration over what is seen by intellectuals as an Enlightenment process that was stifled.[21] The confluence of economic success, social harmony, and cultural coherence that has been linked to persisting Confucian values in these East Asian societies has nevertheless carried a certain attraction, even for Western observers.[22]

The patterns of these other East Asian societies are suggestive on the cultural level for anticipating how China might negotiate the transition to mass higher education, especially if ongoing political authoritarianism allows little leeway for critical cultural reflection. A striking feature of all three societies is the importance of the private sector, with around 70 percent of all enrollments being privately funded and an elite public sector setting overall standards and dominating top-level employment opportunities.[23] A second feature is the tendency for the elite public sector to be male dominated, while women students are over-represented in the lower echelons and in the private sector. A third feature, in Taiwan and South Korea, has been a very strong emphasis on the sciences and engineering in enrollments up until the final stage of expansion, when social sciences were given somewhat greater leeway. This suggests a technocratic vision of economic and social change and a strong commitment to national manpower planning.

In the present Chinese context, expansion will necessarily depend on greatly increased familial and personal contributions to higher education. The main policy question is whether this funding will find its way mainly into public institutions, with an expansion of enrollments encouraged at all levels, but most especially in the best institutions that head the system, or whether a mass private sector is encouraged to cater to those who either prefer this choice or do not qualify for the higher standards of the public sector. A small number of private or "people-run" institutions had gained approval for state-certified programs at the short-cycle level by 1993,[24] and many more are seeking this status. However, present indications are that the public sector will be expected to carry the main burden of expansion,[25] though it is not clear at what level.

On the issue of female participation, the Chinese record under socialism was somewhat better than the situation in other East Asian societies at a similar economic development level. However, recent developments in the market economy suggest women students could be disadvantaged under conditions of increasing hierarchy and find themselves drawn into the lower echelons of the system. Urban women could well choose practical programs in local institutions that lead to secure urban jobs, given the difficulties they face seeking professional employment, while rural women are less likely than rural men to get financial support from their families for any level of higher education.

On the issue of curricular emphasis, in 1990, China still had 68 percent of all enrollments in various scientific fields, indicating patterns similar to those of Taiwan and Korea at a similar stage. There is thus the possibility of a massive expansion of enrollments in the social sciences, which tend to be at low cost, as part of the transition to a mass system. The key question here is what part of the system will be encouraged to develop these programs. Will they be encouraged in the best national institutions, or in cheap local or private institutions designed to serve market needs directly?

This chapter will deal with the same three themes that have been explored in earlier chapters—the knowledge map, the gender map, and the geographical map. As an exercise in envisioning a preferred future, it will attempt to sketch out the kinds of changes in pattern and structure that might move the Chinese university toward a mass institution that draws upon progressive dimensions of its own cultural heritage, as well as aspects of Marxist emancipatory thought and other progressive traditions that have been introduced over the century. I will try to draw the lines clearly and firmly, setting this ideal against the persisting cultural patterns of hierarchy and support for political authoritarianism that are derived from elements of the Confucian tradition and have historically been supported by aspects of Russian and European thought.

The Knowledge Map

In considering possibilities for a more holistic integrative approach to knowledge in the higher curriculum in China, one that would allow universities to play a transformative role in social change, it may be helpful to go back to the reflections in chapter 3 on Bernstein's notion of the collection code and the integrated code as they related to the antithesis between Soviet and Maoist patterns in the struggles of the 1950s and the Cultural Revolution. We noted the weakened classification and framing of curricular knowledge during the Cultural Revolution, as disciplinary boundaries among different fields of knowledge were deemphasized and there were conscious attempts to link all areas of knowledge toward emancipatory and revolutionary practice in both the arenas of social change and such grass-roots economic change as rural industrialization. Mao's vision was a powerful one, and it had deep roots in a progressive thread of Chinese epistemology, going back to Ming neo-Confucian concerns with the unity of knowledge and action, and earlier.[26] The tragedy of the period lay in the fact that those who might have been best able to realize this vision in actual educational and curricular patterns—the intellectuals and teachers—were the main targets of attack. The movement thus ended up in a kind of destructive anarchism, with cruel personal vendettas destroying even the pretense of revolutionary educational achievements.

Nevertheless, we have noted how the nonformal or adult system of higher education, which found expression in July 21 universities during the Cultural Revolution period, and was rooted much farther back in various kinds of nonformal education from the early part of the century,[27] continued to develop throughout the reform decade as a kind of second thread in the higher education system. It first played an important role in enabling the generation of cadres appointed during the Cultural Revolution to gain the needed knowledge and qualifications for the modernization drive and then, in the second half of the decade, it absorbed a growing number of secondary school graduates who were unable to gain entrance to the formal system.

While the content of its programs were increasingly upgraded on the patterns of the formal system over this period, its overall ethos, teaching style, and approach retained some of the legacy of the past, and also a sense of pride in this historical connection. With the rapid expansion of formal higher education beginning to take off in the early 1990s, the adult higher education system is now increasingly threatened, as more and more secondary school graduates find their way into the formal system through new self-paying programs, attracted by qualifications that have a higher social prestige. The fact that most major national institutions have developed colleges of adult education over the reform decade, thus connecting the adult and formal systems, suggests that the time has come for some kind of systemic integration between the two streams. Existing independent adult institutions could ally themselves with appropriate formal institutions, and the national entry examinations for the two systems could be integrated. With effective evaluation and appropriate mechanisms for assuring standards of quality, this could be mutually enhancing and provide an important basis for linking the higher curriculum to an indigenous context.[28]

While the nonformal or adult system retains vital links to China's own progressive and revolutionary traditions of knowledge, the formal system has been the main vehicle for interaction with an international knowledge community, and for the revision and revitalization of programs across the knowledge spectrum from the humanities to the technological sciences during the 1980s. I would argue that only the combined force of these two sets of cultural and epistemological patterns is likely to be able to stand against the patterns of hierarchy, narrow specialization, and ideological control that have formed the opposite curricular pole in China's historical experience.

Let me turn now to the curricular achievements of the reform decade that have been briefly sketched in chapter 4. We have already noted the impulse toward more comprehensive patterns of knowledge, with all universities seeking to broaden their curricular coverage, and quite a remarkable development of social science and humanities programs in institutions originally designated as highly specialist technical institutes. In addition to this general broadening of the curriculum, there has been a redefinition of specializations and departments in broader terms, with the introduction of elective courses and more emphasis on basic theoretical foundations, and also an attempt to group departments within colleges that would encourage cooperation among programs.

Most importantly, throughout this whole process, university intellectuals have themselves redefined course content and reshaped teaching programs, reveling in the new freedoms that were given to them as they left behind the detailed, state-defined teaching plans of an earlier period, and exercised their own judgment over what needed most to be known within broad official definitions of each specialization. In my many visits to universities at different levels within the system, and discussions with faculty in the academic programs office (*jiaowu chu*), it became evident to me that much greater autonomy and individuality was expressed in prestigious national-level institutions, as they defined program content, than in provincial or local-level institutions, which felt the need to seek legitimacy by following national guidelines more closely.

It might be possible to conceptualize the present change process in terms of a movement from the strong classification and framing of the Soviet-derived patterns, which were essentially restored in the late 1970s, toward new forms of integration, with weakened boundaries among disciplines, in a situation where intellectuals themselves have enjoyed increasing autonomy and freedom of academic expression. Also, a substantial percentage of all faculty in national institutions have had the opportunity for study and research abroad, resulting in an eclectic set of external influences on curricular content and teaching methods. This is a striking contrast to the Cultural Revolution period, where Maoist orthodoxy and Maoist epistemology more or less strangled the possibilities for the development of a culturally authentic curriculum in their very inception. Yet for effective movement in this direction, both the values of China's own progressive knowledge traditions and the critical adaptation of external influences are needed, as China's earlier historical experience demonstrates. For this reason the integration of the adult higher education system into the formal system could have real significance.

A further institutional development that could offer a supportive framework to this kind of ongoing change is the impulse toward institutional amalgamation that has resulted from a new policy, expressed in the 1993 reform document, and intended to enhance excellence. This is popularly called the 2/1/1 engineering project (*er yao yao gongcheng*) and refers to expressed intentions of the state to identify and give special financial support to 100 of the best universities by the twenty-first century.[29] This idea has stimulated provincial authorities and central ministries to position their institutions in such a way as to qualify for selection into this elite group. The result has been mergers of two or more institutions, with special financial support from provincial authorities, and in some cases ministry authorities, to ensure strong profiles for particular institutions that are under consideration.

The whole process could be seen as a remarkable reversal of the "reordering of colleges and departments" that took place under Soviet guidance between 1952 and 1955, one that could well lead to the emergence of institutions that have some similarities in curricular ethos with the comprehensive institutions of the Nationalist period. At the same time they will be large in scale, and truly multi-functional institutions.

A few examples may serve to illustrate potential trends. Recently in Chengdu, Sichuan province, Sichuan University, a comprehensive university of the arts and sciences with a history going back to the 1920s, has combined with the Chengdu University of Science and Technology, a polytechnic university founded in the early 1950s. The combined enrollment of these two institutions is around 22,000, making it the largest university in China. Both institutions were originally administered by the State Education Commission, making this merger relatively smooth. The new factor in their situation, however, is substantial financial support from the Sichuan provincial government.[30]

Another example of potential cooperation from the southwest is Chongqing University, the major polytechnical university of the region, which is considering amalgamation with the Southwest Institute of Political Science and Law, and the Chongqing Institute of Architecture, both of which shared common roots with Chongqing University in the pre-Liberation period. Such a merger would be a direct reversal of the patterns imposed by the Soviet model in 1952. What makes it problematic, however, is the fact that these two institutions are under the jurisdiction of distinct national ministries, while Chongqing University is under the State Education Commission.[31]

A third interesting case is the creation of a very large university in Shanghai at the municipal level, with the combination of Shanghai University of Science and Technology, Shanghai Industrial University, and Shanghai University. The first two of these institutions were founded in the Great Leap Forward period as an expression of the impulse to bring together basic and applied sciences, while the third was founded in the early 1980s, on the basis of the branch campuses set up by major national universities such as Fudan and Tongji, to provide enhanced higher education opportunities for local Shanghai students. Interestingly, three major national universities in Shanghai—Fudan, Shanghai Jiaotong, and Shanghai University of International Studies—apparently felt so threatened by this merger that they have jointly sought a contract for support from the Shanghai government.[32]

Many other mergers are now under discussion. If existing adult and television universities could be appropriately integrated into the very best of these institutions, this would make possible a combination of the best scholars in the formal system, with their manifold international interactions, and scholars associated with the nonformal system who take pride in China's progressive heritage. This would be a new type of Chinese university, large in size, comprehensive in curricular provision, and providing conditions for the integration of the best from international currents of scholarship within Chinese progressive traditions. With the abolition of the national job assignment system, graduates of these institutions would find their way into different levels and echelons of government and society, from the national level right down to the grass roots.

Since many mergers involve institutions at the top level of the higher education system, we can be fairly certain that the faculty of these new-style mass institutions will be some of the most creative and productive scholars in the system. Under the conditions we have envisaged they would be able to exercise a much more significant social role than in the past. Student enrollments have been highly restricted at the elite keypoint institutions that head the system, and it is only most recently that they have been allowed to recruit increasing numbers of self-paying students under adjustments to the national enrollment plan. Colleges for students in the adult system are also fairly recent. In the past, the influence of China's best scholars was thus limited to a small group of elite students, most of whom moved into positions in the national-level bureaucracy or went abroad. A movement toward massive, multipurpose institutions at the top of the system would make possible a much broader social influence for these faculty, as a larger body of graduates goes out into all echelons of society. The potential for the best universities to make a transformative contribution to political and social change would thus be enhanced.

This picture is of course an idealized sketch of a possible direction of change that can be seen in the present situation. One could just as easily sketch out a negative picture of future developments. This is a picture that would emphasize the increased hierarchy likely to result from the policy of special support for 100 elite institutions, and anticipate patterns similar to those of other East Asian societies. An increasingly stratified and hierarchical set of institutions would emerge, with most of the expansion within the system taking place in its lower echelons. Low-level public and newly emerging private institutions would capitalize on the kinds of commercialization of knowledge already in evidence, providing cheap programs in areas of popular demand such as finance, trade, and foreign languages to meet market needs, while the best institutions would be protected as an elite and limited in the social science programs they are allowed to offer. This would effectively prevent the kinds of broad social influence that could have come from mass universities, with their implications for the strengthening of civil society and democratic change. One can see the appeal of such patterns to political authorities anxious to retain strict social control, though needing to ensure adequate human resources for the modernization process.

THE GENDER MAP

Throughout this volume, I have tried to include the contribution made by women to the evolving story of China's universities, yet there has been a striking inadequacy of detailed information in many periods, as well as real difficulty in identifying and elaborating the perspectives of Chinese women on the change process. In the early period we saw a situation in which a small number of women from relatively elite backgrounds took part in study abroad programs from the late nineteenth century, and some found their way into missionary colleges. Beginning in 1919, women were first accepted into national universities, and through the Beijing Women's Normal University they were able to have a substantial voice in scholarly and political circles during the 1920s. Subsequently, under both Nationalist and Communist development projects, women were pressured into giving up their agenda for the broader goals of revolution or nationalistic construction.[33] While they had a voice and a role within these broader agendas, the limited numbers participating in higher education and cadre training in both contexts ensured that it was a subordinate role.

From the 1950s, women's participation in formal higher education grew steadily, reaching a height of 33 percent during the Cultural Revolution decade when the popularization of secondary education, and the cessation of the national higher education entry examinations, facilitated their entry to higher education. The subsequent restoration of the examinations in 1977 and 1978, caused women's participation to drop to 24 percent initially, but by the mid-1980s, it had climbed back to 30 percent and by the end of the decade was nearing 34 percent.

Women faculty increased in number and proportion gradually over the whole period after 1949, reaching 20.6 percent by 1965, 25.8 percent by 1980, and 29.1 percent by 1990. The socialist job assignment system assured women graduates relatively equal career opportunities with men, and teaching in higher education was regarded as an appropriate outlet for professional women. As a result, the representation of women in China's higher education faculty has been considerably higher than in other Asian countries.[34] In extensive interviews carried out with women faculty in Northwest China in 1993, which have been described in chapter 6, we found none among them who felt they had suffered serious discrimination in their professional lives due to gender, although many had harrowing experiences to recount concerning what they had suffered from political oppression during the Cultural Revolution and other mobilization campaigns.

By the early 1990s, women's representation in the ranks of faculty under aged thirty had already reached 37 percent nationwide, and was continuing to increase. This has been mainly the result of a process of default, as an increasing number of male faculty have left the university for careers in business, and male graduate students have chosen not to enter university careers. There is thus an interesting situation in the 1990s, in which women faculty and students are positioned to have increasing influence within the university, just as university positions become less attractive relative to new avenues opened up with the market reforms. Still, the university retains a vitally important role in the economic and social change process, as mounting social demand pushes it rapidly toward a mass system. The fascinating question is what contribution women faculty might make to the vision outlined above of multipurpose universities in the top echelon of the higher education system having a wide social influence.

Will Chinese women faculty bring a special consciousness as women to the kinds of curricular change that have been described above? How might they strengthen the university's transformative potential? How might they use its agency in their own struggle against the new kinds of gender discrimination that have emerged with the market reforms?

In reflecting on these questions, perhaps we should go back to the discussion in the beginning of chapter 2, which noted similarities and differences in the relation between women and the academy in the West and China. In both societies, women were formally excluded from institutionally defined higher learning in around the thirteenth century, with the emergence of universities in medieval Europe and the triumph of Zhu Xi's version of neo-Confucian orthodoxy in China. In the European context, the development of modern science, the mechanistic vision of the natural world that followed, and the university's role in nation-building were all developments that took place before women found their way into academe. Thus women within the Western university have given considerable effort to feminist epistemology as a form of understanding that seeks both to critique and to supersede the fragmented, mechanistic universe of male science and industrialism.[35]

For Chinese women, the situation is somewhat different. Modern science and the mechanistic/industrial vision never had the roots in Chinese culture that they had in the West, but were bodies of knowledge and understanding pragmatically introduced and used for nationalistic ends in the Chinese environment. The success of the Cultural Revolution in entirely dethroning and eliminating the Soviet version of these knowledge patterns and institutional structures suggests how tenuous were their roots in the Chinese cultural environment. Traditional Chinese philosophy, both Confucianism and Daoism, had an integrative holistic understanding of the human and natural worlds and their interconnections, being thus in a sense closer to feminist ways of knowing. Knowledge was always a seamless whole, with theory and practice, the natural and social worlds, the moral and factual dimensions of reality interacting in integral ways.[36] China has even been seen as a kind of eternal feminine, attractive and desirable to the West precisely because it never adopted the forms of knowledge for power that had made Western imperialism so successful.[37]

We have also noted how early Chinese revolutionaries such as Chen Duxiu, feeling China's oppression in the global context, had a particular empathy for women within their own society, since they felt Chinese women bore the double oppression of China's national humiliation and Chinese feudal subordination.[38] Chinese women have clearly faced a different struggle in the modern context than their Western sisters. They have also had resources in traditional culture and epistemology that were at once more feminine and more threatening to femininity than Western knowledge patterns. Due to its holism and integration, the Confucian world view left no place for women to take a stand outside of its all-embracing discourse.[39] Daoism has often been seen as an alternative ground, less structured and hierarchical, giving women a less formalized role within its patterns, yet it too subjected the feminine to the service of male interests.[40] Perhaps only Buddhist educational patterns and institutions in traditional China provided some kind of space for Chinese women's thought and action.

Encompassed by patterns of discourse and thought that have made it very difficult for them to assert a voice, Chinese women seem to have been trapped by the very femininity of the culture in which they have found themselves. While they had a brief period of self expression and action in the decade after May 4th, both Nationalist and Communist projects of modernity and socialist construction constrained them to operate within new official discourses. No space was given them for the development of theories and perspectives of their own. Given these circumstances, it is not surprising that we have had difficulty identifying a distinctive feminine contribution to the historical development of the university, even though Chinese women were there from a relatively early period.

Recent developments in Chinese feminism indicate, however, that women are finding a voice at present and are beginning to create programs of women's studies that conform neither to official Communist categories nor to Western feminist positions. This has become possible within the greater autonomy of Chinese universities in the reform period, and with the emergence of a degree of intellectual freedom. The development of Chinese women's perspectives has been seen as moving through three stages by Tani Barlow.[41] First they critiqued the role of *funu* [women], which was provided for them by Communist orthodoxy, a role that most of them had never identified with. Then they moved to a conception of *nuxing* (the female gender), which emphasized all those aspects of femininity denied to women within proletarian political discourse. The third stage Barlow elaborates by reference to the term *nuren*, [women as humans], as Chinese women develop a literature that claims for themselves a distinctive piece of the cultural humanism that had historically excluded them.

One of the key figures in the development of a Chinese feminism that conforms neither to Communist political rhetoric and institutions, nor to Western feminism, is Li Xiaozhang, whose ideas have been introduced in chapter 4. She stands out as a national leader in efforts underway to develop a strong women's studies movement within Chinese higher education, and a women's literature that gives voice to Chinese women.

What contribution might this play to the broader agenda sketched out above of large multipurpose universities at the top echelon of the higher education system having both a strong academic profile and the potential to contribute to social transformation? A recent article by a Chinese woman sociologist calls for multidisciplinary research within women's studies that will address some of the problems emerging in the market economy. It should be research that can be used by women in their struggle for justice, not merely academic research. "This obviously differs from the scholasticism of the halls of traditional sociology, where scholars pay attention only to publishing articles and piling up endless theoretical arguments, activities that have very little to do with people's real lives. In other words, the birth and development of women's studies itself is a kind of 'revolution' against traditional scholasticism. Consequently, women's studies scholars should use their own unique methods and styles of research to make a contribution toward this discipline."[42] This scholar goes on to comment that anthropological method seems far more appropriate to understanding the Chinese context than sociological method, indicating that the role of various disciplines could change under the impact of women's studies. Clearly there is an opportunity at present for women to assert themselves in the university community. They may be able to link certain disciplines more integrally to real problems of Chinese society. They may also be able to push universities in new directions, in terms of research and teaching.

After sketching out this hopeful picture of how women's studies and the presence of an increasingly large contingent of women faculty in Chinese universities might support the university's transformative role, we should also consider opposing tendencies in the situation. A recent article on the dilemma facing Western universities under pressures of globalization has distinguished "market knowledge" and "social knowledge" as expressing opposite responses of the university to global economic pressures.[43] While women's ways of knowing could do much to strengthen "social knowledge" in the higher curriculum in China, women faculty and students are being swept along by pressures for market knowledge in the increasing commercialization going on. We have already noted in the Northwest how many women faculty are concerned about female students responding passively to the new forms of discrimination in employment opportunities, and adapting to pressures that are likely to push them to seek simpler and more marketable types of qualification.

Thus it is not hard to anticipate that if an intensified stratification develops, following an East Asian pattern, as the Chinese university moves into the mass stage, women students are likely to be increasingly concentrated in lower echelons of the system, while men will dominate the elite echelons that open up employment in higher levels of government and industry. The triumph of market knowledge, as the dominant rationale for the university curriculum, could well have particularly severe effects on women students and faculty.

THE GEOGRAPHICAL MAP

The third theme that has run through this story of the Chinese university has been that of geography, with the central dilemma being how the university, an essentially Western institution introduced to China in the late nineteenth century, could become connected to China's vast hinterland and become a fully Chinese institution, not merely part of a Westernized enclave in a few coastal cities. The geographical issue also connects to the great divide between urban and rural China, and the issue of how far the university has become accessible to rural students in different periods.

China's first modern universities very naturally developed in coastal cities, Beiyang gongxue in Tianjin in 1895, Nanyang in Shanghai in 1896, and the Imperial University in Beijing in 1898. Although late Qing legislation for higher education, passed in 1902 and 1903, did not address the issue of the geographical distribution of higher education in any explicit way, there was an implicit assumption that it would follow the bureaucratic patterns of traditional higher learning, and we have seen that almost every province or region had a college of political science and law from an early period, although other higher institutions developed much more quickly in coastal areas.

From the early Republican period, however, there was considerable official concern about the geographical distribution of modern higher education. The idea of identifying university districts, and developing regional plans for higher education, reappeared over and over in the years before and after May 4th. Probably the most ambitious scheme of all was that of Cai Yuanpei, which was introduced in 1927–1928, when he took the leadership of the Nationalist university council. It soon faltered in the face of popular resistance and governmental weakness. Only in the Sino-Japanese War period, from 1937 to 1945, did modern universities find their way to the hinterland areas of central, northwestern, and southwestern China. We have noted in chapter 2 how both the higher curriculum and research were affected by this process, developing much closer links than ever before with China's own cultural and historical roots.

Under the Communist regime, the politics of geography were of considerable importance, and chapter 3 has detailed the results of the movement lasting from 1952 to 1955, called the "reorganization of colleges and departments." The six regional systems of higher education that emerged might be seen as a fulfillment, in certain ways, of Cai Yuanpei's dream of a rationally ordered set of patterns that assured the presence of universities and of each type of professional school, in all parts of the country. However, we have seen from chapters 5 and 6 how the mechanistic character of the centrally orchestrated reorganization that took place, with centers and peripheries created within each region, resulted in permanent inequalities among provinces within each region ever since.

Perhaps the most organically rooted and enduring movement for geographical participation took place in 1958, when each province took the initiative to create new provincial-level institutions, many of which embodied forms of curricular integration and local knowledge that directly challenged the narrow specialization of the Soviet model. Thus universities of science and technology, comprehensive universities, and colleges of traditional Chinese medicine were among the new institutions springing up at this period. In some cases, these became vigorous intellectual centers at the provincial or municipal level, and they may have a significant role in the new type of institution that is emerging. A case in point is the new institution recently created in Shanghai through the merger of three local institutions, which intends to compete for excellence with national universities such as Fudan and Jiaotong.

How might the vision of the multipurpose university, depicted earlier in this chapter, relate to geographical issues in the present and future of Chinese higher education? It is my sense there is tremendous potential in hinterland regions to preserve and build upon the academic and social strength of institutions created in the 1940s and 1950s through patterns that would encourage the combination of two or three of the best institutions, either provincial or national, in a particular region, and foster multidimensional programs, including graduate, undergraduate, adult, and short-term professional education. These institutions could be encouraged to recruit students nationwide, and to capitalize on their combination of academic excellence, a somewhat traditional academic spirit, and the much lower living costs than are found in coastal areas. On the one hand, they would continue their work of education and professional training for the province or region, with governmental or industrial subsidies for local students recruited under commissioned or directed training programs and committed to work in local settings where they are needed on graduation. On the other hand, they could attract fee-paying students from all over the country who would benefit from their excellent standards, and also bring a certain cosmopolitanism to the campus environment. In addition to continuing and enhanced support for local students at different levels, government and industry should ensure that these hinterland institutions have appropriate access to research funding, both vertical and horizontal, so that the talents of faculty are fully used. This kind of a student body and research opportunity would provide incentives for faculty to stay and develop their careers, rather than escaping to coastal areas or to business opportunities.

The development of large, multi-functional mass institutions in China's hinterland areas would offer the possibility of an appropriate concentration of resources from central and provincial sources so that the academic strengths built up over thirty years of socialism were not dissipated and lost under market pressures. It would be entirely natural and expected for there to be a somewhat less vigorous development of short-cycle and nonformal institutions, due to the lack of strong economic incentives, but with this kind of education integrated within the university, it should be possible to maintain some equivalence of resources and opportunities between hinterland and coastal areas.

One of the most important aspects of the geographical issue is that relating to student access, particularly the access of rural students to higher education. The working out of policies whereby those students who can afford to pay appropriately for higher education do so, while scholarships, bursaries, or loans support those who cannot, is one of the main issues on the agenda at present. In a remarkable departure from former practices, whereby all higher education finances were provided from the state, most institutions now depend on student fees and various kinds of research or development contracts for anywhere between 10 percent and 50 percent of their income, as we have seen in chapters 5 and 6. On the one hand, this situation shows some promise for the university to connect itself both to economic development needs and social demand. On the other, however, it could well lead to the exclusion of qualified students, particularly those from rural areas, who are not able to pay fees, and may find it difficult to adapt to the idea of loans for higher education study. The way in which this situation is dealt with on the level of national policy will be of great importance. The fact that rural youth in hinterland areas are more likely to be disadvantaged than those in coastal areas, where there is greater economic dynamism, indicates the particular importance of maintaining and strengthening multi-functional universities at the regional and provincial level in the hinterland.

This issue is also closely linked to the question of the role of private higher institutions in the reform process. There can be little doubt about the rising tide of social demand for higher education, and also a degree of economic prosperity that makes it feasible for students and their families, in some areas at least, to contribute an increasing proportion of the cost. Given this situation, it is not surprising that a large number of private or people-run (*minban*) institutions have come into being and are seeking registration with the government and the right to provide state-certified programs at the short-cycle or undergraduate level. So far only a very few have been certified, mainly for the short-cycle level.[44] If this kind of development were encouraged by the government, over time a situation similar to that in other East Asian countries could develop, with much of the lower-level university programming provided on a private basis, and the government maintaining a monopoly over a relatively small elite sector.

The disadvantage of such a development in the Chinese context would lie in the way it encouraged widening geographical disparities between coastal and hinterland parts of the country. It is unlikely that private institutions would flourish in the hinterland, and we have already seen how programs for self-paying students in coastal areas have begun to attract some of the best students away from hinterland regions. Geographical inequalities would probably be further exacerbated by such a development. Far better, I would argue, to allow the best institutions, at the top echelon of the system, to expand massively and absorb fee-paying students who might choose a good hinterland institution rather than a poorer coastal one. These institutions would be much more able to guarantee quality than private ones, and would in effect be making use of a kind of academic capital developed over thirty years of socialism as they expanded their programs. Furthermore, their faculty would be likely to teach in ways that would contribute to profound social understanding, as well as good professional standards. By contrast, private institutions could easily be diploma mills that absorb substantial student fees for profit, and provide certificates with little guarantee of quality. Their programs are likely to be cheap substitutes for real social learning.

Thus the policy choices lying before the government at present, both with relation to student fees and financing, and with relation to the patterns of expansion that will be encouraged in the higher education system, have profound implications for the geographical distribution of higher education and for the degree to which rural students, especially those from hinterland areas, are able to gain access.

A final plea for a strong emphasis on support for large multi-purpose universities in the hinterland would relate this both to issues of the knowledge map and the gender map. We have seen already how deeply the Chinese university was changed and indigenized during the Sino-Japanese War, and in the present period of globalization, hinterland universities in China may have a crucial role to play in ensuring enduring connections to China's indigenous knowledge patterns. In addition, we have seen the particular and growing strength of women faculty and students in hinterland regions, indicating the possibility of a particularly dynamic role for women within this kind of setting.

INTERNATIONAL INTERACTIONS AND THE CHINESE UNIVERSITY

This chapter has been an exercise in envisioning and persuasion, rather than a purely academic discussion of the future of the Chinese university. I am deeply aware of the crudity of argument and roughness of the brush strokes sketched out. Nevertheless, I am convinced that this vision of a Chinese university that would draw on progressive dimensions of its indigenous tradition and would flourish in hinterland regions where it is closely connected to Chinese soil, is a preferred direction for the future. I am also aware of how fragile the vision is, and how easily China could get caught up in the development of a market university, highly stratified, producing knowledge for direct economic use, yet lacking either vision or resources for social change or cultural authenticity.

In this final section of chapter 7, I'd like to reflect a little on the kinds of international interaction that might support the emergence of the type of university that has been envisioned, setting these against the kinds of interaction that are likely to push China farther and farther along the road of a stratification of higher education structures and a marketization of the higher curriculum.

The first point that is very clear, I think, is the need to move beyond programs that emphasize faculty training or professional training of various kinds. These have dominated many of the aid programs, and have certainly had their value. But there is now a need to proceed to joint identification of theoretical and practical problems and joint research, which allows for a balanced contribution from both the Chinese and foreign sides. There needs to be a recognition of the vital contribution that may be made by

Chinese culture and China's social experience to the definition and elaboration of research and development projects. In a sense, the many projects for academic and professional training of Chinese personnel both abroad and in China have now laid a strong foundation for this next step. The mass university, with its comprehensive connections to all dimensions of the Chinese context, both elite and popular, would be an ideal milieu for the fostering of such mutually enriching activity.

Secondly, external agencies entering into academic or development cooperation with China should specifically seek a balance in emphasis on different knowledge areas and provide opportunities for mutual activity in aesthetic, moral, and social areas of knowledge, as well as technical dimensions of the social and natural sciences. We have already noted the proclivity of the Chinese government for supporting only the technical dimensions of international knowledge cooperation, fields such as engineering and management that are likely to have direct benefits for economic change and cause little disturbance in terms of social or political change. This approach has been justified by reference to the need to maintain China's cultural autonomy, and assert a strong Chinese identity in the modernization process.

The actual outcome of this repression of social and political debate and this reification of traditional culture, however, has been a tendency on the part of students and intellectuals to admire all things Western. There are great difficulties in having real discourse over cultural authenticity when definitions of culture have been taken over for political purposes. Under these conditions any substantive criticism of Western ideas, or attempts to champion Chinese cultural perspectives, are immediately suspect as supportive of the political regime. An awareness of these complex problems among those designing projects of cultural and academic cooperation from outside of China could lead to the identification and development of projects in areas such as history, sociology, anthropology, law, political science, and economics that would result in genuine communicative action and mutual transformation.

In a powerful commentary on ways in which the African university might pursue cultural authenticity, Ali Mazrui developed ideas about the domestication of foreign knowledge through application to the local context; its diversification, with contributions from many different civilizational contexts being sought; and finally the visionary project of counter-penetration, as elements of what is unique in its own cultural and epistemological resources are introduced to a wider world.[45] China has reached a stage already whereby some dimensions of Marxist thought have been domesticated, as well as some other threads from European political and economic thought.

It has also been remarkably adept at diversification during the reform decade, with a wide range of interactions in knowledge and culture around the globe, contrasting to the uni-dimensional knowledge relations it had with the Soviet Union in the 1950s. I am convinced that China now stands on the brink of real possibilities of counter-penetration, as many dimensions of its cultural and social knowledge, as well as its successful economic experience, capture interest in the global community. However, there may need to be a substantial shift in thinking in bilateral aid agencies and organizations for national cultural exchange if their China projects are to become channels for this kind of mutual interaction. Notions of superiority and an impulse to maintain the role of teacher remain strong, even though highly practical considerations of mutual trade and economic benefit have, in reality, become more and more important in bilateral relations

Hopefully, China's universities will play an important role in the future, not only as channels of new knowledge and technology for needed areas of economic and social development within China, but also in introducing to a wider world progressive dimensions of Chinese culture and lessons learned from China's social development over a dramatic century of change. The twentieth century began a little early for modern higher education, with the establishment, in 1895, of the first institution destined to be a university and so to stand between the worlds of European and Chinese culture and epistemology, a place where deep conflicts were inevitable. Finally, in 1995, with the close of the century only five years away, it is possible to see how the working out of those conflicts has served to bring East and West somewhat closer together.

NOTES

1. This approach to scholarship is best exemplified in work associated with the World Order Models Project (WOMP), with scholars such as Johann Galtung, Samuel Kim, Ali Mazrui, and Rajni Kothari, as discussed in the Introduction to this volume.

2. Ding Gang, "'Wu Si' qianhou de shuyuan yanjiu yu Zhongguo daxue de fazhan" [Research on the Shuyuan before and after May 4th, and the Development of Chinese Universities], paper presented at the conference on "Indigenous Knowledge and Cultural Interchange: Challenges to the Idea of the University," Yuelu Shuyuan and Hunan University, May 23–27, 1994.

3. Vilma Seeberg, "Access to Higher Education: Targeted Recruitment Reform Under Economic Development Plans in the People's Republic of China," *Higher Education* Vol. 25, no. 3, March 1993, p. 178.

4. It is interesting to note how recent Chinese analyses of the character of the higher education system, and the challenges posed to it by economic change and pressures for expansion, readily admit it has been a highly elite system up to the present time. See, for example, Mao Rong, "Gaodeng jiaoyu de dazhonghua yu shichang jingji," [The Massification of Higher Education and the Market Economy] in *Xinhua wenzhai*, October 1994, pp. 163–166. This article suggests three possible choices for

the future structure of higher education in China: a multi-level, multi-functional structure, emphasizing diversity, a pyramid structure, with a small number of elite institutions, and a large basis at lower levels, emphasizing service to the market, or a dual structure which divides responsibility between national and local governments, and represents a new version of the old idea of "walking on two legs." My analysis will strongly support the first of these three options, but this author does not go into details on which of these possibilities is thought to be most likely.

5. World Bank, *China: Management and Finance of Higher Education*, Report No. 5912-CHA, Projects Department, East Asia and Pacific Regional Office, 1986, p. 11.

6. This policy is analyzed in detail in R. Hayhoe, "China's Universities Since Tiananmen: A Critical Assessment." *China Quarterly*, 134 (June 1993): 295–296.

7. In an interview by the author with senior researchers at the State Education Commission's Policy Research Center, April 30, 1993, the planned projection for the year 2000 was given as 7 million, with 3.5 million in the formal system, and 3.5 million in the adult system. By October of 1993, this figure had been revised to 6 million, with only 2.5 million in the adult sector, as revealed to members of a World Bank team doing an overall assessment of the higher education system. These figures were again confirmed during the second visit of the World Bank team in May 1994.

8. The issue of the scale and pace of expansion of the higher education system has been under close study by the Development Research Institute of the State Education Commission for some time, and the literature on mass higher education is well understood. For an excellent analysis from a Chinese official perspective, see Tan Songhua, "Woguo gaodeng jiaoyu fazhan zhanlue ruogan wenti de tantou," [A Discussion of Various Problems Relating to the Development Strategy for Higher Education in China], *Zhongguo gaodeng jiaoyu yanjiu* [Chinese Higher Education Research], February 1994, pp. 24–30. This article confirms present intentions of the State Education Commission to support expansion of the system the point where it provides access to 7 to 8 percent of the age cohort by the year 2000. The article contains an interesting reflection on the history of higher education, noting how earlier impulses toward the broadening of access had foundered due to the lack of a strong economic foundation for expansion. Generally, the article emphasizes the inefficiency of the Soviet-derived system, due to the relatively small size of enrollments in most institutions, and their specialized curricular orientation. This has resulted in the overlapping of provision by institutions administered from national ministries and provincial governments. Mergers and the development of larger-scale institutions are encouraged in this article.

9. George Bereday, *Universities for All: International Perspectives on Mass Higher Education* (San Francisco: Jossey Bass, 1973), especially chapter 8.

10. Martin Trow, *Problems in the Transition from Elite to Mass Higher Education* (Berkeley: Carnegie Commission on Higher Education, 1973).

11. Clark Kerr, "The Idea of a Multiversity," in Clark Kerr, *The Uses of the University* (Cambridge, Mass.: Harvard University Press, 1982), p. 41.

12. By 1980, women had equal participation rates at the undergraduate level with men in the United States and Canada. However, women in undergraduate programs in Japan and Korea made up only 42 percent and 32 percent of their respective student bodies in 1989. In 1990, women made up 53 percent of all graduate students in the United States and 45 percent in Canada, while the parallel figure for Korea was 22 percent, and for Japan 15 percent. See the *UNESCO Statistical Yearbook, 1991*. U.S. figures come from U.S. Department of Commerce, *Statistical Abstract of the United States, 1992* (Washington, D.C.: U.S. Government Printing Office, 1992).

13. Each province has a somewhat different situation, though in all universities are public and under provincial jurisdiction. In Ontario recently, the Council of Ontario Universities, representing fifteen universities, is recommending a fee increase

that would mean students would pay 30 percent of the actual cost of their university education.

14. I have done a detailed comparative analysis of this phenomenon in R. Hayhoe, "An Asian Multiversity? Comparative Reflections on the Transition to Mass Higher Education in East Asia," *Comparative Education Review*, Vol. 39, no. 3, August 1995.

15. Ikuo Amano, "Continuity and Change in the Structure of Japanese Higher Education," in Ikuo Amano and William Cummings (eds.), *Changes in the Japanese University* (New York: Praeger, 1979): 10–39.

16. Taijin Shin, "The Connections between Education and National Development in East Asian Countries: With Special Reference to the Structural Analysis of Higher Education and Economic Growth in the Republic of Korea," unpublished Ph.D. thesis, University of Toronto, 1993.

17. Erwin Epstein and Wei-fan Kuo, "Higher Education," in Douglas Smith (ed.), *The Confucian Continuum* (New York: Praeger, 1991), p. 193.

18. Kumiko Fujimura-Fanselow and Anne E. Imamura, "The Education of Women in Japan," in Edward Beauchamp (ed.), *Windows on Japanese Education* (Westport, Connecticut: Greenwood Press, 1991); In-ho Lee, "Work, Education and Women's Gains: The Korea Experience," in Jill Kerr Conway and Susan C. Bourque, *The Politics of Women's Education* (Ann Arbor: University of Michigan Press, 1993).

19. Juergen Habermas, *The Structural Transformation of the Public Sphere* (Cambridge, Mass.: M.I.T. Press, 1989).

20. Teruhisa Horio, *Educational Thought and Ideology in Modern Japan* (Tokyo: University of Tokyo Press, 1988).

21. Vera Schwarcz, *The Chinese Enlightenment* (Berkeley: University of California Press, 1987), tells the story of this lifelong pursuit for a group of Chinese intellectuals associated with the May 4th Movement of 1919, some of whom spent their latter years in Taiwan. Teruhisa Horio's *Educational Thought and Ideology in Modern Japan* (Tokyo: University of Tokyo Press, 1988), could be seen as a parallel analysis of the betrayal of Enlightenment values in Japan. For Korea, a similar concern is voiced in Uchang Kim, "The Autonomous Development of the University in Korea," in *The University and the Future World* (Seoul: Yonsei University Press, 1985): 149–178.

22. See, for example, Douglas Smith, *The Confucian Continuum*, chapter 1. See also William T. de Bary, *East Asian Civilizations: A Dialogue in Five Stages* (Cambridge, Mass.: Harvard University Press, 1988), and Ronald Dore, *Taking Japan Seriously: A Confucian Perspective on Leading Economic Issues* (London: Athlone, 1987).

23. Roger Geiger, in his typology of private higher education, depicts this as a restricted public sector and a mass private sector, in contrast to the parallel public and private sectors in the United States and the comprehensive public and peripheral private sectors in Canada and Europe. See R.L. Geiger, "Public and Private Sectors in Higher Education: A Comparison of International Patterns," in *Higher Education*, Vol. 17, 1988, pp. 699–711.

24. Xu Dunhuang, Xian Liting, and Liu Dawei, "Guanyu juban minban gaodeng xuexiao ruogan wenti de tantou," [A Discussion of Various Problems Relating to the Management of People-run Schools] in *Zhongguo gaodeng jiaoyu*, no. 10, 1994, pp. 4–5. This article reports that ten "people-run" or private higher institutions, seven in the regular sector, three in the adult sector, had been approved by the State Education Commission.

25. Mao Rong, "Gaodeng jiaoyu de dazhonghua yu shichang jingji," p. 165.

26. It is interesting to see a revival of interest in Mao's ideas in recent years, affirming their continuing relevance to China's future, in spite of the Cultural Revolution disaster. See, for example, Wu Wei and Li Zhengxin, "Mao Zedong he Zhongguo de chuantong jiaoyu," [Mao Zedong and China's traditional education] in *Jiaoyu yanjiu*, no. 4, 1994, p. 11; Ouyang Yu, "Mao Zedong guanyu ren de quanmian fazhan sixiang chutan," [A Preliminary Discussion of Mao Zedong's Thinking on the

Whole Development of the Person], in *Jiaoyu yanjiu* [Educational Research], no. 2, 1994, pp. 6–9, 27, and Dali Yin, "Reforming Chinese Education: Context, Structure, and Attitudes in the 1980s," in *Compare*, Vol. 23, no. 2, 1993.

27. Paul Bailey, *Reform the People: Changing Attitudes Toward Popular Education in Early Twentieth Century China* (Edinburgh: Edinburgh University Press, 1990).

28. In fact, it is unlikely that the two systems will be integrated, as those responsible for the adult system and its resources see it as in their interest to maintain a discrete identity, in spite of the difficulty of attracting good students. This comes across clearly in a recent interview with an official from the adult education bureau of the State Education Commission. See *Zhongguo jiaoyu bao*, July 13, 1994, p. 1.

29. Wang Zhonglie and Wu Zhenyao, "Zhongdian jianshe—yipi gaodeng xuexiao he zhongdian xueke," [Priority Development—A Group of Higher Institutions and Priority Areas of Study] in *Zhongguo gaodeng jiaoyu* [Chinese Higher Education], nos. 7–8, July–August 1993.

30. I had the privilege of visiting this institution and hearing the story of their amalgamation firsthand, while participating in a World Bank study of China's higher education in May 1994.

31. A similar situation seems not to have hindered the amalgamation of five institutions in Beijing that belong to diverse ministries: The University of International Trade and Business, the Beijing College of Chemical Engineering, the Beijing University of Traditional Chinese Medicine, the Beijing College of Fashion Design, and the China College of Finance. See *Renmin ribao* [People's Daily], April 21, 1994, p. 4.

32. See *Renmin ribao*, May 14, 1994, p. 3. It is interesting to note how this kind of competition among institutions enhances the speed of expansion, especially in those regions where there is a strong economic infrastructure. Thus the municipality of Shanghai has already reached a situation where 20 percent of the age cohort entered higher education by 1991, in contrast to a national level of about 3.5 percent of the age cohort. See Mao Rong, "Gaodeng jiaoyu de dazhonghua," p. 165.

33. Christina Gilmartin, "Gender, Political Culture, and Women's Mobilization," in C. Gilmartin, G. Hershatter, L. Rofel, and T. White (eds.), *Engendering China* (Cambridge, Mass.: Harvard University Press, 1994), pp. 195–225, shows how well-developed the women's movement was within the Nationalist party in the 1920s, and subsequently how it became "curtailed by the dual operations of nationalism and patriarchy." (p. 224). There are many parallel analyses for the Communist period, perhaps the most comprehensive one being Judith Stacey, *Patriarchy and Socialist Revolution in China* (Berkeley: University of California Press, 1983).

34. According to the *UNESCO Statistical Yearbook 1991*, 3.11, only 15 percent of higher education faculty in Japan were women in 1989, and 18 percent in Korea.

35. See, for example, Sandra Harding, *The Science Question in Feminism* (Ithaca, N.Y.: Cornell University Press, 1986), *Whose Science, Whose Knowledge? Thinking from Women's Lives* (Ithaca: Cornell University Press, 1991), and *Feminist Epistemology: Social Science Issues* (Bloomington: Indiana University Press, 1987); see also Carolyn Merchant, *The Death of Nature: Women, Ecology, and the Scientific Revolution* (San Francisco: Harper and Row, 1980).

36. Mary Belenky et al., *Women's Ways of Knowing* (New York: Basic Books, 1986).

37. Rey Chow, *Women and Chinese Modernity: The Politics of Reading between West and East* (Minneapolis: University of Minnesota Press, 1991), gives an evocative analysis of this way of thinking, with special reference to Bertolucci and the film *The Last Emperor*.

38. Chen Dongyuan, *Zhongguo funu shi* (Shanghai: Shangwu chubanshe, 1937), pp. 366–368.

39. This point is well put by Rey Chow in chapter 2 of *Women and Chinese*

Modernity (p. 61): "The ubiquitous nature of Confucianism as a monitoring social system that encompasses all aspects of Chinese cultural life means that 'individual' ontological freedom, which remains to this day a valid source of resistance against systemized ideology in the West, is much more difficult to establish in China."

40. Charlotte Furth, "Rethinking Van Gulik: Sexuality and Reproduction in Traditional Chinese Medicine," in Gilmartin et al. (eds.) *Engendering China*, p. 145, makes the following comment: "China scholars are accustomed to portraying Confucian patriarchy as misogynist in its emphasis on ritual hierarchy privileging yang while confining women to subordinate social and domestic roles. Daoism, by contrast, is portrayed as doctrinally inclined to privilege yin and honor the female, and these metaphorical religious figurations of gender are presumed to go hand in hand with a greater social and sexual equalitarianism. Yet the classical bedchamber manuals teaching Daoist secrets of longevity portray an aristocratic and lavishly polygamous society where very young women were exploited as sexual handmaidens—the stereotype of a royal harem."

41. Tani E. Barlow, "Politics and Protocols of Funu: (Un)Making National Women," in Gilmartin et al. (eds.), *Engendering China*, pp. 339–359.

42. Chen Yiyun, "Out of the Traditional Halls of Academe: Exploring New Avenues for Research on Women," in Gilmartin et al. (eds.), *Engendering China*, p. 78.

43. Howard Buchbinder, "The Market-Oriented University and the Changing Role of Knowledge," in *Higher Education* (Amsterdam), Vol. 26, no. 3, October 1993.

44. Xu Dunhuang, Xian Litang, and Liu Dawei, "Guanyu juban minban gaodeng xuexiao ruogan wenti de tantou," in *Zhongguo Gaodeng jiaoyu*, no. 10, 1994, pp. 4–5.

45. Ali A. Mazrui, "The African University as a Multinational Corporation," in Ali Mazrui, *Political Values and the Educated Class in Africa* (London: Heinneman, 1978), pp. 282–319.

SELECTED BIBLIOGRAPHY

Abe, Hiroshi, "Borrowing from Japan: China's First Modern Education System," in Hayhoe and Bastid, *China's Education and the Industrialized World*, pp. 57–80.

Altbach, Philip, *The Knowledge Context* (Albany, N.Y.: SUNY Press, 1986).

Amano, Ikuo, "Continuity and Change in the Structure of Japanese Higher Education," in I. Amano and W. Cummings (eds.), *Changes in the Japanese University* (New York: Praeger, 1979), pp. 10–39.

Arnove, Robert, "World Systems Theory and Comparative Education," in *Comparative Education Review*, Vol. 24, no. 2, February 1980, pp. 48–62.

Artz, Frederick, *The Development of Technical Education in France 1500–1850* (Cambridge, Mass., and London: Society for the History of Technology and M.I.T. Press, 1966).

Ashby, Eric, *Universities: British, Indian, African* (London: Weidenfield and Nicolson, 1966).

Ayers, William, *Chang Chih-tung and Educational Reform in China* (Cambridge, Mass.: Harvard University Press, 1971).

Bai, Zhou, "Guanyu dangqian gaodeng xuexiao shizi duiwu xianzhuang de diaocha baogao," [Report on a Survey Concerning the Contemporary Situation of the Faculty Contingent in Higher Institutions], in *Zhongguo gaodeng jiaoyu*, no. 12, December 1993, pp. 21–22.

Bailey, Paul, *Reform the People: Changing Attitudes towards Popular Education in Early Twentieth-Century China* (Edinburgh: Edinburgh University Press, 1990).

Barlow, Tani E., "Politics and Protocols of Funu: (Un)Making National Women," in C. Gilmartin, et al. (eds.), *Engendering China* (Cambridge, Mass.: Harvard University Press, 1994), pp. 339–359.

Barnard, H.C., *Education and the French Revolution* (Cambridge: Cambridge University Press, 1969).

Barnett, A. Doak, *China's Far West: Four Decades of Change* (Boulder, Colo.: Westview Press, 1993).

Bastid, Marianne, *Educational Reform in Early Twentieth-Century China*, translated by Paul Bailey (Ann Arbor: Center for Chinese Studies, University of Michigan, 1988).

———, "L'argument économique dans les réformes de l'enseignement en Chine au XXe siècle," in *Interchange*, Vol. 19, nos. 3/4, Fall/Winter 1988.

———, "Servitude or Liberation? The Introduction of Foreign Educational Practices and Systems to China from 1840 to the Present," in R. Hayhoe and M. Bastid (eds.), *China's Education and the Industrialized World*.

Becker, C.H., Falski, M., Langevin, P., and Tawney, R.H., *The Reorganization of Education in China* (Paris: League of Nations Institute of Intellectual Cooperation, 1932).

Beijing shifan daxue xiaoshi 1902–1982 [A History of Beijing Normal University] (Beijing: Beijing shifan daxue chubanshe, 1982).

Belenky, Mary, et al., *Women's Ways of Knowing: The Development of Self, Voice, and Mind* (New York: Basic Books, 1986).

Ben-david, Joseph, *American Higher Education: Directions Old and New* (New York: McGraw-Hill, 1972).

Bereday, George, *Universities for All: International Perspectives on Mass Higher Education* (San Francisco: Jossey-Bass, 1973).

Bergère, Marie Claire, "Tiananmen 1989: Background and Consequences," in T. Saich and M. Dassu (eds.), *The Reform Decade* (London: Kegan Paul International, 1992), pp. 132–150.

Bernstein, Basil, "On the Classification and Framing of Educational Knowledge," in Michael Young (ed.), *Knowledge and Control* (London: Collier Macmillan, 1971).

Bernstein, Thomas, *Up to the Mountains and Down to the Villages: The Transfer of Youth from Urban to Rural China* (New Haven: Yale University Press, 1977).

Biggerstaff, Knight, *The Earliest Modern Government Schools in China* (Port Washington, New York: Kennikat Press, 1972).

Black, George, and Munro, Robin, *Black Hands of Beijing: Lives of Defiance in China's Democracy Movement* (New York: John Wiley and Sons, 1993).

Borisov, O.B., and Koloskov, B.T., *Soviet-Chinese Relations 1945–1970* (Bloomington and London: Indiana University Press, 1975).

Buchbinder, Howard, "The Market-oriented University and the Changing Role of Knowledge," in *Higher Education*, Vol. 26, no. 3, 1993.

Bulliet, W., *The Patricians of Nishapur: A Study in Medieval Islamic Social History* (Cambridge, Mass.: Harvard University Press, 1972).

Burris, Maryann, "To Serve China: Medical Schools and Modernization in the People's Republic of China," unpublished Ph.D. dissertation, Stanford University, 1990.

Cai, Yuanpei, *Cai Yuanpei xuanji* [Selected Writings of Cai Yuanpei] (Beijing: Zhongguo shuju, 1959).

Carnoy, Martin, *Education and Cultural Imperialism* (New York: MacKay, 1974).

Chaffee, John, *The Thorny Gates of Learning in Sung China* (Cambridge: Cambridge University Press, 1985).

Chan, Anita, *Children of Mao* (London: Macmillan, 1985).

Chan, Hoi-man, "Modernity and Revolution in Chinese Education: Towards an Analytical Agenda of the Great Leap Forward and the Cultural Revolution," in R. Hayhoe (ed.), *Education and Modernization: The Chinese Experience*, pp. 73–102.

Chan, Ming, and Dirlik, Arif, *Schools into Fields and Factories: Anarchists, the Guomindang and the National Labor University in Shanghai, 1927–1937* (Durham, N.C., and London: Duke University Press, 1991).

Chan, Wing-tsit, *Chu Hsi: Life and Thought* (Hong Kong: Chinese University Press, 1984).

Chang, Chung-li, *The Chinese Gentry: Studies in Their Role in the Nineteenth Century* (Seattle: University of Washington Press, 1955).

Chao, Chung, and Yang, I-fan, *Students in Mainland China* (Kowloon, Hong Kong: Union Research Institute, 1962).

Chen, Dongyuan, *Zhongguo funu shenghuo shi* [A History of the Lives of Chinese Women] (Shanghai: Shangwu chubanshe, 1937).

——, *Zhongguo jiaoyushi* [A History of Chinese Education] (Shanghai: Commercial Press, 1936).

Chen, Lifu, *Zhanshi jiaoyu xingzheng huiyi* [Recollections of Educational Administration During the War] (Taiwan: Commercial Press, 1973).

Chen, Qingzhi, *Zhongguo jiaoyushi* [A History of Chinese Education] (Shanghai: Commercial Press, 1936).

Chen, Theodore, *Chinese Education since 1949: Academic and Revolutionary Models* (New York: Pergamon, 1981).

———, *The Thought Reform of Chinese Intellectuals* (Westport, Conn.: Hyperion Press, 1958).

Chen, Xuexun, and Tian Zhengping (eds.), *Liuxue jiaoyu* [The Education of Students Abroad] (Shanghai: Shanghai jiaoyu chubanshe, 1991).

Chen, Yiyun, "Out of the Traditional Halls of Academe: Exploring New Avenues for Research on Women," in C. Gilmartin et al. (eds.), *Engendering China* (Cambridge, Mass.: Harvard University Press, 1994).

Chen, Yuanhui (ed.), *Zhongguo jindai jiaoyushi ziliao huibian* [A Collection of Material on Recent Chinese Educational History], 3 vols., (Shanghai: Shanghai jiaoyu chubanshe, 1990–1991).

Cheng, Fangwu, *Zhanhuo zhong de daxue* [A University Under Fire] (Beijing: Renmin daxue chubanshe, 1982).

Cherrington, Ruth, *China's Students: The Struggle for Democracy* (London: Routledge and Kegan Paul, 1991).

Chiang, Yung-chen, "Social Engineering and the Social Sciences in China, 1989–1949," unpublished Ph.D. dissertation, Harvard University, 1986.

Chinese Universities and Colleges: A Guide to Institutions of Higher Education in China (Beijing: Higher Education Press, 1989).

Chow, Ray, *Women and Chinese Modernity: The Politics of Reading Between West and East* (Minneapolis: University of Minnesota Press, 1991).

Chung, Shih, *Higher Education in China* (Hong Kong: Union Research Institute, 1953).

Churchward, L.G., *The Soviet Intelligentsia* (London: Routledge and Kegan Paul, 1973).

Cohen, Paul, *China and Christianity: The Missionary Movement and the Growth of Chinese Anti-Foreignism, 1860–1870* (Cambridge, Mass.: Harvard University Press, 1963).

Compayré, Gabriel, *Abelard and the Origin and Early History of Universities* (New York: Ams Press, 1969).

Croizier, Ralph, "Traditional Medicine in Modern China," in G.B. Risse (ed.), *Modern China and Traditional Chinese Medicine* (Springfield, Ill.: Charles C. Thomas, 1973).

Croll, Elizabeth, *Feminism and Socialism in China* (London: Routledge and Kegan Paul, 1978).

Dangdai Zhongguo gaodeng shifan jiaoyu ziliao xuan [Selected Materials on Contemporary Chinese Higher Normal Education] (Shanghai: Huadong shida chubanshe, 1986).

Dardess, John, *Confucianism and Autocracy: Professional Elites in the Founding of the Ming Dynasty* (Berkeley: University of California Press, 1983).

Davin, Delia, "Imperialism and the Diffusion of Liberal Thought: British Influences on Chinese Education," in Hayhoe and Bastid (eds.), *China's Education and the Industrialized World*, pp. 33–56.

de Bary, William T., *East Asian Civilizations: A Dialogue in Five Stages* (Cambridge, Mass.: Harvard University Press, 1988).

de Bary, William T., and Chaffee, John, *Neo-Confucian Education: The Formative Stage* (Berkeley: University of California Press, 1989).

de Bary, William T., and Haboush, J.K. (eds.), *The Rise of Neo-Confucianism in Korea* (New York: Columbia University Press, 1985).

Department of Planning and Construction, State Education Commission, P.R.C., *Educational Statistics Yearbook of China 1990* (Beijing: People's Education Press, 1991).

———. *Educational Statistics Yearbook of China 1991/1992* (Beijing: People's Education Press, 1992

———. *Essential Statistics of Education in China for 1992* (March 1993).

Department of Planning, Ministry of Education, P.R.C., *Achievement of Education in China: Statistics 1949–1983* (Beijing: Renmin jiaoyu chubanshe, 1984).

Dewitt, Nicholas, *Soviet Professional Manpower* (Washington, D.C.: National Science Foundation, 1955).

Ding, Gang, and Liu, Qi, *Shuyuan yu Zhongguo wenhua* [Academies and Chinese Culture] (Shanghai: Shanghai jiaoyu chubanshe, 1992).

Ding, Gang, "'Wu Si' Qianhou de shuyuan yanjiu yu Zhongguo daxue de fazhan," [Research on the *Shuyuan* before and after May 4th and the Development of Chinese Universities], paper presented at the conference on "Indigenous Knowledge and Cultural Interchange: Challenges to the Idea of the University," Yuelu *Shuyuan* and Hunan University, May 23–27, 1994.

Ding, Gang, *Zhongguo fojiao jiaoyu: Ru fo dao jiaoyu bijiao yanjiu* [Chinese Buddhist Education: Comparative Research on Confucian, Buddhist, and Daoist Education] (Chengdu: Sichuan jiaoyu chubanshe, 1988).

Djung, Lu-Dzai, *A History of Democratic Education in Modern China* (Shanghai: Commercial Press, 1934).

Dong, Chuncai (ed.), *Zhongguo geming gendi jiaoyushi* [A History of Education in the Chinese Revolutionary Base Areas], 3 vols., (Beijing: Jiaoyu kexue chubanshe, 1991, 1993).

Dore, Ronald, *Education in Tokagawa Japan* (London: Athlone, 1984).

Drake, Earl, "World Bank Transfer of Technology and Ideas to India and China," in R. Hayhoe (ed.), *Knowledge Across Cultures: Universities East and West* (Toronto: OISE Press, Wuhan: Hubei Education Press, 1993), pp. 237–254.

Duggan, Stephen, *A Critique of the Report of the League of Nations Mission of Educational Experts to China* (New York: Institute of International Education, January 1933).

Duiker, William, *Ts'ai Yuan-p'ei: Educator of Modern China* (University Park and London: Pennsylvania State University Press, 1977).

Durkheim, Emile, *The Evolution of Educational Thought* (London: Routledge and Kegan Paul, 1977).

Elleman, Bruce, "The Soviet Union's Secret Diplomacy Concerning the Chinese Eastern Railway, 1924–1925," in *Journal of Asian Studies*, Vol. 53, no. 2, May 1994, pp. 459–486.

Elman, Benjamin, *From Philosophy to Philology: Intellectual and Social Aspects of Change in Late Imperial China* (Cambridge, Mass.: Harvard East Asian Monographs, 1984).

Elman, Benjamin, and Woodside, Alexander (eds.), *Education and Society in Late Imperial China, 1600–1900* (Berkeley: University of California Press, 1994).

Epstein, Irving (ed.), *Chinese Education: Policies, Problems, and Prospects* (New York: Garland Publishing, 1991).

Findley, Dru, "The Impact of Recent Events in China on International Professional and Academic Exchanges and Related Development Activities," Ford Foundation, Beijing Office, August 31, 1989.

Fitzpatrick, Sheila, *Education and Social Mobility in the Soviet Union, 1921–1934* (Cambridge: Cambridge University Press, 1979).

Franke, Wolfgang, *The Reform and Abolition of the Traditional Chinese Examination System* (Cambridge, Mass.: Harvard University Press, 1960).

Fraser, Steward, *Chinese Communist Education: Records of the First Decade* (Nashville, Tennessee: Vanderbilt University Press, 1965).

Freyn, Hubert, *Chinese Education in the War* (Shanghai: Kelly and Walsh, 1940).

Fujimura-Fanselow, Kumiko, and Imamura, Anne, "The Education of Women in Japan," in Edward Beauchamp (ed.), *Windows on Japanese Education* (Westport, Conn.: Greenwood Press, 1991).

Furth, Charlotte, "Rethinking Van Gulik: Sexuality and Reproduction in Traditional Chinese Medicine," in C. Gilmartin et al. (eds.), *Engendering China* (Cambridge, Mass.: Harvard University Press, 1994).

Galtung, Johann, "Conflict on a Global Scale: Social Imperialism and Sub-Imperialism—Continuities in the Structural Theory of Imperialism," in *World Development*, Vol. 4, no. 3, March 1976, pp. 153–165.

———, "A Structural Theory of Imperialism," in *Journal of Peace Research*, Vol. 8, 1972, pp. 81–117.

———, *The True Worlds: A Transnational Approach* (New York: Free Press, 1980).

Gardner, John, "Study and Criticism: The Voice of Shanghai Radicals," in Christopher Howe (ed.), *Shanghai: Revolution and Development in an Asian Metropolis* (Cambridge: Cambridge University Press, 1981).

Geiger, Roger, "Public and Private Sectors in Higher Education: A Comparison of International Patterns," in *Higher Education*, Vol. 17, 1988, pp. 699–711.

Gilmartin, Christina, "Gender, Political Culture, and Women's Modernization," in C. Gilmartin et al. (eds.), *Engendering China*, pp. 195–225.

Gilmartin, Christina, Hershatter, Gail, Rofel, Lisa, and White, T. (eds.), *Engendering China* (Cambridge, Mass.: Harvard University Press, 1994).

Gittings, John, *Survey of the Sino-Soviet Dispute* (London: Oxford University Press, 1968).

Goldman, Merle, *Sowing the Seeds of Democracy in China: Political Reform in the Deng Xiaoping Era* (Cambridge, Mass.: Harvard University Press, 1994).

Goldman, Rene, "The Rectification Campaign at Peking University, May–June 1957," in *China Quarterly*, no. 12, October–December 1964, pp. 53–63.

Grieder, Jerome, *Hu Shi and the Chinese Renaissance: Liberalism in the Chinese Revolution, 1917–1937* (Cambridge, Mass.: Harvard University Press, 1970).

Gruson, Pascale, *L'Etat Enseignant* (Paris: Mouton, 1978).

Guenther, Isolde, "A Study of the Evolution of the Technische Hochschule," unpublished Ph.D. dissertation, University of London Institute of Education, 1972.

Guisso, Richard, and Johannesen, Stanley, *Women in China: Current Directions in Historical Scholarship* (Lewiston, N.Y.: Edwin Mellen Press, 1981).

Guy, R. Kent, *The Emperor's Four Treasuries: Scholars and the State in the Late Ch'ien-Lung Era* (Cambridge, Mass.: Harvard University Press, 1987).

Habermas, Juergen, *The Structural Transformation of the Public Sphere* (Cambridge, Mass.: M.I.T. Press, 1989).

———, *The Theory of Communicative Action*, 2 vols. (Boston: Beacon Press, 1984, 1987).

Haddad, Wadi et al., *Education and Development: Evidence of New Priorities* (Washington, D.C.: The World Bank, 1990).

Hamrin, Carol Lee, and Cheek, Timothy (eds.), *China's Establishment Intellectuals* (New York and London: M.E. Sharpe, 1986).

Harding, Sandra, *Feminist Epistemology: Social Science Issues* (Bloomington: Indiana University Press, 1987).

———, *The Science Question in Feminism* (Ithaca, N.Y.: Cornell University Press, 1986).

———, *Whose Science, Whose Knowledge? Thinking about Women's Lives* (Ithaca, N.Y.: Cornell University Press, 1991).

Harrell, Paula, *Sowing the Seeds of Change: Chinese Studies, Japanese Teachers 1895–1905* (Stanford, Calif.: Stanford University Press, 1992).

Harris, Robin, *A History of Higher Education in Canada* (Toronto: University of Toronto Press, 1978).

Hay, Stephen, *Asian Ideas of East and West: Tagore and His Critics in Japan, China, and India* (Cambridge, Mass.: Harvard University Press, 1970).

Hayek, F.A, *The Counter Revolution of Science* (Indianapolis, Ind.: Liberty Press, 1979).

Hayford, Charles, *To the People: James Yen and Village China* (New York: Columbia University Press, 1990).

Hayhoe, Ruth, "China, Comparative Education, and World Order Models Theory," in *Compare*, 16:1, 1986, pp. 65–80.

———, *China's Universities and the Open Door* (New York: M.E. Sharpe, and Toronto: OISE Press, 1989).

———, "China's Universities since Tiananmen: A Critical Assessment," in *China Quarterly*, no. 134, June 1993.

———, "Chinese Universities and the Social Sciences," in *Minerva*, Vol. XXXI, no. 4, 1993, pp. 478–503.

———, *Contemporary Chinese Education* (London: Croom Helm, 1984).

——— (ed.), *Education and Modernization: The Chinese Experience* (Oxford: Pergamon, and Toronto: OISE Press, 1992).

———, "Student Enrollment and Job Assignment Issues," in *China News Analysis*, no. 1481, March 15, 1993.

———, "Shanghai as Mediator of the Educational Open Door," in *Pacific Affairs*, Vol. 61, no. 2, Summer 1988.

Hayhoe, Ruth, and Bastid, Marianne (eds.), *China's Education and the Industrialized World: Studies in Cultural Transfer* (New York: M.E. Sharpe, and Toronto: OISE Press, 1987).

Hayhoe, Ruth, and Lu, Yongling (eds.), *Ma Xiangbo and the Mind of Modern China* (New York: M.E. Sharpe, forthcoming).

Henan daxue xiaoshi, 1912–1984 [An Institutional History of Henan University 1912–1984] (Informal publication, May 1985).

Henze, Juergen, "The Formal Education System and Modernization," in R. Hayhoe (ed.), *Education and Modernization: The Chinese Experience* (Toronto: OISE Press, 1992).

———, "Higher Education: The Tension between Quality and Equality," in R. Hayhoe (ed.), *Contemporary Chinese Education* (London: Croom Helm, 1984).

Hinton, William, *Hundred-Day War* (New York: Monthly Review Press, 1972).

Ho Ping-ti, *The Ladder of Success in Imperial China: Aspects of Social Mobility, 1368–1911* (New York and London: Columbia University Press, 1962).

Hofstadter, Richard, and Metzger, Walter, *The Development of Academic Freedom in the United States* (New York and London: Columbia University Press, 1955).

Holmes, Brian, *Comparative Education: Some Considerations of Method* (London: George Allen and Unwin, 1981).

Horio, Teruhisa, *Educational Thought and Ideology in Modern Japan* (Tokyo: University of Tokyo Press, 1988).

Hsia, Ronald, "The Intellectual and Public Life of Ma Yin-ch'u," in *China Quarterly*, no. 6, April–June 1961.

Hu, C. T., "Chinese People's University: Bastion of Marxism-Leninism," in R.F. Butts and W.B. Niblett (eds.), *The World Yearbook of Education: Universities Facing the Future* (London: Evans Bros., 1972), pp. 63–74.

Hu, Shi Ming, and Seifman, Eli, *Toward a New World Outlook: A Documentary History of Education in the People's Republic of China, 1949–1976* (New York: Ams Press, 1976).

Huang, Meizhen, Shi, Yanhua, and Zhang, Yun (eds.), *Shanghai daxue shiliao* [Historical Materials on Shanghai University] (Shanghai: Fudan daxue chubanshe, 1984).

Huang, Shiqi, "Nonformal Education and Modernization," in R. Hayhoe (ed.), *Education and Modernization: The Chinese Experience* (Oxford: Pergamon, 1992).

Hucker, Charles, "The Tong-lin Movement of the Late Ming Period," in John Fairbank (ed.), *Chinese Thought and Institutions* (Chicago: University of Chicago Press, 1957), pp. 132–162.

Humboldt, Wilhelm von, "On the Spirit and the Organizational Framework of Intellectual Institutions," in *Minerva*, Vol. 8, April 1970, pp. 242–250.

Hunan shifan daxue wushi nian [Hunan Normal University Over Fifty Years]

(Changsha: Hunan jiaoyu chubanshe, 1988).

Israel, John, "The Idea of Liberal Education in China," in R. Morse (ed.), *The Limits of Reform in China* (Boulder, Colo.: Westview Press, 1983).

———, "Southwest Associated University: Preservation as an Ultimate Value," in Paul K.T. Sih (ed.), *Nationalist China during the Sino-Japanese War, 1937–1945* (Hicksville, N.Y.: Exposition Press, 1977).

———, *Student Nationalism in China, 1927–1937* (Stanford, Calif.: Stanford University Press, 1966).

Jacobsen, Harold, and Oksenberg, Michael, *China's Participation in the IMF, the World Bank, and GATT: Towards a Global Economic Order* (Ann Arbor: University of Michigan Press, 1990).

Jiang, Naiyong, "The Plight of Job Placement for Female College Graduates," in *Chinese Education*, Vol. 25, no. 1, Spring 1992, pp. 48–52.

Jiaoyu faling [Educational Laws and Regulations] (Shanghai: Zhonghua shuju, 1947).

Jin, Binghua and Yi, Jizhuo, "*Guoqing yu Rensheng* [National Conditions and Life Issues] (Shanghai: Renmin chubanshe, 1990).

Johnston, William, *Russia's Educational Heritage* (Pittsburgh, Pa.: Carnegie Press, 1950).

Ju, Jin (ed.), *Yapian zhanzheng shiqi jiaoyu* [Education in the Period of the Opium Wars] (Shanghai: Shanghai jiaoyu chubanshe, 1990).

Keenan, Barry, *Academy Revival and the Management of China's Education in the Lower Yangtze Region, 1865–1911* (Berkeley: Institute of East Asian Studies, University of California, 1994).

Keenan, Barry, *The Dewey Experiment in China* (Cambridge, Mass.: Harvard University Press, 1977).

Kelly, Gail, and Altbach, Philip, *Education and the Colonial Experience* (London: Transaction Books, 1984).

Kerr, Clark, "The Idea of a Multiversity," in Clark Kerr, *The Uses of the University* (Cambridge, Mass.: Harvard University Press, 1982).

Kim, Samuel, *China, the U.N., and World Order* (Princeton, N.J.: Princeton University Press, 1979).

Kim, Samuel, *The Quest for a Just World Order* (Boulder, Colo.: Westview Press, 1984).

Klochko, Mikhail A., *A Soviet Scientist in Red China* (New York: Praeger, 1964).

Korol, Alexander, *Soviet Education for Science and Technology* (New York: john Wiley and Sons and the Technology Press of M.I.T., 1957).

Kothari, Rajni, *Footsteps into the Future* (New York: The Free Press, 1974).

Kozoku, Ono, *Chinese Women in a Century of Revolution, 1850–1950* (Stanford, Calif.: Stanford University Press, 1989).

Kreissler, Françoise, "Technical Education as a Key to Cultural Cooperation: The Sino-German Case," in Hayhoe and Bastid, *China's Education and the Industrialized World*, pp. 81–96.

Kristeva, Julia, *About Chinese Women* (London: Marion Boyars, 1974).

Kwong, Julia, *Chinese Education in Transition: Prelude to the Cultural Revolution* (Montreal: McGill-Queens University Press, 1979).

———, *Cultural Revolution in China's Schools* (Stanford: Hoover Institution Press, 1988).

Lampton, David, *Health, Conflict, and the Chinese Political System* (Ann Arbor: Center for Chinese Studies, 1974).

Lardy, Nicholas, "Economic Recovery and the First Five-Year Plan," in J.K. Fairbank and D. Twitchett (eds), *The Cambridge History of China*, Vol. 14 (Cambridge: Cambridge University Press, 1987).

Lee, Inho, "Work, Education, and Women's Gains: The Korean Experience, " in Jill Kerr Conway and Susan C. Bourque (eds.), *The Politics of Women's Education* (Ann Arbor: University of Michigan Press, 1993).

Lee, Sungho, "The Emergence of the Modern University in Korea," in P. Altbach and V. Selvaratnam, *From Dependence to Autonomy: The Development of Asian Universities* (Amsterdam: Kluwer Academic Publishers, 1989), pp. 227–256.

Lee, Thomas H.C., *Government Education and Examinations in Sung China* (Hong Kong: Chinese University Press, 1985).

Lenin, V.I., *Imperialism and the Highest Stage of Capitalism* (New York: International Publishers, 1939).

Levenson, Joseph, *Confucian China and Its Modern Fate*, 3 vols. (London: Routledge and Kegan Paul, 1958, 1964, 1965).

Li, Caidong (ed.), *Bailudong shuyuan shilue* [The Evolution of the White Deer Academy] (Beijing: Jiaoyu kexue chubanshe, 1989).

Li, Tiangang, "The Anglo-Chinese College and East-West Cultural Understanding," paper presented at the conference on "Knowledge Across Cultures: Universities East and West," Ontario Institute for Studies in Education, Toronto, Canada, October 11–14, 1992.

———, "The Chinese Academy of Literary Standards and Ma Xiangbo's Educational Thought," paper delivered at the Conference on the History of Missionary Universities in China, Nanjing Normal University, June 1991.

Li, Wen-Lang, "Changing Status of Women in the PRC,: in Shao-chuan Leng (ed.), *Changes in China: Party, State, and Society* (New York: University Press of America, 1989).

Li, Yu-ning (ed.), *Chinese Women through Chinese Eyes* (New York: M.E. Sharpe, 1992).

Liaoning gaodeng xuexiao yange [The Evolution of Higher Educational Institutions in Liaoning] (Shenyang: Liaoning renmin chubanshe, 1983).

Lilge, Frederic, *The Abuse of Learning: The Failure of the German University* (New York: Macmillan, 1948).

Lin, Yusheng, *The Crisis of Chinese Consciousness: Radical Antitraditionalism in the May 4th Era* (Madison: University of Wisconsin Press, 1979).

Linden, Allen B., "Politics and Education in Nationalist China: The Case of the University Council 1927–1928," in *Journal of Asian Studies*, Vol. XXVIII, no. 4, August 1968, pp. 763–776.

Lindsay, Michael, *Notes on Educational Problems in Communist China, 1941–1947* (New York: Institute of Pacific Relations, 1950).

Liu, Boji, *Guangdong shuyuan zhidu* [The *Shuyuan* System of Guangdong] (Taiwan: Taiwan shudian, 1958).

Liu, Haifeng, "Zhongguo gaodeng xuexiao de xiaoshi zhuisu wenti," [The Problem of Founding Dates in the Institutional Histories of Chinese Higher Education] in *Jiaoyu yanjiu*, no. 5, 1994, pp. 63–75.

Liu, Shao-ch'i, *Collected Works of Liu Shao-ch'i*, Vol. II, (Hong Kong: Union Research Institute, 1969).

Lu, Runlin, et al. (eds.), *Lanzhou daxue xiaoshi 1909–1989* [An Institutional History of Lanzhou University] (Lanzhou: Lanzhou daxue chubanshe, 1990).

Lu, Shuxiang, and Wang, Haifen (eds.), *Mashi wentong duben* [A Reader on the Ma Brothers' Grammar] (Shanghai: Shanghai jiaoyu chubanshe, 1986).

Lubot, Eugene, "Ts'ai Yuan-p'ei: From Confucian Scholar to Chancellor of Peking University," unpublished Ph.D. dissertation, Ohio State University, 1970.

Lucas, AnElissa, *Chinese Medical Modernization: Comparative Policy Continuities, 1930s-1980s* (New York: Praeger, 1982).

Lui, Adam Yuen-chung, *The Hanlin Academy: Training Ground for the Ambitious, 1644–1850* (Hamden, Conn.: Archon Books, 1981).

Lutz, Jessie, *China and the Christian Colleges* (Ithaca, New York, and London: Cornell University Press, 1971).

Ma, Kanwen, "Chinese Medicine and the West," in R. Hayhoe (ed.), *Knowledge Across Cultures: Universities East and West* (Toronto: OISE Press, Wuhan: Hubei

Education Press).

MacFarquhar, Roderick, *The Hundred Flowers Campaign and the Chinese Intellectuals* (New York: Octagon Books, 1974).

Mak, Grace, "The People's Republic of China," in G. Kelly (ed.), *International Handbook of Women's Education* (Westport, Conn.: Greenwood Press, 1988).

Makdisi, George, *The Rise of Colleges: Institutions of Higher Learning in Islam and the West* (Edinburgh: Edinburgh University Press, 1981).

Mao, Lirui, and Shen, Guangqun (eds.), *Zhongguo jiaoyu tongshi* [A Comprehensive History of Chinese Education], 6 vols. (Jinan: Shandong jiaoyu chubanshe, 1988).

Mao, Rong, "Gaodeng jiaoyu de dazhonghua yu shichang jingji," [The Massification of Higher Education and the Market Economy] in *Xinhua wenzhai*, October 1994, pp. 163–166.

Mao, Tse-tung, "On Contradiction," in C.T. Hu, *Chinese Communist Education* (New York: Teachers College, Columbia University, 1962).

———, *Selected Works of Mao Tse-tung*, Vols. I–III (Peking: Foreign Languages Press, 1967–1975).

Martin, W.A.P., *Hanlin Papers* (London: Trubner, 1880).

Marx, Karl, *The German Ideology* (Moscow: Progress Publishers, 1976).

Mazrui, Ali A., "The African University as a Multinational Corporation," in A. Mazrui, *Political Values and the Educated Class in Africa* (London: Heinneman, 1978).

———, *A World Federation of Cultures* (New York: Free Press, 1974).

McLean, Martin, "Educational Dependency" in *Compare* 13:1, 1983, pp. 25–42.

McLelland, Charles, *State, Society, and University in Germany, 1700–1914* (Cambridge: Cambridge University Press, 1980).

Menzel, Joanna, *The Chinese Civil Service: Career Open to Talent?* (Boston: D.C. Heath, 1963).

Merchant, Carolyn, *The Death of Nature: Women, Ecology, and the Scientific Revolution* (San Francisco: Harper and Row, 1980).

Meskill, John, *Academies in the Ming Dynasty* (Tucson: University of Arizona Press, 1982).

Meyer, Charles, *Histoire de la Femme Chinoise* (Paris: J. Clattes, 1986).

Minden, Karen, *Bamboo Stone: The Evolution of a Chinese Medical Elite* (Toronto: University of Toronto Press, 1994).

Miyazaki, Ichisada, *China's Examination Hell: The Civil Service Examinations of Imperial China* (New York and Tokyo: Weatherhill, 1977).

Monroe, Paul, *China: A Nation in Evolution* (New York: Macmillan, 1928).

Moody, Joseph, *French Education Since Napoleon* (New York: Syracuse University Press, 1978).

Nakayama, Shigeru, "Independence and Choice: Western Impacts on Japanese Higher Education," in P. Altbach and V. Selvaratnam, *From Dependence to Autonomy* (Amsterdam: Kluwer Academic Publishers, 1989), pp. 97–104.

Neugebauer, Ernst, *Anfange pädagogischer Entwicklungshilfe unter dem Völkerbund in China 1931 bis 1935* (Hamburg: Mitteilungen des Institutes für Asienkunde, 1971).

Noble, David, *World Without Women: The Christian Clerical Culture of Western Science* (New York: Alfred Knopf, 1992).

Orleans, Leo A., *Chinese Students in America: Policies, Issues, and Numbers* (Washington, D.C.: National Academy Press, 1988).

———, *Professional Manpower and Education in Communist China* (Washington, D.C.: National Science Foundation, 1960).

Ouyang Yu, "Mao Zedong guanyu ren de quanmian fazhan sixiang chutan," [A Preliminary Discussion of Mao Zedong's Thinking on the Whole Development of the Person], in *Jiaoyu yanjiu*, no. 2, 1994, pp. 6–9, 27.

Pepper, Suzanne, *China's Education Reform in the 1980s: Policies, Issues, and Historical Perspectives* (Berkeley: University of California Institute of East Asian Studies, 1990).

——, *Civil War in China: The Political Struggle, 1945–1949* (Berkeley: University of California Press, 1980).

——, "New Directions in Education," in J.K. Fairbank and D. Twitchett (eds.), *The Cambridge History of China*, Vol. 14 (Cambridge: Cambridge University Press, 1987).

Piolet, J.B., *La France en Dehors; les missions catholiques françaises au XIXe siècle*, Tome III (Paris: Armand Colin, c. 1900).

Popper, Karl, *Conjectures and Refutations* (London: Routledge and Kegan Paul, 1963).

——, *The Logic of Scientific Discovery* (London: Hutchinson, 1959).

——, *The Open Society and Its Enemies* (London: Routledge and Kegan Paul, 1970).

Price, Ronald, *Marxism and Education in China and Russia* (London: Croom Helm 1977).

Prost, Antoine, *L'Enseignement en France, 1800–1967* (Paris: Armand Colin, 1968).

Qian Duansheng, "Higher Education Takes a New Path," in *China Reconstructs*, September–October 1953.

Qinghua daxue xiaoshi gao [Draft History of Qinghua University] (Beijing: Zhonghua shuju, 1981).

Qu, Shipei, *Kangri zhanzheng shiqi jiefang qu gaodeng jiaoyu* [Higher Education in Liberation Areas During the Anti-Japanese War Period] (Beijing: Beijing daxue chubanshe, 1985).

Rai, Shirin, *Resistance and Reaction: University Politics in Post-Mao China* (Hemel Hempstead: Harvester Wheatsheaf and St. Martin's Press, 1991).

Raibaud, Martine, "L'enseignement catholique en Chine sous la République de 1912–1949," thèse de doctorat, Université de Paris VII, 1991.

Rankin, Mary Backus, *Early Chinese Revolutionaries: Radical Intellectuals in Shanghai and Chekiang, 1902–1911* (Cambridge, Mass.: Harvard University Press, 1971).

Rashdall, Hastings, *The Universities of Europe in the Middle Ages*, 3 vols. (Oxford: Clarendon Press, 1895).

Reynolds, Douglas, *China 1898–1912: The Xinzheng Revolution and Japan* (Cambridge, Mass.: Council on East Asian Studies, Harvard University, 1993).

Ringer, Fritz, *The Decline of the German Mandarins* (Cambridge, Mass.: Harvard University Press, 1969).

——, *Education and Society in Modern Europe* (Bloomington and London: Indiana University Press, 1979).

——, *Fields of Knowledge: French Academic Culture in Comparative Perspective, 1890–1920* (Cambridge: Cambridge University Press, 1992).

Robertson, D. MacLaren, *A History of the French Academy, 1635–1910* (New York: G.W. Dillingham, 1910).

Rosen, Stanley, "Women, Education, and Modernization," in R. Hayhoe, *Education and Modernization: the Chinese Experience* (Oxford: Pergamon, 1992).

Ross, Heidi, *China Learns English: Language Learning and Social Change in the People's Republic* (New Haven and London: Yale University Press, 1993).

Rothblatt, Sheldon, *The Revolution of the Dons: Cambridge and Society in Victorian England* (London: Faber and Faber, 1968).

Saich, Tony, "The Reform Decade in China: The Limits to Revolution from Above," in T. Saich and M. Dassu (eds.), *The Reform Decade*.

Saich, Tony, and Dassu, Marta (eds.), *The Reform Decade* (London: Kegan Paul International, 1992).

Sakharov, Andrew, "The Threat to Intellectual Freedom," in J.L. Nogee, *Man, State, and Society in the Soviet Union* (London: Pall Mall Press, 1972).

Schwarcz, Vera, *The Chinese Enlightenment: Intellectuals and the Legacy of the May*

4th Movement of 1919 (Berkeley: University of California Press, 1986).

Schwartz, Benjamin, *In Search of Wealth and Power: Yen Fu and the West* (Cambridge, Mass.: Harvard University Press, 1964).

Seeberg, Vilma, "Access to Higher Education: Targeted Recruitment Reform Under Economic Development Plans in the People's Republic of China," in *Higher Education*, Vol. 25, no. 2, March 1993.

Selden, Mark, *The Yenan Way in Revolutionary China* (Cambridge, Mass.: Harvard University Press, 1971).

Seybolt, Peter, *Revolutionary Education in China: Documents and Commentary* (New York: International Arts and Sciences Press, 1973).

———, "Yenan Education and the Chinese Revolution," unpublished Ph.D. dissertation, Harvard University, 1969.

Sheng Langxi, *Zhongguo shuyuan zhidu* [The Chinese *Shuyuan* System] (Shanghai: Zhonghua shuju, 1934).

Shin, Taijin, "The Connections Between Education and National Development in East Asian Countries: with Special Reference to the Structural Analysis of Higher Education and Economic Growth in the Republic of Korea," unpublished Ph.D. dissertation, University of Toronto, 1993.

Shirk, Susan, *Competitive Comrades: Career Incentives and Student Strategies in China* (Berkeley: University of California Press, 1982).

Shu, Xincheng, *Zhongguo jindai jiaoyushi ziliao* [Materials on Recent Chinese Educational History], 3 vols. (Beijing: Renmin jiaoyu chubanshe, 1979).

Siu, Bobby, *Women of China: Imperialism and Women's Resistance, 1900–1949* (London: Zed Press, 1982).

Smith, Douglas (ed.), *The Confucian Continuum: Educational Modernization in Taiwan* (New York: Praeger, 1991).

Smith, Robert, *The École Normale Supérieure and the Third Republic* (Albany, N.Y.: State University of New York Press, 1982).

Spence, Jonathan, *The Search for Modern China* (New York: W.W. Norton and Co., 1990).

Song, Yijun, "A Comparative Study of the Aid Policies of the World Bank and the Canadian International Development Agency in Chinese Higher Education: A Synthesis of Different Perspectives," unpublished Ed.D. thesis, University of Toronto, 1994.

Stacey, Judith, *Patriarchy and Socialist Revolution in China* (Berkeley: University of California Press, 1983).

Stranahan, Patricia, *Yan'an Women and the Communist Party* (Berkeley: Center for Chinese Studies, Institute of East Asian Studies, 1983).

Sun, E-Tu Zen, "The Growth of the Academic Community 1912–1949," in J. Fairbank and A. Feuerwerker (eds.), *The Cambridge History of China*, Vol. XIII, part 2 (Cambridge: Cambridge University Press, 1986), pp. 396–412.

Tan, Shen, "A Study of Women and Social Change," in *Social Sciences in China*, Vol. XV, no. 2, Summer 1994, pp. 65–73.

Tan, Songhua, "Woguo gaodeng jiaoyu fazhan zhanlue ruogan wenti de tantou," [A Discussion of Various Problems Relating to the Development Strategy for Higher Education in China] in *Zhongguo gaodeng jiaoyu yanjiu*, February 1994, pp. 24–30.

Tao, Yinghui, "Cai Yuanpei yu Zhongyang yanjiuyuan," [Cai Yuanpei and the Academica Sinica] in Zhongyang yanjiuyuan, *Jindai yanjiusuo jikan*, Vol. 7 June 1978, pp. 1–51.

Teiwes, Frederick, "Establishment and Consolidation of the New Regime," in J.K. Fairbank and D. Twitchett (eds.), *The Cambridge History of China*, Vol. 14 (Cambridge: Cambridge University Press, 1987).

Teng, Ssu-yu, "Chinese Influence on the Western Examination System," in *Harvard Journal of Asiatic Studies*, Vol. 7, no. 4, 1942.

Tian, Jinghai, Gong, Yizhou, and Pen, Jun, "Daxue biyesheng de xintai diaocha fenxi," [Analysis of a Survey of University Graduates' State of Mind] in *Gaodeng shifan jiaoyu yanjiu*, no. 2, February 1992, pp. 41–48; also in *Gaodeng jiaoyu*, September 1992, pp. 61–68.

Tibawi, A.L., "Origin and Character of Al-Madrasah," in A.L. Tibawi, *Arabic and Islamic Themes* (London: Luzac, 1974).

Trow, Martin, *Problems in the Transition from Elite to Mass Higher Education* (Berkeley: Carnegie Commission on Higher Education, 1973).

Tsang, Chiu-sam, *Society, Schools, and Progress in China* (London: Pergamon, 1968).

Tsurumi, E. Patricia, *Japanese Colonial Education in Taiwan, 1895–1945* (Cambridge, Mass.: Harvard University Press, 1977).

UNESCO Statistical Yearbook 1991 (Paris: UNESCO, 1992).

Unger, Jonathan, *Education under Mao: Class and Competition in Canton Schools, 1960–1980* (New York: Columbia University Press, 1982).

U.S. Department of Commerce, *Statistical Abstract of the United States 1992* (Washington, D.C.: U.S. Government Printing Office, 1992).

Wallerstein, Immanuel, *The Politics of the World Economy: The States, the Movements and the Civilizations* (Cambridge: Cambridge University Press, 1984).

Wang, Hsueh-wen, *Chinese Communist Education: The Yenan Period* (Taiwan: Institute of International Relations, 1975).

Wang, Minghan, and Heng, Jun, *Xibei shifan daxue xiaoshi* [An Institutional History of Northwest Normal University] (Xining: Qinghai renmin chubanshe, 1989).

Wang, Ruilan, Zhang, Hui, and Jiang, Bo, "Gaodeng jiaoyu fei junheng fazhan de xianshi sikao," [Realistic Reflections on the Uneven Development of Higher Education] in *Jiaoyu yanjiu*, no. 4, 1993, pp. 46–48.

Wang, Xiangrong, *Riben jiaoxi* [Japanese Teachers] (Beijing: Sanlian chubanshe, 1987).

Wang, Y.C., *Chinese Intellectuals and the West* (Chapel Hill: University of North Carolina Press, 1966).

Wang, Zhonglie, and Wu, Zhenyao, "Zhongdian jianshe—yipi gaodeng xuexiao he zhongdian xueke," [Priority Development—A Group of Higher Institutions and Priority Areas of Study] in *Zhongguo gaodeng jiaoyu*, nos. 7–8, July–August 1993.

Weber, Max, *The Methodology of the Social Sciences* (New York: Free Press, 1949).

West, Philip, *Yenching University and Sino-Western Relations, 1916–1952* (Cambridge, Mass.: Harvard University Press, 1976).

Wolfe, Marjorie, and Witke, Roxane (eds.), *Women in Chinese Society* (Stanford, Calif.: Stanford University Press, 1975).

Woodside, Alexander, *Vietnam and the Chinese Model: A Comparative Study of Vietnamese and Chinese Government in the First Half of the Nineteenth Century* (Cambridge, Mass.: Council of East Asian Studies, Harvard University, 1988).

World Bank, *China: Management and Finance of Higher Education*, Report No. 5912-CHA, Projects Department, East Asia and Pacific Regional Office, 1986).

Wu, Haiqing, "The Current Status of Women Professors in China," in *Chinese Education*, Vol. 25, no. 1, Spring 1992, pp. 53–55.

Wu, Wei and Li, Zhengxin, "Mao Zedong yu Zhongguo chuantong jiaoyu," [Mao Zedong and Chinese Traditional Education], in *Jiaoyu yanjiu*, no. 4, 1994.

Xiao, Chaoren, et al., *Beijing daxue xiaoshi* [A History of Beijing University] (Shanghai: Shanghai jiaoyu chubanshe, 1981).

Xiaoshi bianxiezu [School History Editing Group] (ed.), *Huazhong ligong daxue de sishi nian* [The Forty Years of Central China University of Science and Technology] (Wuhan: Huazhong ligong daxue chubanshe, 1993).

Xibei daxue xiaoshi gao [A Draft History of Northwest University] (Xi'an: Xibei daxue chubanshe, 1987).

Xibei nongye daxue xiaoshi [An Institutional History of Northwest Agricultural University] (Xi'an: Shaanxi renmin chubanshe, 1986).

Xinan lianda ji Yunnan shida jianxiao wushi zhounian jinian ji [A Memorial Collection of the 50th Anniversary of the establishment of Southwest Associated University and Yunnan Normal University] (Kunming: Special issue of *Yunnan shida xuebao*, 1988).

Xiong, Mingan, *Zhongguo gaodeng jiaoyushi* [A History of Chinese Higher Education] (Chongqing: Chongqing chubanshe, 1983).

Xu, Dunhuang, Xian, Liting, and Liu, Dawei, "Guanyu juban minban gaodeng xuexiao ruogan wenti de tantou," [A Discussion of Various Problems Relating to the Management of People-run Schools], in *Zhongguo gaodeng jiaoyu*, no. 10, 1994, pp. 4–5.

Xu, Qingyu, "Luetan shishi '2/1/1 gongcheng' de ruogan xiangguan yinsu" [A Brief Discussion of Various Related Factors in Carrying Out the 2/1/1 Engineering Project] in *Jiaoyu yanjiu*, no. 3, 1994, pp. 42–45.

Yan'an ziran kexueyuan shiliao [Historical Materials on the Yan'an Natural Sciences College] (Beijing: Zhonggong dangshi ziliao chubanshe, 1986).

Yao, Esther Lee, *Chinese Women Past and Present* (Mesquite, Tex.: Ide House, 1983), pp. 75–82.

Yao, Qihe, et al. (eds.), *Huazhong Ligong daxue de sishi nian* [The Forty Years of Central China University of Science and Technology] (Wuhan: Huazhong ligong daxue chubanshe, 1993).

Yates, Frances, *The French Academy in the Sixteenth Century* (London: Warburg Institute, University of London, 1947).

Yeh, Wen-hsin, *The Alienated Academy: Culture and Politics in Republican China 1919–1937* (Cambridge, Mass.: Council on East Asian Studies, Harvard University, 1990).

Yen, Maria, *The Umbrella Garden: A Picture of Student Life in Red China* (New York: Macmillan, 1954).

Yin, Chiling, *Reconstruction of Modern Educational Organizations in China* (Shanghai: Commercial Press, 1924).

Yin, Dali, "Reforming Chinese Education: Context, Structure, and Attitudes in the 1980s," in *Compare*, Vol. 23, no. 2, 1993.

Yin, Qiping, and White, Gordon, "The Marketization of Chinese Higher Education: A Critical Assessment," in *Comparative Education*, Vol. 30, no. 3, 1994, pp. 217–237.

Young, Marilyn, *Women in China: Studies in Social Change and Feminism* (Ann Arbor: Center for Chinese Studies, University of Michigan, 1973).

Zhang, Liuquan, *Zhongguo shuyuan shihua* [The Evolution of the Chinese *Shuyuan*] (Beijing: Jiaoyu kexue chubanshe, 1981).

Zhao, Andong, "Jianguo chuqi gaodeng jiaoyu gaige," [Higher Education Reform in the Early Period of National Construction] in Yu, Li (ed.), *Xiandai jiaoyu sixiang yanlun* [Introductory Discussions on Contemporary Educational Thought] (Shanghai: Huadong shifan daxue chubanshe, 1986).

Zhong, Wenhui, "China's Participation in the World Community: A Study of Chinese Scholarly Communication," unpublished Ed.D. thesis, University of Toronto, 1992.

Zhongguo jiaoyu gaijin hui [China Educational Progress Society] (ed.), *Zhongguo jiaoyu tongji gailan* [A Survey of Chinese Educational Statistics] (Shanghai: Commercial Press, 1923).

Zhongguo jiaoyu nianjian [China Education Yearbook] (Shanghai: Kaiming shudian, 1934).

Zhongguo jiaoyu nianjian 1949–1981 [Chinese Education Yearbook 1949–1981] (Beijing: Zhongguo dabaike quanshu chubanshe, 1984).

Zhongguo renmin daxue dashiji [A Chronology of Events at China People's University, July 1937–February 1992] (Beijing: Zhongguo renmin daxue gaodeng jiaoyu yanjiushi yu xiaoshi bianxiezu, 1992).

Zhongguo renmin gongheguo jiaoyu dashiji 1949–1982 [A Record of Educational Events in the PR China 1949–1992] (Beijing: Jiaoyu kexue chubanshe, 1983).

Zhongnan caijing daxue xiaoshi 1949–1988 [An Institutional History of the Central South University of Finance and Economics, 1949–1988] (Wuhan: Zhongnan caijing daxue chubanshe, 1988).

Zhou, Ju, "Mei Su gaodeng jiaoyu jingyan yu woguo gaodeng jiaoyu gaige," [The American and Soviet Experience of Higher Education and Higher Educational Reform in Our Country] in *Zhongguo shehui kexue*, no. 3, 1984, pp. 3–20.

Zhou, Yutong, *Zhongguo xiandai jiaoyushi* [A History of Contemporary Chinese Education] (Shanghai: Liangyou tushu gongsi, 1934).

Zhu, Weizheng, "Confucius and Traditional Chinese Education: An Assessment," in R. Hayhoe, *Education and Modernization: The Chinese Experience.*

Zhu Youxian (ed.), *Zhongguo jindai xuezhi shiliao* [Historical Materials on the Educational System in Recent Chinese History], 6 vols. (Shanghai: Huadong shida chubanshe, 1983–1991).

Zhuang, Hunming, *Kangzhan shiqi Zhongguo gaodeng jiaoyu zhi yanjiu* [Research on Chinese Higher Education in the Period of the Anti-Japanese War], unpublished Ph.D. dissertation, Sili Zhongguo wenhua xueyuan, lishixue yanjiusuo, 1979.

Index

Germany xvi, 6, 43, 45, 138, 163, 189, 234
girls' education 34, 39, 40, 42
Goldman, Merle 116
grandes écoles 6
Great Leap Forward xiii, xxi, 17, 22, 74,
    87, 88, 90, 101, 127, 171
    educational reforms 92–98, 254
Guanghua University 80
Guangxi University 80
Guangzhou Foreign Languages Institute
    160, 164–165, 169, 179, 180
Guangzhou Foreign Trade Institute 169
guilds 4, 11, 14
guozijian 10, 41
    origin and definition 11

Habermas, Juergen xiii, 139
Hanlin Academy xxi, 10, 11, 13, 35, 41
Hanxia kaowenyuan 44
Harbin Polytechnical University 79, 102
Harvard University 253
Hawkins xviii
He Bingdi xvii
Heilongjiang University 95
Henan University 165, 172–173
Hengyang Normal College 165
Henze, Juergen xviii
hierarchy 253–254, 261
Higginson, J.H., xxii
higher education
    in the Central South region 151–156
    in the Northwest 204–208
    number of institutions in China 42, 47,
        52, 56, 81, 96–97, 118, 128
Holland 17
Holmes, Brian xiv
Horio, Teruhisa 255
Hu Shi 47, 250
Hua Hengfeng 45
Huanan College for Women 39
Huanan University of Technology 154
Huang Yanpei 85
Huazhong Agricultural University 164–165,
    171
Huazhong Normal University 80, 83, 84, 154
Huazhong University of Science and
    Technology 80, 104–106, 154, 163,
    164–165, 168–169, 172, 173, 178,
    182, 185, 186, 235
Hubei Normal University 157
Hubei University 95, 157, 166
Huizhou Normal College 165
Humboldt, Wilhelm von 7
Hunan Agricultural University 165
Hunan Normal University 165, 173

Hunan Self-Study University 22, 85
Hunan University 80, 164–165, 170, 182
Hundred Day Reform 19, 33, 41
Hundred Flowers Movement 90

IDRC 171
Imperial University 19, 41, 116, 266
imperialism 4, 15, 16, 29
    links to culture 18–22
    Soviet version of 15, 16, 17, 22
incorporation of colleges and universities
    14–15
India 4, 15, 16, 49
Inner Mongolia Engineering College 96
institutional histories xvi, 77
intellectual authority xxi, 13, 63, 74, 77, 117
intellectual freedom 13, 62, 63, 74, 91, 117,
    133, 142, 264
international activities of universities 134–142
    bilateral cultural and academic projects
        137–139
    bilateral development projects 139–142,
        163
    in the Central South 162–164
    in the Northwest 217, 232–236
    interviews xv, 239
Islamic education 14
Israel, John xvii
ius ubique docendi 4, 12

Japan 13, 16, 40, 140, 189, 217, 252,
    254–255
    Imperial University 19
Japanese educational influences in China
    19, 32, 35, 40, 41
Japanese teachers 40
Jesuit college 7, 38
Jesuit curriculum 38
Jianghan Vocational University 165–166, 173
Jiangnan Manufacturing Bureau 45
Jiaotong University 3, 37, 49, 81, 202, 235,
    260, 267
JICA 140
Jilin University 80
Jinan University 169
Jinling college 39
Jinling University
job assignment system 83, 84, 87, 89, 120,
    128–129, 131, 154, 175, 177–8,
    225, 226, 251, 260
joint doctoral program xviii
July 21 universities 103, 104, 257

Kairov, I.A. 83
Kang Keqing 60

research 58, 94, 122, 124–125, 126, 136–137, 139, 157, 270–271
  in the Central South 160–162, 181–184
  in education 84
  funding of 124–125, 161, 192, 217, 228–231
  in the Northwest 228, 241
  relation to teaching 9, 122, 124
  of women 265
returnees 189–192, 234–244
revolutionary schools 39
Richards, Timothy 18, 41, 49
Ringer, Fritz 7
Rockefeller Foundation 192
Rosen, Stanley xviii
Ross, Heidi xviii, xxii
Royal Asia Society 44
Royal Society 44
Russell, Bertrand 49
Russia 234

Sakharov, Andrei 8
Schwarcz, Vera 45
science and technology 29–30, 94, 103
scientific knowledge 45, 50, 249
scientific method 17
secondary education 88–89, 99–100, 204, 206
self-strengthening 32–33
  institutions 36–37
Seybolt, Peter xvii
Shaanbei Public Institute (North China United University) 61, 82
Shaanxi Normal University 218–219, 230
Shaanxi University of Finance and Economics 219–220, 225
Shaanxi University of Technology 203
Shandong Medical University 202
Shandong University 80, 81, 155
Shanghai Academy of Social Sciences 95
Shanghai Industrial University 260
Shanghai Institute of Finance and Economics 95
Shanghai International Studies University 210, 260
Shanghai Machine Tools Plant 102
Shanghai No. 1 Medical University 202, 224
Shanghai University 50, 60, 260
Shanghai University of Science and Technology 260
Shanxi University 18
Sheng Xuanhuai 37
Sheng Yugui 37
Shenzhen University 155–156, 165–166, 173, 184, 185, 186

Shils, Edward xxii
shuyuan 9, 10, 12, 15, 33, 34, 74, 116, 249
  origin 11
  relation to state 11
  teaching methods 12, 61
  tradition 22–23, 61, 85, 93, 96, 116, 250
Sichuan Medical College 96
Sichuan University 80, 259
Singapore 16
Sino-Japanese War xx, 31, 32, 51, 55–58, 73, 88, 172, 201, 270
  movement of universities 56, 88, 127, 201, 267
Sixty Articles 98
social responsibility 117, 125, 142
social sciences 50, 57, 60, 77, 79, 82, 83, 95, 103, 105, 123, 125, 168, 170, 241, 255, 271
South China Institute of Technology 81
Southwest Associated University 57
Southwest China 79
Southwest Normal University 80
Soviet experts xvi, 77, 79, 84, 98, 250
Soviet influence in China 20–22, 31, 35, 60, 77, 84–85, 90, 101, 117
Soviet tutelage xxi, 17
Soviet Union 6, 16, 73, 77, 98, 217, 252, 272
Soviet university 13
sowon 14
specialist knowledge 6, 8, 35, 101
SSHRCC xv, xxii
St. Johns University 50, 80
state and education
  in Communist China 93
  in France 6, 85
  in Germany 7
  Leninist views 8
  in the Soviet Union 8–9, 85
  in traditional China 9, 11, 77
structural theory of imperialism xiii, 15, 17, 18
students
  activism 53
  admission 5, 48, 54
  adult 180–181
  contract 176, 214, 268
  directed enrollment 177, 215
  geographical flows 154–157, 175, 208–210
  graduate 131, 133, 154, 211–212, 224, 228, 235
  rural 89, 100–101, 128, 156–157, 164, 166–167, 215, 243–244, 256, 268–270